Charles Dickens
A Critical Study

Gadshill Place from the Gardens

Charles Dickens

A Critical Study

GEORGE GISSING

NONSUCH

First published 1898
Copyright © in this edition Nonsuch Publishing, 2007

Nonsuch Publishing
Cirencester Road, Chalford, Stroud, Gloucestershire, GL6 8PE
www.nonsuch-publishing.com

Nonsuch Publishing is an imprint of NPI Media Group

British Library Cataloguing in Publication Data.
A catalogue record for this book is available from the British Library.

ISBN 978 1 84588 237 2

Typesetting and origination by NPI Media Group
Printed in Great Britain

Contents

Illustrations

Introduction to the
Modern Edition

The first time I read an excellent work, it is to me just as if I gained a new friend; and when I read over a book I have perused before, it resembles the meeting of an old one.

George Gissing was born in Wakefield, Yorkshire, on 22 November 1857. As a young child, he was an avid reader and gladly took advantage of the extensive family library in his childhood home. He enjoyed literature—both reading and writing—and won many acclaimed prizes for his poetry.

Gissing enjoyed a relatively stable childhood until his father died in 1870. After his father's death, he felt he had lost the main guiding force in his intellectual development and this—the first of a number of unfortunate circumstances—would have a profound and negative effect on Gissing and his future outlook on life.

At the age of fifteen he won a scholarship to Owens College, Manchester, but his prospects were quickly ruined when he was caught stealing money from the students' cloakroom—money which he had planned to give to a young prostitute named Nell Harrison, with whom he had recently become infatuated. Gissing was imprisoned for a month and subsequently sent to America. He returned to England in 1877, jobless, penniless and friendless.

He later endured a wearisome relationship with his first wife, a persistent drunkard who he finally paid to move away permanently. He married his second wife, Edith Underwood, in February 1891, but again things did not work out. She was widely known to be violent and mentally unstable, and was eventually committed to an asylum.

Despite the distressing state of his marital and financial affairs, Gissing continued to write, and managed to get an extensive amount of work published. Above all, he recognised its financial worth:

Literature nowadays is a trade. Putting aside men of genius, who may succeed by mere cosmic force, your successful man of letters is your skilful tradesman. He thinks first and foremost of the markets.

In addition to over one hundred short stories, a travel book, a range of literary criticism and enough letters to fill several volumes, Gissing wrote and had published an impressive twenty-one novels, the two most well known of which were *New Grub Street* (1891) and *The Odd Women* (1893). Many of Gissing's novels—*The Nether World* (1889) in particular—explicitly tackle the complexity of London slum life and convey, in startlingly intricate detail, the atmosphere and character of the poverty-stricken nineteenth-century London streets.

Gissing left one novel—*Veranilda*—unfinished at the time of his death. He died on 28 December 1903 in a rented villa at Ispoure near St Jean Pied de Port in south-west France, at the age of only forty-six; he suffered from severe emphysema. His body is buried in the English cemetery at St Jean de Luz on the Bay of Biscay. Since his death, a number of his works have, sadly, gone out of print, but a range of Gissing's works are still available and, more recently, many books are justifiably being brought back into print.

In his lifetime, Gissing acquired a number of erudite and literary acquaintances, including Grant Allen, George Meredith, W. H. Hudson and, perhaps most notably, H. G. Wells. One of his more modern readers—and an evident enthusiast of his literary works—was George Orwell, who wrote extensively of Gissing's writings in a review essay of 1948. In particular, he focused on his fictional works, celebrating their unique style and approach to the distinctive scenes of everyday London life, while revelling in their robust handling of typically taboo subject matter. He wrote:

Gissing was not a writer of picaresque tales, or burlesques, or comedies, or political tracts: he was interested in individual human beings, and the fact that he can deal sympathetically with several different sets of motives, and makes a credible story out of the collision between them, makes him exceptional among English writers ... Certainly there is not much of what is usually called beauty, not much lyricism, in the situations and characters that he chooses to imagine, and still less in the texture of his writing. His prose, indeed, is often disgusting.

Gissing's work attracted a range of criticism from his contemporaries, both positive and negative. Sadly, not all his readers expressed the natural enthusiasm of Orwell almost sixty years after his work came under public scrutiny for the first time. Gissing's untimely death unfortunately pushed the majority of his fictional works into obscurity, while his writings on Dickens were soon to be overshadowed by those of the more easy-going G. K. Chesterton.

Charles Dickens: a Critical Study was first published in 1898. By the time the book appeared on the public scene, Gissing had—through the publication of his novels—already made for himself a reputation as the author of gloomy and pessimistic portrayals of late Victorian life. C. K. Shorter remarked in his 'Literary Letter' in the *Illustrated London News* that it was:

> a curious irony to have given Mr Gissing the task of appreciating Dickens. The one writer makes poverty so much more depressing than it really is, the other so much more joyous than it is.

Indeed the two writers were far apart in their representations of London, but Gissing was clearly influenced by Dickens, believing his literature worthy of such extensive and detailed criticism. He acknowledged Dickens' literary faults and weaknesses, but can also be seen to pay enthusiastic homage to his illustrious predecessor. Temple Scott, in his 1924 introduction to Gissing's book, argues, '[there was not] in English Literature a more fulfilling estimate of the writings of Dickens than Gissing's critical study, which is at once finely judicious and deliberately appreciative.' The openness and sincerity of his detailed account made a refreshing change to the typically generalised approach of other contemporary critics.

The book was widely reviewed, mainly attracting positive criticism. In America too, it was acclaimed as the first piece of thorough and level-headed criticism on Dickens to be published. As a result, Gissing received an unexpected proposal from the publisher of Methuen, inviting him to write introductions to the new Rochester editions of Dickens' works. He wrote eleven of these celebrated introductions in the space of eighteen months, and although these new editions were not particularly popular, Gissing had made a name for himself worldwide.

By the time of his death Gissing had become in the eyes of his contemporaries one of the best-ever Dickens specialists. In the words of G. K. Chesterton—his supposed rival—Gissing was among 'the soundest of the Dickens critics, a man of genius.'

This edition also includes an essay on 'Dickens-Land' by J. A. Nicklin, which examines the relationship between Dickens, his works and the places that he knew; a dictionary of characters, places, etc., in his novels and stories; and notes on the illustrations by F. G. Kitton.

Charles Dickens
A Critical Study

George Gissing

I

His Times

More than forty years have elapsed since the death of Charles Dickens. The time which shaped him and sent him forth is so far behind us, as to have become a matter of historical study for the present generation; the time which knew him as one of its foremost figures, and owed so much to the influences of his wondrous personality, is already made remote by a social revolution of which he watched the mere beginning. It seems possible to regard Dickens from the stand-point of posterity; to consider his career, to review his literary work, and to estimate his total activity, as belonging to an age clearly distinguishable from our own.

When Queen Victoria came to the throne Charles Dickens was twenty-five years old. To say that he was twenty in the year 1832 is to point more significantly the period of his growth into manhood. At least a year before the passing of that Reform Bill which was to give political power to English capitalism (a convenient word of our day) Dickens had begun work as a shorthand writer, and as journalist. Before 1837 he had written his *Sketches*, had published them in volumes which gave some vogue to the name of "Boz", and was already engaged upon *Pickwick*. In short, Dickens's years of apprenticeship to life and literature were those which saw the rise and establishment of the Middle Class, commonly called "Great"—of the new power in political and social England which owed its development to coal and steam and iron mechanism. By birth superior to the rank of proletary, inferior to that of capitalist, this young man, endowed with original genius, and with the invincible vitality demanded for its exercise under such conditions, observed in a spirit of lively criticism, not seldom of jealousy, the class so rapidly achieving wealth and rule. He lived to become, in all externals, and to some extent in the tone of his mind, a characteristic member of this privileged society; but his criticism of its foibles, and of its grave shortcomings, never ceased. The landed proprietor of Gadshill could not forget (the great writer could never desire to forget) a miserable childhood imprisoned in the limbo of squalid London; his grudge against this memory was in essence a *class* feeling; to the end his personal triumph gratified him, however unconsciously, as the vindication of a social claim.

Walter Scott, inheriting gentle blood and feudal enthusiasm, resisted to the last the theories of '32; and yet by irony of circumstance owed his ruin to commercial enterprise. Charles Dickens, humbly born, and from first to last fighting the battle of those in like estate, wore himself to a premature end in striving to found his title of gentleman on something more substantial than glory. The one came into the world too late; the other, from this point of view, was but too thoroughly of his time.

A time of suffering, of conflict, of expansion, of progress. In the year of Dickens's birth (1812) we read of rioting workmen who smash machinery, and are answered by the argument of force. Between then and 1834, the date of the Poor Law Amendment Act, much more machinery is broken, power-looms and threshing-engines, north and south; but hungry multitudes have no chance against steam and capital. Statisticians, with rows of figures, make clear to us the vast growth of population and commerce in these same years; we are told, for instance, that between 1821 and 1841 the people of Sheffield and of Birmingham increased by 80 per cent. It is noted, too, that savings-bank deposits increased enormously during the same years: a matter for congratulation. Nevertheless, with the new Poor Law comes such a demand for new workhouses that in some four-and-twenty years we find an expenditure of five millions sterling in this hopeful direction. To be sure, a habit of pauperdom was threatening the ruin of the country—or of such parts of it as could not be saved by coal and steam and iron. Upon the close of the Napoleonic wars followed three decades of hardship for all save the inevitably rich, and those who were able to take time by the forelock; so that side by side we have the beginnings of vast prosperity and wide prevalence of woe. Under the old law providing for the destitute by means of outdoor relief, pauperdom was doubtless encouraged; but the change to sterner discipline could not escape the charge of harshness, and among those who denounced the new rule was Dickens himself. Whilst this difference of opinion was being fought out, came a series of lean years, failure of harvests, and hunger more acute than usual, which led to the movement known as Chartism (a hint that the middle-class triumph of '32 was by no means a finality, seeing that behind that great class was a class, numerically at all events, much greater); at the same time went on the Corn-law struggles. Reading the verses of Ebenezer Elliott, one cannot but reflect on the scope in England of those days for a writer of fiction who should have gone to work in the spirit of the Rhymer, without impulse or obligation to make his books amusing. But the novelist of homely life was already at his task, doing it in his own way, picturing with rare vividness the England that he knew; and fate had blest him with the spirit of boundless mirth.

There are glimpses in Dickens of that widespread, yet obscure, misery which lay about him in his early years. As, for instance, where we read in *Oliver Twist*, in the description of the child's walk to London, that "in some villages large painted boards were fixed up, warning all persons who begged within the district, that they would be sent to jail". And in his mind there must ever have been a background of such knowledge, influencing his work, even when it found no place in the scheme of a story.

In a rapid view of the early nineteenth century, attention is demanded by one detail, commonly forgotten, and by the historian easily ignored, but a matter of the first importance as serving to illustrate some of Dickens's best work. In 1833, Lord Ashley (afterwards Lord Shaftesbury) entered upon his long strife with stubborn conservatism and heartless interest on behalf of little children who worked for wages in English factories and mines. The law then in force forbade children under thirteen years of age to engage in such labour for more than thirteen hours a day; legislators of that period were so struck by the humanity of the provision that no eloquence could induce them to think of superseding it. Members of the reformed House of Commons were naturally committed to sound economic views on supply and demand; they enlarged upon the immorality of interfering with freedom of contract; and, when Lord Ashley was guilty of persevering in his anti-social craze, of standing all but alone, year after year, the advocate of grimy little creatures who would otherwise have given nobody any trouble, howling insult, or ingenious calumny, long served the cause of his philosophic opponents.

Let anyone who is prone to glorify the commercial history of nine-teenth-century England search upon dusty shelves for certain Reports of

Commissioners in the matter of children's employments at this time of Lord
Ashley's activity, and there read a tale of cruelty and avarice which arraigns
the memory of a generation content so infamously to enrich itself. Those
Reports make clear that some part, at all events, of modern English prosperity results from the toil of children (among them babies of five and six),
whose lives were spent in the black depths of coal-pits and amid the hot roar
of machinery. Poetry has found inspiration in the subject, but no verse can
make such appeal to heart and conscience as the businesslike statements of
a Commission. Lord Ashley's contemporaries in Parliament dismissed these
stories with a smile. Employers of infant labour naturally would lend no ear
to a sentimental dreamer; but it might have been presumed that at all events
in one direction, that of the Church, voices would make themselves heard
in defence of "these little ones". We read, however, in the philanthropist's
Diary: "In very few instances did any mill-owner appear on the platform
with me; in still fewer the representatives of any religious denomination".
This quiet remark serves to remind one, among other things, that Dickens
was not without his reasons for a spirit of distrust towards religion by law
established, as well as towards sundry other forms of religion—the spirit
which, especially in his early career, was often misunderstood as hostility
to religion in itself, a wanton mocking at sacred things. Such a fact should
always be kept in mind in reading Dickens. It is here glanced at merely for
its historical significance; the question of Dickens's religious attitude will
call for attention elsewhere.

Dickens, if any writer, has associated himself with the thought of suffering childhood. The circumstances of his life confined him, for the most
part, to London in his choice of matter for artistic use, and it is especially the
London child whose sorrows are made so vivid to us by the master's pen. But
we know that he was well acquainted with the monstrous wickedness of that
child labour in mines and mills; and, find where he might the pathetic little
figures useful to him in his fiction, he was always speaking, consciously, to
an age remarkable for stupidity and heartlessness in the treatment of all its
poorer children. Perhaps in this direction his influence was as great as in any.
In recognizing this, be it remembered for how many years an Englishman of
noble birth, one who, on all accounts, might have been thought likely to sway
the minds of his countrymen to any worthy end, battled in vain and amid all
manner of obloquy, for so simple a piece of humanity and justice. Dickens
had a weapon more efficacious than mere honest zeal. He could make people
laugh; and if once the crowd has laughed with you, it will not object to cry a
little—nay, it will make good resolves, and sometimes carry them out.

It was a time by several degrees harsher, coarser, and uglier than our own. Take that one matter of hanging. Through all his work we see Dickens preoccupied with the gallows; and no wonder. In his *Sketches* there is the lurid story of the woman who has obtained possession of her son after his execution, and who seeks the aid of a doctor, in hope of restoring the boy to life; and in so late a book as *Great Expectations* occurs that glimpse of murderous Newgate, which is among his finest things. His description of a hanging, written to a daily paper, is said to have had its part in putting an end to public executions; but that was comparatively late in his life; at his most impressionable time the hanging of old and young, men and women, regularly served as one of the entertainments of Londoners. Undoubtedly, even in Dickens's boyhood, manners had improved to some extent upon those we see pictured in Hogarth; but from our present stand-point the difference, certainly in poorer London, is barely appreciable. It was an age in which the English character seemed bent on exhibiting all its grossest and meanest and most stupid characteristics. Sheer ugliness of everyday life reached a limit not easily surpassed; thickheaded national prejudice, in consequence of great wars and British victories, had marvellously developed; aristocracy was losing its better influence, and power passing to a well-fed multitude, remarkable for a dogged practicality which, as often as not, meant ferocious egoism. With all this, a prevalence of such ignoble vices as religious hypocrisy and servile snobbishness. Our own day has its faults in plenty: some of them perhaps more perilous than the worst here noted of our ancestors; but it is undeniably much cleaner of face and hands, decidedly more graceful in its common habits of mind.

One has but to open at any page of *Pickwick* to be struck with a characteristic of social life in Dickens's youth, which implies so much that it may be held to represent the whole civilization in which he was born and bred. Mr Pickwick and his friends all drank brandy; drank it as the simplest and handiest refreshment, at home or abroad; drank it at dawn or at midnight, in the retirement of the bed-chamber, or by the genial fireside; offered it as an invitation to good-fellowship, or as a reward of virtue in inferiors; and on a coach-journey, whether in summer or winter, held it among the indispensable comforts. "He", said Samuel Johnson, "who aspires to be a hero, must drink brandy"; and in this respect the Pickwickians achieve true heroism. Of course they pay for their glory, being frequently drunk in the most flagrant sense of the word; but to say that they "come up smiling" after it, is to use an inadequate phrase—however appropriate to those times; he would indeed have been a sorry Pickwickian who owned to a morning s headache. If such a thing existed, unavowed, there was the proverbial remedy at hand—"a hair of the dog". It is conceivable that, in an age to come, a student of *Pickwick* may point, as an obvious explanation of the marvellous flow of vitality and merriment among the people of Dickens's day, to their glorious beverage, doubtless more ethereal and yet more potent than any drink known to later mortals—the divine liquor called brandy.

Amid this life of the young century—cruel, unlovely, but abounding in vital force—there arose two masters in the art of fiction. To one of them was given the task of picturing England on its brighter side, the world of rank and fashion and wealth, with but rare glances (these, however, more noteworthy than is generally recognized) at the populace below. The other had for his field that vast obscurity of lower town life which till then had never been turned to literary uses. Of the country poor, at a somewhat earlier date, admirable presentment had been made in the verse of Crabbe, a writer (in truth the forerunner of what is now called "realism") whose most unmerited neglect may largely be accounted for by the unfortunate vehicle of his work, the "riding-rhyme", which has lost its charm for the English ear; but poverty amid a wilderness of streets, and that class of city population just raised above harsh necessity, no one had seriously made his theme in prose or verse. Thackeray and Dickens supplement each other, and, however wide apart the lives they depict, to a striking degree confirm each other's views of a certain era in the history of England. In their day, both were charged with partiality, with excessive emphasis. Both being avowedly satirists, the charge can be easily understood, and to a certain point may be admitted. In the case of Dickens, with whom alone I am here concerned, it will be part of my endeavour to vindicate him against the familiar complaint that, however trustworthy his background, the figures designed upon it, in general, are mere forms of fantasy. On re-reading his work, it is not thus that Dickens's characters, on the whole, impress me. With reserves which will appear in the course of my essay, I believe him to have been, what he always claimed to be, a very accurate painter of the human beings, no less than of the social conditions, he saw about him. He has not a wide scope; he is always noticeably at his best in dealing with an ill-defined order of English folk, a class (or classes) characterized by dulness, prejudice, dogged individuality, and manners, to say the least, unengaging. From this order he chose the living figures of his narrative, and they appear to me, all in all, no less truly representative than the persons selected by Thackeray to illustrate a higher rank of life. Readers of

Dickens who exclaim at the "unreality" of his characters (I do not here speak of his conduct of a story) will generally be found unacquainted with the English lower classes of today; and one may remark in passing that the English people is distinguished among nationalities by the profound mutual ignorance which separates its social ranks.

One often hears it said that Dickens gives us types, not individuals; types, moreover, of the most abstract kind, something like the figures in the old Moralities: embodied hypocrisy, selfishness, pride, and so on, masking as everyday mortals. This appears to me an unconsidered judgment. Dickens's characters will pass before us and be attentively reviewed; speaking of them generally, I see in them, not abstractions, but men and women of such loud peculiarities, so aggressively individual in mind and form, in voice and habit, that they for ever proclaim themselves the children of a certain country, of a certain time, of a certain rank. Clothed abstractions do not take hold upon the imagination and the memory as these people of Dickens did from the day of their coming into life. The secret of this subtle power lay in the reality of the figures themselves. There are characters in Dickens (meant, moreover, to be leading persons of the drama) which have failed thus to make good their being; their names we may remember, but all else has become shadowy; and what is the reason of this vanishment, in contrast with the persistence of figures less important? Simply that here Dickens *has* presented us with types, abstractions. The social changes of the last sixty years are not small; but to anyone who really knows the lower middle class in London it will be obvious that many of the originals of Dickens still exist, still pursue the objectionable, or amusing, tenor of their way, amid new names and new forms of ugliness. Sixty years ago, grotesques and eccentricities were more common than nowadays; the Englishman, always angular and self-assertive, had grown flagrant in his egoism during the long period of combat with menacing powers; education had not set up its grindstone for all and sundry; and persons esteemed odd even in such a society abounded among high and low. For these oddities, especially among the poorer folk, Dickens had an eager eye; they were offered to him in measure overflowing; nowadays he would have to search for them amid the masses drilled into uniformity, but there they are—the same creatures differently clad. Precisely because his books are rich in extravagances of human nature is Dickens so true a chronicler of his day and generation.

A time of ugliness: ugly religion, ugly law, ugly relations between rich and poor, ugly clothes, ugly furniture. What would Charles Dickens have made of all this had his genius been lacking in the grace of humour? Yet it is not his humour alone that will preserve him for the delight of young and old, no less than for the instruction of the studious. In his work there is a core of perpetuity; to find it we must look back upon the beginnings of his life, and on the teaching which prepared him for his life's endeavour.

II

The Growth of Man and Writer

Needless to recount in detail the biography of Charles Dickens. Living, he was regarded with a warmth of personal interest such as no other English writer ever inspired; all the facts of his life which could rightly become public property (and some with which the public had no concern) were known to every contemporary reader; and as yet they seem in no risk of being forgotten.

By accident he was not born a Londoner, but his life in London began while he was yet a child. His earliest impressions, however, were received at Rochester and Chatham, where he went to what was called a school, and in the time at his own disposal began to educate himself in his own way by reading the eighteenth-century novelists. A happy thing for Dickens, and for us, that he was permitted to pass these few years of opening life elsewhere than in London. He speaks of himself as "not a very robust child sitting in by-places near Rochester Castle, with a head full of Partridge, Strap, Tom Pipes, and Sancho Panza"; better from every point of view, than if he had gained his first knowledge of English life and fiction amid the brick walls of Camden Town. Dickens always had a true love of the country, especially of that which is near to picturesque old towns of historic interest; and this most precious characteristic, to which we owe some of the sweetest, freshest pages in his work, might never have developed in him but for the early years at Rochester. Very closely has he linked his memory with that district of Kent, nowadays, of course, like most other districts easily accessible from London, all but robbed of the old charm. At Rochester begin the adventurous travels of Mr Pickwick; near Rochester stands the house of Gadshill; and it was Rochester that he chose for the scene of his last story, the unfinished *Edwin Dread*.

With London came unhappiness. *David Copperfield* has made universally familiar that figure of the poor little lad slaving at ignoble tasks in some by-way near the River Thames. David works for a wine-merchant,

The " Bull " Inn, Rochester

cleaning bottles; his original had for taskmasters a firm of blacking-makers. We know how sorely this memory rankled in the mind of the successful author; he kept the fact from his wife till long after marriage, and, we are told, could never bear to speak to his children of that and the like endurances. This I have seen mentioned as proof of a kind of sensitiveness not to be distinguished from snobbery. Dickens would not, like Josiah Bounderby in *Hard Times*, proclaim from the house-tops that he had been a poor boy toiling for a few shillings a week, and assuredly he would have preferred to look back upon a childhood like to that of his friends and neighbours; but much of his shrinking from this recollection was due to the fact that it involved a grave censure upon his parents. "It is wonderful to me", he writes, in the fragment of autobiography preserved by Forster (*Life*, Bk. I, chap. 2), "how I could have been so easily cast away at such an age. It is wonderful to me that, even after my descent into the poor little drudge I had been since we came to London, no one had compassion enough on me—a child of singular abilities, quick, eager, delicate, and soon hurt, bodily or mentally—to suggest that something might have been spared, as certainly it might have been, to place me at any common school. Our friends, I take it, were tired out. No one made any sign. My father and mother were quite satisfied. They could hardly have been more so, if I had been twenty years of age, distinguished at a Grammar School, and going to Cambridge." In this passage the tone of feeling is unmistakable; as the boy had suffered from a sense of undeserved humiliation, so did the man feel hurt in his deepest sensibilities whenever he reflected on that evil time. His silence regarding it was a very natural reserve.

In middle age we find Dickens saying about his father, that the longer he lived, the better man he thought him. To us the elder Dickens is inevitably Mr Micawber, and who shall say that he has no affection for that type of genial impecuniosity? To his father, no doubt, the novelist owed the happy temperament which had so large a part in his success; plainly, he owed little more. Of his mother, only one significant fact is recorded: that when at length an opportunity offered for the boy's escape from his drudgery in the blacking warehouse, Mrs Dickens strongly objected to any such change. An unpleasant topic; enough to recognise in passing, that this incident certainly was not without its permanent effect on the son's mind.

The two years of childish hardship in London (1822-1824), which have resulted in one of the most picturesque and pathetic chapters that English literature can show, were of supreme importance in the growth of the novelist. Recollections of that time supplied him with a store of literary material upon which he drew through all the years of his best activity. In the only possible way he learnt the life of obscure London: himself a part of it, struggling and suffering in its sordid welter, at an age when the strongest impressions are received. It did not last long enough to corrupt the natural sweetness of his mind. Imagine Charles Dickens kept in the blacking warehouse for ten years; picture him striving vainly to find utterance for the thoughts that were in him, refused the society of any but boors and rascals, making, perhaps, a futile attempt to succeed as an actor, and in full manhood measuring the abyss which sundered him from all he had hoped; it is only too easy, knowing the character of the man so well, to conceive what would have resulted. But at twelve years old he was sent to school, and from that day never lost a step on the path of worldly success. In spite of all, he was one of fortune's favourites; what he had undergone turned to his ultimate advantage, and the man who at twenty-four found himself the most popular author of his time and country, might well be encouraged to see things on the cheery side and to laugh with his multitudinous public.

Dickens's biographer makes a fanciful suggestion that the fact of his having observed low life at so tender an age (from ten to twelve) accounts for the purity of tone with which that life is treated in the novelist's works. In its proper place I shall take a different view of Dickens's method in this matter;

it is not to be supposed for a moment that the boy, familiar with London on its grimiest side, working in cellars, inhabiting garrets, eating in cookshops, visiting a debtor's prison (his father was in detention for a time), escaped the contamination of his surroundings. London in all its foulness was stamped on the lad's memory. He escaped in time, that was all, and his fortunate endowment did the rest.

The year 1825, then, saw him at a day-school in North London: the ordinary day-school of that time, which is as much as to say that it was just better than no school at all. One cannot discover that he learnt anything there, or from any professed teacher elsewhere, beyond the very elements of common knowledge. And here again is a point on which throughout his life Dickens felt a certain soreness; he wished to be thought, wished to be, a well-educated man, yet was well aware that in several directions he could never make up for early defects of training. In those days it was socially more important than now to have received a "classical education", and with the classics he had no acquaintance. There is no mistaking the personal note in those passages of his books which treat of, or allude to, Greek and Latin studies in a satirical spirit. True, it is just as impossible to deny that, in this particular field of English life, every sort of insincerity was rampant. Carlyle (who, by the by, was no Grecian) threw scorn upon "gerund-grinding", and with justice; Dickens delighted in showing classical teachers as dreary humbugs, and in hinting that they were such by the mere necessity of the case. Mr Feeder, B.A., grinds, with his Greek or Latin stop on, for the edification of Toots. Dr Blimber snuffles at dinnertime, "It is remarkable that the Romans—", and every terrified boy assumes an air of impossible interest. Even Copperfield's worthy friend, Dr Strong, potters in an imbecile fashion over a Greek lexicon which there is plainly not the slightest hope of his ever completing. Numerous are the side-hits at this educational idol of wealthy England. For all that, remember David's self-congratulation when, his school-days at an end, he feels that he is "well-taught"; in other words, that he is possessed of the results of Dr Strong's mooning over dead languages. Dickens had far too much sense and honesty to proclaim a loud contempt where he knew himself ignorant. For an example of the sort of thing impossible to him, see the passage in an early volume of the Goncourts' Diary, where the egregious brothers report a quarrel with Saint-Victor, a defender of the Ancients; they, in their monumental fatuity, ending the debate by a declaration that a French novel called *Adolphe* was from every point of view preferable to Homer. Dickens knew better than this; but, having real ground for satire in the educational follies of the day, he indulged that personal pique which I have already touched upon, and doubtless reflected that he, at all events, had not greatly missed the help of the old heathens in his battle of life. When his own boys had passed through the approved curriculum of Public School and University, he viewed the question more liberally. One of the most pleasing characters in his later work, Mr Crisparkle in *Edwin Drood*, is a classical tutor, and without shadow of humbug; indeed, he is perhaps the only figure in all Dickens presenting a fair resemblance to the modern type of English gentleman.

There is no use in discussing what a man might have done had he been in important respects another man than he was. That his lack of education meant a serious personal defect in Dickens appears only too plainly through-out the story of his life; that it shows from time to time as a disadvantage in his books there is no denying. I am not concerned with criticism such as Macaulay's attack upon *Hard Times*, on the ground that it showed a hopeless misconception of the problems and methods of Political Economy; it seems to me that Dickens here produced a book of small merit, but this wholly apart from the question of its economic teaching. One feels, however, that the faults of such a book as *Hard Times* must, in some degree, be attrib-uted to Dickens's lack of acquaintance with various kinds of literature, with various modes of thought. The theme, undoubtedly, is admirable, but the manner of its presentment betrays an extraordinary *naïveté*, plainly due to untrained intellect, a mind insufficiently stored. His work offers several such instances. And whilst on this point, it is as well to remember that Dickens's contemporaries did not join unanimously in the chorus of delighted praise which greeted each new book; now and then he met with severe criticism from the graver literary organs, and in most cases such censure directed itself against precisely this weakness. It was held that Dickens set himself to treat of questions beyond his scope, and made known his views with an acrimony altogether unjustified in one who had only prejudice, or, at best, humane sentiment, to go upon. Some of his letters prove how keenly he felt this kind of criticism, which of course had no effect but to confirm him in his own judgments and habits of utterance. In truth, though there were numbers of persons who could point out Dickens's shortcomings as a thinker, only one man could produce literature such as his, enriching a great part of the human race with inestimable gifts of joy and kindness. He went his way in spite of critics, and did the work appointed him.

Of the results of his neglected boyhood as they appear in the details of his life, something will be said hereafter. It would have been wonderful if from such beginnings there had developed, by its own force, a well-balanced character. In balance, in moderation, Dickens was at times conspicuously lacking, whether as man or artist. Something more of education, even in the common sense of the word, would assuredly have helped to subdue this fault in one so largely endowed with the genial virtues. He need not have lost his originality of mind. We can well enough conceive Charles Dickens ripening to the degree of wisdom which would have assured him a more quietly happy, and therefore a longer, life. But to that end other masters are needed than such as pretended to, and such as really did, instruct the unregarded son of the navy pay-officer.

If one asks (as well one may) how it came to pass that an uneducated man produced at the age of three-and-twenty a book so original in subject and treatment, so wonderfully true in observation, and on the whole so well written as *Sketches by Boz*, there is of course but one answer: the man had genius. But even genius is not independent of external aid. "Pray, sir" asked someone of the elder Dickens, "where was your son educated?" And the parent replied, "Why, indeed, sir,—ha! ha! — he may be said to have educated himself!" How early this self-instruction began we have already had a hint in that glimpse of the child sitting by Rochester Castle "with a head full of Partridge, Strap, Tom Pipes and Sancho Panza". Sancho Panza, it may perhaps be presumed, is known even to the present generation; but who were those others? Indeed, who knows anything nowadays of the great writers who nourished the young mind of Dickens? Smollett, Fielding—perhaps, after all, it is as well that these authors do not supply the amusement of our young people. When eight or nine years old, Charles Dickens read them rapturously, all but got them by heart, and he asserts, what may be readily believed, that they did him no jot of harm. But these old novelists are strong food: a boy who is to enrich the literature of the world may well be nourished upon them; other boys, perchance, had better grow up on milder nutriment.

The catalogue of his early reading is most important; let it be given here, as Dickens gives it in *David Copperfield*, with additions elsewhere supplied. *Roderick Random, Peregrine Pickle, Humphrey Clinker, Tom Jones, The Vicar of Wakefield, Don Quixote, Gil Blas, Robinson Crusoe, The Arabian Nights,* and *Tales of the Genii*; also volumes of Essayists: *The Tatler, The Spectator, The Idler, The Citizen of the World,* and a *Collection of Farces* edited by Mrs Inchbald. These the child had found in his father's house at Chatham; he carried them with him in his head to London, and there found them his solace through the two years of bitter bondage. The importance of this list lies not merely in the fact that it certifies Dickens's earliest reading; it remained throughout his whole life (with very few exceptions) the sum of books dear to his memory and to his imagination. Those which he read first were practically the only books which influenced Dickens as an author. We must add the Bible (with special emphasis, the New Testament), Shakespeare, Ben Jonson, and Sterne; among his own contemporaries, Scott and Carlyle. Therewith we may close this tale of authors whom he notably followed through his youth of study and his career as man of letters. After success came to him (and it came so early) he never had much time for reading, and probably never any great inclination. We are told that he especially enjoyed books of travel, but they served merely as recreation. His own travels in Europe supplied him with no new authors (one hears of his trying to read some French novelist, and finding the dialogue intolerably dull), nor with any new mental pursuit. He learned to speak in French and Italian, but made very little use of the attainment. Few really great men can have had so narrow an intellectual scope. Turn to his *practical* interests, and there indeed we have another picture; I speak at present only of the book-lore which shaped his mind, and helped to direct his pen.

To this early familiarity with English classics is due the remarkable command of language shown even in his first sketches. When I come to speak of Dickens's style, it will be time enough to touch upon faults which are obvious; vulgarisms occur in his apprentice work, but the wonder is that they were not more frequent; assuredly they must have been, but for the literary part of that self-education which good fortune had permitted him. A thorough acquaintance with the books above mentioned made him master of that racy tongue which was demanded by his subject, and by his way of regarding it. Destined to a place in the list of writers characteristically English, he found in the works of his predecessors a natural inheritance, and without need of studious reflection came equipped to his task.

No, they are not read nowadays, the old masters of the English novel; yet they must needs be read by anyone who would understand the English people. To the boy Dickens, they presented pictures of life as it was still going on about him; not much had altered; when he himself began to write fiction, his scenes, his characters, made a natural continuance of the stories told by Smollett, Fielding, Sterne, and Goldsmith. To us, at the beginning of the twentieth century, *Nicholas Nickleby* tells of a social life as far away as that described in *Roderick Random*; yet in another respect these books are nearer to us, of more familiar spirit, than the novel—whatever it may be—newest from the press and in greatest vogue. They are a part of our nationality; in both of them runs our very life-blood. However great the changes on the surface of life, England remains, and is likely to remain, the same at heart with the England of our eighteenth-century novelists. By communing with them, one breaks through the disguises of modern fashion, gauges the importance of "progress", and learns to recognize the historically essential. Before the end of this essay, I shall have often insisted on the value of Dickens's work as an expression of national life and sentiment. Born, of course, with the aptitude for such utterance, he could not have had better schooling than in the lumber-room library at Chatham. There he first heard the voice of his own thoughts. And to those books we also must turn, if the fury of today's existence leave us any inclination or leisure for a study of the conditions which produced Charles Dickens.

His choice of a pseudonym for the title-page of his *Sketches* is significant, for, as he tells us himself, "Boz" was simply a facetious nasal contraction, used in his family, of a nickname "Moses", the original Moses being no other than the son of Dr Primrose in the *Vicar of Wakefield*. There is a peculiar happiness in this close link between Goldsmith and Dickens, spirits so much akin in tender humanity. Indeed, Dickens had a special affection for the *Vicar of Wakefield*. When thinking of his first Christmas book (and who could more have delighted in the *Carol* than Oliver Goldsmith?), he says that he wishes to write a story of about the same length as *The Vicar*. One could easily draw a parallel between the two authors; and it is certain that among the influences which made Dickens, none had more importance than the example of Goldsmith's fiction.

A word is called for by the two books, among those mentioned above, which are least connected with English traditions and English thought. The *Arabian Nights* and *Tales of the Genii* were certainly more read in Dickens's day than in ours; probably most children at present would know nothing of Eastern romance but for the Christmas pantomime. Oddly enough, Dickens seems to make more allusions throughout his work to the *Arabian Nights* than to any other book or author. He is not given to quoting, or making literary references; but those fairy tales of the East supply him with a good number of illustrations, and not only in his early novels. Is it merely fanciful to see in this interest, not of course an explanation, but a circumstance illustrative, of that habit of mind which led him to discover infinite romance in the obscurer life of London? Where the ordinary man sees nothing but everyday habit, Dickens is filled with the perception of marvellous possibilities. Again and again he has put the spirit of the *Arabian Nights* into his pictures of life by the river Thames.

Some person annoyed him once by speaking of his books as "romances", and his annoyance is quite intelligible, for a "romance" in the proper sense of the word he never wrote; yet the turn of his mind was very different from that exhibited by a modern pursuer of veracity in fiction. He sought for wonders amid the dreary life of common streets; and perhaps in this direction also his intellect was encouraged when he made acquaintance with the dazzling Eastern fables, and took them alternately with that more solid nutriment of the eighteenth-century novel.

The Essayists must have done much for the refining of his intelligence; probably his reading of Addison and Steele came nearer to education, specially understood, than anything else with which he was occupied in boyhood. Long afterwards, when he had thought of a periodical publication (which was to become *Household Words*), he wrote about it to Forster: "I strongly incline to the notion of a kind of *Spectator* (Addison's) —very cheap and pretty frequent". How strange it sounds to our ears! What editor would nowadays dream of taking Addison as his model? But Dickens was so much nearer to the age of graceful leisure, and, on one side of his personality, had profited so well by its teaching.

Of Sir Walter Scott he does not seem often to have spoken, though there is evidence in one of his American speeches that he truly admired that greater spirit. And it seems to me that Scotts influence is not to be mistaken in the narrative of *Barnaby Rudge*.

One artist there was, an artist with the brush and burin, of whom it may be said that Dickens assuredly learnt, though I cannot see a possibility of comparing their work, as Forster and others have done. The genius of Hogarth differed widely from that of the author of *Pickwick*, but it was inevitable that his profound studies of life and character should attract, even fascinate, a mind absorbed in contemplation of poverty and all its concomitants. Added thereto was the peculiar interest in the artist's name, which resulted to Dickens from his marriage at the age of twenty-four with Miss Hogarth, this lady claiming descent from her great namesake. Both men were strenuous moralists, but it would be hard to show any other point of resemblance in their methods of presenting fact. As to their humour, I am unable to find anything in Hogarth which can for a moment be compared with that quality in Dickens. Hogarth smiles, it is true, but how grimly! There prevails in him an uncompromising spirit of which the novelist had nothing whatever. Try to imagine a volume of fiction produced by the artist of *Gin Lane*, of *The Harlot's Progress*, and put it beside the books which, from *Pickwick* onwards, have been the delight of English homes. Puritans both of them, Hogarth shows his religion on the sterner side; Dickens, in a gentle avoidance of whatsoever may give offence to the pure in heart, the very essence of his artistic conscience being that compromise which the other scorned. In truth, as artists they saw differently. Dickens was no self-deceiver; at any moment his steps would guide him to parts of London where he could behold, and had often beheld, scenes as terrible as any that the artist struck into black and white; he looked steadily at such things, and, at the proper time, could speak of them. But when he took up the pen of the story-teller, his genius constrained him to such use, such interpretation, of bitter fact as made him beloved, not dreaded, by readers asking, before all else, to be soothingly entertained. On this point I shall have more to say presently. Enough here, that the great limner undoubtedly helped to concentrate the young writer's mind on subjects he was to treat in his own way. Evidence, were it needed, is found in the preface to *Oliver Twist*, where, after speaking of the romantic types of rascality then popular in fiction, he declares that only in one book has he seen the true thief depicted, namely, in the works of Hogarth.

With one artist of his own time Dickens was brought into close relations. The *Sketches* were illustrated by George Cruikshank; so was *Oliver Twist*, and a foolish bit of gossip, troublesome at the time, would have it that Oliver's history had come into being at the suggestion of certain drawings of Cruikshank's own. For my own part, I can enjoy only a few of the famous etchings in these early books; it appears to me that a man of less originality than Cruikshank's, the late Fred Barnard, has done better work in his pictures to the novels, better in the sense of more truly illustrative. But in their leaning to the grotesque, Dickens and Cruikshank were so much alike that one can at all events understand the baseless story which Dickens took all possible trouble to refute. Some years afterwards, when Cruikshank published his picture called *The Bottle*, intended as a blow in the cause of temperance, Dickens spoke and wrote of it with high admiration, though he had fault to find with the manner in which its lesson was conveyed. There could not but exist much sympathy between these workers on lines so similar in different arts; but beyond the fact of Dickens's liking for the artist's designs from the beginning of his own career, nothing, so far as I know, can be advanced in proof of his having been guided or prompted by Cruikshank's genius.

It was in imitation of his father's example that Dickens, by learning shorthand, prepared himself to become, first a reporter in one of the offices in Doctors'-Commons (the remarkable region so well known from *David Copperfield*), and after that in the gallery of the House. Thus far had he got at nineteen. With the vivacious energy which was always his leading characteristic, he made himself, forthwith, a journalist of mark in the sphere to which he was restricted. Prior to this, whilst earning his livelihood as a clerk in an attorney's office, he had somehow read a good deal at the British Museum, and had devoted most of his evenings to the theatre. It may safely be said that the evening amusement was much more important in its results than any formal study he undertook; unless, indeed,—a not improbable conjecture—he, like Charles Lamb, sought the reading-room of the Museum chiefly for dramatic literature. At this time of his life, Dickens had resolved upon a theatrical career; whether as dramatist or actor he did not much mind, feeling equal to either pursuit. His day's drudgery, however thoroughly performed, was endured only in the hope of release as soon as he found his chance upon the stage. Of course he would have succeeded in either capacity, though with a success far less brilliant than fate had in store for him. He did in the end become, if not strictly an actor, at all events a public entertainer whose strongest effects were produced by the exercise of melodramatic talent; as an amateur, he acted frequently throughout his life. His attempts at dramatic authorship—*The Strange Gentleman*, a farce played in 1836; *The Village Coquettes*, a libretto, produced in the same year; and *The Lamplighter*, a farce written in 1838, but never acted—gave no serious proof of his powers in this direction; they were hurriedly thrown off at the time when his literary fame was already beginning. But in the year or two before he wrote his *Sketches*, when the consciousness of vague ability and high ambition made him restive in his mechanical calling of shorthand writer, he applied to the manager of Covent Garden Theatre for an opportunity of showing what he could do. The accident of illness interfered with an appointment granted him, and, owing to advance in journalism, the application was not renewed. Plainly Dickens came very near indeed to entering upon the actor's life, and so close throughout is his connection with the theatrical world, that one cannot glance at this incident as a mere detail in the story of his youth. It declares a natural bent of mind, not the passing inclination which is so often felt by lads more or less gifted.

When, in the full enjoyment of his power, Dickens amused himself and served charitable ends by getting up dramatic performances, we note a significance in his selection of a play. He chose Ben Jonson's *Every Man in His Humour*, himself taking the part of Bobadil. How early he read Ben Jonson, I am unable to say; I should like to be assured that it was in those hours spent at the British Museum, when all his work yet lay before him. One can well imagine the delight of Dickens in a first acquaintance with rare Ben. Forster gives an excellent description of the zeal and gusto with which his friend entered into the character of Bobadil; how for some weeks he actually *became* Bobadil, talking him and writing him on every opportunity. What more natural than his enjoyment of the sterling old writer whose strength lay in the exhibition of extravagant humours! Dickens had no such life about him as the Elizabethan; in comparison, his world was starved and squalid; but of the humours of the men he knew—*humours* precisely in Jonson's sense—he made richer use than anything in that kind known to English literature since the golden age. All Dickens might be summed in the title of Jonson's play; no figure but is representative of a "humour", running at times into excesses hardly surpassed by Ben himself. On several occasions (1845-50) he acted in this comedy, and one can hardly doubt that it helped to confirm his tendency to exuberance of grotesque characterization.

So much, then, for that part of his self-education which came from books. Meanwhile life had been supplying him with abundant experience, which no one knew better than Dickens how to store and utilize. Théophile Gautier, an observer of a very different type, says somewhere of himself: "*Toute ma valeur, c'est que je suis un homme pour qui le monde visible existe*"; in Dickens this was far from the sole, or the supreme, quality; but assuredly few men have known so well how to use their eyes. A student is commonly inobservant of outward things; Dickens, far from a bookish youth, looked about him in those years of struggle for a livelihood with a glance which missed no minutest feature of what he saw. We are told that his eyes were very bright, impressing all who met him with a sense of their keenness. Keen they were in no ordinary sense; for they pierced beneath the surface, and (in Lamb's phrase) discerned the *quiddity* of common objects. Everything he looked upon was registered in his mind, where at any moment he could revive the original impression, and with his command of words, vital, picturesque, show the thing to others.

His work as attorney's clerk lasted for not quite two years (1827-28); his reporter-ship in the courts of Doctors'-Commons seems to have been of even shorter duration; but in this time he probably acquired most of his knowledge of the legal world, which was shown first of all in *Pickwick*, and continued to appear, in one form or another, throughout his books. For exactitude of observation, this group of professional figures, from office-boy up to judge, is the most valuable thing in Dickens. It strikes one as noteworthy, on the other hand, that he never cared to use his experience of journalism. Practically, he once attempted to resume his connection with the press, and became editor of *The-Daily News*—for not quite three weeks

(1846); but the novels (unless we take account of the caricatures in *Pickwick*) have no concern with that side of literary life. Within limits the picture is supplied by Thackeray. But Dickens might have put to wonderful service his memories of the time when he reported for the *True Sun*, the *Mirror of Parliament*, and the *Morning Chronicle* (1831-36). He told the story, long afterwards, in one of the best and brightest of his speeches, that given at the dinner of the Newspaper Press Fund in 1865; when, speaking to a generation which travelled by steam, he recalled how he had been upset in almost every description of vehicle known in this country, and had carried reports to his editor in the teeth of difficulties insuperable by any man of merely common energy and resource. What use he made of his experiences in travel by highway and byway, we know well, for these are among his characteristic. Never is Dickens more joyously himself than when he tells of stage-coach and posting-vehicles. He tried his hand at a description of the railway, but with no such gusto, no such success. His youth belonged to the pre-locomotive time, the time of jolly faring on English roads—jolly in spite of frost and rain, and discomforts innumerable. All this he has made his own, and he learned it as a newspaper reporter

For the acquiring of knowledge of his own country he could hardly have been better placed. Hither and thither he sped, north and south, east and west, to report the weighty words of orators now long forgotten. He saw most English towns; he marked with pleasure the hamlets and villages; of inns, great and small, he learnt all that man is capable of learning. And in that old England, there was more of the picturesque, more of the beautiful, than we see today. I have insisted upon the ugliness of the life of that time; indeed, it can hardly be exaggerated; but there is another aspect of Dickens's England, one which might be illustrated with ample detail from all his better books. Side by side with the increase of comfort (or of luxury), with that lightening of dark places which is surely good, goes on the destruction of so much one would fain preserve. Think, for instance, of Yarmouth, as seen in *David Copperfield*, and the Yarmouth of this year's railway advertisements. What more need be said!

Not only, then, in London, but through the length and breadth of the land, Dickens was seeing and studying his countrymen. Nothing that he learnt embittered him, any more than had his own hardships in the years happily gone by; but he noted many a form of suffering, with the tyranny, great or small, the hypocrisy and the thickheadedness which were responsible for it; and when his time came, he knew how to commend these things to the sympathy, the indignation, the mirth of larger audiences than any author had yet controlled. Overflowing with the enjoyment of life, he naturally found more sunshine than gloom, whether in crowded streets, or by the wayside with its scattered wanderers. Now, as always, he delighted in the amusements of the people, in fairs and shows, and every sort of humble entertainment. A conjurer, a fortune-teller, a shabby acrobat, a cheap-Jack—one and all were irresistible to him; he could not pass a menagerie, a circus, a strolling troop of players; the squeak of Punch had as much charm for him as for any child. Merely to mention such folk is to call up a host of reminiscences from the books which bear his name. He had not the vagabond nature which we see, for instance, in George Borrow; he is a man of the town, of civilization; but the forms of vagabondage which arise amid a great population, quaint survivals, ragged eccentricities, laughter-moving incarnations of rascality and humbug, excited his unfailing interest. He lived to take his place in a society of wealth, culture, and refinement; but his heart was always with the people, with the humble-minded and those of low estate. Among these he had found the material for his genius to work upon, and, most important of all, among these he learnt to make himself the perfect mouthpiece of English homeliness.

In *Oliver Twist* we come upon a casual mention, quite serious, of "continental frivolities". The phrase is delightfully English, and very characteristic of Dickens's mind when he began to write. Ten years later he would not have used it; he outgrew that narrowness; but it was well that he knew no better at five-and-twenty. Insularity in his growing time was needful to him, and must be counted for a virtue.

A year before Queen Victoria's accession, appeared, in two volumes, *Sketches by Boz, illustrative of Everyday Life and Everyday People*, a collection of papers which had already seen the light in periodicals. This book came from a 'prentice hand, but it contains in germ all the future Dickens. Glance at the headings of the pages; here we have the Beadle and all connected with him, London streets, theatres, shows, the pawnshop, Doctors'-Commons, Christmas, Newgate, coaching, the River; here we have a satirical picture of Parliament, fun made of cheap snobbery, a rap on the knuckles of sectarianism. Hardly a topic associated with Dickens in his maturity is missing from the earliest attempts. What could be more prophetic than the title of the opening chapters—*Our Parish*? With the Parish — a large one, indeed—Dickens to the end concerned himself; therein lay his force, his secret of vitality. He began with a rapid survey of his whole field; hinting at all he might accomplish, indicating the limits he was not to pass.

He treats at once of the lower middle class, where he will be always at his best; with the class below it, with those who literally earn bread in the sweat of their brows, he was better acquainted than any other novelist of his time, but they figure much less prominently in his books. To the lower middle class, a social status so peculiarly English, so rich in virtues yet so provocative of satire, he by origin belonged; in its atmosphere he always breathed most freely, and had the largest command of his humorous resources. Humour is a characteristic of *Boz*, but humour undeveloped, tentative; merely a far-off promise of the fruit which ripened so rapidly. There is joking about the results of matrimony, a primitive form of facetiousness which belongs to the time and the class, and which it took Dickens a good many years to shake off. Vulgarity was, of course, inseparable from his subject, and that the young author should have been himself involved in the charge is easily understood. A vulgar expression may be here and there discovered (I mean, of course, in the author's own words), but the tone of the whole work is as far from vulgarity as that of the eighteenth-century sketches and meditations of which we are occasionally reminded. As for the form, it strikes one as more original than that of the subsequent books. No one, indeed, had ever made such use as this of materials taken from the very dust-heap of decent London life; such common paltry stuff of the town, yet here so truthfully described, with such intimate touches, such glimpses of mirthful motive, as come only from the hand of the born artist. Veracity I take to be the high merit of these sketches. Dickens has not yet developed his liking for the grotesquely original; he pictures the commonplace, with no striving for effect, and admirably succeeds. Some of these descriptions of the town in its various aspects, day and night, he never surpassed; they abound in detail, yet never by any chance admit a false note. His persons live and move; you may encounter nearly all of them today, affected by the course of time, but still recognizable from his fine portraiture. It was no slight achievement for a youth of four-and-twenty, this putting on record once for all of so large and significant a portion of English life.

Therewith ended Dickens's apprenticeship. He had stored his material, was on the point of attaining full command of his powers. When next he sat down to write he produced a masterpiece.

III

The Story-Teller

A glance over the literary annals of the time during which Dickens was apprentice to his craft shows us, in fiction, the names of Disraeli, Peacock, Mrs Norton, Bulwer, Ainsworth, and Marryat. One and all signify little to the coming master, though he professed a high esteem for the romances of Lord Lytton, and with Captain Marryat shared the tradition of the eighteenth-century novelists. Tennyson had already come forth; Browning had printed a poem; *Sartor Resartus* had "got itself published", and was waiting for readers. In another sphere, *Tracts for the Times* were making commotion; regarding which matter the young student of life doubtless had already his opinion. It is of more interest to note that in 1832 were established *Chambers's Journal and Knight's Penny Magazine*; indicative of the growth of a new public, a class of readers which no author had hitherto directly addressed, and which was only to be reached by publication in the cheapest form. From the preface to *Oliver Twist* we learn that romances of highwaymen had much vogue, of course among the populace, and about this time Ainsworth responded to the demand with his *Jack Sheppard*. Against this prevalent glorification of rascality Dickens directed his first novel, properly so called.

Pickwick cannot be classed as a novel ; it is merely a great book. Everyone knows that it originated in the suggestion of a publisher that the author of *Sketches by Boz* should write certain facetious chapters to accompany certain facetious drawings; it was to be a joke at the expense of Cockney sportsmen. Dickens obtained permission to write in his own way. Of the original suggestion there remains Mr Winkle with the gun; for the rest, this bit of hackwork became a good deal more than the writer himself foresaw. Obviously he sat down with only the vaguest scheme; even the personality of his central figure was not clear to him. A pardonable fault, when the circumstances are known, but the same defect appears in all Dickens's earlier books; he only succeeded in correcting it when his imaginative fervour had begun to cool, and in the end he sought by the artifices of an elaborate plot to make up for the decline of qualities greatly more important. In considering Dickens as an artist, I propose first of all to deal with the construction of his stories. Let it be understood that in the present chapter I discuss the novels solely from this point of view, postponing consideration of those features of the master's work which are his strength and his glory.

However ill-constructed, *Pickwick*, I imagine, was never found uninteresting. One may discourse about it in good set terms, pointing out that it belongs to a very old school of narrative, and indicating resemblances with no less a work than *Don Quixote*—Mr Pickwick and Sam Weller being in some degree the antitypes of the Knight of La Mancha and Sancho. Intrigue there is none (save in the offices of Messrs. Dodson and Fogg). The thing is aimed at the reader's diaphragm, and, by ricochet, touches his heart. Lord Campbell declared that he would rather have written *Pickwick* than be Chief Justice of England; yet here we have simply the rambles and accidents and undignified escapades of certain Londoners, one of them accompanied by a manservant, whom he picked up as boots at an inn; we have a typical London landlady, a breach-of-promise case, and a debtors' prison. What unpromising material, in the year 1837, for any author but the one who knew how to make immortal use of it!

As in the *Sketches* we found the germ of all Dickens, so in this second book, not yet a novel, may we mark tendencies soon to have full development. The theme itself admitting no great variety of tone, we have the time-honoured device of episodic stories; one of them shows that melodramatic bent which was to be of such importance in future books; another, the tale of Gabriel Grub, gives, thus early, a hint of the Christmas fantasies which so greatly strengthened their author's hold on the popular admiration and love. The close gives us our first example of Dickens's resolute optimism. Everybody (or all but everybody) is to be made happy for ever after; knavish hearts are softened by gratitude, and those of the good beat high in satisfied benevolence. This is the kind of thing that delights the public, and lucky would be the public if it were often offered to them with a rich sincerity like that of Dickens.

With *Oliver Twist* we take up the tradition of English novel-writing; at once we are reminded of the old books in the library at Chatham. Scenes and people and tone are new, but the manner is that long ago established. As for construction, there is a little, and a very little, more of it than in *Pickwick* ; it is badly managed, so badly, that one seeks to explain the defect

The "Old White Hart" Inn, Southwark

by remembering that the early part of *Oliver* and the last part of *Pickwick* were in hand simultaneously. Yet not in this book alone did Dickens give proof of an astonishing lack of skill when it came to inventing plausible circumstances. Later, by sheer force of resolve, he exhibited ingenuity enough, often too much for his purpose; but the art of adapting simple probabilities to the ends of a narrative he never mastered. In his plots, unfortunately, he is seldom concerned with the plain motives of human life. (Observe that I am speaking of his *plots*.) Too often he prefers some far-fetched eccentricity, some piece of knavishness, some unlikely occurrence, about which to weave his tale. And this, it seems to me, is directly traceable to his fondness for the theatre. He planned a narrative as though plotting for the stage. When the necessities of intrigue did not weigh upon him—as happily was so often the case in his roomy stories—he could forget the footlights; at the first demand for an "effect", gas and limelight are both turned on. Cannot we often hear the incidental music? Dickens's love for the stage was assuredly a misfortune to him, as author and as man.

In the idle mysteries which are made to surround Oliver, and in the incredible weakness of what is meant to be the darkest part of the story, we have pure stage-work. Chapter XVII contains a passage ridiculing the melodrama of the time, a tissue of medieval villanies; what Dickens himself did, in these worst moments of his invention, was to use the motives of standard melodrama on a contemporary subject. Even the dialogue occasionally proves this. "Wolves tear your throats!" growls Bill Sikes, fleeing from his pursuers—a strange exclamation for a London burglar. And again, when brought to bay after the murder he calls one of the horrified thieves "this screeching Hell-Babe"—a phrase natural enough on the boards of the Adelphi Theatre, but incongruous in a London slum. That part of the book in which Rose Maylie and her lover appear smacks rather of the circulating library than of the stage. We read of Rose in distress that "a heavy wildness came over her soft blue eyes". I cannot remember that Dickens was ever again guilty of such a phrase as this; but the theatric vice appears in his construction to the end.

In the years 1838 and 1839 he did far too much. *Nicholas Nickleby* was begun long before the end of *Oliver Twist*, as *Oliver* was begun before the end of *Pickwick*. Ill-considered engagements so pressed upon him that in February, 1839, we find him appealing to his publisher for patience, and expressing an opinion that "the conduct of three different stories at the same time, and the production of a large portion of each every month, would have been beyond Scott himself". It came as a natural result of his sudden and great success. Finally, he put himself at ease by a simple refusal to be bound by his undertakings; an extreme step, but one which has to be balanced against the interested calculations of a shrewd publisher.

It is plain that *Nickleby* suffered from these circumstances of undue stress; in spite of its popularity, and of merits presently to be recognized, it is the least satisfactory of the group of books written before Dickens's first visit to America. Five books in five years, from *Pickwick* in 1837 to *Barnaby Rudge* in 1841—a record nothing like that of Scott, but wonderful as the work of a man with only half Scott's length of experience to draw upon. *Nickleby* being much longer than its predecessor, the faulty construction is more felt, and becomes a weariness, an irritation; that is to say, if one thinks of the matter at all, which one never should in reading Dickens. Again we are involved in melodrama of the feeblest description; towards the end of the story there are wastes of stagey dialogue and action, unreadable by any but the very young. All this is quite unworthy of the author; but, following upon *Oliver*, it indicated the limits of his power as a novelist. Dickens never had command of "situation", though he was strong in incident. A great situation must be led up to by careful and skilful foresight in character and event—precisely where his resources always failed him. Thus, scenes which he intended, and perhaps thought, to be very effective, fall flat through their lack of substance. A mature reader turns away in disgust, and, if he belong to a hasty school of modern criticism, henceforth declares that Dickens is hopelessly antiquated, and was always vastly over-praised.

Here, for the last time, we have episodic stories; admissible enough in a book which, for all its faults, smacks so of the leisurely old fiction. In *The Old Curiosity Shop*, which came next, there is more originality of design: one does not smell the footlights, but has, instead, delicious wafts of freshness from the fields and lanes of England. Of course' we find an initial vice of construction, inseparable from Dickens's habit at that time of beginning to write without any settled scheme. Master Humphrey opens with talk of himself, enters upon a relation of something that befell him in his wanderings, and of a sudden—the author perceiving this necessity—vanishes from the scene, which is thenceforth occupied by the figures he has served to introduce. In other words, readers of the periodical called *Master Humphrey's Clock* having shown some impatience with its desultory character, Dickens converted into a formal novel the bit of writing which he had begun as sketch or gossip. Nowadays it would be all but impossible for a writer of fiction, who by any accident should have written and published serially a work with such a fault of design, to republish it in a volume without correcting the faulty part; a very slight degree of literary conscientiousness, as we understand it, would impose this duty; nay, fear of the public would exact it. But such a thing never occurred to Dickens. Conscientious he was in matters of his art, as we shall have occasion to notice, but the art itself was less exacting in his day; a multitude applauded, and why should he meddle with what they had so loudly approved? In the same way we find Walter Scott coming one fine day upon an old manuscript of his own—two or three chapters of a romance long ago begun and thrown aside. He reads the pages, smiles over them, and sits down to complete the story. In reading the proofs of *Waverley*, if not before, Scott must have been well aware of the great gap between its two portions, of the difference of style, the contrast of tone: the early chapters so obviously an experiment, the latter mature and masterly. It would have taken him a very few hours to rewrite the beginning; but why? The whole thing was done for his amusement. The public, in its turn, was something more than amused. And our grave Art of Fiction, a stern task-mistress, had nothing to do with the matter.

For the rest, *The Old Curiosity Shop* is greatly superior from this point of view to the previous novels. The story has more of symmetry; it moves more regularly to its close, and that close is much more satisfying; it remains in one's mind as a whole, with no part that one feels obtrusive or incongruous or wearily feeble. In writing the last portion, Dickens was so engrossed by his theme that he worked at unusual hours, prolonging the day's labour into the night—never, of course, a habit with a man of his social instincts. The book gained thereby its unity of effect. It is a story in the true sense, and one of the most delightful in our language.

Last of this early group—product of continuous effort through five of the happiest years that man ever lived—comes *Barnaby Rudge*, which is in part a story of private life, in part a historical novel. The two portions are not well knit together; the interest with which we begin is lost in far wider interests before we end; nevertheless *Barnaby* is free from Dickens's worst vices of construction. Granting the imperfection of the scheme, it is closely wrought, and its details are not ill-contrived. One defect forced upon our attention is characteristic of Dickens: his inability to make skilful revelation of circumstances which, for the purpose of the story, he has kept long concealed. This skill never came to him; with apology for so disrespectful a word, he must be held to have bungled all his effects of this kind, and there can be no doubt that the revealing of the mystery of *Edwin Drood* would have betrayed the old inability. Permit Dickens to show us the life he knew in its simple everyday course, and he is unsurpassed by any master of fiction; demand from him a contrived story, and he yields at once to the very rank and file of novelists.

A peculiarity of this book is the frequent opening of a chapter with several lines of old-fashioned moralizing, generally on the compensations of life. Later, Dickens found a happy substitute for this kind of thing in his peculiar vein of good-humoured satire, which had a more practical if a narrower scope.

The year 1842 was a turning-point in his career. He paid his first visit to America, and came back with his ideas enlarged on many subjects. After publishing *American Notes*, and the first of his Christmas books, the *Carol*, he completed, in 1844, what is in some respects the greatest of his works, *Martin Chuzzlewit*. The fact that such a judgment is possible shows how little the characteristic merit of Dickens's writings has to do with their completeness as works of art; for a novel more shapeless, a story less coherent than *Martin Chuzzlewit*, will not easily be found in any literature. Repeated readings avail not to fix it in one's mind as a sequence of events; we know the persons, we remember many a scene, but beyond that all is a vague reminiscence. I repeat, that one can only feel astonishment at the inability of such a man as Dickens to scheme better than this. Had he but trusted to some lucid narrative, however slight! Misled by the footlights, he aims at a series of "effects", every one void of human interest, or, at best, an outrage upon probability. He involves himself in complications which necessitate leaps and bounds of perverse ingenuity. And at last, his story frankly hopeless, he cuts through knots, throws difficulties into oblivion, and plays up his characters to a final rally; so sure of his touch upon the readers' emotions that he can disregard their bewilderment. The first chapter, a very dull, long-drawn piece of ridicule directed against the supposed advantages of "birth", has nothing whatever to do with the story; the book would gain by its omission. Dickens in a splenetic mood (a rare thing) is far from at his best. *Chuzzlewit* surpasses all his novels in the theatrical conventionality of its great closing scene—its grand finale (see Chapter LII). Around old Martin (at the centre of the stage) are grouped all the dramatis personae, whether they have any business there or not; Mrs Gamp, Poll Sweedlepipe, and young Bailey coming in without rhyme or reason, simply to complete the circle. It is magnificent: the brilliant triumph of stage tradition. But it does not suffice; something more is needed that the reader's appetite for a cheerful ending may have entire satisfaction; therefore, before the book closes, who should turn up in the heart of London but that very family of miserable emigrants whom Martin and Tapley had left behind them in the wild west of America! Here they are, at the foot of the Monument, close by Todgers'—arrived on purpose to shake hands with everyone, and to fill the cup of benevolent rejoicing. What man save Dickens ever dared so much; what man will ever find the courage to strike that note again!

It is necessary to bear in mind that these novels appeared in monthly parts—twenty of them—and that the author began publishing with only three or four parts completed. Such a mode of writing accounts for many things. Dickens admitted certain disadvantages, but always held that this was the best way of pursuing his art. Of course the novel became an improvisation. In beginning *Chuzzlewit*, he had no intention whatever of sending his hero to America; the resolve was taken, suddenly, when a declining sale proved that the monthly instalments were not proving so attractive as usual. Impossible ever to make changes in the early chapters of a story, however urgently the artist's conscience demanded it; impossible, in Dickens's case, to see mentally as a whole the work on which he was engaged. What he had written, he had written; it had to serve its purpose. One can only lament that such were the defects of his inimitable qualities.

The next great book was not finished till 1848; meanwhile there had been travel and residence on the Continent—a bright chapter in Dickens's life, but without noteworthy influence on his work. His Italian sketches are character-istic of the man; one cannot say more. Among the Alps he wrote *Dombey and Son*, not without trouble due to the unfamiliar surroundings. "You can hardly imagine", he declares to Forster, "what infinite pains I take, or what extraordi-nary difficulty I find in getting on *fast* ... I suppose this is partly the effect of two years' ease, and partly of the absence of the streets and numbers of figures. I can't express how much I want these. It seems as if they supplied something to my brain, which I cannot bear, when busy, to lose." In truth, away from London he was cut off from the source of his inspiration; but he had a memory stored with London pictures. He tells us, and we can well believe him, that, whilst writing, he saw every bed in the dormitory of Paul's school, every pew in the church where Florence was married. In which connection it is worth mentioning that not till the year 1855 did Dickens keep any sort of literary memorandum-book. After all his best work was done, he felt misgivings which prompted him to make notes. A French or English realist, with his library of documents, may muse over this fact—and deduce from it what he pleases.

Dombey is the first of the novels which have a distinct moral theme; its subject is Pride. Here there is no doubt that Dickens laid down the broad outlines of his story in advance, and adhered to them; we feel that the book is built up with great pains, with infinite endeavour to make a unity. The advance is undeniable (of course we have lost something, for all that), but one cannot help noticing that with the death of Paul ends a novel which is complete in itself, a novel more effective, I think, than results from the prolonged work. Dickens tells, in letters, of the effort it cost him to trans-fer immediately all the interest of his story from the dead boy to his sister Florence; the necessity for it was unfortunate. As usual, we have loud mel-odrama side by side with comedy unsurpassed for its delicate touches of truth and fancy. The girl Alice and her disreputable mother, pendants to Edith Dombey and Mrs Skewton, are in mid-limelight; perhaps Dickens never so boldly defied the modesty of nature as here, both in character and situation. An instance of farfetched and cumbrous contrivance, with gross improbability added to it, is Mr Dombey's discovery of the place to which his wife has fled. Nothing easier than to bring about the same end by simple and probable means; but Dickens had an "effect" in view—of the kind that so strangely satisfied him. His melodrama serves an end which is new in *Dombey*, though afterwards of frequent occurrence: that of bringing together, in strangely intimate relations, figures representing social extremes. Dickens came to delight in this. His best use of the motive is in *Bleak House*; and a striking instance occurs in the last pages he ever wrote.

It was whilst telling the story of little Paul, a victim of excessive paren-
tal care, that, perhaps by force of contrast, the novelist looked back upon
his own childhood, and thought of turning it to literary use. We learn from
Forster (Book i, chapter 2) that in the year 1847 was written a chapter of
reminiscences which Dickens at first intended to be the beginning of an autobiography. Wisely, no doubt, he soon abandoned this idea; but the memory
of his own sad childhood would not be dismissed, and it made the ground-
work of his next novel (1850), *David Copperfield*. Dickens held this to be his
best book, and the world has agreed with him. In no other does the narrative
move on with such full sail from first to last. He wrote from his heart; picturing completely all he had suffered as a child, and even touching upon the
domestic trouble of his later life. It is difficult to speak of *David Copperfield*
in terms of cool criticism, but for the moment I am concerned only with
its form, and must put aside the allurement of its matter. Once more, then,
combined with lavish wealth of description, character, pathos, humour, we
meet with poverty of invention, abuse of drama. All the story of Emily (after
her childhood) is unhappily conceived. (Of course this part of the book was
at once dramatized and acted.) Such a subject lay wholly beyond Dickens's
scope, and could not be treated by him in any but an unsatisfactory way.
The mysteries surrounding Mr Wickham, the knaveries of Uriah Heep, have
no claim upon our belief; intrigue half-heartedly introduced merely because
intrigue seems necessary; even Mr Micawber, in all his robust reality, has to
walk among these airy figments, and play his theatrical part. In the scene
between Emily and Rosa Dartle (Chapter L) the orchestra plays very loudly
indeed; every word has its accompanying squeak or tremolo. But enough;
one has not the heart to dwell upon the shortcomings of such a book.

It may be noted, however, with what frankness Dickens accepts the
conventionality of a story told in the first person. David relates in detail
conversations which take place before he is born, and makes no apology for
doing so. Why should he? The point never occurs to the engrossed reader. In
Bleak House, where the same expedient is used (in part), such boldness is not
shown, though the convention still demands abundant sacrifice of probability in another way. Finally, in *Great Expectations* we have a narrative in the
first person, which, granting to the narrator nothing less than Dickens's own
equipment of genius, preserves verisimilitude with remarkable care, nothing
being related, as seen or heard, which could not have been seen or heard by
the writer. This instance serves to show that Dickens did become conscious
of artistic faults, and set himself to correct them. But, in the meantime, he
had touched the culmination of his imaginative life, and a slight improve-

ment in technical correctness could not compensate the world's loss when his characteristic strength began to fail and his natural force to be abated.

Bleak House (1853) is constructed only too well. Here Dickens applied himself laboriously to the perfecting of that kind of story he had always had in view, and produced a fine example of theatrical plot. One cannot say, in this case, that the intrigue refuses to be remembered; it is a puzzle, yet ingeniously simple; the parts fitting together very neatly indeed. So neatly, that poor untidy Life disclaims all connection with these doings, however willingly she may recognize for her children a score or so of the actors. To be sure there are oversights. How could Dickens expect one to believe that Lady Dedlock recognized her lover's handwriting in a piece of work done by him as *law-writer*—she not even knowing that he was so employed? What fate pursued him that he could not, in all the resources of his brain, hit upon a device for such a simple end more convincing than this? Still, with an end not worth attaining, the author here wrought successfully. The story is child's play compared with many invented, for instance, by Wilkie Collins; but in combination with Dickens's genuine powers, it produces its designed effect; we move in a world of choking fog and squalid pitfalls, amid plot and counterplot, cold self-interest and passion over-wrought, and can never refuse attention to the magician who shows it all.

I have left it to this place to speak of the sin, most gross, most palpable, which Dickens everywhere commits in his abuse of "coincidence". *Bleak House* is the supreme example of his recklessness. It seems never to have occurred to him, thus far in his career, that novels and fairy tales (or his favourite *Arabian Nights*) should obey different laws in the matter of incident. When Oliver Twist casually makes acquaintance with an old gentleman in the streets of London, this old gentleman of course turns out to be his relative, who desired of all things to discover the boy. When Steerforth returns to England from his travels with Emily, his ship is of course wrecked on the sands at Yarmouth, and his dead body washed up at the feet of David Copperfield, who happened to have made a little journey to see his Yarmouth friends on that very day. In *Bleak House* scarcely a page but presents some coincidence as glaring as these. Therein lies the worthlessness of the plot, which is held together only by the use of coincidence in its most flagrant forms. Grant that anything may happen just where or when the interest of the story demands it, and a neat drama may pretty easily be constructed. The very boldness of the thing prevents readers from considering it; indeed most readers take the author's own view, and imagine every artificiality to be permitted in the world of fiction.

Dickens was content to have aroused interest, wonder, and many other emotions. The conception of the book is striking; the atmosphere could hardly be better; even the melodrama (as in Krook's death by spontaneous combustion) justifies itself by magnificent workmanship. No doubt the generality of readers are wise, and it is pedantry to object to the logical extremes of convention in an art which, without convention, would not exist.

One wishes that Esther Summerson had not been allowed to write in her own person—or rather to assume, with such remarkable success, the personality of Charles Dickens. This well-meaning young woman, so blind to her own merits, of course had no idea that she was a great humorist and a writer of admirable narrative; but readers (again the reflective few) are only too much impressed by her powers. Again one closes his eyes, and suffers a glad illusion. But for the occasional "I" one may easily enough forget that Miss Summerson is speaking.

I must pass rapidly over the novels that remain. Of *Little Dorrit* (1855), as of *Martin Chuzzlewit*, who can pretend to bear the story in mind? There is again a moral theme: the evils of greed and vulgar ambition. As a rule, we find this book dismissed rather contemptuously; it is held to be tedious, and unlike Dickens in its prevalent air of gloom. For all that, I believe it to contain some of his finest work, some passages in which he attains an artistic finish hardly found elsewhere; and to these I shall return. There were reasons why the book should be lacking in the old vivacity—never indeed to be recovered, in so far as it had belonged to the golden years of youth; it was written in a time of domestic unhappiness and of much unsettlement, the natural result of which appeared three years later, when Dickens left the study for the platform. As a narrative, *Little Dorrit* is far from successful; it is cumbered with mysteries which prove futile, and has no proportion in its contrasting parts. Here and there the hand of the master is plainly weary.

More so, however, in the only other full-length novel which he lived to complete. None of his books is so open to the charge of tedious superfluity as *Our Mutual Friend* (1865); on many a page dialogue which is strictly no dialogue at all, but mere verbosity in a vein of forced humour, drags its slow length along in caricature of the author at his best. A plot, depending on all manner of fantastic circumstances, unfolds itself with dreary elaboration, and surely delights no one. Yet I have a sense of ingratitude in speaking thus of *Our Mutual Friend*; for in it Dickens went far towards breaking with his worst theatrical traditions, and nowhere, I think, irritates one with a violent improbability in the management of his occurrences. The multiplication of wills, as Dickens insisted in reply to criticism, need not trouble anyone who reads the newspapers; at worst it lacks interest. With anything, however, but gratification, one notes that the author is adapting himself to a new time, new people, new manners. Far behind us are the stage-coach and the brandy-drinkers; the age, if more respectable, has become decidedly duller. Even so with Dickens; he feels the constraint of a day to which he was not born, and whilst bending himself to its demands, succeeds only in making us regret the times gone by.

For new schools of fiction have meanwhile arisen in England. Charlotte Brontë has sent forth her three books; Kingsley is writing, and Charles Reade, and Anthony Trollope; George Meredith, and, later, George Eliot, have begun their careers. We are in the time of "The Origin of Species". A veteran in every sense but the literal, Dickens keeps his vast popularity, but cannot hope to do more than remind his readers (and his hearers) of all that he had achieved.

Of *Hard Times*, I have said nothing; it is practically a forgotten book, and little in it demands attention. Two other short novels remain to be mentioned (the Christmas books belong to a class that does not call for criticism in this place), and one of them, *Great Expectations* (1861), would be nearly perfect in its mechanism but for the unhappy deference to Lord Lytton's judgment, which caused the end to be altered. Dickens meant to have left Pip a lonely man, and of course rightly so; by the irony of fate he was induced to spoil his work through a brother novelist's desire for a happy ending—a strange thing, indeed, to befall Dickens. Observe how finely the narrative is kept in one key. It begins with a mournful impression—the foggy marshes spreading drearily by the seaward Thames—and throughout recurs this effect of cold and damp and dreariness; in that kind Dickens never did anything so good. Despite the subject, we have no stage fire—except around the person of Mr Wopsle, a charming bit of satire, recalling and contrasting with the far-off days of *Nickleby*. The one unsatisfactory feature is the part concerned with Miss Havisham and Estella. Here the old Dickens survives in unhappy fashion; unable to resist the lure of eccentricity, but no longer presenting it with the gusto which was wont to be more than an excuse. Passing this, one can hardly over-praise the workmanship. No story in the first person was ever better told.

Of the *Tale of Two Cities* (1859) it is impossible to speak so favourably. Like *Barnaby Rudge*, an historical novel, it is better constructed than that early book, but by no means so alive. In his two novels dealing with a past time, Dickens attacks the two things he most hated in the present: religious fanaticism and social tyranny. *Barnaby* is in all senses a charac-

Cooling Church

teristic book. The *Tale of Two Cities* can hardly be called so in anything but its theme. The novelist here laid a restraint upon himself; he aimed deliberately at writing a story for the story's sake; the one thing he had never yet been able to do. Among other presumed superfluities, humour is dismissed. To some readers the result appears admirable; for my part, I feel the restraint throughout, miss the best of my author, and, whilst admitting that he has produced something like a true tragedy, reflect that many another man could have handled the theme as well, if not better. It leaves no strong impression on my mind; even the figure of Carton soon grows dim against a dimmer background.

In the autumn of 1867 Dickens left England on his second voyage across the Atlantic, to give that long series of public readings which shattered his health and sent him back a doomed man. Upon this aspect of his public life something will be said in a later chapter. The spring of 1868 saw him return, and before the end of the year he had entered upon a series of farewell readings in his own country. Defiant of the gravest physical symptoms,—it was not in the man's nature to believe that he could be beaten in anything he undertook,—he laboured through a self-imposed duty which would have tasked him severely even in the time of robust health, and finally took leave of his audience on the 5th of April, 1870. Meanwhile (in a few months of rest to which he was constrained by medical advice) he had begun the writing of a new book, which was to appear in twelve monthly numbers, instead of the old heroic twenty; its name, *The Mystery of Edwin Drood*. Six numbers only were finished. As an indication of the disturbance of mental habit caused by the author's life as a public entertainer, Forster mentions that Dickens miscalculated the length (in print) of his first two parts by no less than twelve pages: ominous error in one who had rarely found his calculation in this matter wrong even by a line. Beyond the sixth part, only a disjointed scene was written. He worked in his garden house at Gadshill—the home endeared to him by Shakespearean associations—till the evening of the 8th of June, and an hour or two later was seized by fatal illness. The next day he died.

Edwin Drood would probably have been his best-constructed book: as far as it goes, the story hangs well together, showing a care in the contrivance of detail which is more than commonly justified by the result. One cannot help wishing that Dickens had chosen another subject—one in which there was neither mystery nor murder, both so irresistibly attractive to him, yet so far from being the true material of his art. Surely it is unfortunate that the last work of a great writer should have for its theme nothing more human than a trivial mystery woven about a vulgar deed of blood. For this, it seems to me, his public readings may well have been responsible. In the last series he had made a great impression by his rendering (acting, indeed) of the death of Nancy in *Oliver Twist*. The thing, utterly unworthy of him in this shape, had cost him great pains; his imagination was drenched with gore, preoccupied with a sordid horror. Casting about him for a new story, he saw murder at the end of every vista. It would not have been thus if he had lived a calmer life, with natural development of his thoughts. In that case we might have had some true successor to *David Copperfield*. His selection of scene was happy and promising—the old city of his childhood, Rochester. The tone, too, of his descriptive passages is much more appropriate than the subject. But Dickens had made his choice in life, and therefrom inevitably resulted his course in literature.

IV

Art, Veracity, and Moral Purpose

It is a thankless task to write of such a man as Dickens in disparaging phrase. I am impatient to reach that point of my essay where I shall be at liberty to speak with admiration unstinted, to dwell upon the strength of the master's work, and exalt him where he is unsurpassed. But it is necessary to clear the way. So great a change has come over the theory and practice of fiction in the England of our times that we must needs treat of Dickens as, in many respects, antiquated. To be antiquated is not necessarily to be condemned, in art or anything else (save weapons of slaughter); but as the result of the last chapter we feel that, in one direction, Dickens suffers from a comparison with novelists, his peers, of a newer day, even with some who were strictly his contemporaries. We have now to ask ourselves in what other aspects his work differs markedly from our present conception of the art of novel-writing. It will be seen, of course, that, theoretically, he had very little in common with the school of strict veracity, of realism—call it what you please; the school which, quite apart from extravagances, has directed fiction into a path it is likely to pursue for many a year to come. Hard words are spoken of him by young writers whose zeal outruns their discretion, and far outstrips their knowledge; from the advanced posts of modern criticism any stone is good enough to throw at a novelist who avows and glories in his moral purpose; who would on no account bring a blush to the middle-class cheek; who at any moment tampers with truth of circumstance, that his readers may have joy rather than sorrow. Well, we must look into this matter, and, as Captain Cuttle says, take its bearings. Endeavouring to judge Dickens as a man of his time, we must see in what spirit he approached his tasks; what he consciously sought to achieve in this pursuit of story-telling. One thing, assuredly, can never become old-fashioned in any disdainful sense; that is, sincerity of purpose. Novelists of today desire above everything to be recognized as sincere in their picturing of life. If Dickens prove to be no less honest, according to his lights, we must then glance at the reasons which remove him so far from us in his artistic design and execution.

Much fault has been found with Forster's *Biography*, which is generally blamed as giving undue prominence to the figure of the biographer. I cannot join in this censure; I prefer to echo the praise of Thomas Carlyle: "So long as Dickens is interesting to his fellow-men, here will be seen, face to face, what Dickens's manner of existing was". Carlyle, I conceive, was no bad judge of a biography; as a worker in literature he appreciated this vivid presentment of a fellow-worker. I should say, indeed, that there exists no book more inspiriting and fortifying to a young man beginning his struggle in the world of letters (especially, of course, to the young novelist) than this of Forster's. And simply because it exhibits in such rich detail the story, and the manner, of Dickens's work; showing him at his desk day by day, recounting his hidden difficulties, his secret triumphs; in short, making the man live over again before us the noblest portion of his life.

One thing to be learnt from every page of the biography is the strenuous spirit in which Dickens wrought. Whatever our judgment as to the result, his zeal and energy were those of the born artist. Passages numberless might he quoted from his letters, showing how he enjoyed the labour of production, how he threw himself into the imaginative world with which he was occupied, how impossible it was for him to put less than *all* his splendid force into the task of the moment. A good instance is the following. He writes to tell his friend Forster of some private annoyance, which had threatened to upset his day's work. "I was most horribly put out for a little while; for I had got up early to go to work, and was full of interest in what I had to do. But having eased my mind by that note to you, and taken a turn or two up and down the room, I went at it again, and soon got so interested that I blazed away till nine last night; only stopping ten minutes for dinner. I suppose I wrote eight printed pages of *Chuzzlewit* yesterday. The consequence is that I could finish it today, but am taking it easy, and making myself laugh very much" (Forster, Book iv, chapter 2.) Year after year, he keeps his friend minutely informed by letter of the progress he makes with every book; consults him on endless points, great and small; is inexhaustible in gossip about himself, which never appears egoistic because of the artistic earnestness declared in every syllable. With no whit less conscientiousness did he discharge his duties as editor of a magazine. We find him writing to Forster: "I have had a story"—accepted from an imperfectly qualified contributor—"to hack and hew into some form for *Household Words* this morning, which has taken me four hours of close attention". Four hours of Dickens's time, in the year 1856, devoted to such a matter as this!—where any ordinary editor, or rather his assistant, would have contented himself with a few blottings and insertions, sure that "the great big stupid public", as Thackeray called it, would be no better pleased, toil how one might. To Dickens the public was not everything; he could not rest until the deformities of that little bit of writing were removed, and no longer offended his eye.

Even so. On the other hand, having it in mind to make a certain use of a character in *Dombey and Son*, he seriously asks Forster: "Do you think it may be done, without making people angry?"

Here is the contradiction so irritating to Dickens's severer critics, the artistic generation of today. What!—they exclaim—a great writer, inspired with a thoroughly fine idea, is to stay his hand until he has made grave inquiry whether Messrs. Mudie's subscribers will approve it or not! The mere suggestion is infuriating. And this—they vociferate—is what Dickens was always doing. It may be true that he worked like a Trojan; but what is the use of work, meant to be artistic, carried on in hourly fear of Mrs Grundy! Fingers are pointed to this, that, and the other Continental novelist; can you imagine *him* in such sorry plight? Why, nothing would have pleased him better than to know he was outraging public sentiment! In fact, it is only when one *does* so that one's work has a chance of being good!

All which may be true enough in relation to the speakers. As regards Dickens, it is irrelevant. Dickens had before him no such artistic ideal; he never desired freedom to offend his public. Sympathy with his readers was to him the very breath of life; the more complete that sympathy, the better did he esteem his work. Of the restrictions laid upon him he was perfectly aware, and there is evidence that he could see the artistic advantage which would result from a slackening of the bonds of English delicacy; but it never occurred to him to make public protest against the prejudices in force. Dickens could never have regarded it as within a storyteller's scope to attempt the conversion of his readers to a new view of literary morals. Against a political folly, or a social injustice, he would use every resource of his art, and see no reason to hesitate; for there was the certainty of the approval of all good folk. To write a novel in a spirit of antagonism to all but a very few of his countrymen would have seemed to him a sort of practical *bull*; is it not the law of novel-writing, first and foremost, that one shall aim at pleasing as many people as possible?

In his preface to *Pendennis* Thackeray spoke very plainly on this subject. He honestly told his readers that they must not expect to find in his novel the whole truth about the life of a young man, seeing that, since the author of *Tom Jones*, no English writer had been permitted such frankness. The same thing is remarked by Dickens in a letter which Forster prints; a letter written from Paris, and commenting on the inconsistency of English people, who, living abroad and reading foreign authors, complain that "the hero of an English book is always uninteresting". He proceeds: "But O my smooth friend, what a shining impostor you must think yourself, and what an ass you must think me, when you suppose that by putting a brazen face upon it you can blot out of my knowledge the fact that this same unnatural young gentleman (if to be decent is to be necessarily unnatural), whom you meet in those other books and in mine, *must* be presented to you in that unnatural aspect by reason of your morality, and is not to have, I will not say any of the indecencies you like, but not even any of the experiences, trials, perplexities, and confusions inseparable from the making or unmaking of all men!" (Forster, Book xi, chapter i). This he clearly saw; but it never disturbed his conscience, for the reason indicated. Thackeray, we may be sure, thought much more on the subject, and in graver mood; and as a result, he allowed himself more liberty than Dickens—not without protest from the many-headed. There existed this difference between the two men. Thackeray had a kind of strength not given to his brother in art.

Only in one way can the public evince its sympathy with an author—by purchasing his books. It follows, then, that Dickens attached great importance to the varying demand for his complete novels, or for the separate monthly parts at their time of issue. Here again is a stone of stumbling for the disinterested artist who reads Dickens's life. We may select two crucial examples.

After the first visit to America began the publication of *Martin Chuzzlewit*, and it was seen at once that the instalments from month to month were less favourably received than those of the earlier books. The sixty thousand or so of regular purchasers decreased by about two thirds. "Whatever the causes," says Forster, "here was the undeniable fact of a grave depreciation of sale in his writings, unaccompanied by any falling off either in themselves or in the writer's reputation. It was very temporary; but it was present, and to be dealt with accordingly" (Book iv, chapter 2.) Dickens's way of dealing with it was to make his hero suddenly resolve to go to America. Number Four closed with that declaration, and its results were seen, we are told, in an additional two thousand purchasers. Forster's words, of course, represent Dickens's view of the matter, which amounts to this: that however thoroughly assured an author may be that he is doing his best, a falling-off in the sale of his work must needs cause him grave mental disturbance; nay, that it must prompt him, as a matter of course, to changes of plan and solicitous calculation. He is to write, in short, with an eye steadily fixed upon his publisher's sale-room; never to lose sight of that index of popular approval or the reverse. That phrase "to be dealt with accordingly" is more distasteful than one can easily express to anyone with a tincture of latter-day conscientiousness in things of art. As I have said, it can be explained in a sense not at all dishonourable to Dickens; but how much more pleasant would it be to read in its place some quite unparliamentary utterance such, for example, as Scott made use of when William Blackwood requested him to change the end of one of his stories!

It sounds odd to praise Scott, from this point of view, at the expense of Dickens. As a conscientious workman Dickens is far ahead of the author of *Waverley*, who never dreamt of taking such pains as with the other novelist became habitual. We know, too, that Scott avowedly wrote for money, and varied his subjects in accordance with the varying public taste. But let us suppose that his novels had appeared in monthly parts, and that such an experience had befallen him as this of Dickens; can we easily imagine Walter Scott, in an attitude of commercial despondency, anxiously deliberating on the subject of his next chapter? The thing is inconceivable. It marks the difference not only between two men, but two epochs. Not with impunity, for all his generous endowments, did Dickens come to manhood in the year 1832—the year in which Sir Walter said farewell to a world he no longer recognized.

The other case which I think it worth while to mention is that of Dickens's first Christmas story, the *Carol*. In those days Christmas publications did not come out three or four months before the season they were meant to celebrate. The *Carol* appeared only just before Christmas Eve; it was seized upon with enthusiasm, and edition followed edition. Unluckily, the publisher had not exercised prudence in the "cost of production"; the profits were small, and as a consequence we have the following letter, addressed to Forster in January, 1844: "Such a night as I have passed! I really believed I should never get up again until I had passed through all the horrors of a fever. I found the *Carol* accounts awaiting me, and they were the cause of it. The first six thousand copies show a profit of £230! and the last four will yield as much more. I had set my heart and soul upon a thousand clear. What a wonderful thing it is that such a great success should occasion me such intolerable anxiety and disappointment! My year's bills, unpaid, are so terrific, that all the energy and determination I can possibly exert will be required to clear me before I go abroad." (Book iv, chapter 2.) Now this letter is very disagreeable reading; for, at so early a stage in its writer's career, it points already to the end. Those "terrific" bills— had they been less terrific, say, by only one quarter, and had they been consistently kept at a point below the terrify-ing—how much better for Dickens himself and for the world! It could not be. The great middle class was growing enormously rich with its coal-mines and steam-engines, and the fact of his being an artist did not excuse a mem-ber of that class from the British necessity of keeping up appearances. So we have all but the "horrors of a fever" because a little book, which Thackeray rightly called "a national benefit", brought in only a certain sum of money! In his perturbation Dickens does himself injustice. He had *not* "set his heart and soul" on a thousand pounds; he never in all his life set his heart and soul on wealth. "No man", he said once, in talk with friends, "attaches less importance to the possession of money, or less disparagement to the want of it, than I do"; and he spoke essential truth. It would be quite unjust to think of Dickens as invariably writing in fear of diminishing sales, or as trembling with cupidity whenever he opened his publishers' accounts. To understand the whole man we must needs remark the commercial side of him; but his genius saved him from the worst results of the commercial spirit.

It was not only of money that he stood in need. Remember his theatri-cal leanings, and one understands without difficulty how important to him was the stimulus of praise. From the early days, as has often been observed, the relations between Dickens and his public were notably personal; in his study, he sat, as it were, with hearers grouped about him, conscious of their presence, happily, in quite another way than that already noticed. Like the actor (which indeed he ultimately became), his desire was for instant applause. Dickens could never have struggled for long years against the lack of appreciation. In coldness towards his work he would have seen its literary condemnation, and have turned to a new endeavour. When the readers of *Martin Chuzzlewit* fall off he is troubled, first and foremost, by the failure of popular sympathy. He asks himself; most anxiously, what the cause can be; and, with a touching deference to the voice of the crowd, is inclined to think that he has grown less interesting. For observe that Dickens never conceives himself, when he aims at popularity, as writing *down* to his audience. Of that he is wholly incapable; for that he has too much understanding of the conditions of literary success. Never yet was great popularity, in whatsoever class, achieved by deliberate pursuit of a low ideal. The silliest story which ever enjoyed a vast vogue among the silliest readers was a true representation of the author's mind; for only to writing of this kind—sincere though in foolishness—comes a response from multitudes of readers. Dickens might alter his intention, might change his theme; but he never did so with the thought that he was condescending. In this respect a true democrat, he believed, probably without ever reflecting upon it, that the approved of the people was necessarily the supreme in art. At the same time, never man wrought more energetically to justify the people's choice.

How does this attitude of mind affect Dickens's veracity as an artist concerned with everyday life? In what degree, and in what directions, does he feel himself at liberty to disguise facts, to modify circumstances, for the sake of giving pleasure or avoiding offence?

Our "realist" will hear of no such paltering with "truth". Heedless of Pilate's question, he takes for granted that the truth can be got at, and that it is his plain duty to set it down without compromise; or, if less crude in his perceptions, he holds that truth, for the artist, is the impression produced on *him*, and that to convey this impression with entire sincerity is his sole reason for existing. To Dickens such a view of the artist's duty never presented itself. Art, for him, was art precisely because it was not nature. Even our realists may recognize this, and may grant that it is the business of art to select, to dispose—under penalties if the result be falsification. But Dickens went further; he had a moral purpose; the thing above all others scornfully forbidden in our schools of rigid "naturalism".

Let it not be forgotten that he made his public protest—moderate enough, but yet a protest—against smooth conventionalism. In the preface to *Nicholas Nickleby* he defends himself against those who censured him for not having made his hero "always blameless and agreeable". He had seen no reason, he says, for departing from the plain facts of human character. This is interesting when we call to mind the personality of Nicholas, who must have got into very refined company for his humanity to prove offensive. But the English novel was at a sorry pass in that day, and doubtless Dickens seriously believed that he had taken a bold step towards naturalism (had he known the word). Indeed, was he not justified in thinking so? Who, if not Dickens, founded the later school of English fiction? He who as a young man had unconsciously obeyed Goethe's precept, taking hold upon the life nearest to him, making use of it for literature, and proving that it *was* of interest, could rightly claim the honours of an innovator.

The preface to *Oliver Twist*, in defending his choice of subject, strikes the note of compromise, and at the same time declares in simple terms the author's purpose. After speaking of the romances of highwaymen then in vogue, which he held to be harmful, because so false to experience, he tells how he had resolved to give a true picture of a band of thieves, seeing no reason "why the dregs of life (as long as their speech did not offend the

No. 48 Doughty Street, Mecklenburgh Square

ear) should not serve the purpose of a moral". Here, then, we have it stated plainly that we are not to look for complete verisimilitude in the speech of his characters, and, again, that he only exhibits these characters *in terrorem*, or, at all events, to induce grave thoughts. When I come to discuss in detail Dickens's characterization I shall have to ask how far it is possible truthfully to represent a foul-mouthed person, whilst taking care that the words he uses do not "offend the ear". Here I wish only to indicate the limits which Dickens imposed upon himself. He, it is clear, had no misgiving; to him Bill Sikes and Nancy and Charley Bates were convincing figures, though they never once utter a vile word—which, as a matter of fact, they one and all did in every other breath. He did not deliberately sacrifice truth to refinement. Moreover, he was convinced that he had done a moral service to the world. That both these ends were attained by help of unexampled buoyancy of spirit, an unfailing flow of the healthiest mirth, the kindliest humour, should in consistency appear to us the strangest thing of all—to us who strive so hard for "atmosphere", insist so strongly upon "objectivity" in the author. But in this matter Dickens troubled himself with no theory or argument. He wrote as his soul dictated, and surely could not have done better.

Admitting his limits, accepting them even gladly, he was yet possessed with a sense of the absolute reality of everything he pictured forth. Had the word been in use he must necessarily have called himself a Realist. This is one of the biographical commonplaces concerning Dickens. Everyone knows how he excited himself over his writing, how he laughed and cried with his imaginary people, how he all but made himself ill with grief over the death-bed of little Nell or of Paul Dombey. This means, of course, that his imagination worked with perfect freedom, had the fullest scope, yet never came into conflict with the prepossessions of his public. Permission to write as Smollett and as Fielding wrote could in no way have advantaged Dickens. He was the born story-teller of a certain day, of a certain class. Again, he does not deem himself the creator of a world, but the laboriously faithful painter of that about him. He labours his utmost to preserve illusion. Dickens could never have been guilty of that capital crime against art so light-heartedly committed by Anthony Trollope, who will begin a paragraph in his novels with some such words as these: "Now, if this were fact, and not a story ..." For all that, Trollope was the more literal copier of life. But his figures do not survive as those of Dickens, who did in fact create—created individuals, to become at once and for ever representative of their time.

Whilst at work, no questioning troubled him. But in speaking of the results, he occasionally allows us a glimpse of his mind; we see how he reconciled art with veracity. The best instance I can recall is his comment upon "Doctor Marigold", the Cheap-Jack, of whom he drew so sympathetic a picture. He says, "It is wonderfully like the real thing, of course a little refined and humoured". Note the *of course*. Art was art, not nature. He had to make his Cheap-Jack presentable, to disguise anything repellent, to bring out every interesting and attractive quality. A literal transcript of the man's being would not have seemed to him within his province. But it is just this "refining" and "humouring" which many in our day hold traitorous; the outcome of it is called Idealism.

At times Dickens's idealism goes further, leading him into misrepresentation of social facts. Refining and humouring, even from his point of view, must have their limits; and these he altogether exceeded in a character such as Lizzie Hexam, the heroine of *Our Mutual Friend*. The child of a Thames-side loafer, uneducated, and brought up amid the roughest surroundings, Lizzie uses language and expresses sentiment which would do credit to a lady in whatsoever position. In the same way, the girl called Alice Marlow, who plays so melodramatic a part in *Dombey and Son*, represents a total impossibility, the combination of base origin and squalid life, with striking mental power, strikingly developed. This kind of thing is permissible to no artist who deals with the actual world. Using a phrase germane to our subject, it is morally mischievous. Many a novelist has sinned in this direction; above all, young authors misled by motives alien to art, who delight in idealizing girls of the lower, or lowest class. Dickens had outgrown that stage of pardonable weakness when he wrote *Our Mutual Friend*. He wished, of course, to contrast the low-born Lizzie Hexam with persons, in the same story, of what is called good birth and breeding, and to show her their superior; a purpose which aggravates his fault, the comparison being so obviously unfair. In this connection I recall a figure from Thackeray: the uneducated girl with whom Arthur Pendennis forms a perilous acquaintance. Fanny Bolton is one of the truest characters in all fiction,—so unpleasantly true, that readers ignorant of her class might imagine the author to have drawn her in a spirit of social prejudice. Never was his hand more admirably just. Fanny Bolton is one of the instances I had in mind when I alluded to Thackeray's power in describing other modes of life than that with which his name is associated.

Here Dickens idealized to please himself. In the end, it came to the same thing when we see him hesitating over a design of which he doubted the popular acceptance. Walter Gay, in *Dombey and Son*, whose career is so delightfully prosperous, seemed at one moment about to be condemned to a very different fate. "I think", writes Dickens in a letter, "it would be a good thing to disappoint all the expectations this chapter seems to raise of his happy connection with the story and the heroine, and to show him gradually and naturally trailing away from that love of adventure and boyish light-heartedness, into negligence, idleness, dissipation, dishonesty, and ruin. To show, in short, that common, everyday miserable declension, of which we know so much in our ordinary life." (Forster, Book vi, chapter 2.) Here, indeed, is a suggestion of "realism"; but we know, in reading it, that Dickens could never have carried it out. He adds, "Do you think it may be done, without making people angry?" Certainly it could not; Dickens knew it could not, even when the artist deep within him brooded over the theme; he gave it up almost at once. Forster points out that something of the same idea was eventually used in *Bleak House*. But Richard Carstone, though he wastes his life, does not sink to "dissipation, dishonesty, and ruin". The hand was stayed where the picture would have become too painful alike for author and public—always, or nearly always, in such entire sympathy. The phrase about "making people angry" signifies much less than it would in a novelist of today. It might well have taken the form: "Can I bring *myself* to do this thing?"

To return for a moment to *Our Mutual Friend*, I never look into that book without feeling a suspicion that Dickens originally meant Mr Boffin to suffer a real change of character, to become in truth the miserly curmudgeon which we are told he only pretended to be. Careful reading of the chapters which bear on this point has confirmed my impression; for which, however, there is no support that I know of, in Forster or elsewhere. It may well have been that here again Dickens, face to face with an unpleasant bit of truth, felt his heart fail him. Again he may have asked, "Will it make people angry?" If so—on this I wish to insist—it was in no spirit of dishonest compliance that he changed his plan. To make people angry would have been to defeat his own prime purpose. Granting two possible Mr Boffins: he who becomes a miser in reality, and he who, for a good purpose, acts the miser's part; how much better to choose the Mr Boffin who will end in hearty laughter and overflowing benevolence!

Avoidance of the disagreeable, as a topic uncongenial to art—this is Dickens's principle. There results, necessarily, a rather serious omission from his picture of life. Writing once from Boulogne, and describing the pier as he saw it of an evening, he says, "I never did behold such specimens of the youth of my country, male and female, as pervade that place. They are really in their vulgarity and insolence quite disheartening. One is so fearfully ashamed of them, and they contrast so very unfavourably with the natives." (Forster, Book vii, chapter 4.) But Dickens certainly had no need to visit

Boulogne to study English "vulgarity and insolence"; it blared around him wherever he walked in London, and, had he wrought in another spirit, it must have taken a very large place in every one of his books. He avoided it, or showed it only in such forms as amused rather than disgusted. The Boulogne pier-walker, a significant figure of that day, deserved his niche in fiction; Dickens glanced at him, and passed him by.

Two examples dwell in my memory which show him in the mood for downright fact of the unpleasant sort. More might be discovered, but these, I think, would remain the noteworthy instances of "realism" in Dickens; moments when, for whatever reason, he saw fit to tell a harsh truth without any mitigation. One occurs in the short story of *Doctor Marigold*. We have seen that the figure of the Cheap-Jack was "refined and humoured"; not so that of the Cheap-Jack's wife, the brutal woman who ill-uses and all but kills her child. This picture is remorseless in everyday truth; no humour softens it, no arbitrary event checks the course of the woman's hateful cruelty. The second example is *George Silverman's Explanation*, another short story, which from beginning to end is written in a tone of uncompromising bitterness. Being told by Silverman himself, its consistent gloom is dramatically appropriate and skilful. Here we have a picture of pietistic virulence the like of which cannot be found elsewhere in Dickens; hard bare fact; never a smile to lighten the impression; no interference with the rigour of destiny. Anything but characteristic, this little story is still a notable instance of Dickens's power. Were the author unknown it would be attributed to some strenuous follower of the "naturalist" school.

From his duty, as he conceived it, of teaching a moral lesson, Dickens never departs. He has an unfailing sense of the high importance of his work from this point of view. Not that it preoccupies him, as was the case with George Eliot, and weighs upon him as he writes; naturally and calmly, without suspicion of pose, without troublous searching of conscience, he sees his subject as a moral lesson, and cannot understand the position of an artist to whom such thought never occurs. And his morality is of the simplest; a few plain ordinances serve for human guidance; to infringe them is to be marked for punishment more or less sensational; to follow the path of the just is to ensure a certain amount of prosperity, and reward unlimited in buoyancy of heart. The generality of readers like to see a scoundrel get his deserts, and Dickens, for the most part, gives them abundant satisfaction. No half-measures. When Pecksniff is unmasked, we have the joy of seeing him felled to the ground in the presence of a jubilant company. Nor does this suffice; he and his daughter Cherry, both having forfeited all the sympathies of decent folk, come to actual beggary, and prowl about the murky streets. Nothing more improbable than such an end for Mr Pecksniff or for his daughter—who was very well able to take care of herself; and obviously a deeper moral would be implied in the continued flourishing of both; but Dickens and his public were impatient to see the rascal in the dirt, the shrew beside him. Sampson Brass and his sister, whose crime against society is much more serious, pass their later years in the same squalid defeat; yet we feel assured that the virile Sally, at all events, made a much better fight against the consequences of her rascality. Lady Dedlock, having sinned in a manner peculiarly unpardonable, is driven by remorse from her luxurious home, and expires in one of the foulest corners of London. Remorse alone, however poignant and enduring, would not seem an adequate penalty; we must see the proud lady, the sinful woman, literally brought low, down to the level of the poor wretch who was her accomplice. Ill-doers less conspicuous are let off with a punishment which can be viewed facetiously, but punished they are. It is all so satisfying; it so rounds off our conception of life. Nothing so abhorred by the multitude as a lack of finality in stories, a vagueness of conclusion which gives them the trouble of forming surmises.

Equally of course, justice is tempered with mercy. Who would have the heart to demand rigour of the law for Mr Jingle and Job Trotter? We see them all but starved to death in a debtors' prison, and that is enough; their conversion to honesty gives such scope for Mr Pickwick's delightful goodness that nothing could be more in accord with the fitness of things. Squeers or Mr Brass we will by no means forgive; nay, of their hard lot, so well merited, we will make all the fun we can; but many a pleasant scamp who has shaken our sides shall be put in the way of earning an honest living. Profoundly human, however crude to an age that cannot laugh and cry so readily. Good, sound, practical teaching, which will help the soul of man long after more pretentious work has returned to dust.

Ah, those final chapters of Dickens! How eagerly they are read by the young, and with what a pleasant smile by elders who prize the good things of literature! No one is forgotten, and many an unsuspected bit of happiness calls aloud for gratitude to the author. Do you remember Mr Mell, the underpaid and bullied usher in *David Copperfield*,—the poor broken-spirited fellow whose boots will not bear another mending,—who uses an hour of liberty to visit his mother in the alms-house, and gladden her heart by piping sorry music on his flute? We lose sight of him, utterly; knowing only that he has been sent about his business after provoking the displeasure of the insolent lad Steerforth, Then, do you remember how, at the end of the book, David has news from Australia, delicious news about Mr Micawber, and Mrs Gummidge, and sundry other people, and how, in reading the colonial paper, he suddenly comes upon the name of *Dr Mell*, a distinguished man at the Antipodes? Who so stubborn a theorist that this kindly figment of the imagination does not please him? Who would prefer to learn the cold fact: that Mell, the rejected usher, sank from stage to stage of wretchedness, and died lamentably in the street or the workhouse?

It was not by computing the density of the common brain, by gauging the force of vulgar prejudice, that Charles Dickens rose to his supreme popularity. Nature made him the mouthpiece of his kind, in all that relates to simple emotions and homely thought. Who can more rightly be called an artist than he who gave form and substance to the ideal of goodness and purity, of honour, justice, mercy, whereby the dim multitudes falteringly seek to guide their steps? This was his task in life, to embody the better dreams of ordinary men; to fix them as bright realities, for weary eyes to look upon. He achieved it in the strength of a faultless sympathy; following the true instincts which it is so unjust—so unintelligent—to interpret as mere commercial shrewdness or dulness of artistic perception. Art is not single; to every great man his province, his mode. During at least one whole generation, Charles Dickens, in the world of literature, meant England. For his art, splendidly triumphant, made visible to all mankind the characteristic virtues, the typical shortcomings, of the homely English race.

V

Characterization

The familiar objection to Dickens's characters, that they are "so unreal" (a criticism common in the mouths of persons who would be the last to tolerate downright verity in fiction), is in part explained—in part justified—by the dramatic conduct of his stories. What unreality there is, arises for the most part from necessities of "plot". This may be illustrated by a comparison between two figures wherein the master has embodied so much homely sweetness and rectitude that both are popular favourites. The boatman Peggotty and Joe Gargery the blacksmith are drawn on similar lines; in both the gentlest nature is manifest beneath a ruggedness proper to their callings. There is a certain resemblance, too, between the stories in which each plays his part; childlike in their simple virtues, both become strongly attached to a child—not their own—living under the same roof, and both suffer a grave disappointment in this affection; the boatman's niece is beguiled from him to her ruin, the blacksmith's little relative grows into a conceited youth ashamed of the old companion and the old home. To readers in general I presume that Peggotty is better known than Joe; *David Copperfield* being more frequently read than *Great Expectations*; but if we compare the two figures as to their "reality", we must decide in favour of Gargery. I think him a better piece of workmanship all round; the prime reason, however, for his standing out so much more solidly in one's mind than Little Emily's uncle is that he lives in a world, not of melodrama, but of everyday cause and effect. The convict Magwitch and his strange doings make no such demand upon one's credulity as the story of Emily and Steerforth, told as it is, with its extravagant situations and flagrantly artificial development. Pip is so thoroughly alive that we can forget his dim relations with Satis House. But who can put faith in Mr Peggotty, when he sets forth to search for his niece over the highways and by-ways of Europe? Who can for a moment put faith in Emily herself after she has ceased to be the betrothed of Ham? As easily could one believe that David Copperfield actually overheard that wildly fantastic dialogue in the lodging-house between the lost girl and Rosa Dartle.

Many such examples might be adduced of excellent, or masterly, characterization spoilt by the demand for effective intrigue. We call to mind this or that person in circumstances impossible of credit; and hastily declare that character and situation are alike unreal. And hereby hangs another point worth touching upon. I have heard it very truly remarked that, in our day, people for the most part criticise Dickens from a recollection of their reading in childhood; they do not come fresh to him with mature minds; in general, they never read him at all after childish years. This is an obvious source of much injustice. Dickens is good reading for all times of life, as are all the great imaginative writers. Let him be read by children together with *Don Quixote*. But who can speak with authority of Cervantes who knows him only from an acquaintance made at ten years old? To the mind of a child Dickens is, or ought to be, fascinating—(alas for the whole subject of children's reading nowadays!)—and most of the fascination is due to that romantic treatment of common life which is part, indeed, of Dickens's merit, but has smaller value and interest to the older mind. Much of his finest humour is lost upon children; much of his perfect description, and all his highest achievement in characterization. Taking Dickens "as read", people inflict a loss upon themselves and do a wrong to the author. Who, in childhood, ever cared much for *Little Dorrit*? The reason is plain; in this book Dickens has comparatively little of his wonted buoyancy; throughout, it is in a graver key. True, a house falls down in a most exciting way, and this the reader will remember; all else is to him a waste. We hear, accordingly, that nothing good can be said for *Little Dorrit*. Whereas, a competent judge, taking up the book as he would any other, will find in it some of the best work Dickens ever did; and especially in this matter of characterization; pictures so wholly admirable, so marvellously observed and so exquisitely presented, that he is tempted to place *Little Dorrit* among the best of the novels.

Again, it is not unusual to seek in Dickens's characters for something he never intended to be there; in other words, his figures are often slighted because they represent a class in society which lacks many qualities desired by cultivated readers, and possesses very prominently the distasteful features such a critic could well dispense with. You lay down, for instance, Thackeray's *Pendennis*, and soon after you happen to take up *Dombey and Son*. Comparisons arise. Whilst reading of Major Bagstock, you find your thoughts wandering to Major Pendennis; when occupied (rather disdainfully) with Mr Toots, you suddenly recall Foker. What can be the immediate outcome of such contrast? It seems impossible to deny to Thackeray a great superiority in the drawing of character; his aristocratic Major and his wealthy young jackass are so much more "real", that is to say, so much more familiar, than the promoted vulgarian Bagstock and the enriched whipper-snapper Toots. A hasty person would be capable of exclaiming that Dickens had plainly taken suggestions from Thackeray, and made but poor use of them. Observe, however, that *Dombey and Son* appeared, complete, in 1848; *Pendennis* in 1849. Observe, too, the explanation of the whole matter: that Bagstock and Toots represent quite as truthfully figures possible in a certain class, as do Thackeray's characters those to be found in a rank distinctly higher. If Thackeray (who needed no suggestions from others' books) was indeed conscious of this whimsical parallel, we can only admire the skill and finish with which he worked it out. But assuredly he dreamt of no slight to Dickens's performance. They had wrought in different material. Social distinctions are sufficiently pronounced even in our time of revolution; fifty years ago they were much more so. And precisely what estranges the culti-vated reader in Bagstock and Toots, is nothing more nor less than evidence of their creator's truthfulness.

A wider question confronts one in looking steadfastly at the masterpieces of a novelist concerned with the lower, sometimes the lowest, modes of life in a great city. Among all the names immortalized by Dickens none is more widely familiar than that of Mrs Gamp. It is universally admitted that in Mrs Gamp we have a creation such as can be met with only in the greatest writers; a figure at once individual and typical; a marvel of humorous pre-sentment; vital in the highest degree attainable by this art of fiction. From the day of her first appearance on the stage, Mrs Camp has been a delight, a wonder, a by-word. She stands unique, no other novelist can show a piece of work, in the same kind, worthy of a place beside her; we must go to the very heights of world-literature, to him who bodied forth Dame Quickly, and Juliet's nurse, for the suggestion of equivalent power. Granted, then, that Mrs Gamp has indubitable existence; who and what is she? Well, a so-called nurse, living in Kingsgate Street, Holborn, in a filthy room somewhere upstairs, and summoned for nursing of all kinds by persons more or less well-to-do, who are so unfortunate as to know of no less offensive substi-tute. We are told, and can believe, that in the year 1844 (the date of *Martin Chuzzlewit*) few people did know of any substitute for Mrs Gamp; that she was an institution; that she carried her odious vices and her criminal incom-petence from house to house in decent parts of London. Dickens knew her only too well; had observed her at moments of domestic crisis; had learnt her language and could reproduce it (or most of it) with surprising accuracy. In plain words, then, we are speaking of a very loathsome creature; a sluttish, drunken, avaricious, dishonest woman. Meeting her in the flesh, we should shrink disgusted, so well does the foulness of her person correspond with the baseness of her mind. Hearing her speak, we should turn away in half-amused contempt. Yet, when we encounter her in the pages of Dickens, we cannot have too much of Mrs Gamp's company; her talk is an occasion of uproarious mirth; we never dream of calling her to moral judgment, but laugh the more, the more infamously she sees fit to behave. Now, in what sense can this figure in literature be called a copy of the human original?

I am perfectly aware that this inquiry goes to the roots of the theory of Art. Here I have no space (nor would it be the proper moment) to discuss all the issues that are involved in a question so direct and natural; but if we are to talk at all about the people in Dickens, we must needs start with some understanding of what is implied when we call them true, lifelike, finely presented. Is not the fact in itself very remarkable, that by dint (it seems) of *omitting* those very features which in life most strongly impress us, an artist in fiction can produce something which we applaud as an inimitable portrait? That for disgust he can give us delight, and yet leave us glorying in his verisimilitude?

Turn to another art. Open the great volume of Hogarth, and look at the several figures of women which present a fair correspondence with that of Mrs Gamp. We admire the artist's observation, his great skill, his moral significance, even his grim humour; then—we close the book with a feeling of relief. With these faces who would spend hours of leisure? The thing has been supremely well done, and we are glad of it, and will praise the artist unreservedly; but his basely grinning and leering women must not hang upon the wall, to be looked at and talked of with all and sundry. Hogarth has copied—in the strict sense of the word. He gives us life—and we cannot bear it.

The Mrs Camp of our novel is a piece of the most delicate idealism. It is a sublimation of the essence of Gamp. No novelist (say what he will) ever gave us a picture of life which was not idealized; but there are degrees— degrees of purpose and of power. Juliet's Nurse is an idealized portrait, but it comes much nearer to the real thing than Mrs Gamp; in our middle-class England we cannot altogether away with the free-spoken dame of Verona; we Bowdlerize her—of course damaging her in the process. Mrs Berry, in *Richard Feverel*, is idealized, but she smacks too strongly of the truth for boudoir readers. Why, Moll Flanders herself is touched and softened, for all the author's illusive directness. In Mrs Gamp, Dickens has done his own Bowdlerizing, but with a dexterity which serves only to heighten his figure's effectiveness. Vulgarity he leaves; that is of the essence of the matter; vulgarity unsurpassable is the note of Mrs Gamp. Vileness, on the other hand, becomes grotesquerie, wonderfully converted into a subject of laughter. Her speech, among the basest ever heard from human tongue, by a process of infinite subtlety, which leaves it the same yet not the same, is made an endless amusement, a source of quotation for laughing lips incapable of unclean utterance.

Idealism, then: confessed idealism. But let us take another character from another book, also a woman supposed to represent a phase of low life in London. Do you recall "good Mrs Brown", the hag who strips little Florence Dombey of her clothes? And do you remember that this creature has a daughter, her name Alice Marlow, who—presumably having been a domestic servant, or a shop-girl, or something of the kind—was led astray by Mr Carker of the shining teeth, and has become a wandering nondescript? Now in Alice Marlow we again have idealism; but of a different kind. This child of good Mrs Brown, tramping into London on a bitter night, is found on the roadside and charitably taken home by Mr Carker's sister, neither being aware of the other's identity; and having submitted to this kindness, and having accepted money, the girl goes her way. That same night she learns who has befriended her, and forthwith rushes back (a few miles) through storm and darkness, to fling the alms at the giver. Outlines of a story sufficiently theatrical; but the dialogue! One fails to understand how Dickens brought himself to pen the language which—at great length—he puts into this puppet's mouth. It is doubtful whether one could pick out a single sentence, a single phrase, such as the real Alice Marlow could conceivably have used. Her passion is vehement; no impossible thing. The words in which she utters it would be appropriate to the most stagey of wronged heroines—be that who it may. A figure less lifelike will not be found in any novel ever written. Yet Dickens doubtless intended it as legitimate idealization; a sort of type of the doleful multitude of betrayed women. He meant it for imagination exalting common fact. But the fact is not exalted; it has simply vanished. And the imagination is of a kind that avails nothing on any theme. In Mrs Gamp a portion of truth is omitted; in Alice Marlow there is substitution of falsity. By the former process, true idealism *may* be reached; by the latter, one arrives at nothing but attitude and sham.

Of course omission and veiling do not suffice to create Mrs Gamp. In his alchemy, Dickens had command of the *menstruum* which alone is powerful enough to effect such transmutation as this; it is called humour.

Humour, be it remembered, is inseparable from charity. Not only did it enable him to see this coarse creature as an amusing person; it inspired him with that large tolerance which looks through things external, gives its full weight to circumstance, and preserves a modesty, a humility, in human judgment. We can form some notion of what Mrs Gamp would have become in the hands of a rigorous realist, with scorn and disgust (inevitably implied) taking the place of humour. We reject the photograph; it avails us nothing in art or life. Humour deals gently with fact and fate; in its smile there is forbearance, in its laugh there is kindliness. With falsehood—however well meant —it is incompatible; when it has done its work as solvent, the gross adherents are dissipated, the essential truth remains. Do you ask for the Platonic *idea* of London's hired nurse early in Queen Victoria's reign? Dickens shows it you embodied. At such a thing as this, crawling between earth and heaven, what can one do but laugh? Its existence is a puzzle, a wonder. The class it represents shall be got rid of as speedily as possible; well and good; we cannot tolerate such a public nuisance. But the type shall be preserved for all time by the magic of a great writer's deep-seeing humour, and shall be known as Mrs Gamp.

For a moment, contrast with this masterpiece a picture in which Dickens has used his idealism on material more promising, though sought amid surroundings sufficiently like those seen in the description of Kingsgate Street. The most successful character in his stories written to be read at Christmas is Mrs Lirriper. She belongs to a class distinguished then, as now, by its uncleanness, its rapacity, its knavery, its ignorance. Mrs Lirriper keeps a London lodging-house. Here, in depicting an individual, Dickens has not typified a class. He idealizes this woman, but finds in her, ready to his hand, the qualities of goodness and tenderness and cheery honesty, so that there is no question of transmuting a subject repulsive to the senses. Mrs Lirriper is quite possible, even in a London lodging-house; in the flesh, however, we should not exactly seek her society. Her talk (idealized with excellent adroitness) would too often jar upon the ear; her person would be, to say the least, unattractive. In the book, she has lost these accidents of position: we are first amused, then drawn on to like, to admire, to love her. An unfortunate blemish—the ever-recurring artificiality of story—threatens to make her dim; but Mrs Lirriper triumphs over this. We bear her in memory as a person known—a person most unhappily circumstanced, set in a gloomy sphere; but of such sweet nature that we forget her inevitable defects, even as we should those of an actual acquaintance of like character.

In looking back on the events of life, do we not see them otherwise than, at the time, they appeared to us? The harsh is smoothed ; the worst of everything is forgotten; things pleasant come into relief. This (a great argument for optimism) is a similitude of Dickens's art. Like Time, he obscures the unpleasing, emphasizes all we are glad to remember. Time does not falsify; neither does Dickens, whenever his art is unalloyed.

Let us turn to his literary method. It is that of all the great novelists. To set before his reader the image so vivid in his own mind, he simply describes and reports. We have, in general, a very precise and complete picture of externals—the face, the gesture, the habit. In this Dickens excels; he proves to us by sheer force of visible detail how distinct was the mental shape from which he drew. We learn the tone of voice, the trick of utterance; he declared that every word spoken by his characters was audible to him. Then does the man reveal himself in colloquy; sometimes once for all, sometimes by degrees, in chapter after chapter—though this is seldom the case. We know these people because we see and hear them.

In a few instances he added deliberate analysis; it was never well done, always superfluous. Very rarely has analysis of character justified itself in fiction. To Dickens the method was alien; he could make no use whatever of it. In the early book which illustrates all his defects, *Nicholas Nickleby*, we have some dreary pages concerned with the inner man of Ralph Nickleby; seeing that the outer is but shadowy, these details cannot interest; they show, moreover, much crudity and conventionality of thought. Later, an analysis is attempted of Mr Dombey—very laborious, very long. It does not help us in the least to understand Paul's father, himself one of the least satisfactory of Dickens's leading persons. One may surmise that the author felt something of this, and went out of his wonted way in an endeavour to give the image more life.

It results from Dickens's weakness in the devising of incident, in the planning of story, that he seldom develops character through circumstance. There are conversions, but we do not much believe in them; they smack of the stage. Possibly young Martin Chuzzlewit may be counted an exception; but there is never much life in him. From this point of view Dickens's best bit of work is Pip, in *Great Expectations*: Pip, the narrator of his own story, who exhibits very well indeed the growth of a personality, the interaction of character and event. One is not permitted to lose sight of the actual author; though so much more living than Esther Summerson, Pip is yet embarrassed, like her, with the gift of humour. We know very well whose voice comes from behind the scenes when Pip is describing Mr Wopsle's dramatic venture. Save for this, we acknowledge a true self-revelation. What could be better than a lad's picture of his state of mind, when, after learning that he has "great expectations", he quits the country home of his childhood and goes to London? "I formed a plan in outline for bestowing a dinner of roast beef and plum-pudding, a pint of ale, and a gallon of condescension upon everybody in the village" (chapter xix). It is one of many touches which give high value to this book.

As a rule, the more elaborate Dickens's conception of character, the smaller his success in working it out. Again and again he endeavoured to present men and women of exceptionally strong passions: the kind of persons who make such a figure on the boards, where they frown and clench their fists, and utter terrible phrases. It began in *Oliver Twist* with the man called Monk; in *Barnaby* came the murderer; in *Chuzzlewit* appears the puppet known as old Martin, a thing of sawdust. Later, the efforts in this direction are more conscientious, more laboured, but rarely more successful. An exception, perhaps, may be noted in Bradley Headstone, the lover of Lizzie Hexam, whose consuming passion here and there convinces, all the more for its well-contrived contrast with the character of the man whom Lizzie prefers. Charley Hexam, too, is lifelike, on a lower plane. The popular voice pleads for Sydney Carton; yes, he is well presented—but so easy to forget. Think, on the other hand, of the long list of women meant to be tragic, who, one and all, must be judged failures. Edith Dombey, with her silent wrath and ludicrous behaviour, who, intended for a strong, scornful nature, dumbly goes to the sacrifice when bidden by her foolish mother, and then rails at the old worldling for the miseries needlessly brought upon herself. Rosa Dartle, at first a promising suggestion, but falling away into exaggerations of limelight frenzy. Lady Dedlock and her maid Hortense—which is the more obvious waxwork? Mrs Clennam, in *Little Dorrit*, is wrought so patiently and placed in so picturesque a scene that one laments over her impossibility; her so-called talk is, perhaps, less readable than anything in Dickens. The same book shows us, or aims at showing us, Miss Wade and Tattycoram, from both of whom we turn incredulous. Of Miss Havisham one grudges to speak; her ghostly presence does its best to spoil an admirable novel. Women, all these, only in name; a cause of grief to the lovers of the master, a matter of scoffing to his idler critics. When we come to women of everyday stature, then indeed it is a different thing. So numerous are these, and so important in an estimate of Dickens's power of characterization, that I must give them a chapter to themselves.

Neither at a black-hearted villain was he really good, though he prided himself on his achievements in this kind. Jonas Chuzzlewit is the earliest worth mention; and what can be said of Jonas, save that he is a surly ruffian of whom one knows very little? The "setting" of his part is very strong; much powerful writing goes to narrate his history; but the man remains mechanical. Mr Carker hardly aims at such completeness of scoundreldom, but he would be a fierce rascal—if not so bent on exhibiting his teeth, which remind one of the working wires. Other shapes hover in lurid vagueness. Whether, last of all, John Jasper would have shown a great advance, must remain doubtful. The first half of *Edwin Drood* shows him picturesquely, and little more. We discover no hint of real tragedy. The man seems to us a very vulgar assassin, and we care not at all what becomes of him.

Against these set the gallery of portraits in which Dickens has displayed to us the legal world of his day. Here he painted from nature, and with an artist's love of his subject. From the attorneys and barristers of *Pickwick*, sportive themselves and a cause of infinite mirth in others, to the Old Bailey practitioners so admirably grim in *Great Expectations*, one's eye passes along a row of masterpieces. Nay, it is idle to use the pictorial simile; here are men with blood in their veins—some of them with a good deal of it on their hands. They will not be forgotten; whether we watch the light comedy of Jorkins and Spenlow, or observe the grim gravity of Mr Jaggers, it is with the same entire conviction. In this department of his work Dickens can be said to idealize only in the sense of the finest art; no praise can exaggerate his dexterity in setting forth these examples of supreme realism. As a picture of actual life in a certain small world *Bleak House* is his greatest book; from office-boy to judge, here are all who walk in "the valley of the shadow of the Law". Impossible to run through the list, much as one would enjoy it. Think only of Mr Vholes. In the whole range of fiction there is no character more vivid than this; exhibited so briefly yet so completely, with such rightness in every touch, such impressiveness of total effect, that the thing becomes a miracle. No strain of improbable intrigue can threaten the vitality of these dusty figures. The clerks are as much alive as their employers; the law-stationer stands for ever face to face with Mr Tulkinghorn; Inspector Bucket has warmer flesh than that of any other detective in the library of detective literature. As for Jaggers and Wemmick, we should presume them unsurpassable had we not known their predecessors. They would make a novelist's reputation.

Among the finest examples of characterization (I postpone a review of the figures which belong more distinctly to satire) must be mentioned the Father of the Marshalsea. Should ever proof be demanded—as often it has been—that Dickens is capable of high comedy, let it be sought in the 31st chapter of book i of *Little Dorrit*. There will be seen the old Marshalsea prisoner, the bankrupt of half a lifetime, entertaining and patronizing his workhouse pensioner, old Mr Nandy. For delicacy of treatment, for fineness of observation, this scene, I am inclined to think, is unequalled in all the novels. Of exaggeration there is no trace; nothing raises a laugh; at most one smiles, and may very likely be kept grave by profound interest and a certain emotion of wonder. We are in a debtors' prison, among vulgar folk; yet the exquisite finish of this study of human nature forbids one to judge it by any but the highest standards. The Dorrit brothers are both well drawn; they are characterizations in the best sense of the word; and in this scene we have the culmination of the author's genius. That it reveals itself so quietly is but the final assurance of consummate power.

With the normal in character, with what (all things considered) we may call wholesome normality, Dickens does not often concern himself. Of course there are his homely-minded "little women", of whom more in another place. And there are his benevolent old boys (I call them so advisedly) whom one would like to be able to class with everyday people, but who cannot in strictness be considered here. Walking-gentlemen appear often enough; amiable shadows, such as Tom Pinch's friend Westlock; figures meant to be prominent, such as Arthur Clennam. There remain a few instances of genuine characterization within ordinary limits. I cannot fall in with the common judgment that Dickens never shows us a gentleman. Twice, certainly, he has done so, with the interesting distinction that in one case he depicts a gentleman of the old school; in the other, a representative of the refined manhood which came into existence (or became commonly observable) in his latter years. In John Jarndyce I can detect no vulgarity; he appears to me compact of good sense, honour, and gentle feeling. His eccentricity does not pass bounds; the better we know him the less observable it grows. Though we are told nothing expressly of his intellectual acquirements, it is plain that he had a liberal education, and that his tastes are studious. Impossible not to like and to respect Mr Jarndyce. Compare him with Mr Pickwick, or with the Cheerybles, and we see at once the author's indication of social superiority, no less than his increased skill in portraiture. The second figure, belonging to a changed time, is Mr Crisparkle, for whose sake especially one regrets the unfinished state of *Edwin Drood*. His breezy manner, his athletic habits, his pleasant speech, give no bad idea of the classical tutor who is neither an upstart nor a pedant. Dickens was careful in his choice of names; we see how he formed that of Crisparkle, and recognize its fitness.

Two other names occur to me, which carry with them a suggestion of true gentility—if the word be permitted; but their bearers can hardly rank with

normal personages. Sir Leicester Dedlock, though by no means unsympathetically presented, belongs rather to the region of satire; he is a gentleman,
indeed, and meant to be representative of a class, but his special characteristic overcharges the portrait. Incomparably more of a human being than his
wife, he might, with less satirical emphasis, have been a very true gentleman
indeed. Then, in *Dombey and Son*, does one not remember Cousin Feenix?
The name, this time, is unfortunate; this weak-legged scion of aristocracy
deserved better treatment. For he is no phantasm; has no part with the pup-
pets of supposed high-birth whom Dickens occasionally set up only for
the pleasure of knocking them down again. However incapable of walking straight across a room, however restricted in his views of life, Cousin
Feenix has the instincts of birth and breeding. I think one may say that he
is Dickens's least disputable success in a sketch (it is only a sketch) from the
aristocratic world. His talk does not seem to me exaggerated, and it is unu-
sually interesting; his heart is right, his apprehensions are delicate. That he
should be shown as feeble in mind, no less than at the knees, is merely part
of the author's scheme; and, after all, the feebleness is more apparent than
real. Dickens, moreover, very often associates kindness of disposition with
lack of brains; it connects itself, I fancy, with his attitude towards liberal
education, which has already been discussed, as well as with his Radicalism,
still to be spoken of. No distinctly intellectual person figures in his books;
David Copperfield is only a seeming exception, for who really thinks of
David as a literary man? To his autobiography let all praise be given—with
the reserve that we see the man himself less clearly than any other person
of whom he speaks. Decidedly he is *not* "the hero of his own story". Had
Dickens intended to show us a man of letters, he would here have failed
most grievously; of course he aimed at no such thing; the attempt would
have cost him half his public. And so it is that one never thinks of the good
David as a character at all, never for a moment credits *him*, the long-suffering youth for whom Dora "held the pens", with that glorious endowment of
genius which went to the writing of his life.

Of an average middle-class family in Dickens's earlier time—decent,
kindly, not unintelligent folk—we have the best example in the Meagles
group, from *Little Dorrit*. This household may be contrasted with, say, that
of the Maylies in *Oliver Twist*, which is merely immature work, and with
the more familiar family circles on which Dickens lavishes his mirth and
his benevolence. The Meagles do not much interest us, which is quite right;
they are thoroughly realized, and take their place in social history. Well
done, too, is the Pocket family in *Great Expectations*, an interesting pendant

to that of the Jellybys in *Bleak House*; showing how well, when he chose, Dickens could satirize without extravagance. Mrs Pocket is decidedly more credible than Mrs Jellyby; it might be urged, perhaps, that she belongs to the Sixties instead of to the Fifties, a point of some importance. The likeness in dissimilitude between these ladies' husbands is very instructive. As for the son, Herbert Pocket, he is a capital specimen of the healthy, right-minded, and fairly-educated middleclass youth. Very skilfully indeed is he placed side by side with Pip; each throwing into relief the other's natural and acquired characteristics. We see how long it will take the blacksmith's foster-child (he telling the tale himself) to reach the point of mental and moral refinement to which Herbert Pocket has been bred.

One more illustration of the ordinary in life and character. Evidently Dickens took much pains with Walter Gay, in *Dombey and Son*, meaning to represent an average middle-class boy, high-spirited, frank, affectionate, and full of cheerful ambition. I have already mentioned the darker design, so quickly abandoned; we feel sure its working out would not have carried conviction, for Walter Gay, from the first, does not ring quite true. The note seems forced; we are not stirred by the lad's exuberance of jollity, and he never for a moment awakens strong interest. Is it any better with Richard Carstone,—in whom the tragic idea was, with modification, carried through? Yes, Richard is more interesting; by necessity of his fortunes, and by virtue of artistic effort. He has his place in a book pervaded with the atmosphere of doom. Vivid he never becomes; we see him as a passive victim of fate, rather than as a struggling man; if he made a better fight, or if we were allowed to see more of his human weakness (partly forbidden by our proprieties), his destiny would affect us more than it does. In truth, this kind of thing cannot be done under Dickens's restrictions. Thackeray *could* have done it magnificently; but there was "the great, big, stupid public".

The "gentleman" Dickens loved to contemplate was—in echo of Burns's phrase—he who derives his patent of gentility straight from Almighty God. These he found abundantly among the humble of estate, the poor in spirit; or indulged his fine humanity in the belief that they abounded. A broken squire, reduced to miserly service, but keeping through all faults and misfortunes the better part of his honest and kindly nature; grotesque in person, of fantastic demeanour, but always lovable;—of this dream comes Newman Noggs. A city clerk, grey in conscientious labour for one house, glorying in the perfection of his ledger, taking it ill if his employers insist on raising his salary;—the vision is christened Tim Linkinwater. A young man of bumpkinish appearance, shy, ungainly, who has somehow drifted into the household

The Market-Cross, Salisbury

of a country architect; who nourishes his soul at the church organ; who is so good and simple and reverential that years of experience cannot teach him what everyone else sees at a glance—the hypocritical rascality of his master: he takes shape, and is known to us as Tom Pinch. A village blacksmith, with heart as tender as his thews are tough; delighting above all things in the society of a little child; so dull of brain that he gives up in despair the effort to learn his alphabet; so sweet of temper that he endures in silence the nagging of an outrageous wife; so delicate of sensibility that he perspires at the thought of seeming to intrude upon an old friend risen in life;—what name can be his but Joe Gargery? These, and many another like unto them, did the master lovingly create, and there would be something of sacrilege in a cold scrutiny of his work. Whether or no their prototypes existed in the hurrying crowd of English life, which obscures so much good as well as evil, these figures have fixed themselves in the English imagination, and their names are part of our language. Dickens saw them, and heard them speak; to us, when we choose to enjoy without criticising, they seem no less present. Every such creation was a good deed; the results for good have been incalculable. Would he have been better occupied, had he pried into each character, revealed its vices, insisted on its sordid weaknesses, thrown bare its frequent hypocrisy, and emphasized its dreary unintelligence? Indeed, I think not. I will only permit myself the regret that he who could come so near to truth, and yet so move the affections, as in Joe Gargery, was at other times content with that inferior idealism which addresses itself only to unripe minds or to transitory moods.

The point to be kept in view regarding these ideal figures is that, however little their speech or conduct may smack of earth, their worldly surroundings are shown with marvellous fidelity. Tom Pinch worshipping at the shrine of Pecksniff may not hold our attention; but Tom Pinch walking towards Salisbury on the frosty road, or going to market in London with his sister, is unforgettable. This is what makes the difference between an impossible person in Dickens and the same kind of vision in the work of smaller writers. One cannot repeat too often that, in our literary slang, he "visualized" every character—Little Nell no less than Mr Jaggers. Seeing *them*, he saw the house in which they lived, the table at which they ate, and all the little habits of their day-to-day life. Here is an invaluable method of illusion, if an author can adopt it. Thus fortified, Dickens's least substantial imaginings have a durability not to be hoped for the laborious accuracies of an artist uninspired.

Pass to another group in this scarcely exhaustible world—the confessed eccentrics. Here Dickens revels. An English novelist must needs be occupied to some extent with grotesque abnormalities of thought and demeanour. Dickens saw them about him even more commonly than we of today, and delighted in noting, selecting, combining. The result is seen in those persons of his drama who are frankly given up by many who will defend his verisimilitude in other directions. Mantalini, for example; Quilp, Captain

Cuttle, Silas Wegg, and many another. For Silas Wegg, I fear, nothing can be urged, save the trifle that we know him; he becomes a bore, one of the worst instances of this form of humour weakened by extenuation. Even Dickens occasionally suffered from the necessity of filling a certain space. Think how long his novels are, and marvel that the difficulty does not more often declare itself. Of Mr Boythorn we are accustomed to think as drawn from Landor, but then it is Landor with all the intellect left out; his roaring as gently as any sucking-dove does not greatly charm us, but his talk has good qualities. More of a character, in the proper sense of the word, is Harold Skimpole, whose portrait gave such offence to Leigh Hunt. Now Skimpole is one of the few people in Dickens whom we dislike, and so, *a priori*, demands attention. If we incline to think his eccentricity overdone, be it remembered that the man was in part an actor, and a very clever actor too. Skimpole is excellent work, and stands out with fine individuality in contrast to the representatives of true unworldliness.

To which category belongs Mr Micawber? The art of living without an income may be successfully cultivated in very different moods. It is possible for a man of the most generous instincts to achieve great things in this line of endeavour; but the fact remains that, sooner or later, somebody has the honour of discharging his liabilities. To speak severely of Mr Micawber is beyond the power of the most conscientious critic, whether in life or art; the most rigid economist would be glad to grasp him by the hand and to pay for the bowl of punch over which this type of genial impecuniosity would dilate upon his embarrassments and his hopes; the least compromising realist has but to open at a dialogue or a letter in which Mr Micawber's name is seen, and straightway he forgets his theories. No selfish intention can be attributed to him. His bill might *not* be provided for when he declared it *was*, and, in consequence, poor Traddles may lose the table he has purchased for "the dearest girl in the world", but Mr Micawber had all the time been firmly assured that something would turn up; he will sympathize profoundly with Traddles, and write him an epistle which makes amends for the loss of many tables. No man ever lived who was so consistently delightful—certainly Dickens's father cannot have been so, but in this idealized portraiture we have essential truth. Men of this stamp do not abound, but they are met with, even today. As a rule, he who waits for something to turn up, mixing punch the while, does so with a very keen eye on his neighbour's pocket, and is recommended to us neither by Skimpole's fantastic gaiety nor by Micawber's eloquence and warmth of heart; nevertheless, one knows the irrepressibly hopeful man, full of kindliness, often distinguished by unconscious affectations of speech, who goes through life an unreluctant pensioner on the friends won by his many good and genial qualities. The one point on which experience gives no support to the imaginative figure is his conversion to practical activity. Mr Micawber in Australia does the heart good; but he is a pious vision. We refuse to think of a wife worn out by anxieties, of children growing up in squalor; we gladly accept the flourishing colonist ; but this is tribute to the author whom we love. Dickens never wrought more successfully for our pleasure and for his own fame. He is ever at his best when dealing with an amiable weakness. And in Micawber he gives us no purely national type; such men are peculiar to no country; all the characteristics of this wonderful picture can be appreciated by civilized readers throughout the world. It is not so in regard to many of his creations, though all the finest have traits of universal humanity. Should time deal hardly with him, should his emphasis of time and place begin to weigh against his wide acceptance, it is difficult to believe that the beaming visage of Wilkins Micawber will not continue to be recognized wherever men care for literary art.

This chapter must conclude with a glance at a class of human beings prominent in Dickens's earlier books, but of small artistic interest when treated in the manner peculiar to him. He was fond of characters hovering between eccentricity and madness, and in one case he depicted what he himself calls an idiot, though idiocy is not strictly speaking the form of disease exhibited. Lunatics were more often found at large in his day than in ours; perhaps that accounts for our introduction to such persons as Mrs Nickleby's wooer and Mr Dick; Miss Flite, of course, had another significance. The crazy gentleman on the garden walk, who at once flatters and terrifies Mrs Nickleby, can hardly be regarded as anything but an actor in broad farce; his talk, indeed, is midsummer madness, but is meant only to raise a laugh. In the new century, one does not laugh with such agreeable facility. Mrs Nickleby commands our attention—at a respectful distance; and here, as always, behaves after her kind, illustrating the eternal feminine; but the madman we cannot accept. Betsy Trotwood's *protégé* comes nearer to the recognizable; nevertheless Mr Dick's presence in such a book as *David Copperfield* would seem waste of space, but for certain considerations. He illustrates the formidable lady's goodness and common-sense; he served a very practical purpose, that of recommending rational treatment of the insane; and he had his place in the pages of an author whose humanity includes all that are in any way afflicted, in mind, body, or estate. Moreover, the craze about King Charles's head has been, and is likely to be, a great resource to literary persons in search of a familiar allusion. In passing to *Barnaby Rudge*, we are on different ground. Whatever else, Barnaby is a very picturesque figure, and I presume it was merely on this account that Dickens selected such a hero. In an earlier chapter, I said that this story seemed to me to bear traces of the influence of Scott; its narrative style and certain dialogues in the historical part are suggestive of this. May not the crazy Barnaby have originated in a recollection of Madge Wildfire? Crazy, I call him; an idiot he certainly is not. An idiot does not live a life of exalted imagination. But certain lunatics are of imagination all compact, and Barnaby, poetically speaking, makes a good representative of the class. Of psychology—a word unknown to Dickens—we, of course, have nothing; to ask for it is out of place. The idea, all things considered, cannot be judged a happy one. Whilst writing the latter part of the book Dickens thought for a moment of showing the rioters as led by a commanding figure, who, in the end, should prove to have escaped from Bedlam. We see his motive for this, but are not sorry he abandoned the idea. Probably *Barnby Rudge*, good as it is, would have been still better had the suggestion of a half-witted central figure been also discarded.

VI

Satiric Portraiture

Not only does Dickens give poetic shape to the better characteristics of English life; he is also England's satirist. Often directed against abuses in their nature temporary, his satire has in some part lost its edge, and would have only historic interest but for the great preservative, humour, mingled with all his books; much of it, however, is of enduring significance, and reminds us that the graver faults of Englishmen are not to be overcome by a few years of popular education, by general increase of comfort and refinement, by the spread of a democratic spirit. Some of these blemishes, it is true, belong more or less to all mankind; but in Dickens's England they were peculiarly disfiguring, and the worst of them seem inseparable from the national character.

Much as they loved and glorified him, his countrymen did not fail to make protest when wounded by the force of his satiric portraiture. The cry was "exaggeration". Naturally, this protest was very loud during the publication of *Martin Chuzzlewit*, in which book a vice supposed to be peculiarly English was vigorously dealt with. Dickens used the opportunity of a preface to answer his critics; he remarked that peculiarities of character often escape observation until they are directly pointed out, and asked whether the charge of exaggeration brought against him might not simply mean that he, a professed student of life, saw more than ordinary people. There was undoubted truth in the plea; Browning has put the same thought—as an apology for art—into the mouth of Fra Lippo Lippi. Dickens assuredly saw a great deal more in every day of his life than his average readers in three-score years and ten. But it still remained a question whether, in his desire to stigmatize an objectionable peculiarity, the satirist had not erred by making this peculiarity the whole man. Exaggeration there was, beyond dispute, in such a picture as that of Pecksniff, inasmuch as no man can be so consistently illustrative of an evil habit of mind. There was lack of proportion; the figure failed in human symmetry. Just as, in the same book, the pictures of American life erred through one-sidedness. Dickens had written satire, and satire as pointed, as effective, as any in literature. Let the galled jade wince; there was an outcry of many voices, appealing to common judgment. It might be noted that these same sensitive critics had never objected to "exaggeration" when the point at issue was merely one of art; they became aware of their favourite author's defect only when it involved a question of morals or of national character.

Merely as satirist, however, Dickens never for a moment endangered his popularity. The fact, already noticed, that *Martin Chuzzlewit* found fewer admirers than the books preceding it, had nothing to do with its moral theme, but must be traced to causes, generally more or less vague, such as from time to time affect the reception of every author's work; not long after its completion, this book became one of the most widely read. There is the satire which leaves cold, or alienates, the ordinary man, either because it passes above his head, or conflicts with his cherished prejudices; and there is the satire which, by appealing to his better self,—that is, to a standard of morality which he theoretically, or in very deed, accepts,—commands his sympathy as soon as he sees its drift. What is called the "popular conscience" was on Dickens's side; and he had the immense advantage of being able to raise a hearty laugh even whilst pointing his lesson. Among the rarest of things is this thorough understanding between author and public, permitting a man of genius to say aloud with impunity that which all his hearers say within themselves dumbly, inarticulately. Dickens never went too far; never struck at a genuine conviction of the multitude. Let us imagine him, in some moment of aberration, suggesting criticism of the popular idea of sexual morality! Would it have availed him that he had done the state some service? Would argument or authority have helped for one moment to win him a patient hearing? We know that he never desired to provoke such antagonism. Broadly speaking, he was one with his readers, and therein lay his strength for reform.

As for the charge of exaggeration, the truth is that Dickens exaggerated no whit more in his satire than in his sympathetic portraiture. It is an idle objection. Of course he exaggerated, in all but every page. In the last chapter I pointed to exceptional instances of literal or subdued truthfulness; not by these did he achieve his triumphs; they lurk for discovery by the curious. Granting his idealistic method, such censure falls wide of the mark. We are struck more forcibly when a character is exhibited as compact of knavery or grotesque cruelty, than when it presents incarnate goodness; that is all.

The one question we are justified in urging is, whether his characterization is consistent with itself. In the great majority of cases, I believe the answer must be affirmative. Were it not so, Dickens's reputation would by this time linger only among the untaught; among those who are content to laugh, no matter how the mirth be raised.

His satire covers a great part of English life, public and private. Education, charity, religion, social morality in its broadest sense, society in its narrowest; legal procedure, the machinery of politics, and the forms of government. Licensed to speak his mind, he aims laughingly or sternly, but always in the same admirable spirit, at every glaring abuse of the day. He devotes a whole book, a prodigy of skilful labour, to that crowning example of the law's delay, which had wrought ruin in innumerable homes; he throws off a brilliant little sketch, in a Christmas number, and makes everybody laugh at the absurd defects of railway refreshment-rooms. We marvel at such breadth of untiring observation in the service of human welfare. Impossible to follow him through all the achievements of his satire; I can but select examples in each field, proceeding in the order just indicated.

It is natural that he should turn, at the beginning of his career, to abuses evident in the parish, the school, the place of worship. These were nearest at hand; they stared at him in his observant childhood, and during his life as a journalist. Consequently we soon meet with Mr Bumble, with Mr Squeers, with the Rev. Mr Stiggins. Of these three figures, the one most open to the charge of exaggeration is the Yorkshire schoolmaster; yet who shall declare with assurance that Squeers's brutality outdoes the probable in his place and generation? There is crude workmanship in the portrait, and still more in the picture of Dotheboys, where over-charging defeats its own end. The extraordinary feature of this bit of work is the inextricable blending of horror and jocosity. Later, when Dickens had fuller command of his resources, he would have made Dotheboys very much more impressive; it remains an illustration of super-abundant spirits in a man of genius. We can hardly help an amiable feeling towards the Squeers family, seeing the hearty gusto with which they pursue their monstrous business. The children who suffer under them are so shadowy that we cannot feel the wrong as we ought; such a spectacle should lay waste the heart, and yet we continue smiling. Dickens, of course, did not intend that this gathering of martyred children should have the effect of reality. Enough if he called attention to the existence of a monstrous state of things; reflection shall come afterwards; his immediate business is story-telling, that is to say, amusement. Wonderfully did he adapt means to ends; we find, in fact, that nothing could have been practically more effectual

The "George" Inn, Greta Bridge

than this exhibition of strange gaiety. Mr Bumble, though he comes earlier, is, in truth, better work than Squeers. Read carefully chapter iv of *Oliver Twist*, and you will discover, probably to your surprise, that the "parochial" functionary is, after all, human: in one line—in a delicate touch—we are shown Bumble softened, to the point of a brief silence, by Oliver's pleading for kind usage. No such moment occurs in the history of Squeers. And we see why not. The master of Dotheboys is not meant for a conscientious study of a human being; he is merely the representative of a vile institution. Admit a lurking humanity, and we have suggestion of possible reform. Now the parochial system, bad as it was, seemed a necessity, and only needed a thorough overhauling,—observe the perfectly human behaviour of certain of the guardians before whom Oliver appears; but with the Yorkshire schools, it was root and branch, they must be swept from the earth. I do not think this is refining overmuch; Dickens's genius declared itself so consistently in his adaptation of literary means to ends of various kinds; and, however immature the details of his performance, he shows from the first this marvellous precision in effect.

Dotheboys was of course, even in these bad times, an exceptional method for the rearing of youth. It is not cold-blooded cruelty, but blockheaded ignorance, against which Dickens has to fight over the whole ground of education. We have noticed his attitude towards the system of classical training; the genteel private schools of his day invited satire, and supplied him with some of his most entertaining chapters. Dr Blimber's establishment is a favourable specimen of the kind of thing that satisfied well-to-do parents; genial ridicule suffices for its condemnation. But Dickens went deeper and laid stress upon the initial stages of the absurd system. Mrs Pipchin, however distinct a personality, was not singular in her mode of dealing with children fresh from the nursery. Always profoundly interested in these little people, Dickens, without reaching any very clear conception of reform, well understood the evil consequences of such gross neglect or mistaken zeal as were common in households of every class. He knew that the vices of society could for the most part be traced to these bad beginnings. A leader in this as in so many other directions, he taught his readers to think much of children just at the time when England had especial need of an educational awakening. Not his satire alone, but his so-called sentimentality, served a great purpose, and the death-bed of Paul Dombey, no less than the sufferings of Mr Creakle's little victim, helped on the better day.

Though it has been "proved to demonstration"—by persons who care for such proof—that tenderness of heart led him astray in his bitterness against the new Poor Law, we see, of course, that herein he pursued his humane task, seeking in all possible ways to mitigate the harshness of institutions which pressed hardly upon the poor and weak. He could not away with those who held—or spoke as if they held—that a man had no duty to his fellows beyond the strict letter of the law. In this respect that very poor book, *Hard Times*, has noteworthy significance; but the figures of Gradgrind and Bounderby show how completely he could fail when he dispensed (or all but dispensed) with the aid of humour. Oliver Twist's "old gentleman in the white waistcoat" is decidedly better as portraiture, and as satire more effective. Apologists, or rampant glorifiers, of the workhouse, such as appear in the Christmas Books, need not be viewed too seriously; they stood forth at a season of none too refined joviality, and were in keeping with barons of beef, tons of plum-pudding, and other such heavy extravagances. They do not live in one's mind; nor, I think, does any one of Dickens's persons who are meant to satirize poor-law abuses. In this matter, his spirit did its work, his art not greatly assisting.

But when we come to his lashings of religious hypocrisy, the figures castigated are substantial enough. Always delighted to present a humbug, Dickens can scarce restrain himself when he gets hold of a religious humbug, especially of the coarse type. Brother Stiggins shines immortal in the same pages with Mr Pickwick and the Wellers. Compare with him the Reverend Mr Chadband. They are the same men, but one lived in 1837, the other in 1853. Brother Stiggins is, in plain English, a drunkard; Mr Chadband would think shame of himself to be even once overtaken: he is a consumer of tea and muffins. It suited the author's mood, and the day in which he was writing, to have Mr Stiggins soundly beaten in a pugilistic encounter with Tony Weller, to say nothing of other undignified positions in which the reverend gentleman finds himself; but Mr Chadband may discourse upon "Terewth" in Mr Snagsby's parlour to any length that pleases him with no fear of such outrage. These same discourses are among the most mirth-provoking things in all Dickens: impossible to regard with nothing but contempt or dislike the man who has so shaken our sides. It might be well for the world if the race of Chadband should disappear (a consummation still far out of sight); but the satirist frankly glories in him, and to us he is a joy for ever. This is the best of the full-length pictures; but we have many a glimpse of kindred personages, always shown us with infinite gusto. The Rev. Melchisedech Howler, for instance. With what extravagance of humour, with what a rapture of robust mirth, are his characteristics touched off in a short passage of *Dombey and Son*! I must give myself the pleasure of copying it. "The Rev.

Melchisedech Howler, who, having been one day discharged from the West India Docks on a false suspicion (got up expressly against him by the general enemy) of screwing gimlets into puncheons, and applying his lips to the orifice, had announced the destruction of the world for that day two years, at ten in the morning, and opened a front parlour for the reception of ladies and gentlemen, of the ranting persuasion, upon whom, on the first occasion of their assemblage, the admonition of the Rev. Melchisedech had produced so powerful an effect, that, in their rapturous performance of a sacred jig, which closed the service, the whole flock broke through into a kitchen below and disabled a mangle belonging to one of the fold" (chapter xv). There is a sheer boyishness in this irresistible glee; yet the passage was written more than ten years after *Pickwick*. It is the same all but to the end. Dickens treats a thoroughgoing humbug as though he loved him. Reverent of all true religion, and inclined to bitterness against respectable shortcomings in the high places of the Church, he goes wild with merriment over back-parlour proselytism and the brayings of Little Bethel. Perhaps in this respect alone did he give grave and lasting offence to numbers of people who would otherwise have been amongst his admirers. At a later time, he could draw, or attempt, a sympathetic portrait of a clergyman of the Established Church, in *Our Mutual Friend*, and, in his last book, could speak respectfully of Canons; but with Dissent he never reconciled himself. To this day, I believe, his books are excluded, on religious grounds, from certain families holding austere views. Remembering the England he sets before us, it is perhaps the highest testimony to his power that such hostility did not make itself more felt when he was mocking so light-heartedly at Stiggins and Chadband and the Rev. Melchisedech.

Connected with hypocrisy in religion, but very skilfully kept apart from it, is his finest satiric portrait, that of Mr Pecksniff. Think of all that is suggested in this representative of an odious vice, and marvel at the adroitness with which a hundred pitfalls of the incautious satirist are successfully avoided. A moral hypocrite, an incarnation of middle-class respectability in the worst sense of the word, in the sense so loathed by Carlyle, and by every other man of brains then living; yet never a hint at subjects forbidden in the family circle, never a word to which that relative of Mr Pecksniff, the famous Podsnap, could possibly object. The thing would seem impossible, but that it is done. Let the understanding read between the lines; as in all great art, much is implied that finds no direct expression. Mr Pecksniff walks and talks before us, a cause of hilarity to old and young, yet the type of as ugly a failing as any class or people can be afflicted withal. The book in which he figures is directed against self-interest in all its forms. We see the sagacious swindler, and the greedy dupe whose unscrupulousness ends in murder. We see the flocking of the Chuzzlewit family, like birds of prey, about the sick-bed of their wealthy relative; and among them the gentlemanly architect of unctuous phrase, who, hearing himself called a hypocrite, signalizes his pre-eminence in an immortal remark: "Charity, my dear, when I take my chamber-candlestick to-night, remind me to be more than usually particular in praying for Mr Anthony Chuzzlewit, who has done me an injustice". This man is another than Tartufe; he belongs to a different age, and different country. His religion is not an end in itself; he does not desire to be thought a saint; his prayers are inseparable from the chamber-candlestick, a mere item in the character of British respectability. A like subordination appears in the piety of all Dickens's religious pretenders; their language never becomes offensive to the ordinary reader, simply because it avoids the use of sacred names and phrases, and is seen to have a purely temporal application. Mr Chadband is a tradesman, dealing in a species of exhortation which his hearers have agreed to call spiritual, and to rate at a certain value in coin of the realm; religion in its true sense never comes into question. Mr Pecksniff, of course, might have become a shining light in some great conventicle, but destiny has made him a layman; he published his habit of praying, because to pray (over the chamber-candlestick) was incumbent upon an Englishman who had a position to support, who had a stake in the country. A reputation for piety, however, would not suffice to his self-respect, and to the needs of his business; he adds an all-embracing benevolence, his smile falls like the blessed sunshine on all who meet him in his daily walk. This it is which so impresses the simple-minded Tom Pinch. Tom, a thorough Englishman for all his virtues, would not be attracted by a show of merely religious exaltation; faith must be translated into works. Pecksniff must seem to him good, kind, generous, a great man at his profession, sound and trustworthy in all he undertakes. In other words, the Pecksniff whom Tom believes in is the type of English excellence, and evidently no bad type to be set before a nation. Such men existed, and do, and will; we talk little about them, and it is their last desire that we should; they live, mostly in silence, for the honour of their race and of humankind. But, since the Puritan revolution, it has unhappily seemed necessary to our countrymen in general to profess in a peculiar way certain peculiar forms of godliness, and this habit, gradually associated with social prejudices arising from high prosperity, results in the respectable man. Analysing this person down to his elements, Carlyle found it an essential, if not *the* essential, that he should "keep a gig". Mr

Pecksniff's gig, one remembers, was no very imposing vehicle; it looked "like a gig with a tumour". "Let us be moral", says the great man (happening at that moment to be drunk); and here we get to the honest root of the matter. Though the Englishman may dispense with a gig and remain respectable, he must not be suspected of immorality. "Let us contemplate existence", pursues the inebriate sage. We do so, we English, and find that the term morality (more decidedly than religion) includes all that, in our souls, we rate most highly. According to his recognized morality (sexual first and foremost), do we put trust in a man. We are a practical people; we point to our wealth in evidence; and our experience has set it beyond doubt that chastity of thought and act is a nation's prime safeguard.

Could we but be satisfied with the conviction, and simply act upon it! It is not enough. We must hold it as an article of faith that respectability not only does not err, but knows not temptation. A poet who never asked to be thought respectable has put into words we shall not easily forget his thought about immorality:

"I waive the quantum o' the sin,
The hazard of concealing;
But och! it hardens a' within,
And petrifies the feeling!"

The quantum of the sin is so grave, the hazard of concealing so momentous, in English eyes, that we form a national conspiracy to exhibit English nature as distinct, in several points, from the merely human. Hence a characteristic delicacy, a singular refinement, resulting at its best in very sweet and noble lives; hence, also, that counterbalancing vice which would fain atone for vice in the more usual sense of the word. Though all within may be hopelessly hardened, the feeling petrified into a little idol of egoism, outwardly there shall be a show of everything we respect. "Homage to virtue", quotha? Well and good, were it nothing more. But Mr Pecksniff takes up his parable, his innumerable kindred hold forth in the marketplace. Respectability cannot hold its tongue, in fact; and the language it affects is wont to be nauseous.

Lower than Pecksniff, but of obvious brotherhood with him, stands Uriah Heep. This example of a low-born man, who, chancing to have brains, deems it most expedient to use them for dishonest purposes, will not yield in the essentials of respectability to the best in the land. He is poor, he is 'umble, but his morals must not for a moment be doubted. The undisguisable fact of poverty is accepted and made the most of; it becomes his tower of strength.

Mr Pecksniff, conscious of a well-filled purse, assumes a certain modesty of demeanour—a foretaste, by the by, of that affectation in rich people which promises such an opportunity for satire in our own day. Uriah Heep wallows in perpetual humility; he grovels before his social superiors, that he may prove to them his equality in soul. With regard to this slimy personage, we note at once that he is a victim of circumstances, the outcome of a bad education and of a society affected with disease. His like abounded at the time; nowadays they will not so easily be discovered. The doctrine that "A man's a man for a' that" has taken solid shape, and our triumphant democracy will soon be ashamed of a motto so disparaging. But Heep saw no prospect when he stood upright; only when he crawled did a chance of issue from that too humble life present itself. "Remember your place!"—from his earliest years this admonition had sounded for him. This prime duty is ever present to his mind; it prompts him to avow, in and out of season, that he belongs to a very 'umble family, that he is himself the 'umblest of mortals. Meanwhile the man's vitals are consumed with envy, hatred, and malice. He cannot respect himself; his training has made the thing impossible; and all men are his enemies. When he is detected in criminal proceedings we are hard upon him, very hard. Dickens cannot relent to this victim of all that is worst in the society he criticises. Had Uriah stopped short of crime, something might have been said for him, but the fellow is fatally logical. Logic of that kind we cannot hear of for a moment; in our own logic of the police-court and the assizes we will take remarkably good care that there is no flaw.

Pecksniff and Uriah have a certain amount of intellect. In his last book Dickens presents us with the monumental humbug who is at the same time an egregious fool. Mr Sapsea very honestly worships himself; he is respectability weighing a good many stone, with heavy watch-guard and expensive tailoring. By incessant lauding of his own virtues to a world always more or less attentive when such a speaker carries social weight, Sapsea has developed a mania of self-importance. His thickness of hide, his stolidity, are well displayed, but it seems to me that in this case Dickens has been guilty of a piece of exaggeration altogether exceeding the limits of art; perhaps the one instance where his illusion fails to make us accept an extravagance even for a moment. I refer to Sapsea's inscription for his wife's tomb (*Edwin Drood*, chapter iv). Contrasting this with anything to be found in Pecksniff or Uriah Heep, we perceive the limits of his satire, strictly imposed by art, even where he is commonly held to have been most fantastic.

Dickens applied with extraordinary skill the only method which, granted all his genius, could have ensured him so vast a sway over the public of that

No. 146 High Street, Rochester

time. His art, especially as satirist, lies in the judicious use of emphasis and iteration. Emphasis alone would not have answered his purpose; the striking thing must be said over and over again till the most stupid hearer has it by heart. We of today sometimes congratulate ourselves on an improvement in the public taste and intelligence, and it is true that some popular authors conciliate their admirers by an appeal in a comparatively subdued note. But—who has a popularity like to that of Dickens? Should there again rise an author to be compared with him in sincerity and universality of acceptance, once more will be heard that unmistakable voice of summons to Goodman Dull. We are educated, we are cultured; be it so; but, to say the least, some few millions of us turn with weariness from pages of concentrated art. Fifty years ago the people who did *not* might have been gathered from the English-speaking world into a London hall, without uncomfortable crowding. Dickens well understood that he must cry aloud and spare not; he did it naturally, as a man of his generation; he, and his fellow reformers, educators, popular entertainers, were perforce vociferous to the half-awakened multitudes. Carlyle was even more emphatic, and reiterated throughout a much longer life. Education notwithstanding, these will again be the characteristics of any writer for whom fate reserves a gigantic popularity in the century just beginning.

Yes, it is quite true that Mr Micawber, Mr Pecksniff, Uriah Heep, and all Dickens's prominent creations say the same thing in the same way, over and over again. The literary exquisite is disgusted, the man of letters shakes his head with a smile. Remember: for twenty months did these characters of favourite fiction make a periodical appearance, and not the most stupid man in England forgot them between one month and the next. The method is at the disposal of all and sundry; who will use it to this effect?

In his satires on "high life", Dickens was less successful than with the middle class. I have spoken of Sir Leicester Dedlock and Cousin Feenix, both well done, the latter especially, and characterizations worthy of the author, but they hold no place in the general memory. His earliest attempt at this kind of thing was unfortunate; Lord Frederick Verisopht and Sir Mulberry Hawk are on a par with the literary lady in *Pickwick*, who wrote the ode to an Expiring Frog—an exercise of fancy which has no relation whatever to the facts of life. Possibly the young author of *Nicholas Nickleby* fancied he had drawn a typical baronet and a lord; more likely he worked with conscious reference to the theatre. In *Little Dorrit* we are introduced to certain high-born or highly-connected people, who make themselves deliberately offensive, but their names cannot be recalled. Much better is the study of an ancient worldling in Edith Dombey's mother, Mrs Skewton. Her paralytic seizure, her death in life, are fine and grisly realism; but we do not accept Mrs Skewton as a typical figure. Too obvious is the comparison with Thackeray's work; Dickens is here at a grave disadvantage, and would have done better not to touch that ground at all. Perhaps the same must be said of his incursions into political satire; and yet, one would be loth to lose the Circumlocution Office. Though by the choice of such a name he seems to forbid our expecting any picture of reality, there seems reason to believe that those pages of *Little Dorrit* are not much less true than amusing; at all events they are admirably written. Of the Barnacle family we accept readily enough the one who is described as bright and young; indeed, this youngster is a good deal of a gentleman, and represents the surviving element of that day's Civil Service; under a competitive system, he alone would have a chance. His relatives have significance enough, but very little life. Dickens wrote of them in anger, which was never the case in his satiric masterpieces. Anger abundantly justified, no doubt; but at the same time another critic of the English government was making heard his wrathful voice (it came from Chelsea), and with more of the true prophetic vehemence. Dickens did not feel at home in this Barnacle atmosphere; something of personal feeling entered into his description of its stifling properties. He could write brilliantly on the subject, but not with the calmness necessary for the creation of lasting characters.

The upstarts of commerce and speculation came more within his scope. Montague Tigg keeps a place in one's recollection, but chiefly, I think, as the impecunious braggart rather than as the successful knave. There is an impressiveness about Mr Merdle, but perhaps rather in the description of his surroundings than in the figure of the man himself; readers in general know nothing of him, his name never points a paragraph. The Veneerings, in *Our Mutual Friend*, seem better on a re-reading than in a memory of the acquaintance with them long ago. This is often the case with Dickens, and speaks strongly in his favour. They smell of furniture polish; their newness in society is a positive distress to the nerves; to read of them is to revive a sensation one has occasionally experienced in fact. Being but sketches, they are of necessity (in Dickens's method) all emphasis; we never lose sight of their satiric meaning; their very name (like that of the Circumlocution Office) signals caricature. At this point Dickens connects himself once more with literary traditions; we are reminded of the nomenclature of English drama; of Justice Greedy, of Anthony Absolute, Mrs Malaprop, and the rest. It is only in his subordinate figures, and rarely then, that he falls into this bad habit, so destructive of illusion. For the most part, his names are aptly selected, or invented with great skill—skill, of course, different from that of Balzac, who aims at another kind of effectiveness. Gamp, Micawber, Bumble, Pipchin—to be sure they are so familiar to us that we associate them inevitably with certain characters, but one recognizes their exquisite rightness. Pecksniff is more daring, and touches the limit of fine discretion. In a very few cases he drew upon that list of grotesque names which anyone can compile from a directory, names which are generally valueless in fiction just because they really exist; Venus, for example.

Anything but a caricature, though as significant a figure as any among these minor groups, is Mr Casby in *Little Dorrit*, the venerable grandsire, of snowy locks and childlike visage; the Patriarch, as he is called, who walks in a light of contemplative benevolence. Mr Casby is a humbug of a peculiarly dangerous kind; under various disguises he is constantly met with in the England of today. This sweetly philosophic being owns houses, and those of the kind which we now call slums. Of course he knows nothing about their evil condition; of course he employs an agent to collect his rents, and is naturally surprised when this agent falls short in the expected receipts. It pains him that human nature should be so dishonest; for the sake of his tenants themselves it behoves him to insist on full and regular payment. When, in the end, Mr Casby has his impressive locks ruthlessly shorn by the agent risen in revolt against such a mass of lies and cruelty and unclean selfishness, we feel that the punishment is inadequate. This question of landlordism should have been treated by Dickens on a larger scale; it remains one of the curses of English life, and is likely to do so until the victims of house-owners see their way to cut, not the hair, but the throats, of a few selected specimens. Mr Casby, nowadays, does not take the trouble to assume a sweet or reverend aspect; if he lives in the neighbourhood of his property, he is frankly a brute; if, as is so often the case, he resides in a very different part of the town, his associates are persons who would smile indeed at any affectation of sanctity. In this, and some other directions, hypocrisy has declined among us. Our people of all classes have advanced in the understanding of business, a word which will justify most atrocities, and excuse all but every form of shamelessness.

That rich little book, *Great Expectations*, contains a humbug less offensive than Casby, and on the surface greatly amusing, but illustrative of a contemptible quality closely allied with the commercial spirit. Seen at a distance Mr Pumblechook is a source of inextinguishable laughter; near at hand he is seen to be a very sordid creature. A time-server to his marrow, he adds the preposterous self-esteem which always gave Dickens so congenial an opportunity. Here we have a form of moral dishonesty peculiar to no one people. Mr Pumblechook's barefaced pretence that he is the maker of Pip's fortune, his heavy patronage whilst that fortune endures, and his sour desertion of the young man when circumstances alter, is mere overfed humanity discoverable all the world over. He has English traits, and we are constrained to own the man as a relative; we meet him as often as we do the tailor who grovels before the customer unexpectedly become rich. Compare him with the other embodiments of dishonesty, and it is seen, not only what inexhaustible material of this kind lay at Dickens's command, but with what excellent art he differentiates his characters.

Less successful are the last pieces of satiric drawing I can find space to mention. In this chapter, rather than in the next, is the place for Mrs Jellyby, who loses all distinction of sex, and comes near to losing all humanity, in her special craze. Women have gone far towards such a consummation, and one dare not refuse to admit her possibility; but the extravagance of the thing rather repels, and we are never so assured of Mrs Jellyby as of Mr Pecksniff. Unacceptable in the same way is that fiercely charitable lady who goes about with her tracts and her insolence among the cottages of the poor. One knows how such persons nowadays demean themselves, and we can readily believe that they behaved more outrageously half a century ago; but being meant as a type, this religious female dragoon misses the mark; we refuse credence and turn away.

Caricature in general is a word of depreciatory meaning. I have already made it clear how far I am from agreeing with the critics who think that to call Dickens a caricaturist, and to praise his humour, is to dismiss him once for all. It seems to me that in all his very best work he pursues an ideal widely apart from that of caricature in any sense; and that in other instances he permits himself an emphasis, like in kind to that of the caricaturist, but by its excellence of art, its fine sincerity of purpose, removed from every inferior association. To call Mrs Gamp a caricature is an obvious abuse of language; not less so, I think, to apply the word to Mr Pecksniff or to Uriah Heep. Occasionally, missing the effect he intended, Dickens produced work which invites this definition; at times, again, he deliberately drew a figure with that literary overcharging which corresponds to the exaggeration, small or great, of professed caricaturists with the pencil. His finest humour, his most successful satire, belongs to a different order of art. To be convinced of this one need but think of the multiplicity of detail, all exquisitely finished, which goes to make his best-known portraits. Full justice has never been done to this abounding richness of invention, this untiring felicity of touch in minutiae innumerable. Caricature proceeds by a broad and simple method. It is no more the name for Dickens's full fervour of creation, than for Shakespeare's in his prose comedy. Each is a supreme idealist.

VII

Women and Children

With female readers Dickens was never a prime favourite. One feels very sure that they contributed little or nothing to the success of *Pickwick*. In the angelic *Oliver* they began, no doubt, to find matter of interest, and thence onward they might "take to" the triumphant novelist for the pathos of his child-life and to some extent because of his note of domesticity. But on the whole it was for men that Dickens wrote. Today the women must be very few who by deliberate choice open a volume of his works.

The humorist never strongly appeals to that audience. Moreover, it is natural enough that a writer so often boisterous, who deals so largely with the coarser aspects of life, who gives us very little of what is conventionally called tenderness, and a good deal of bloodthirsty violence, should yield to many others in women's choice. For certain of them, Dickens is simply "vulgar"— and there an end of it; they can no more read him with pleasure than they can his forerunners of the eighteenth century. In a class where this might not be honestly felt as an objection, he is practically unknown to mothers and daughters who devote abundant leisure to fiction of other kinds; and representatives of this public have been known to speak of him with frank dislike. One reason, it seems, for such coldness in presumably gentle hearts goes deeper than those which first suggest themselves. If George Eliot was of opinion that Shakespeare shows himself unjust to women, and on that account could not wholly revere him, we need not be surprised that average members of her sex should see in Dickens something like a personal enemy, a confirmed libeller of all who speak the feminine tongue.

For, setting aside his would-be tragic figures, the Lady Dedlocks and Edith Dombeys of whom enough has been said; neglecting also for the moment his exemplars in the life of home (doubtfully sympathetic to female readers of our day); it is obvious that Dickens wrote of women in his liveliest spirit of satire. Wonderful as fact, and admirable as art, are the numberless pictures of more or less detestable widows, wives, and spinsters which appear throughout his books. Beyond dispute, they must be held among his finest work; this portraiture alone would establish his claim to greatness. And I think it might be forcibly argued that, for incontestable proof of Dickens's fidelity in reproducing the life he knew, one should turn in the first place to his gallery of foolish, ridiculous, or offensive women.

These remarkable creatures belong for the most part to one rank of life, that which we vaguely designate as the lower middle class. In general their circumstances are comfortable; they suffer no hardship—save that of birth, which they do not perceive as such; nothing is asked of them but a quiet and amiable discharge of household duties ; they are treated by their male kindred with great, often with extraordinary, consideration. Yet their characteristic is acidity of temper and boundless licence of querulous or insulting talk. The real business of their lives is to make all about them as uncomfortable as they can. Invariably, they are unintelligent and untaught; very often they are flagrantly imbecile. Their very virtues (if such persons can be said to have any) become a scourge. In the highways and by-ways of life, by the fireside, and in the bed-chamber, their voices shrill upon the terrified ear. It is difficult to believe that death can stifle them; one imagines them upon the threshold of some other world, sounding confusion among unhappy spirits who hoped to have found peace.

There needs no historical investigation to ascertain the truthfulness of these presentments. Among the poorer folk, especially in London, such women may be observed today by any inquirer sufficiently courageous; they are a multitude that no man can number; every other house in the cheap suburbs will be found to contain at least one specimen—very often two, for the advantage of quarrelling when men are not at hand. Education has done little as yet to improve the tempers and the intellects of women in this rank. A humorist of our time suggests that sheer dulness and monotony of existence explains their unamiable habits, that they quarrel because they can get no other form of excitement. I believe there is some truth in this, but it does not cover the whole ground. Many a woman who frequents theatres and music-halls, goes shopping and lives in comparative luxury, has brought the arts of ill-temper to high perfection. Indeed, I am not sure that increase of liberty is not tending to exasperate these evil characteristics in women vulgarly bred; if Dickens were now writing, I believe he would have to add to his representative women the well-dressed shrew who proceeds on the slightest provocation from fury of language to violence of act. Mrs Varden does not dream of assaulting her husband, for in truth she loves him; Mrs Snagsby is in genuine terror at the thought that the deferential law-stationer may come to harm. Nowadays these ladies would enjoy a very much larger life, would systematically neglect their children (if they chose to have any), and would soothe their nerves, in moments carefully chosen, by flinging at the remonstrant husband any domestic object to which they attached no special value.

Through his early life Dickens must have been in constant observation of these social pests. In every lodging-house he entered, such a voice would surely be sounding. His women use utterance such as no male genius could have invented; from the beginning he knew it perfectly, the vocabulary, the syntax, the figurative flights of this appalling language. "God's great gift of speech abused" was the commonplace of his world. Another man, obtaining his release from those depths, would have turned away in loathing; Dickens found therein matter for his mirth, material for his art. When one thinks of it, how strange it is that such an unutterable curse should become, in the artist's hands, an incitement to joyous laughter! As a matter of fact, these women produced more misery than can be calculated. That he does not exhibit this side of the picture is the peculiarity of Dickens's method; a defect, of course, from one point of view, but inseparable from his humorous treatment of life. Women who might well have wrecked homes, are shown as laughable foils for the infinite goodness and patience of men about them. Justly, by the by, a matter of complaint to the female critic. Weller, and Varden, and Snagsby, and Joe Gargery are too favourable specimens of the average husband; in such situations, one or other of them would certainly have lost his patience, and either have fled the country, or have turned wife-beater. Varden is a trifle vexed now and then, but he clinks it off at his cheery anvil, and restores his jovial mood with a draught from Toby. Mr Snagsby coughs behind his hand, is nervously perturbed, and heartily wishes things were otherwise, but never allows himself a harsh word to his "little woman". As for Joe Gargery, what could be expected of the sweetest and humanest temper man was ever blest withal? No, it is decidedly unfair. Not even Jonas Chuzzlewit (who, of course, has a martyr of a wife) can outbalance such a partial record of long-suffering in husbands.

It is worth while to consider with some attention these promoters of public mirth. *Pickwick* would have been incomplete without this element of joviality, and we are not likely to forget the thorn in the flesh of Mr Weller, senior. Sam's father is responsible, I suppose, for that jesting on the subject of widows, which even today will serve its turn on the stage or in the comic paper; it is vulgar, to be sure, but vulgarity in *Pickwick* becomes a fine art; we cannot lose a word of the old coaching hero. Mrs Weller it is hard to describe in moderate terms; taking the matter prosaically, she has all the minor vices that can inhere in woman; but the mere mention of her moves to chuckling. On her death-bed, we are given to understand, she saw the error of her ways. Such persons occasionally do, but her conversion comes a trifle late. Enough for Dickens that we are touched by the old man's spirit of forgiveness. It is the bit of light in a picture felt, after all, to be grimy enough; the bit of sweet and clean humanity which our author always desires to show after he has made his fun out of sorry circumstance. In *Oliver Twist*, the feminine note grows shriller; we have Mrs Sowerberry, sordid tyrant and scold, and the woman who becomes Mrs Bumble. We are meant to reflect, of course, that the "porochial" dignitary gets only his deserts; he who marries with his eye upon a pair of silver sugar-tongs, and is a blustering jackass to boot, can hardly be too severely dealt with. So Mrs Bumble exhibits her true self for her husband's benefit, and, so far as we know, does not repent of her triumphs as an obese virago. *Barnaby Rudge* is enriched with Mrs Varden and her handmaid Miggs. Now of Mrs Varden it can be said that she typifies a large class of most respectable wives. She is not coarse, she is not malignant, she is not incapable of good-humour; but so much value does she attach to the gleams of that bright quality, that not one is suffered to escape her until her household has been brought to the verge of despair by her persistent sourness and sulkiness. No reason whatever can be assigned for it; when she takes offence, it pleases her to do so. She has in perfection all the illogicality of thought, all the maddening tricks of senseless language, which, doubtless for many thousands of years, have served her like for weapons. It is an odd thing that evolution has allowed the persistence of this art, for we may be quite sure that many a primitive woman paid for it with a broken skull. Here it is, however, flourishing, and like to flourish. The generations do not improve upon it; this art of irritation has long ago been brought to its highest possible point. Who knows? A future civilization may discover lapses of common-sense and a finesse of fatuous language unknown to Mrs Varden. For the present, she points a limit of possibility in these directions. Her talk is marvellously reported; never a note of exaggeration, and nothing essential ever forgotten. The same is always to be noted in Dickens's idiotic women; their phrases might have been taken down by a phonograph for reproduction in literature. Such accuracy is a very great thing indeed; few novelists can compare in it with Dickens. His men he may permit to luxuriate in periods obviously artificial; their peculiarities are sometimes overdone, their talk becomes a fantasia of the author's elaboration, but with his women (of

the class we are reviewing) it is never so. Partly, no doubt, because one cannot exaggerate what is already exaggerated to the n'th power; but it was very
possible to miss the absolutely right in such a maze of imbecilities, and I
believe that Dickens does it never.

Mrs Varden repents, Mrs Varden is stricken with remorse, Mrs Varden
becomes a model wife. Let the Jew believe it! Not even on her death-bed
did it happen, but simply because she had a fright in the Gordon riots.
Yes; for one week, or perchance for two, she might have affected (even felt)
penitence; after that, Heaven pity poor Gabriel for having taken her at her
word! The thing is plainly impossible. Such women, at her age, are incapable
of change; they will but grow worse, till the pangs of death shake them. Mrs
Varden would have lingered to her ninetieth year, mopping and mowing
her ill-humour when language failed, and grinning illogicality with tooth-
less gums. She is converted, to make things pleasant for us. We thank the
author's goodness, and say, 'tis but a story.

Miggs, the admirer of Sam Tappertit, is idiocy and malice combined.
To tell the truth, one does not much like to read of Miggs: we feel it is
all a little hard upon women soured by celibacy. Dickens's time *was* hard
indeed on the unwilling spinster, and we do not think it an amiable trait.
Nowadays things are so different; it is common to find spinsters who are
such by choice, and not a few of them are doing good work in the world.
Sixty years ago, every unmarried woman of a certain age was a subject of
open or covert mockery: she had failed in her chase of men, and must be
presumed full of rancour against both sexes. As for Miggs, of course the
detestable Mrs Varden was largely answerable for her evil qualities; when
the handmaid was turned out of doors, the mistress should by rights have
gone with her. She amuses a certain class of readers, but has not much
value either as humour or satire or plain fact.

There looms upon us the lachrymose countenance of Mrs Gummidge.
This superannuated nuisance serves primarily, of course, to illustrate the
fine qualities of the Peggotty household; that she is borne with for one day
says indeed much for their conscientious kindness. The boatman, delicately
sympathetic, explains her fits of depression by saying that she has "been
thinking of the old 'un". Possibly so, and the result of her mournful reflection is that she behaves with monstrous ingratitude to the people who keep
her out of the workhouse. " Im a lone lorn creature, and everything goes
contrairy with me." This vice of querulousness is one of the most intolerable
beheld by the sun. Dickens merely smiles; and of course it is large-hearted in
him to do so: he would have us forbearing with such poor creatures, would

have us understand that they suffer as well as cause suffering to others. One acknowledges the justice of the lesson. But we have not done with Mrs Gummidge; together with the Yarmouth family, she emigrated to Australia, and there—became a bright, happy, serviceable woman! Converted, she, by the great grief that had befallen her friends; made ashamed of whining over megrims when death and shame were making havoc in the little home. Well, it may have been so; but Mrs Gummidge was very old for such a ray of reason to pierce her skull. In any case, we do not think of her in Australia. She sits for ever in the house on Yarmouth sands (sands not yet polluted by her kin from Whitechapel), and shakes her head and pipes her eye, a monument of selfish misery.

Behold Mrs Snagsby. To all Mrs Varden's vices this woman adds one that may be strongly recommended for the ruin of domestic peace when the others have failed—if fail they can. She is jealous of the little law-stationer; she imagines for him all manner of licentious intrigues. That such imagination is inconsistent with the plainest facts of life in no way invalidates its hold upon Mrs Snagsby's mind. She will make things as unpleasant as possible in the grimy house in Cook's Court; the little man shall have rest neither day nor night; his life shall become a burden to him. And goodness knows that the house, at the best of times, falls a good deal short of cheerfulness. There is Guster. Who shall restrain a laugh, hearing of Guster? Plainly described, this girl is an underpaid, underfed, and overworked slavey, without a friend in the world,—unless it be Mr Snagsby,—and subject to frequent epileptic fits. And we roar with laughter as often as she is named! It is Dickens's pleasure that we shall do so, and, if it comes to defence of so strange a subject of humour, one can only say that, from a certain point of view, everything in this world is laughable. Look broadly enough, and it is undoubtedly amusing that such a woman as Mrs Snagsby should coarsely tyrannize over a poor diseased creature, who toils hard and lives on a pittance. But, in strictness, the humour here perceivable is not of the kind we usually attribute to Dickens; it has something either of philosophic sublimity or of mortal bitterness. For my own part, I think Dickens points, in such situations as this, to larger significances than were consciously in his mind. I may return to the matter in speaking expressly of his humour; here we are specially concerned with the exhibition of Mrs Snagsby's personality. Happily, she undergoes no moral palingenesis; by the date of *Bleak House* her creator had outgrown the inclination for that kind of thing. We are sure that she made the deferential little man miserable to the end of his days; and when she had buried him, she held forth for many years more on the martyrdom of her married life.

She is decidedly more hateful than Mrs Varden, by virtue of her cruelty to the girl, and more of a force for ill by virtue of her animal jealousy. In short—a most amusing figure.

It certainly is a troublesome fact for sensitive female readers that this, a great English novelist of the Victorian age, so abounds in women who are the curse of their husbands' lives. A complete list of them would, I imagine, occupy nearly a page of this book. Mrs Jellyby I have already discussed. I have spoken of the much more lifelike Mrs Pocket, a capital portrait. I have alluded to the uncommon realism of Dr Marigold's wife. A mention must at least be made of Mrs Macstinger, who, as Mrs Bunsby, enters upon such a promising field of fresh activity. But there remains one full-length picture which we may by no means neglect, its name Mrs Joe Gargery.

Mrs Gargery belongs to Dickens's later manner. In such work as this, his hand was still inimitably true, and his artistic conscience no longer allowed him to play with circumstance as in the days of Mrs Varden. The blacksmith's wife is a shrew of the most highly developed order. If ever she is good-tempered in the common sense of the word, she never lets it be suspected; without any assignable cause, she is invariably acrid, and ready at a moment's notice to break into fury of abuse. It gratifies her immensely to have married the softest-hearted man that ever lived, and also that he happens to be physically one of the strongest; the joy of trampling upon him, knowing that he who could kill her with a backhand blow will never even answer the bitterest insult with an unkind word! It delights her, too, that she has a little brother, a mere baby still, whom she can ill-use at her leisure, remembering always that every harshness to the child is felt still worse by the big good fellow, her husband. Do you urge that Dickens should give a cause for this evil temper? Cause there is none—save of that scientific kind which has no place in English novels. It is the peculiarity of these women that no one can conjecture why they behave so ill. The nature of the animals—nothing more can be said.

Notice, now, that in Mrs Gargery, though he still disguises the worst of the situation with his unfailing humour, Dickens gives us more of the harsh truth than in any previous book. That is a fine scene where the woman, by a malicious lie, causes a fight between Joe and Orlick; a true illustration of character, and well brought out. Again, Mrs Joe's punishment. Here we are very far from the early novels. Mrs Gargery shall be brought to quietness; but how? By a half-murderous blow on the back of her head, from which she will never recover. Dickens understood by this time that there is no other efficacious way with these ornaments of their sex. A felling and stunning and all but killing blow, followed by paralysis and slow death. A sharp remedy, but no whit sharper than the evil it cures. Mrs Gargery, under such treatment, learns patience and the rights of other people. We are half sorry she cannot rise and put her learning into practice, but there is always a doubt. As likely as not she would take to drinking, and enter on a new phase of ferocity.

Of higher social standing, not perhaps better educated but certainly better bred, are the women who acknowledge their great exemplar in Mrs Nickleby. This lady—all things considered, the term may be applied without abuse—has passed the greater part of her life in a rural district, and morally she belongs, I think, rather to the country than the town; there is a freshness about her, a *naïveté* not—up to a certain point —disagreeable; her manners and conversation are suggestive of long afternoons, and evenings of infinite leisure. Mrs Nickleby is, above all, well-meaning; according to her lights she is gracious and tolerant; she has natural affections, and would be sincerely distressed by a charge of selfishness. Unhappily the poor woman has been born with the intellectual equipment of a Somerset ewe. It would be a delicate question of psychology to distinguish her from the harmless, smiling idiot whom we think it unnecessary and cruel to put under restraint. One may say, indeed, that this defect is radical in all Dickens's female characters; the better-hearted succeed in keeping it out of sight—in the others it becomes flagrant and a terror. Sixty years ago there was practically no provision in England for the mental training of women. Sent early to a good school, and kept there till the age, say, of one-and-twenty, Mrs Nickleby would have grown into a quite endurable gentlewoman, aware of her natural weakness, and a modest participant in general conversation. Allowed to develop in her own way, and married to a man only less unintelligent than herself, she puts forth a wonderful luxuriance of amiable fatuity. Thoughts, in the strict sense of the word, she has none; her brain is a mere blind mechanism for setting in motion an irresponsible tongue; together they express in human language the sentiments of the ewe aforesaid. Mr Nickleby died in the prime of life; what else could be the fate of a man doomed to listen to this talk morning, noon, and night? With Mrs Nickleby one cannot converse; she understands the meaning of nothing that is said to her; she is incapable of answering a question, or of seeing the logical bearings of any statement whatsoever. One conviction is impressed upon her (pardon the word) mind: that throughout life she has invariably said and done the right thing, and that other persons, in their relations with her, have been as invariably wrong. Let events turn how they may, they do but serve to confirm her complacent position. Having exerted herself to the utmost in urging a particular line of conduct, which, on trial, proves to have been the worst that could have been followed, Mrs Nickleby blandly reminds her victims that she had known from the first, and repeatedly declared, what would be the result of such manifest imprudence. Should this lead to an outbreak of masculine impatience, not to say anger, the good lady receives a nervous shock, under which she pales, and pants, and falters as the domestic martyr, the victim of surprising unreason and brutality. As it happens, she does not bring her children to the gutter and herself to the workhouse; we acknowledge the providence that watches over exemplary fools. And after all, as men must laugh at something, it is as well that they should find in Mrs Nickleby matter for mirth. She is ubiquitous, and doubtless always will be. She cannot be chained and muzzled, or forbidden to propagate her kind. We must endure her, as we endure the caprices of the sky. An ultimate fact of nature, and a great argument for those who decline to take life too seriously.

This was early work of Dickens, but not to be improved upon by any increase of experience or of skill. A good many years later, he produced suggestive of her; for she was at all times an exception in the vulgar world, and her like have since been schooled into the self-restraint, of which, under favourable conditions, they are perfectly capable. The species of sentimentality seen in Flora was at that time fed upon songs and verses congenial to the feeble mind; born thirty years later, Flora would have been led to a much better taste in that direction, with the result of greater self-command in all. She is a kind soul, and doubtless became a very pleasant, even useful, friend of little Mrs Clennam. Such a woman is only dangerous when she feels that the law has surrendered to her a real live man—has given him, bound hand and foot, to her care and her mercy. As a maid, as a widow, she will do no harm, nor wish to do any, beyond distressing the tympanum and tasking the patience of anyone with whom she genially converses.

One does not venture to begin praising work such as this. Eulogy would lose itself in enthusiasm. Pass, rather, to the gallery of women who are neither married shrews nor well-meaning pests, yet each peculiar for her mental and moral vice. We glance at Miss Squeers. Fanny, it is plain, has relatives in the pages of Smollett; one seems to remember a damsel in *Roderick Random* of whom, perhaps, the less said the better; the intercourse between Miss Squeers and Nicholas brings this chapter to mind, and points a change alike in national manners and in literature. As a wife, Fanny would pass into that other category with which we have done. Her London parallel is perhaps Sophy Wackles, from whom Mr Swiveller had so narrow and so fortunate

an escape. Such maidens as these, Dickens must have had many opportunities of observing; his social canvas would have been imperfect without
them. Though it seems unjust to put her in this place, I must mention Susan
Nipper, the nurse of Florence Dombey. Susan begins well on the pattern of
her class; she is snappy, and brief-tempered, fond of giving smacks and pull-
ing hair; one sees no reason why with favouring circumstances she should
not develop into a nagger of distinction. But something is observable in
her which imposes caution on prophecy; we see that Susan, though a mere
domestic, has a very unusual endowment of wit; she is sharp in retort, but
also in perception; in any case she cannot become a mere mouthing idiot. In
course of time we see that she has a good heart. And so it comes to pass that,
in spite of origin and evil example, the girl grows in grace. She is fortunately
situated; her sweet young mistress does her every kind of good; and when
she marries Mr Toots we have no misgivings whatever as to that eccentric
gentleman's happiness.

Then, typical of a very large class indeed, comes Mrs Crupp, who "does
for" David Copperfield in his chambers. It is unnecessary to use the short
words which would adequately describe Mrs Crupp; enough to say that
she stands for the baser kind of London landlady—a phrase which speaks
volumes. Some day it will cause laughter, indeed, and something else, to
think that young men beginning life as students, and what not, should have
fallen, as a matter of course, into the hand of Mrs Crupp. Her name smells
of strong liquor; it includes all dishonesty and uncleanliness. The monstros-
ity of her pretensions touches the highest point of the ludicrous. What,
then, is one to say of Sarah Gamp, of Betsy Prig, considered as women? Of
Mrs Gamp in another aspect I have spoken at some length; she is one of
those figures in Dickens to which one necessarily returns, again and again;
as art, the very quintessence of his genius; as social fact, worthy of repeated
contemplation. After all, women they are, these sister hags of the birth and
death chamber. Mrs Gamp has her own ideas of tender emotion; she is
touched by the sight of an undertaker's children "playing at berryings down
in the shop, and follerin' the order-book to its long home in the iron safe!"
Be it remarked that there is an appreciable difference between Mrs Gamp's
nature and that of Mrs Prig; we are clearly shown that Betsy is the harder,
coarser, more mercenary of the twain. If well plied with spirits and pickled
cucumber, Sarah Gamp might be capable of an elementary generosity; it is
our perception of this which helps to keep the creature amusing, where she
might so easily sink below everything but our contemptuous disgust. Betsy
Prig is of a lower order, even socially; one may be sure that she had much less

to do with the better class of clients. There is in her a spitefulness, a greedy malignancy, not found in the nurse of Kingsgate Street; where Mrs Gamp would exhibit hostility in astounding contortions of thick-throated phrase, irresistibly laughable, Betsy Prig would fall into the mere language of the gutter. Their quarrel (one of the great things in literature) makes proof of this, though Dickens's most adroit idealism avoids the offensiveness of the real dialogue. As a girl—try to imagine Sarah Gamp as a young girl!—we know where and how she lived, what examples she had. It was practically Hogarth's London which saw her birth and breeding; but the London of today is well able to produce such women; one catches a glimpse of her life in the market streets, and the public-houses. Well, as a girl she must have been very plump and good-humoured, with quaint turns of speech, foretelling the eloquence of her prime. Mr Ruskin has well pointed out the broad distinction between this London jargon and anything worthy of being called a dialect (by the by, the dialect on which London has exercised its deforming influence is that of Essex, where a confusion of *v* and *w*, no longer heard in town, may still be noticed); he adds that the speech of Mrs Gamp is pure vulgarity, its insurpassable illustration. And the woman herself (one lingers over her affectionately) may be dismissed as vulgarity incarnate. Her profession, her time, even her sex, may, from this point of view, be called accidents. Desiring to study the essential meaning of the *vulgar*, one turns from every living instance, every acute disquisition, and muses over Sarah Gamp.

When we speak of the working-class, we understand something quite distinct from, though not of necessity inferior to, the classes represented by all these women; though Mrs Gargery, no doubt, belongs to that social order. With the working-class household, Dickens, I think, is never entirely successful; one reason among others being that he shrinks from criticising the very poor. In the homes of toilers his great heart has its way, and he can only in general show us such people at their best. But one recalls two working-class women, who, however gently drawn, are living characters: Polly Toodle and Mrs Plornish. Paul Dombey's nurse, who would have it considered in the wages if she is to be called "out of her name", and who as the mother of Rob the Grinder suffers so many anxieties, may fairly stand for a good woman of the proletary; and how very favourably she compares with ordinary women in the class (for reasons of money) just above her! She is not vulgar, and, as a typical good wife in that rank, need not be so; for it is easier to escape such taint in the house of the engine-driver Toodle than in Mr Snagsby's upstairs parlour. Mrs Plornish, the plasterer's wife, is likewise an excellent creature marked by more peculiarity; her firm belief that she makes herself intelligible to a foreigner by grotesque distortion of the English tongue is one of the truest and most amusing things in Dickens. Many a Mrs Plornish honestly supposes that in order to speak foreign languages, it is only necessary—as I once heard one of them remark—to "learn how to twist the mouth". This is an innocent conviction, which disturbs nobody's peace. We like Mrs Plornish, too, for her tenderness to the old father from the workhouse, and her sincere admiration when he pipes his thin little song. These women are blessed with a good temper, the source of everything enjoyable in life. However poor and ignorant, they shed about them the light of home. It is a type that does not much change, so far; and one thinks with misgivings of the day when that increased comfort which is their due, shall open to such women the dreadful possibilities of half-knowledge.

Come the eccentrics; of all classes, of all tempers; the signal for mirth. Here, I suppose, must be introduced the sister of Sampson Brass; though one finds it difficult to think of Miss Sally as feminine. She has the courage of her opinions, and shows something like heroism in scoundreldom, when brought face to face with the criminal law. One never met Miss Brass, but it is very possible that Dickens did. Later, he omits the ferocity from his grotesques. Miss Mowcher, we are told, was meant originally to play a very ugly part in the story of Emily and Steerforth, but an odd incident, nothing less than the reception of a letter from Miss Mowcher herself, led Dickens to use the character in quite another way, making it point a lesson of charity. Mr Dombey's friend Miss Tox is a first-rate toady, if the word may be used of one so respectable and kind-hearted; she represents, with abundance of oddity, the army of genteel old maids, as the term was in that day understood. Miss Tox is out of date, or very nearly so; today she finds much better occupation than in prostrating herself before Mr Dombey, or jealously watching the Major, or looking after her canaries; her goodness is reinforced by knowledge, and her presence is a blessing in many of the dark places of our vast city. Eccentric, indeed, but on a fine basis of sense and character, is the immortal Betsy Trotwood. Wasted in her time, or nearly so; no scope for her, beyond the care of Mr Dick, varied by assaults upon seaside donkeys (the quadrupeds). To be sure, she is the making of David, but that came accidentally. But Miss Trotwood is in advance of her age; victim of a bad marriage, she does not see in this an all-sufficient destiny; where others would have passed their life in tears and tracts, Miss Betsy sets about making for herself a rational existence. We all know her—in various disguises, and should not be sorry to meet her more frequently. For the woman of sense and character is the salt of the earth; with however flagrant peculiarities, may she increase and multiply!

One remembers Miss La Creevy, in her way no less admirably independent. That she got her living by the travesty of art was a misfortune which neither she nor any of her contemporaries (half a dozen perhaps excepted) saw in that light, for she is of the Earliest Victorian. Memorable, too, is the little doll's dressmaker in *Our Mutual Friend*, whose "bad child", her boneless drunkard of a father, keeps her leisure so fully occupied. But they are too numerous for several mention, these quaint examples of more or less distorted womankind—distorted by evil circumstances, and then ridiculed by the world responsible for their abnormalities. Dickens looked on them with tenderness, and makes us like, or respect, them, even whilst we laugh. He saw, too, the larger questions involved in their existence; but on these it was no part of his mission as a story-teller to insist. Had he uttered his whole thought it would hardly have satisfied us for whom a new century has begun. His view of the possibilities of womanhood becomes tolerably clear when we turn to his normal types of marriageable maiden.

In *Pickwick* there are several of them, and we think them vulgar. They must be called young ladies; they are in an easy position, and find it occupation enough to amuse themselves. Speaking plainly, Dickens as a young man could hardly have a just criterion of refinement; the damsels of Dingley Dell were probably as like ladies as anything he had seen. Does he mean them to be delicate in thought and speech and behaviour? Or is he designedly showing us the decent girl of an unrefined class? Their little screams—their shrill laughter—their amorous facetiousness—you will not find that kind of thing now at Dingley Dell; and even then, I fancy, it was rather out of place in the home of a country gentleman. Put these girls at Pentonville, and the picture excites no uneasiness.

Mrs Varden, we know, had a daughter, and the blushing, laughing, petulant Dolly has always been a favourite. Has she not even given her name to millinery? For my own part, I see in Dolly her mother restored to youth, and notwithstanding the Gordon riots, notwithstanding Joe Willet's loss of an arm in "the Salwanners, in America where the war is", I feel an unpleasant certainty as to Dolly's conduct when she becomes a matron. It was (and is) precisely because so many men admire the foolish in girlhood that at least an equal number deplore the intolerable in wives. Dolly is a sort of kitten. This comparison is used by George Eliot of Hefty Sorrel, and George Eliot used it advisedly; she knew very well indeed what comes of human kittenishness. The reader perhaps inter-

poses, smilingly protests, that this is considering altogether too curiously;
would hint, with civility, at a defect in appreciation of humour. But no;
Dickens's humour and delightfulness are as much to me as to any man living. For the moment, I write of him as the social historian of his day, and
endeavour to disclose his real thoughts concerning woman. To Dickens,
Dolly Varden was an ideal maiden; one, to be sure, of several ideals which
haunt the young man's brain. It is nothing to him that Dolly is totally
without education, and that her mother's failings are traceable first and
foremost to that very source. Instruction was needless for sweet seventeen; it tended, if anything, to blue-stockingism. Dolly's business in graver
hours is to look after stockings of a more common hue. For relaxation,
she may smirk and simper and tell little fibs, and smile treacherous little smiles, and on occasion drop a little tear, which means nothing but
pique or selfish annoyance. This is the very truth of Dolly. But she wore
a delicious hat, and had a dainty little mouth, and was altogether so very
kittenish; and to the end of time poor Gabriel Varden, poor Joe Willet,
will find these things irresistible.

Passing to a book written nearly a quarter of a century after *Barnaby
Rudge*, I discover Dolly in a new incarnation; she has learnt somewhat,
she obeys a stricter rule of decorum, and her name is now Bella Wilfer.
I admit that Miss Wilfer belongs to a slightly, very slightly, higher grade
of society, but in those five-and-twenty years all things had advanced. Of
Bella one easily grants the charm, and one admires her for not being more
spoilt by good fortune; we perceive, however, the old traits; we tremble,
now and then, at lurking kittenishness. It is permitted us to behold Bella
as wife and mother, and we see her doing well in both relations; but the
peril is not past. There will come a day when her husband is less fascinated
by pretty ways, when he wants a little intellectual companionship by his
fireside, and that moment must test Bella's mettle. Dolly would have made
hopeless failure, reproducing Mrs Varden in the sourest particulars. Bella,
perchance, had her self-respect strengthened by the example of her time,
and fought down the worst of the feminine.

Between *Barnaby* and *Our Mutual Friend*, Dickens had portrayed many
girls. Early come the daughters of Mr Pecksniff, Charity and Mercy, "not
unholy names, I hope". They are masterpieces, finished to the nail. Here—I
cannot remind the reader too often of this fact in regard to Dickens's
women—one discerns absolutely nothing of "exaggeration"; not a word, not
a gesture, goes beyond the very truth. Here the master would have nothing
to learn from later art; he is the realist's exemplar. How admirably are these

No. 1 Devonshire Terrace, Regent's Park

sisters likened and contrasted! That Jonas Chuzzlewit's wife becomes broken in spirit, meek, morally hopeful, is no instance of such literary optimism as one has noticed elsewhere, but a strict development of character. Her sister's rancorous appetency, with its train of consequences, belongs no less to nature. The artist must glory in these figures, so representative, so finely individualized. Public merriment has, of course, done them only the scantiest justice; their value cannot be appraised in laughter. They are among the most precious things left to us by Victorian literature.

Together with them, let me speak of Fanny Dorrit. In the London of today there is a very familiar female type, known as the shop-girl. Her sphere of action is extensive, for we meet her not only in shops, strictly speaking, but at liquor-bars, in workrooms, and, unfortunately, sometimes in the post-office, to say nothing of fifty other forms of employment open to the under-bred, and more or less aggressive, young woman. Dickens saw nothing like so much of her, but he has drawn her portrait, with unerring hand, in Fanny Dorrit. Her first characteristic is a paltry and ignorant ambition, of course allied with vanity; she is crudely selfish, and has only the elementary scruples of her sex. Withal, there glimmers in her, under favouring circumstance, a vulgar good-nature; if she has much to spare she will bestow it upon those she likes, and at all times she prefers to see cheerfulness around her. In a time of social transition, when the womankind of labourer and office-man tend to intermingle, and together gall the kibes of the daughters of quick-growing capital, Fanny becomes a *question*. It is not easy to get her taught, either in literature or good manners; it is not easy to recompense her services, such as they are, on a scale which makes her free of the temptation ever present to this class. When she marries, her knowledge of domestic duties is found to be on a par, say, with that of a newspaper-boy; her ideas as to expenditure resemble those of a prima donna. Miss Dorrit, we know, had an unhappy training; but not worse in degree, though different in kind, from that of her modern parallel. Dickens did not know how significant was the picture when working at its details in the year of the Crimean War. Before his death he must have had many opportunities of recalling, and reflecting upon, the features of that young person.

It occurs to one how little love-making there is in all his books. This results, in part, from the fact of his dealing with a class which is anything but sentimental, and as little endowed with imagination as any order of civilized beings discoverable throughout the world; partly, again, from his own practical nature. Little Dorrit has her love story, and at one moment it is well told; the chapter describing her travel in Italy deserves high praise. But, on the whole, Amy Dorrit is not a success in characterization. Florence Dombey is, no doubt, in love, but we never think of it as more than the affection of a child; one forms no image whatever of her married life with Walter Gay. Then there is the shadowy betrothed of Richard Carstone, a good girl, to be sure, but remarkably placid. Esther Summerson cannot count, she has no existence. A favourite with readers of her own sex is Lizzie Hexam, and, putting aside her impossibility, Dickens has perhaps made her his most sympathetic love-heroine. One credits her with loyalty, with ardour; she is more nearly a poetical figure than that of any other girl in his books. Of Little Emily I find it difficult to say more than had its place in a previous chapter. She belongs to the stage, where such a story as hers is necessarily presented in the falsest possible light. Let us note one thing, however. Out of regard for what we call propriety, is it not obvious that this girl is shown to us as acting with something like cold-blooded deliberation, the simplest form of true immorality? We have no hint of her temptation, and it really looks very much as if she had calculated the probable advantages of flight with Steerforth. I have always felt the same with regard to the central incident of *Adam Bede*; it comes upon one, at the first reading, as a moral shock. So determined are these novelists not to offend our precious delicacy, that in the upshot they offend it beyond endurance, springing upon us, so to speak, the results of uncontrollable passion, without ever allowing us to suspect that such a motive was in play. The effect of this is a sort of grossness, which dishonours our heroine. So far as we are permitted to judge, there is much reason in the insults hurled at Emily by the frantic Rosa Dartle—a pretty result, indeed, of all our author's delicate gliding over slippery places.

The Emperor Augustus, we are told, objected to the presence of women at the public games when athletes appeared unclad; but he saw nothing improper in their watching the death combats of gladiators. May we not find a parallel to this in the English censorship? To exhibit the actual course of things in a story of lawless (nay, or of lawful) love is utterly forbidden; on the other hand, a novelist may indulge in ghastly bloodshed to any extent of which his stomach is capable. Dickens, the great writer, even appears on a public platform and recites with terrible power the murder of a prostitute by a burglar, yet hardly a voice is raised in protest. Gore is perfectly decent; but the secrets of an impassioned heart are too shameful to come before us even in a whisper.

On this account I do not think it worth while to speak of Nancy, or of other lost creatures appearing in Dickens. But read, I beg, that passage of *Little Dorrit* where Amy herself and her idiot friend Maggy, wandering about the streets at night, are addressed by a woman of the town (Book i, chapter 14); read that passage, and wonder that the same man who penned this shocking rubbish could have written in the same volume pages of a truthfulness beyond all eulogy.

Little Em'ly has, after all, but a subordinate part in *David Copperfield*. The leading lady is Dora. Dora is wooed, Dora is wed—the wooing and wedding of a butterfly. Yet it is Dickens's prettiest bit of love, and I shall scarce find it in my heart to criticise the "little Blossom", the gauze-winged fairy of that "insubstantial, happy, foolish time". Dora is Dolly Varden volatilized; every fault is there, prevented from becoming vice only by utter lack of purpose. The featherbrained little creature has no responsibility; as reasonably would one begin to argue with her toy dog, Jip, when he takes his stand on the cookery book. I have said that we cannot look in *Copperfield* for any true picture of an author's daily life; but, worse than that, we have very comical misrepresentation. Think only of David at his desk and Dora holding the pens! Pray, how much work was our friend likely to get through with that charming assistance? But it is all a fantasy and defies the test of common daylight. Take Dora seriously, and at once you are compelled to ask by what right an author demands your sympathy for such a brainless, nerveless, profitless simpleton. Enter into the spirit of the chapter, and you are held by one of the sweetest dreams of humour and tenderness ever translated into language.

There is no better illustration of Dickens's progress with the time than a comparison of his heroine in *Edwin Drood* with those of the early books. I think it is a great misfortune that we so abruptly lost sight of Rosa Bud; if, as seemed likely, the development of her character was to go on throughout the story, she would have been by far the best of Dickens's intelligent and sympathetic women. At first we have misgivings; Dolly Varden and Dora and others of our old acquaintances seem blended in Miss Twinkleton's pupil; a tricksy and provoking little person, whose reason for not knowing her own mind is probably the old one—that she has no mind to know. But presently we understand; the girl—little more than a child—is in a false position, and suffers under it very consciously. A few pages more, and we see her behaving with rational force of character, the silly prettiness is thrown aside; Rosa declares herself as sensible and just and kind a girl as one could wish to meet. In the days of *Copperfield*, Dickens could not have managed this characterization; in the days of *Barnaby Rudge* he could as soon have created Rosalind. Change of times, growth of experience, widening of artistic consciousness and power—all are evident in this study which was never to be completed. He laughs at Miss Twinkleton and her establishment, but we have an assurance that Rosa Bud was receiving a much better education than fell to the lot of girls thirty years before; even as we feel convinced that Mr Crisparkle's tuition was a vast improvement upon that of Dr Blimber. It is possible, of course, that *Edwin Drood*'s paltry "mystery", with its blood and opium, would have ousted Rosa from the scene; perhaps we had seen the best of her. None the less, she remains a real and interesting little woman, and we should much have liked to watch the course of her affection for Tartar.

A "little woman". The phrase is inevitable in speaking of Dickens's pets. A Lady Dedlock might have stature; a Betsy Trotwood even might be of average height; but Em'ly and Amy and Ruth, Dolly and Dora and Esther, must all be tiny vessels for their great virtues. Shakespeare took another view of this matter; but Shakespeare was not concerned with the lower middle-class of the nineteenth century. There is agreement, I am told, among trustworthy observers that the stature of English women has notably increased during the last two or three decades; a natural consequence of improvement in the conditions of their life. In Dickens's day, when girls took no sort of exercise, fed badly, and (amid London streets) never breathed fresh air, of course they were generally diminutive. And among all the little women he presents to us, who exhibits more concentrated charm of littleness than Ruth Pinch?

I have left her to the last, because she will serve us as the type of all that Dickens really admired in woman. Truth to tell, it was no bad ideal. Granted that the world must go on very much in the old way, that children must be born and looked after, that dinners must be cooked, that houses must be kept sweet, it is hard to see how Ruth Pinch can ever be supplanted. Ruth is no imbecile—your thoroughly kind-hearted and home-loving woman never will be; with opportunities, she would learn much, even beyond domestic limits, and still would delight in her dainty little aprons, her pastry-board and roller. Ruth would be an excellent mother; when, in the latter days, she sat grey-haired and spectacled, surely would her children arise and call her blessed. A very homely little woman, to be sure. She could not be quite comfortable with domestics at her command; a little house, a little garden, the cooking her own peculiar care, a little maid for the little babies—this is her dream. But never, within those walls, a sound of complaining or of strife, never a wry face, acidly discontented with the husband's doings or sayings. Upon my word—is it a bad ideal?

There are those who surmise that in the far-off time when girls are uni-versally well-taught, when it is the exception to meet, in any class, with the maiden or the wife who deems herself a natural inferior of brother, lover, husband, the homely virtues of Ruth Pinch will be even more highly rated than in the stupid old world. There are those who suspect that our *servant-question* foretells a radical change in ways of thinking about the life of home; that the lady of a hundred years hence will be much more competent and active in cares domestic than the average shopkeeper's wife today; that it may not be found impossible to turn from a page of Sophocles to the boiling of a potato, or even the scrubbing of a floor. When every spendthrift idiot of a mistress, and every lying lazybones of a kitchen-wench, is swept into Time's dust-bin, it may come to pass that a race of brave and intelligent women will smile sister-like at this portrait of little Ruth. They will prize Dickens, instead of turning from him in disgust or weariness; for in his pages they will see that ancient deform-ity of their sex, and will recognize how justly he pointed out the way of safe reform; no startling innovation, no extravagant idealism, but a gentle insistence on the facts of human nature, a kindly glorifying of one humble little woman, who saw her duty, and did it singing the while.

A word or two about the children whom he loved to bring into his books, and to make pathetic or amusing. First, of course, we see little Nell; we see her, because she is the mid-figure in a delightful romance; but her face is not very plain to us. She is innocence walking among grotesque forms of suffering and wrong; simplicity set amid quaint contortions. Her death is not the dying of a little girl, but the vanishing of a beautiful dream. Oliver

Twist is no more real, and certainly less interesting. Into what sort of man did this astonishing lad develop? The children of Dotheboys are writhing ghosts; perhaps they had lived in some other world, and were bad boys, and afterwards came into Squeers' hands for purification. Sally Brass's poor little slavey is, on the other hand, well realized; a good study of childhood brought to the verge of idiocy by evil treatment. Tiny Tim serves his admirable purpose in a book which no one can bear to criticise; we know that he *did* die, but in his little lifetime he has softened many a heart. Next rises the son and heir of "our friend Dombey". Dickens believed that little Paul was one of the best things he had ever done; contemporary readers were much excited about the child, whose "old-fashioned" ways became a by-word. I do not find it difficult to accept Paul's enquiry about what the waves were saying (in spite of a most dreadful song, made of that passage, which sounds in my ears from long ago), and of a surety I give more credit to Paul's death-bed speeches than to those of the child in *Our Mutual Friend*, who bequeathed a kiss to "the boofer lady"; but on the whole, Mr Dombey's hope has only a little more of substance than little Nell. His sister Florence is prettiness and gentleness; an abstraction which affects us not. Passing to young David Copperfield, it is a different matter. Here we have the author's vision of his own childhood, and he makes it abundantly convincing. This part of *Copperfield* is one of the narratives which every reader illustrates for himself; the poor little lad stands plain before us, as we read, and in our memory. The picture, I should say, suggests very faithfully an artist's early years, his susceptibility, his abnormal faculty of observation, the vivid workings of his mind and heart. Dickens told Forster that this bit of autobiography might be worthy to stand on the shelf together with the corresponding part of that written by Holcroft. Holcroft is forgotten, I suppose; if the mention of him leads a stray reader to his book, that reader's time will not be wasted.

Of Dickens's true and deep sympathy with childhood there can be no doubt; it becomes passionate in the case of little ones doomed to suffering by a cruel or careless world. In all his excellent public speeches, perhaps the best and most moving passage is that which describes a poor baby he saw in Scotland, a wasting little mortal, whose cradle was an old egg-box; where, he says, it lay dumb and pitiful, its eyes seeming to wonder "why, in the name of an All-merciful God, such things should be". In his novels, we like those children best, of whom we obtain only a passing glimpse, the reason, again, being that remorseless necessity of drama which spoils so many of his older people. But in one case he has written a whole story about children, and these toddlers the most lifelike to be found in his pages. It is the story put into the mouth of Boots at the Holly Tree. Accept the fantasy, and these little actors are wonderfully well shown; their talk is true, their behaviour—down to the crossness of the bride-elect when she gets tired—as truly observed as it is mirth-provoking. No wonder that Boots at the Holly Tree was one of the "readings" most acceptable to Dickens's audience. If he must needs read in public, he could not have chosen a piece more likely to keep sweet his personal memory with those who heard him.

VIII

Humour and Pathos

To write of Dickens at all, is to presuppose his humour. The plan of my essay has necessitated a separate consideration of the various features of his work, and at moments it may have appeared that I found fault without regard to a vast counterbalance; but it was never possible for me to lose sight of that supreme quality of his genius which must be now dwelt upon with undivided attention. It was as a humorist that Dickens made his name; and in a retrospect of his life's activity one perceives that his most earnest purposes depended for their furtherance upon this genial power, which he shares with nearly all the greatest of English writers. Holding, as he did, that the first duty of an author is to influence his reader for good, Dickens necessarily esteemed as the most precious of his gifts that by virtue of which he commanded so great an audience. Without his humour, he might have been a vigorous advocate of social reform, but as a novelist assuredly he would have failed; and as to the advocacy of far-reaching reforms by men who have only earnestness and eloquence to work with, English history tells its tale. Only because they laughed with him so heartily, did multitudes of people turn to discussing the question his page suggested. As a story-teller pure and simple, the powers that remain to him, if humour be subtracted, would never have ensured popularity. Nor, on the other hand, would they have availed him in the struggle for artistic perfection, which is a better thing. Humour is the soul of his work. Like the soul of man, it permeates a living fabric which, but for its creative breath, could never have existed.

In his earliest writing we discover only the suggestion of this quality. The *Sketches* have a touch of true humour, but (apart from the merits of acute observation and great descriptive power) there is much more of merely youthful high spirits, tending to the farcical. Such a piece as *The Tuggs's at Ramsgate* is distinct farce, and not remarkably good of its kind. This vein Dickens continued to work throughout his career, and often with great success. One must distinguish between the parts of his writing which stir to mere hilarity, and his humour in the strict sense of the word. It is none of my business to define that term, which has long ago been adequately expounded; enough that the humorist has by no means invariably a chuckle in his throat; at moments of his supreme success, he will hardly move us to more of merriment than appears in a thoughtful smile. But there is a perfectly legitimate, and tolerably wide, range for the capers of a laughing spirit, and as a writer of true farce I suppose Dickens has never been surpassed. *Pickwick* abounds in it, now quite distinct from, and now all but blending with, the higher characteristic. One can imagine that the public approval of his *Sketches* had given the author an impetus which carried him of a sudden into regions of extravagant buoyancy and mirthfulness. The first few pages are farce of the frankest. Winkle, Snodgrass, and Tupman remain throughout farcical characters, but not so Mr Pickwick himself. Farce is the election at Eatanswill, and the quarrel of the rival Editors, and many another well-remembered passage. Only a man of genius has the privilege of being so emphatically young. "Though the merriment was rather boisterous, still it came from the heart and not from the lips; and this is the right sort of merriment after all." How could one better describe, than in these words from the book itself, that overflowing cheeriness which conquered Dickens's first public! Or take the description of old Wardle coming through the early sunshine to bid Mr Pickwick good morning,—"out of breath with his own anticipations of pleasure". Alas! old gentlemen, however jolly, do not get breathless in this fashion; but the young may, and Dickens, a mere boy himself, was writing for the breathless boyhood of many an age to come.

The farce in his younger work always results from this exuberance of spirits; later, he introduces it deliberately; with conscious art—save perhaps at those moments when the impulse of satire is too much for him. One easily recalls his best efforts in this direction. The wild absurdity of the Muffin Company at the beginning of *Nickleby* shows him still in his boyish mood, and the first chapter of *Chuzzlewit* finds him unluckily reverting to it at the moment when he was about to produce a masterpiece of genuine humour. Mr Mantalini is capital fun; he never quite loses his hold upon one, and to the end we shall laugh over the "demnition egg" and the "demnition bow-wows". At this stage Dickens was capable of a facetiousness of descriptive phrase which hints the peril involved in a reputation such as he had won. "Madame Mantalini wrung her hands for grief and rung the bell for her husband; which done, she fell into a chair and a fainting fit simultaneously." When he had written that passage, and allowed it to stand, his genius warned him; I remember nothing so dangerous in aftertime. Quilp, at his best, is rich entertainment; in Dick Swiveller we touch higher things. The scene between little David Copperfield and the waiter (chapter v) seems to me farce, though very good; country innkeepers were never in the habit of setting a dish-load of cutlets before a little boy who wanted dinner, and not even the shrewdest of waiters, having devoured them all, could make people believe that it was the little boy's achievement; but the comic vigour of the thing is irresistible. Better still is the forced marriage of Jack Bunsby to the great MacStinger. Here, I think, Dickens reaches his highest point. We cannot call it "screaming" farce; it appeals not only to the groundlings. Laughter holding both his sides was never more delightfully justified; gall and the megrims were never more effectually dispelled. It is the ludicrous in its purest form, tainted by no sort of unkindliness, and leaving behind it nothing but the wholesome aftertaste of self-forgetful mirth.

We may notice how Dickens makes use of farcical extravagance to soften the bitterness of truth. When Sally Brass goes down into the grimy cellar-kitchen to give the little slavey her food, we are told that she cut from the joint "two square inches of cold mutton", and bade her victim never say that she had not had meat in *that* house. This makes one laugh; who can refrain? If he had avoided exaggeration, and shown us the ragged, starving child swallowing the kind of meal which was really set before her, who could have endured it? The point is vastly important for an understanding of Dickens's genius and his popularity. That "two square inches" makes all the difference between painful realism and fiction universally acceptable; it is the secret of Dickens's power for good. Beside it may be set another instance. Judy Smallweed, in *Bleak House*, likewise has her little slavey over whom she tyrannizes; a child, too, who has won our sympathy in a high degree, and whom we could not bear to see brutally used. She is brutally used; but then Judy Smallweed is a comical figure; so comical that no one takes her doings with seriousness. Harsh words and broken meats are again provocative of laughter, when in very truth we should sob. With Dickens's end in view, how wise his method! After merriment comes the thought: "But what a shame!" And henceforth the reader thinks sympathetically of poor little girls, whether ruled by vicious trollops or working under easier conditions. Omit the jest—and the story becomes too unpleasant to remember.

Between Dickens's farce and his scenes of humour the difference is obvious. In Mantalini or Jack Bunsby we have nothing illuminative; they amuse, and there the matter ends. But true humour always suggests a thought, always throws light on human nature. The humorist may not be fully conscious of his own meaning; he always, indeed, implies more than he can possibly have thought out; and therefore it is that we find the best humour inexhaustible, ever fresh when we return to it, ever; as our knowledge of life increases, more suggestive of wisdom.

Both the Wellers are creations strictly humorous. For one thing, each is socially representative; each, moreover, is a human type, for ever recognizable beneath time's disguises. Be it noticed that neither the old coachman nor his son is ever shown in a grotesque, or improbable, situation; there is no cutting of capers, even when they make us laugh the loudest. The fantastic is here needless; nature has wrought with roguish intention, and we are aware of it at every moment of their common life. No one takes Mantalini to his heart; but Tony and Sam become in very truth our friends, and for knowing them, improbable as it might seem, we know ourselves the better. They are surprising incarnations of the spirit of man, which is doomed to inhabit so variously. The joke consists in perceiving how this spirit adjusts itself to an odd situation, reconciles itself with queerest circumstance. In old Weller, it is a matter of stress; his difficulties, never too severe, bring out the quaint philosophy of the man, and set us smiling in fellowship. Sam, at ease in the world, makes life his jest, and we ask nothing better than to laugh with one who sees so shrewdly, feels so honestly. Sam cannot away with a humbug—in this respect, Dickens's own child. Put him face to face with Job Trotter, and how his countenance shines, how his tongue is loosed! It is a great part of Sam's business in life to come into genial conflict with Job Trotter; his weapon of mockery is in the end irresistible, and a Cockney serving-man strikes many a stroke for the good of humankind. Of course he does not know it; that is our part, as we look on, and feel in our hearts the warmth of kindly merriment, and give thanks to the great humorist who teaches us so much.

To survey all his humorous characters would be to repeat, in substance, the same remarks again and again. I have no space for a discussion, from this point of view, of the figures which have already passed before us. But of Mrs Gamp one word. She sometimes comes into my thought together with Falstaff, and I am tempted to say that there is a certain propriety in the association. Where else since Shakespeare shall we find such force in the humorous presentment of gross humanity? The two figures, of course, stand on different planes. In Falstaff, intellect and breeding are at issue with the flesh, however sorely worsted; in Sarah Gamp, little intellect and less breeding are to be looked for, and the flesh has its way; but I discover some likeness of character. If Betsy Prig's awful assertion regarding Mrs Harris must be held as proved, is there not a hint of resemblance between the mood that elaborated this delicious fiction and the temper native to the hero of Gadshill? A fancy; let it pass. But to my imagination the thick-tongued, leering, yet half-genial woman walks as palpably in Kingsgate Street as yon mountain of a man in Eastcheap. The literary power exhibited in one and the other portrait is of the same kind; the same perfect method of idealism is put to use in converting to a source of pleasure things that in life repel or nauseate; and in both cases the sublimation of character, of circumstance, is effected by a humour which seems unsurpassable.

From a mention of Mrs Harris, one passes very naturally to Spenlow and Jorkins—an only less happy bit of humour. Of course it was taken straight from life; we know that without any authority; at this moment, be sure of it, more than one Mr Spenlow is excusing his necessity or his meanness with the plea of Mr Jorkins's inflexibility. But only the man of genius notes such a thing, and records it for ever among human traits.

Very rich is Dickens's humour in those passages which serve rather as illustrations of manners than of individual character. Take the scene at Mrs Kenwigs's confinement—a shining chapter in the often weak and crude pages of *Nickleby*. So quietly it is done, yet so vividly; never a note of the extravagant; every detail of the scene set before us as it must have been shown in fact, but invested with such mirthful significance. Or, again, the servants' hall at Mr Dombey's; so much better, because done with so much more geniality, than the life that went on upstairs. Or Mr Guppy giving his friend Jobling a dinner at the chop-house; where we hear the chink of plates and glasses, and feel hungry at Jobling's acceptance of each new succulent suggestion, and see the law-clerk's wink as he reckons up with Polly the waitress. Among things supreme stands "Todgers's". Whenever I chance to come within sight of the Monument, it is not of the fire of London that I think, but of Todgers's; one feels that the house must be still existing, discoverable by sufficiently earnest search. It is inconceivable that any age which has not outgrown our language should forget this priceless description: every line close-packed with humorous truth. And how generous the scale! Here is no "hitting off" in a page or so; a broad canvas filled with detail that never tires, and no touch ever superfluous. Not only are the inhabitants of Todgers's made real to us, collectively and individually, by the minutest portraiture; but the very building and its furniture fix themselves in the mind, so described that each room, each table, becomes symbolic, instinct with a meaning which the ordinary observer would never have suspected. The grim old city of London has of a sudden revealed to us a bit of its very self, and we see in it a museum of human peculiarities, foibles, and vices. There this little group of people lives squeezed amid the brick-and-mortar labyrinth; each so vastly important to himself, so infinitesimal in the general view. They remind us of busy ants, running about with what seems such ridiculous earnestness; yet we know that their concerns are ours, and turn from laughing at them—to go and do likewise.

The subtlest bit of humour in all Dickens's books is, to my mind, that scene I have already mentioned as a triumph of characterization, the Father of the Marshalsea entertaining his old pensioner Nandy. But public favour turns to pictures of life that have more familiarity. Dickens was always happy when dealing with that common object of his time—nothing like so common nowadays—the travelling show: were it dramatic or equestrian, waxworks or Punch and Judy. From Mr Crummles and his troupe in *Nickleby* down to Chops the Dwarf in a story written for *All the Year Round*, he never failed in such humorous picturing. Codlin and Short are typical instances. These figures never become farcical; they are always profoundly true, and amuse by pure virtue of their humanity. Akin to this order of beings is another with which he had remarkable acquaintance—the inn waiter. Read again (or only too possibly read for the first time) the waiter's autobiography in *Somebody's Luggage*. Here is no satire, but very fact made vocal; made, at the same time, such a delightful example of unconscious self-disclosure that we cannot sufficiently wonder at the author's sympathetic knowledge.

No one has equalled him in bringing out the humours of stupidity. One of his masterpieces is old Willet, the landlord of the Maypole. Willet is all but a born idiot, in the proper sense of the word; and that "all but" becomes in Dickens's hand the opportunity for elaborate portraiture. You may compare the man with the weakest-minded of Dickens's lower-class women (whichever that may be), and find in the parallel a rich subject of speculation. Being masculine, Willet is sparing of his words; his great resource is a blank stare of imbecile resentment, implying an estimate of his own importance at which the very gods might stand fixed between amaze and laughter. Inimitable the skill with which this asserter of human dignity is shown at last suffering from mental shock—a shock so severe that it almost reduces him to the condition of a deaf-mute. We had thought it impossible that he could fall intellectually lower; when it comes, we can only acknowledge the author's reserve of power. There he sits, amid the wreck of his fine old inn, staring at his old-time companion, the kitchen boiler. Seeing him thus, we have it brought to mind that he really was, in his way, a capable landlord, and had kept the Maypole spick and span for many a long year; which possibly suggests an aspect of English character, and English conservatism, not out of keeping with some of Dickens's views on such subjects.

I must not omit mention of those sketches of genuine grotesques—not Quilp-like extravagances—which now and then flash upon us at some odd moment of the story: wonders of swift character-drawing, and instinct with humour. The finest examples I can remember are the figure of Mr Nadgett, in *Chuzzlewit* (chapter xxvii), and that of the old woman called Tamaroo, in the same book (chapter xxxii). Language cannot do more in the calling up of a vivid image before the mind; and this result is mainly traceable to the writer's humorous insight. There could be no better illustration of the difference between Dickens's grasp and presentment of a bit of human nature, a bit of observable fact, and that method which the critics of today, inaccurately but intelligibly, call photographic. Nadgett, the tracker of sordid mysteries, and Tamaroo, successor of young Bailey at Todgers's, acquire an imaginative importance like in kind (however different in degree) to that of the grandest figures in fiction. Every stroke of such outlines is a manifestation of genius.

Inseparable from the gift of humour is that of pathos. It was Dickens's misfortune that, owing to habits of his mind already sufficiently discussed, he sometimes elaborated pathetic *scenes*, in the theatrical sense of the word. I do not attribute to him the cold insincerity so common in the work of playwrights; but at times he lost self-restraint and unconsciously responded to the crude ideals of a popular audience. Emphasis and iteration, however necessary for such hearers, were out of place in pathetic narrative. Thus it comes about that he is charged with mawkishness, and we hear of some who greatly enjoy his humour rapidly turning the pages meant to draw a tear. Chiefly, I suppose, it is the death of Paul Dombey that such critics have in mind; they would point also to the death of Jo, the crossing-sweeper, and to that of little Nell. On a re-perusal of these chapters, I feel that nothing can be said in defence of Jo; on his death-bed he is an impossible creature, and here for once moral purpose has been undeniably fatal to every quality of art. Regarding the other narratives, it strikes me that they have been too hastily condemned. The one line which describes the death of Paul's mother is better, no doubt, than the hundreds through which we follow the fading of Paul himself; but these pages I cannot call mawkish, for I do not feel that they are flagrantly untrue. The tear may rise or not—that depends upon how we are constituted—but we are really standing by the bed of a gentle little child, precociously gifted and cruelly overwrought, and, if the situation is to be presented at all, it might be much worse done. Such pathos is called "cheap". I can only repeat that in Dickens's day, the lives, the happiness of children were very cheap indeed, and that he had his purpose in insisting on their claims to attention. As for the heroine of *The Old Curiosity Shop*, distaste for her as a pathetic figure seems to me unintelligent. She is a child of romance; her death is purely symbolical, signifying the premature close of any sweet, innocent, and delicate life. Heaven forbid that I should attribute to Dickens a deliberate allegory; but, having in mind those hapless children who were then being tortured in England's mines and factories, I like to see in little Nell a type of their sufferings; she, the victim of avarice, dragged with bleeding feet along the hard roads, ever pursued by heartless self-interest, and finding her one safe refuge in the grave. Look back upon the close of that delightful novel, and who can deny its charm? Something I shall have to say presently about the literary style; but as a story of peaceful death it is beautifully imagined and touchingly told.

Of true pathos Dickens has abundance. The earliest instance I can call to mind is the death of the Chancery prisoner in *Pickwick*, described at no great length, but very powerful over the emotions. It worthily holds a place amid the scenes of humour enriching that part of the book. We feel intensely the contrast between the prisoner's life and that which was going on in the free world only a few yards away; we see in his death a pitiful-ness beyond words. A scene in another book,—*Bleak House*,—this, too, connected with that accursed system of imprisonment for debt, shows Dickens at his best in bringing out the pathos of child-life. The man known to Mr Skimpole as "Coavinses" has died, and Coavinses' children, viewed askance by neighbours because of their father's calling, are living alone in a garret. They are presented as simply as possible—nothing here of stage emphasis—yet the eyes dazzle as we look. I must quote a line or two. "We were looking at one another," says Esther Summerson, "and at these two children, when there came into the room a very little girl, childish in figure but shrewd and older-looking in the face—pretty faced too—wearing a womanly sort of bonnet much too large for her, and dry-ing her bare arms on a womanly sort of apron. Her fingers were white and wrinkled with washing, and the soap-suds were yet smoking which she wiped off her arms. But for this, she might have been a child playing at washing and imitating a poor working-woman with a quick observation of the truth." It is Charley, of course, who had found a way to support herself and the younger ones. We see how closely the true pathetic and a "quick observation" are allied. Another picture shown us in Esther's nar-rative, that of the baby's death in the starved labourer's cottage, moves by legitimate art. Still more of it is felt in the story of Doctor Marigold, the

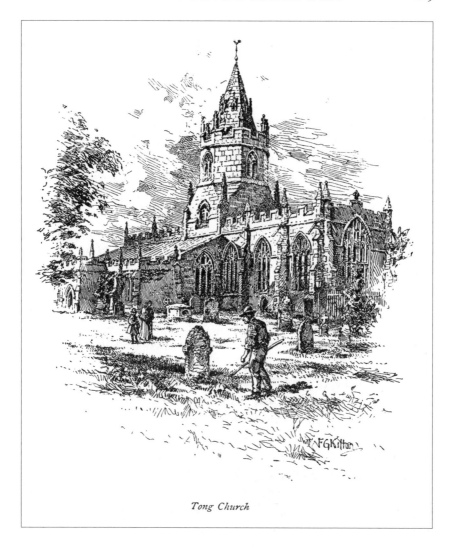

Tong Church

Cheap-Jack, whose child is dying in his arms, whilst for daily bread he plays buffoon before the crowd. This is a noble piece of work, and defies criticism. The tale is told by the man himself as simply as possible; he never insists upon the pitifulness of his position. We hear his whispers to the child, between his hoarse professional shoutings and the guffaws in front; then he finds his word of tenderness brings no response—he looks closer—he turns from the platform. A piece of work that might atone for literary sins far worse than Dickens ever committed.

Little Dorrit is strong in pathos, as in humour. Dickens's memories of childhood made his touch very sure whenever he dealt with the squalid prison-world, and life there was for him no less fertile in pathos than death. Very often it is inextricably blended with his humour; in the details of the Marshalsea picture, who shall say which element of his genius prevails? Yet, comparing it with the corresponding scenes in *Pickwick*, we perceive a sub-dual of tone, which comes not only of advancing years, but of riper art; and as we watch the Dorrits step forth from the prison door, it is another mood than that which accompanied the release of Mr Pickwick. Pathos of this graver and subtler kind is the distinguishing note of *Great Expectations*, a book which Dickens meant, and rightly meant, to end in the minor key. The old convict, Magwitch, if he cannot be called a tragical personality, has feeling enough to move the reader's deeper interest, and in the very end acquires through suffering a dignity which makes him very impressive. Rightly seen, is there not much pathos in the story of Pip's foolishness? It would be more manifest if we could forget Lytton's imbecile suggestion, and restore the original close of the story.

To the majority of readers it seemed—and perhaps still seems—that Dickens achieved his best pathos in the Christmas books. Two of those stories answered their purpose admirably; the other two showed a flagging spirit; but not even in the *Carol* can we look for anything to be seriously compared with the finer features of his novels. The true value of these little books lies in their deliberate illustration of a theme which occupied Dickens's mind from first to last. Writing for the season of peace, good-will, and jollity, he sets himself to exhibit these virtues in an idealization of the English home. The type of domestic beauty he finds, as a matter of course, beneath a humble roof. And we have but to glance in memory through the many volumes of his life's work to recognize that his gentlest, brightest humour, his simplest pathos, occur in those unexciting pages which depict the everyday life of poor and homely English folk. This is Dickens's most delightful aspect, and I believe it is the most certainly enduring portion of what he has left us.

His genius plays like a warm light on the characteristic aspects of homely England. No man ever loved England more; and the proof of it remains in picture after picture of her plain, old-fashioned life—in wayside inns and cottages, in little dwellings hidden amid the city's vastness and tumult, in queer musty shops, in booths and caravans. Finding comfort or jollity, he enjoys it beyond measure, he rubs his hands, he sparkles, he makes us laugh with him from the very heart. Coming upon hardship and woe, he is moved as nowhere else, holds out the hand of true brotherhood, tells to the world his indignation and his grief. There would be no end of selecting passages in illustration, but we must recall a few for the mere pleasure of the thing. Try to imagine the warmest welcome of a cosy little inn, at the end of a long lonely road, on a night of foul weather; you must needs have recourse to the Jolly Sandboys, where Nell and her grandfather and the wandering showmen all found shelter. "There was a deep ruddy blush upon the room, and when the landlord stirred the fire, sending the flames skipping and leaping up—when he took off the lid of the iron pot, and there rushed out a savoury smell, while the bubbling sound grew deeper and more rich, and an unctuous steam came floating out, hanging in a delicious mist above their heads—when he did this, Mr Codlin's heart was touched" (*Old Curiosity Shop*, chapter xxviii). And whose is not? What dyspeptic exquisite but must laugh with appetite over such a description?

As good is the picture of Ruth Pinch at the butcher's. "To see him slap the steak before he laid it on the block, and give his knife a sharpening, was to forget breakfast instantly. It was agreeable, too,—it really was—to see him cut it off, so smooth and juicy. There was nothing savage in the act. Although the knife was large and keen, it was a piece of high art. ... Perhaps the greenest cabbage-leaf ever grown in a garden was wrapped about this steak before it was delivered over to Tom. But the butcher had a sentiment for his business, and knew how to refine upon it. When he saw Tom putting the cabbage-leaf into his pocket awkwardly, he begged to be allowed to do it for him; 'for meat', he said with some emotion, 'must be humoured and not drove'!" (*Chuzzlewit*, chapter xxxix). Reading this, how does one regret that Dickens should have filled with melodrama many a page which might have been given to the commonest doings of the humble street!

There is a great chapter of *The Old Curiosity Shop* (chapter xxxix), where Kit and Barbara, with their respective mothers, with little Jacob, too, and the Baby, go to spend the evening at Astley's. It would have seemed impossible to get so much kindly fun out of a group of the London poor. Dickens does it by dint of his profound, his overflowing sympathy with them. He glows with delight when *they* are delighted; he understands precisely what they enjoy, and why; it does his very soul good to hear Kit's guffaws and the screaming laugh of little Jacob. Where else in literature is there such infinite good-feeling expressed with such wondrous whimsicality? After the circus, Kit takes all his companions to have an oyster supper (by the way, in those days, as Sam Weller assures us, poverty and oysters always went together). And not one of them enjoyed the meal more than he who gaily described it. How the London poor should love Dickens! But—with his books always obtainable—they can scarce be said to read him at all.

Remember that such a scene as this was *new* in literature, a bold innovation. Dickens had no model to imitate when he sat down to tell of the joys of servant-lads and servant-girls with their washerwomen and sempstress mothers. But in spirit he continues the work of two writers whom he always held dear, Goldsmith and Sterne. Goldsmith's sweetness and compassion, Sterne's sensitive humanity, necessarily had their part, and that no small one, in forming Dickens. There is a foretaste of his humour in Moses ("Boz", as we know), the son of the Vicar of Wakefield, and in the would-be fine company; there is a palpable hint to him in the Vicar preaching among poor prisoners. Turning to Uncle Toby, to Corporal Trim, we are perforce reminded of those examples of grotesque goodness, of sweet humility under the oddest exteriors, upon which Dickens lavished his humour and his love.

Captain Cuttle is as well known as any of them. In what terms of literary criticism shall one describe that scene (*Dombey*, chapter xlix) where the Captain sits in Solomon Gills's parlour and Florence mixes his grog for him? It is a sort of fairy tale of modern life. No one can for a moment believe that two such persons ever were in such relations; but so irrelevant an objection never occurs to us. All we know is, that a spell is laid upon us; that we pass from smiles to laughter, and from laughter to smiles again. Who ever paused to think that the old coasting Captain, Mrs MacStinger's lodger, must have been in person and manners and speech not a little repulsive to a young lady straight from a great house in the west of London? It is not germane to the matter. These are actors in the world of humour and imagination, raised above the inessentials of life. Dickens's thought was to make a picture delightful to every heart which can enjoy fun, respect innocence, and sympathize with kindness. Moreover, he wished to point a contrast between the stately house, inhabited by wealth and pride, the atmosphere of which had grown poisonous from the evil passions nurtured in it; and the little back parlour of a shop somewhere amid the City's noisiest streets, where the homeliest—and therefore the most precious—virtues have a secure abode. Fleeing from the home that is none, the mansion where her womanly instincts have been outraged, Florence betakes herself to this poor haven of refuge, and lives there guarded and honoured as any queen in her palace. What could make stronger appeal to the sensibilities of English readers? No national foible is here concerned: we respond with the very best that is in us. We feel that these are the ideals of English life. We are proud of the possibility underlying a fancy of such irresistible charm.

For his own fame, Dickens, I think, never puts his genius to better use than in the idealization of English life and character. Whatever in his work may be of doubtful interest to future time, here is its enduring feature. To be truly and profoundly national is great strength in the maker of literature. What a vast difference from all but every point of view between Dickens and Tennyson; yet it is likely enough that these two may survive together as chosen writers of the Victorian age. They are at one in their English sentiment. They excite the same emotion whenever they speak of the English home; none, I think, of their contemporaries touches so powerfully that island note. In Tennyson's glorious range, humour is not lacking; it exercises itself on a theme of the most intimately national significance, and his Northern Farmer will live as long as the poet's memory. Of humour the very incarnation, Dickens cannot think of his country without a sunny smile. In our hearts we love him for it, and so, surely, will the island people for many an age to come.

IX

Style

Dickens is one of the masters of prose, but in a sense that carries qualification. He cannot be compared with Thackeray for flow of pure idiom, for command of subtle melodies. He is often mannered to the last point of endurance; he has one fault which offends the prime law of prose composition. For all that, he made unique use of the English language, and his style must be examined as one of the justifications of his place in literature.

In the beginning it had excellent qualities; his *Sketches* are phrased with vigour, with variety, and with a soundness of construction which he owed to his eighteenth-century studies. Dealing for the most part with vulgarity, his first book is very free from vulgarisms. In one of the earliest letters to Forster, he speaks of "your invite"; but no such abomination deforms his printed pages. Facetiousness is now and then to blame for an affected sentence, and this fault once or twice crops up in later books. Someone in *Pickwick* wears "a grin which agitated his countenance from one auricular organ to the other"; and in *Bleak House*, when grandfather Smallweed threw his cushion at the old woman, we are told that "the effect of this act of jaculation was twofold". Without much effort Dickens kept clear of such pitfalls; what *might* have befallen him but for his fine models and his good sense, we may surmise from the style of certain of his more or less conscious imitators. Slovenly English he never wrote; the nature of the man made it impossible. And in this respect he contrasts remarkably with all save the greatest of his day. As an illustration of what a generally sound writer could permit himself in the hurry of writing a "mere novel", I remember a passage in Henry Kingsley's *Ravenshoe* (chapter xxviii), where a dog is trying to attract his master's attention; we read, with a little shock of surprise, that "the dog wagged his tail and pawed his waistcoat". But Dickens respected both himself and his public—never a common virtue in the everyday English novelist.

The gravest of his faults, from *Oliver Twist* onwards—and he never wholly overcame it—is the habit of writing metrically. He is not alone in this vice. Charles Kingsley illustrates it very badly in some of his prose; especially, I remember, in the *Heroes*. Should any one wish to see how far the trick (unconsciously, of course) can be carried, let him open Richard Jefferies' paper "The Open Air", where he will find several pages written, with very few breaks, precisely in a metre made familiar by Longfellow. As thus: "All the devious brooklet's sweetness | where the iris stays the sunlight; | all the wild woods hold of beauty: | all the broad hills' thyme and freedom: | thrice a hundred years repeated". This, of course, betrays an ear untrained in the harmonies of prose; the worst of it is, that many readers would discover it with delight, and point to it as admirable. A good many years since, I came upon a magazine article entitled "Dickens as a Poet", the absurd aim whereof was to show admiringly how many passages from the novels could be written and read as blank verse. The fact unfortunately cannot be disputed. Dickens wrote thus under the influence of strong emotion. He observed the tendency, speaks of it as something he cannot help, and is not disturbed by it. The habit overcame him in his moods of softness; and therefore is particularly noticeable towards the end of the *Old Curiosity Shop*. When his emotion is indignant, on the other hand, he is not thus tempted; simply as a bit of prose, the paragraph giving a general description of the children at Dotheboys, is good, well-balanced, with no out-of-place rhythm. But turn to a passage quoted by Forster (Book iii, chapter 8) from the *American Notes*; quoted as a fine expression of Dickens's sympathy with the poor. It is nobly felt, most admirably worded; yet the five-foot cadence is flagrant here and there. "But bring him here, upon this crowded deck. | Strip from his fair young wife her silken dress | ... pinch her pale cheek with care and much privation"—and so on. One is half inclined to think that Dickens did it deliberately, regarding it as an improvement on plain prose.

For a style simple, direct, and forcible, one may turn to *Barnaby Rudge*. Taking it all in all, this is perhaps the best written of his novels; best, that is to say, in the sense of presenting the smoothest and closest strain of narrative. There are no irruptions of metre; the periods are flowing, the language is full of subdued energy. Among the first few books it is very noticeable for this peculiar excellence. One reason, possibly, is its comparative shortness. *Nickleby*, on the other hand, has faults of style plainly due to the necessity of writing more than the author wished to say. One of its best-knit chapters is that describing Nicholas's walk from London through Surrey, with Smike. We breathe the very air of the clowns, and smell the sweetness of wayside hedges.

This power of suggesting a country atmosphere is remarkable in Dickens. He hardly ever mentions a tree or flower by its name; he never elaborates— perhaps never even sketches—a landscape; yet we see and feel the open-air surroundings. The secret is his own delight in the road and the meadow, and his infinite power of suggestion in seemingly unconsidered words.

In narrative, he is always excellent when describing rapid journeys. The best coach-drive ever put into words is that of the Muggleton coach, in *Pickwick*. It surpasses the much longer description in *Chuzzlewit*, which comes near to being monotonous after many paragraphs beginning with the same words; it is incredibly exhilarating, and would put a healthy glow, as of a fine frosty morning, into the veins of a man languishing in the trop- ics. We are asked to believe that the story (in *Bleak House*) of the posting journey conducted by Inspector Bucket, came from the pen of Miss Esther Summerson; the brain, at all events, was Dickens's, and working with its most characteristic vigour. He knew every stage covered by the travellers; he saw the gleam of the lamps, the faces they illumined but for a moment; the very horses brought out fresh were his old acquaintances. Such writing is no mere question of selecting and collocating words; there must first be vision, and that of extraordinary clearness. Dickens tells us that in times of worry or of grave trouble he could still write; he had but to sit down at his desk, and straightaway he *saw*. Where—as would happen—he saw untruly, a mere phantasm thrown forward by the mind, his hand at once had lost its cunning. When vision was but a subtly enhanced memory, he never lacked the skill to make it seen by others.

Think of the easy graphic power that Dickens possessed, and compare it for a moment with the results of such laborious effort to the same ends as was put forth by the French novelist Flaubert. On the one hand, here is a man who works hard indeed, and methodically, but whose work is ever a joy to him, and not seldom a rapture. On the other, we have growls and groans; toil advancing at snail's pace, whilst sweat drips from the toiler's brow; lit- tle or no satisfaction to him in the end from all his suffering. And not one page of Flaubert gives proof of sight and grasp equal to that evinced in a thousand of Dickens. This thing cometh not by prayer and fasting, nor by any amount of thinking about art. You have it or you have it not. As a boy or youth Dickens was occupied in *seeing*; as a young man he took his pen and began to write of what he had seen. And the world saw with him—much better than with its own poor, purblind eyes.

In the story of David Copperfield's journey on the Dover road, we have as good a piece of narrative prose as can be found in English. Equally as good, in another way, are those passages of rapid retrospect, in which David tells us of his later boyhood; a concentration of memory perfumed with the sweetest humour. It is not an easy thing to relate with perfect proportion of detail, with interest that never for a moment drops, the course of a year or two of wholly uneventful marriage; but read the chapter entitled "Our Domestic Life" and try to award adequate praise to the great artist who composed it. One can readily suggest how the chapter might have been spoiled; ever so little undue satire, ever so little excess of sentiment; but who can point to a line in which it might be bettered? It is perfect writing; one can say no more and no less.

Another kind of descriptive writing appears in the nineteenth chapter of *Chuzzlewit*: the funeral of old Anthony conducted by Mr Mould. What of the scope declared in a contrast of this chapter with the one in *Copperfield* just mentioned? I should not like to say that one excels the other; I should find it impossible to decide between their merits. Where is the "extravagance" which, we are told, has pronounced Dickens's doom? Mr Mould and his retainers, the whole funeral from house to grave, seems to me realism of the finest; it is clearest vision and narrative, without a hint of effort; and there stands the thing for ever.

A fine piece of the grimly picturesque is Quilp's death. Better, because more human, is the narrative in *Barnaby Rudge* of the day and night before the gaol-delivery when the rioters are to be hung. It has the effect of rapidity, but contains an immense amount of detail, actual and imaginative. Dennis, Hugh, and Barnaby, together in their cell, are seen by us as the swift hours pass, and at the same time we know what is going on without. Of all the broad and the delicate touches in which these pages abound, not one could be omitted as superfluous; and the impression aimed at is obtained with absolute success.

Narrative, of course, includes description; but in description by itself and in elaborate picturing, as distinguished from the hints which so often serve his purpose, Dickens is very strong. Before speaking of the familiar instances let me mention that chapter at the beginning of *Little Dorrit*, which opens with a picture of London as seen on a gloomy Sunday—if the phrase be not tautological. It is very curious reading. For once we have Dickens quite divested of his humour, and beholding the great city in something like a splenetic mood. As conveying an impression, the passage could not be better; it makes us feel precisely what one has felt times innumerable amid the black lifeless houses, under a sky that crushes the spirit. But seldom indeed can Dickens have seen and felt thus. Compare with it his picture of the fog—Mr Guppy's "London particular"—at the opening of *Bleak House*. This darkness visible makes one rather cheerful than otherwise, for we are spectators in the company of a man who allows nothing to balk his enjoyment of life, and who can jest unaffectedly even in such circumstances. Those few pages of *Little Dorrit*, admirable as art, suggest the kind of novels Dickens might have written without his humour. But in that case he would not have written them at all.

His normal manner is seen in the description of the Fleet, in *Pickwick*. It would appear difficult to make a vivid picture of such a place, a picture which convinces, and yet to omit things vile or intolerable to the feelings; but here it is done. The same art manifests itself as in his masterpieces of characterization; something is obscured, nothing falsified. At times, he could make a sketch in what is known as the impressionist manner; rapid, strong, and in the broadest lines suggesting a vast amount of detail; as in the description of the Gordon rioters seen, passing in their drunken fury along the street, from an upper window (*Barnaby*, chapter L). Dickens was rather proud of this passage; he calls attention to it in a letter written at the time. Innumerable the aspects of London presented in his books; what a wonderful little volume might be made by collecting such passages! Of the West-end we have glimpses only; one remembers, however, that very genteel but stuffy corner inhabited by the house of Barnacle, and the similar locality where dwelt Miss Tox. Stately and wealthy London he does not show us; his artistic preference is for the quaint, out-of-the-way quarters, or for the grim and the lurid, out of which he made a picturesque of his own. Writing once from Naples (where he was merely disappointed and disgusted, we can see why), he says, "I am afraid the conventional idea of the picturesque is associated with such misery and degradation that a new picturesque will have to be established as the world goes onward". Conventional his own ideas and presentments certainly were not, but for the most part they *are* closely connected with misery and degradation. Jacob's Island and Tom-all-alone's have the affect of fine, wild etchings lighted only just sufficiently to show broad features and suggest details one does not desire to pry into. Krook's house and its surroundings make an essential part of the world shadowed by Chancery; unutterably foul and stifling, yet so shown as to hold the imagination in no painful way. Dickens views such scenes in a romantic light. It is the property of his genius to perceive romance in the commonplace and the squalid, no less than in clean and comfortable homeliness.

What he can make out of a wretched little room a few feet square, in a close-packed, sordid neighbourhood, is shown in chapter xlvi of *Chuzzlewit*.

Jonas, become a murderer, is lurking in his own house, and chooses a corner of it where he is not likely to be observed. "The room in which he had shut himself up was on the ground-floor, at the back of the house. It was lighted by a dirty sky-light, and had a door in the wall, opening into a narrow, covered passage or blind alley ... It was a blotched, stained, mouldering room, like a vault; and there were water-pipes running through it, which, at unexpected times in the night, when other things were quiet, clicked and gurgled suddenly, as if they were choking." Nothing could be more insignificant, and at the same time more grim. An out-of-doors companion to it may be found in *Great Expectations*. "I came into Smithfield; the shameful place, being all filth and fat and blood and foam, seemed to stick to me. So I rubbed it off with all possible speed by turning into a street where I saw the great black dome of St. Paul's bulging at me from behind a grim stone building which a bystander said was Newgate Prison. Following the wall of the jail, I found the roadway covered with straw to deaden the sound of passing vehicles; and from the quantity of people standing about, smelling strongly of spirits and beer, I inferred that the trials were on" (chapter xx). This is "locality" as good as the bit of human portraiture which follows (Mr Jaggers walking through the throng of his clients); and higher praise could not be bestowed.

I suppose there is no English writer, perhaps no writer in any literature, who so often gives proof of wonderfully minute observation. It is an important source of his strength; it helps him to put people and things before us more clearly than, as a rule, we should ourselves see them. Two examples only can I find room for; but they will suffice. Peggotty's purse, given to little David on his departure from Yarmouth, was found to contain "three bright shillings, which Peggotty had evidently polished up with whiting for my greater delight". And again, little Pip, after being washed by his sister, is led to make the remark: "I suppose myself to be better acquainted than any living authority with the ridgy effect of a wedding-ring, passing unsympathetically over the human countenance". You will come across no such instances as these in any other novelist, of observation, memory, and imaginative force, all evinced in a touch of detail so indescribably trivial; its very triviality being the proof of power in one who could so choose for his purposes among the neglected incidents of life.

When Dickens writes in his pleasantest mood of things either pleasant in themselves, or especially suggestive of humorous reflection, his style is faultless; perfectly suited, that is to say, to the author's aim and to the matter in hand. His Christmas number called *The Holly Tree* begins with a chapter on Inns; we rise from it feeling that on that subject the last word has been

The "Sir John Falstaff" and West Gate, Canterbury

said, and said in the best possible way. His book of collected papers, *The Uncommercial Traveller*, consists almost wholly of such writing. Whether its theme is City of London Churches, or Shy Neighbourhoods, Tramps, or Night-walks, or London Chambers, he is invariably happy in phrase, and in flow of language which, always easy, never falls below the level of literature. In such work he must be put beside the eighteenth-century essayists, whom he always had in mind. His English is not less idiomatic than theirs, and his views of life find no less complete expression through the medium of a style so lightly and deftly handled.

X

The Radical

Dickens's super-abounding energy, and the unrest which frequently came upon him in consequence of private worries, now and then diverted his thoughts from the all-sufficient labours of literature, and made him anxious to try his strength in public life. At one time he carefully inquired as to the possibility of his becoming a stipendiary magistrate; but the replies he received were not encouraging. At another, he fixed his mind on political journalism; and this had practical result in the establishment of the *Daily News*, which paper, as we have seen, he edited for only a few days. A desire to preside in courts of justice was natural enough in the author of *Oliver Twist*; and, like other men of letters much concerned with social questions, he imagined that the columns of a great newspaper would afford him the best possible field for making known his views and influencing the world. One step which has tempted writers from their appointed task he seems never to have seriously contemplated; he received invitations to stand as a Parliamentary candidate, but gave no ear to them.

The term which described him as politician and social reformer is no longer in common use; he was a Radical. This meant, of course, one who was discontented with the slow course of legislation, moving decorously "from precedent to precedent", and with the aristocratic ideas underlying English life; one who desired radical changes, in the direction of giving liberty and voice to the majority of the people. In a day of advancing Socialism, the demands put forward by such men seem timidly tentative. To our mind, Dickens is in most things a Conservative, and never in his intention democratic—using the word in its original sense. We have to remember the reforms actually achieved in his time, to recognize how progressive was the Radical spirit. Dickens's novels had no small part in the good work, and their influence certainly went further than he knew.

Even in the *Sketches* he writes satirically of the House of Commons, and at a later time his attitude towards Parliament was no less contemptuous than Carlyle's. A letter, bearing the date 1855, declares his grave belief that Representative Government was a failure in England, owing to the national vice which was then known as "flunkeyism". At that time he was writing *Little Dorrit*, and had many reasons for discontent with things in general. But he never desired or anticipated a political revolution of the thorough kind. His first visit to America gave him impressions on the subject of Republicanism which were never removed. He writes thence to Forster, 1842, that he trembled for any Radical who should cross the Atlantic, "unless he is a Radical on principle, by reason and reflection, and from the sense of right. I do fear that the heaviest blow ever dealt at liberty will be dealt by this country, in the failure of its example to the earth." If that example had proved to be in any respect hopeful, he would undoubtedly have rejoiced. Later he probably felt some little satisfaction in the thought that the great Republic had not done so greatly better, all things considered, than monarchic England.

He never attained to a theory of reform; it was not in his mind, his character, to elaborate such reflections. What he thought about the bygone story of his country we can read in the series of chapters which he wrote for *Household Words*, and afterwards published as the *Child's History of England*. As literature it is not happy; too often one is reminded (at a great distance certainly) of that disgusting series of books called Comic Histories, which someone or other disgraced himself by writing. Dickens had no serious historical knowledge, and no true understanding of what is meant by history; his volume shows a series of more or less grotesque sovereigns, who play pranks before high heaven at the expense of the multitudes they are supposed to rule by divine right. Most unfortunate would be the child into whose hand this "history" was put. The one clear suggestion we carry away after trying to read it, is that Dickens congratulated himself on living in the nineteenth century, a subject of Queen Victoria. It was part of his Radicalism to speak of "the bad old times", and true history of course not seldom justifies him. After a visit to Chillon, he writes an admirable letter of description, and ends exclaiming—"Good God, the greatest mystery in all the earth, to me, is how or why the world was tolerated by its Creator through the good old times, and wasn't dashed to fragments". The past, to his mind, was much better forgotten. That the world progressed, he never for a moment held in doubt; but the rate of progress was not at all in keeping with his energetic habits.

In a speech on some public occasion he made a political remark, which, from the ambiguity of its wording, caused newspaper discussion; he said that he had little or no faith in the people governing, but faith limitless in the people governed. Obviously, the shrewdest "trimmer" could not have devised a form of words allowing more latitude of interpretation; but what Dickens meant was plain enough to anyone who did not desire to misunderstand him. He explained afterwards that, the first "people" should be spelt with a small initial letter, the second with a capital. But even so, an ambiguity remains, for "the people governed" may mean either a fact or a hypothesis. Dickens intended the former; he could have implied the latter without any contradiction of his views as seen throughout the novels. He was never a democrat; in his heart he always held that *to be governed* was the people's good; only let the governors be rightly chosen. Herbert Spencer has a precious sentence with which Dickens would profoundly have agreed in all its issues: "There is no political alchemy by which you can get golden conduct out of leaden instincts". Dickens knew—no man better —how unfit are the vast majority of mankind to form sound views as to what is best for them, whether in public or private life; he knew that ignorance inevitably goes hand in hand with forms of baseness, and that though the voice of the people must be heard, it cannot always be allowed to rule. This is very moderate doctrine indeed, but it then qualified a man as a good Radical. Not much more advanced was the position of the little band of teachers who called themselves "Christian Socialists", men with whom Dickens very largely sympathized.

He had the sincerest admiration for Carlyle, the sound of whose great guns could not but delight him—at all events when they were directed against the aristocracy and its game-preserving habits. Himself an aristocrat to the core in the nobler and truer sense of the word, and with very little patience for the simpletons and weaklings whom Dickens took to his heart with so warm a charity, Carlyle was yet far more passionate than the novelist on behalf of the poor and hard-driven sons of men. A humorist, he too, and among the greatest, Carlyle could jest but grimly where his eyes fell upon those "hard-entreated brothers"; he felt within himself the wrath of the prophet moved to lift up his voice against the world's injustice. Conscious himself of the ills of poverty, not only in childhood but at the time of life when want breeds gall and bitterness in strong hearts, he could remind the poor of their eternal duties with stoic sternness, but in the next moment turned away to hide a tear. Vastly wider was his vision than that of Dickens, and so much the deeper his compassion. Another great name rightly associated with Radicalism is that of Tennyson. He who wrote *Locksley Hall* and *Maud* had no stinted sympathy with the revolt against pride of place. A hackneyed strophe in *Vere de Vere* expressed the inmost thought of Dickens's heart. Tennyson moved on to other things; he had a larger mission; but no word that stands upon his perfect page did wrong to the ideal of humanity he had followed in his youth. Unable though he was to enter into the poet's highest mood, Dickens held substantially by the same moral and intellectual guidance. Their messages do not contradict, but supplement, each other.

"I exhort my dear children"—thus runs a passage at the close of Dickens's will—"humbly to try to guide themselves by the teaching of the New Testament in its broad spirit, and to put no faith in any man's narrow construction of its letter here and there." It is the essence of his religion; and his religion (oddly as it may sound) had a great deal to do with the tone and teaching of his literary work. We are told that, for a few years, he attended a Unitarian place of worship; but this involved no dogmatic heresy; at all events, no mental travail on religious subjects. It meant only that the clergy of the English church had irritated and disgusted him. The causes of such feeling are not far to seek, but it will be enough here to mention a fact which he emphasizes in one of his letters, that not until the year of grace 1848 did any Bishop of London make his voice heard as to the necessity of providing the poor with better dwellings. One bears in mind what sort of habitations sheltered the poor of London; one remembers also certain events of that very year '48; and the two reflections help to understand Dickens's attitude. Preoccupied always with the thought of Christ's simple teaching, he took trouble to extract, for his children's use, what seemed to him the essential portions of the New Testament; and it would greatly have pleased him could such a little volume have been used for the instruction of the children of the poor. Instead, he saw them brought up on "the church catechism and other mere formularies and subtleties", and he saw their instructors fighting for this mere husk of religion as though it were the Master's vital word—that word, meanwhile, being by most of them assiduously neglected. None the less he returned to the English Church, and to the end remained a member of it. How he looked upon the more aggressive forms of Dissent we know. It would be a libel to say that Dickens clung to the Establishment because it was "respectable", but undoubtedly he did so in part because the Church belonged to that ancient and solid order of things in England which he never wished to see overturned. Many a man of brains still behaves in the same way, for the same reason. Of his religious sincerity, in the broader sense, there can be no possibility of doubt. He was the last man to drag sacred names and associations into his books on trivial pretexts; but whenever he alludes to Christian precept or makes mention of the Teacher himself, it is with a simple reverence very beautiful and touching; words which came from his own heart, and go straight to that of his reader.

We do not nowadays look for a fervent Christianity in leaders of the people. In that, as to several other matters, Dickens was by choice retrospective. Still writing at a time when "infidelity"—the word then used—was becoming rife among the populace of great towns, he never makes any reference to it, and probably did not take it into account; it had no place in his English ideal. I doubt, indeed, whether he was practically acquainted with the "free-thinking" workman. A more noticeable omission from his books (if we except the one novel which I cannot but think a failure) is that of the workman at war with capital. This great struggle, going on before him all his life, found no place in the scheme of his fiction. He shows us poor men who suffer under tyranny, and who exclaim against the hardship of things; but never such a representative wage-earner as was then to be seen battling for bread and right. One reason is plain: Dickens did not know the north of England. With adequate knowledge of a manufacturing town, he would never have written so unconvincingly as in his book *Hard Times*—the opportunity for dealing with this subject. Stephen Blackpool represents nothing at all; he is a mere model of meekness, and his great misfortune is such as might befall any man anywhere, the curse of a drunken wife. The book is a crude attack on materialism, a theme which might, of course, have entered very well into a study of the combatant working-class. But, as I have already pointed out, the working-class is not Dickens's field, even in London. For the purposes of fiction, it is a class still waiting its portrayer; much has been written about it in novels, but we have no work of the first order dealing primarily with that form of life. Mrs Gaskell essayed the theme very faithfully, and with some success; but it was not her best work. I can recall no working-class figures in English novels so truly representative as those in Charlotte Bronte's second book. Given a little wider experience, the author of *Shirley* might have exhibited this class in a masterpiece such as we vainly look for.

I do not forget Rouncewell in *Bleak House*. He is a Radical, vigorous in action and in speech; but then, he happens to be an employer, and not a "hand". His purpose in visiting Chesney Wold is to withdraw from domestic service, as from an unsuitable position, the young girl with whom his son has fallen in love. Mr Rouncewell belongs distinctly to the middle class—the "great" middle class. He is a Radical in the way of becoming a considerable capitalist. Note that Dickens saw no incongruity in these things. He makes it plain to us that the man has risen by honest ability and work; this being so, he has a right to stand firmly, but respectfully, face to face with Sir Leicester Dedlock, or with men of even higher title. It is the middle-class ideal; that which developed together with England's wealth—at the cost of things which we agree to forget. Dickens greatly admires and sympathizes with Mr Rouncewell. Yet, at this distance of time, we feel it rather difficult to understand why the successful iron-founder should be a more sympathetic figure than the honest-hearted baronet. The one represents a coming triumph; the other, a sinking cause; but, in the meantime, it remains very doubtful whether the triumphing order will achieve more for the interests of humanity than that which has received its death-blow. Mr Rouncewell's characteristics are very significant; he is the ideal Englishman in the eye of Dickens, and of most of his contemporaries. The son of a domestic servant—who is herself a model woman, having risen to the position of confidential housekeeper in a great family—he could never for a moment feel ashamed of his origin; nay, on due occasion he will be proud of it; but he is making money, and looks forward to establishing a "family" of his own. Elaborately, yet modestly, he expounds the situation to the wondering Sir Leicester. With a certain semi-conscious self-approval, he makes known to the baronet that it is no uncommon thing for the son of a wealthy manufacturer to fall in love with a working girl, in which event the girl is removed from her lowly position to be suitably educated and prepared for her duties as a middle-class wife. (Observe our progress; Mr Rouncewell would hardly be so complacent in speaking of such love-affairs nowadays; but that by the by.) There is no hint that the mothers of prosperous men should be removed from a place of servitude. Old and new here meet amicably. Mrs Rouncewell would never consent to quit Chesney Wold, where she regards her duties as a high privilege; she "knows her place", and her son, anything but an intentional revolutionist, is quite content that this should be so. The whole scene is a most valuable bit of history. Sir Leicester and his lady, with old Mrs Rouncewell, represent the past; Rouncewell, his son, and the pretty girl in Lady Dedlock's service, stand for the future. All is civilly transacted; the baronet could not behave otherwise than as *noblesse oblige*; the iron-master is very much of a gentleman. Our author is not entirely aware of his success in satire; for Sir Leicester has more reason to marvel at the social change going on about him than Dickens himself perceived.

Honesty, hard work, worldly success—these are the ideal of the new order; and Dickens heartily approves them. Was he not himself a brilliant example of the self-made man? Much more than that, to be sure; and therefore he supplements the commonly admired scheme of things with a humanity of thought which places him above temporary conditions. Read his addresses given to audiences of the new democracy; especially that delivered at the Birmingham and Midland Institute, in which he used the ambiguous phrases, quoted above, about the people governing and governed. Here, as often in public speeches, he expressly declares that study must *not* be undertaken solely for the sake of "getting on", but for the moral and intellectual good resulting to him who studies, and for the power it bestows of doing good to others. He said it with all sincerity; but his audience, we may be sure, kept before them, whilst they listened, the mental image of Mr Rouncewell. When Dickens spoke of Progress, it was thus that the people interpreted him. And of Progress he spoke much and often, convinced as he was that his country was moving steadily towards a better day. Human nature being what it is, a commercial epoch might do much worse than set up Mr Rouncewell as its patron saint. But Sir Leicester, too, had his intimations of futurity; he may, in his darkest moments, have foreseen Chesney Wold fallen into the possession of some lord of millions, who neither knew nor cared anything about the fair traditions of the past, who revelled in vulgar display, and who, by the force of his glaring example, promoted bitterness and warfare between the classes and the nations of mankind. Dickens lived to see the beginnings of plutocracy. He would not have glorified *that* form of progress; but all unconsciously he had his part in bringing it about.

One vice which had formerly been proper to aristocratic circles, that of furious gambling, he saw spreading through society at large, and spoke of it as became him. He chanced to be at Doncaster during the races, and after describing in a letter the scenes of that lively time, he adds, "I vow to God that I can see nothing in it but cruelty, covetousness, calculation, insensibility, and low wickedness". These are honest words. But no man's censure can avail against a national curse which is inseparably connected with the triumph of commercialism.

On its better side, then, Dickens's Radicalism consisted in profound sympathy with the poor, and boundless contempt of all social superiority that is merely obstructive. Speaking of *The Chimes*, he said that it was his wish and hope in this book "to strike a blow for the poor". Many such blows he struck, and that right manfully. Our social experience forbids us to think that his views were always wise. He hated the new Poor Law, merely because it put an end to a ruinous system of outdoor relief and compelled the indigent to live in so-called workhouses. One can only wonder that his feeling so much overcame his robust common-sense. Quite late in his career we come across the old animosity in his description of Betty Higden (*Our Mutual Friend*), one of the least valuable of his pictures of poor life. Old Betty lives in terror of the workhouse, and wishes to die in a ditch rather than be taken care of by the Union. This is intelligible enough; one knows that workhouses are often brutally conducted, and one sympathizes very thoroughly with a loathing of that "charity" which is not at all synonymous with charity in its true sense. But Betty, as a figure in fiction, does not interest us; she is so evidently a mere mouthpiece for criticism of a system; we do not see her, and do not believe in her talk. The practical man only scoffs. And Dickens could so easily have drawn a character at which no scoffing would have been possible.

It is an obvious fault of his work, when he exhibits victims of social wrong, that it takes no due account of the effect of conditions upon character. Think of little Oliver Twist, who has been brought up under Bumble and Company, amid the outcasts of the world, yet is as remarkable for purity of mind as for accuracy of grammar. Oliver, when taken to Fagin's house, is wholly at a loss to conjecture the meaning of words and acts which even a well-bred boy of his age could not fail to understand; the workhouse lad had evidently never heard of pickpockets. Granted that Oliver was of gentle blood, heredity does not go so far as this. Little Dorrit, again: she is the child of the Marshalsea; and think of what that meant, even apart from the fact of her more literal parentage. Yet we find no blemish in her; she has grown up "under the lock" without contracting one bad habit of thought or speech; indeed, one does not know in what way Amy Dorrit could be morally improved. This is optimism of the crudest kind, but to Dickens and to his readers it suggested no troublesome reflections. To show either Oliver or Amy as a creature of pure instincts, struggling and stumbling towards the light and often sinking in despair, would have satisfied neither; the good character must be good in spite of everything, or the Ruler of the universe seems dishonoured.

To us, in a day of sociology, such ideals are uninteresting, and it relieves us when we come across such a capital study of the everyday fact as is seen (*Dombey*) in Mrs Toodle's graceless son, Rob the Grinder. Robert was a charity-boy, and probably a fair specimen of the breed. From the doubtless well-meaning care of the Charitable Grinders he has come forth a very troublesome young rascal; slippery, untruthful, dishonest, and the ready instrument of any mature scoundrel who chooses to throw him a copper. This, notwithstanding the sterling qualities of his father and mother. Rob is quite capable of penitence; it makes him uncomfortable when he knows that his good mother is crying about him; but after every resolution of amendment comes a speedy relapse, and when we at length lose sight of him, it is with no certainty that he will not live to be transported. Excellent characterization, and far more profitable from the point of view of the good Radical than many crossing-sweeper Joes or declaiming Betty Higdens. It goes to the root of the matter. Rob has been infamously neglected by the pretentious folk who made such a merit of supplying him with bread-and-butter and a hideous garb. This was plainly not the way to make a good citizen out of a low-born child —or any other child. It pointed to the need for education other than that supplied by Grinders, however charitable; and from this point of view, Rob is one of the most important of Dickens's social studies.

Whilst speaking of the influence of social conditions, one ought to glance again at the Smallweed family, in *Bleak House*. These creatures, whether it was meant or not, plainly stand for the blighted, stunted, and prematurely old offspring of foggiest London. Impossible, we are told, to conceive of them as having ever been young. Nothing could be truer. These are typical products of a monstrous barbarism masked as civilization; savages amid the smoke and filth and clamour of a huge town, just as much as the dirty grizzled Indian crouched in a corner of his wigwam. Dickens chose to dwell on things more pleasant and, as it seemed to him, better for the soul; but he knew very well that for one Tim Linkinwater there existed five thousand Smallweeds. Not only in the neighbourhood of Chancery do such weeds crop up; it is the pestilent air of crowded brick and mortar that nourishes them. Statisticians tell us that London families simply die out in the third generation; on the whole, one is glad to hear it. Unfortunately, their decay leaves a miasma; and all children so luckless as to breathe it with their daily air shrivel in mind, if not in body, before they have a chance of enjoying youth.

Dickens's remedy for the evils left behind by the bad old times was, for the most part, private benevolence. He distrusted legislation; he had little faith in charitable associations; though such work as that of the Ragged Schools strongly interested him. His saviour of society was a man of heavy purse and large heart, who did the utmost possible good in his own particular sphere. This, too, was characteristic of the age of free-contract, which claimed every man's right to sell himself as best he could, or buy as many other men as his means allowed. At one with Carlyle in scorning the theory that "cash was the sole nexus" between human beings, Dickens would have viewed uneasily any project for doing away with this nexus altogether; which would mean the abolition of a form of beneficence in which he delighted. With what gusto does he write of any red-checked old gentleman who goes about scattering half-sovereigns, and finding poor people employment, and brightening squalid sick-chambers with the finest produce of Covent Garden. In the Christmas Books, he went to pantomimic lengths in this kind of thing; but no one was asked to take Scrooge very seriously, either as a grasping curmudgeon, or when he bawls out of the window his jovial orders for Christmas fare. Figures, however, such as Mr Garland and the Cheerybles and John Jarndyce and many another were presented in all good faith. We may even see Dickens himself playing the part, and very creditably, in that delightful Christmas paper of his, the *Seven Poor Travellers*; where it makes one's mouth water to read of the fare he ordered at the inn for those lucky vagabonds. In the Cheeryble brothers he indulges his humane imagination to the full. That there indeed existed a couple of kind-hearted merchants, who were as anxious to give money as others are to make it, we will believe on the author's assurance; but that anyone ever saw the Cheerybles in the flesh we decline to credit. They are chubby fairies in tights and gaiters; a light not of this world flushes about their jolly forms. Dickens becomes wild with joyous sympathy in telling of their eccentric warm-heartedness, "Damn you, Tim Linkinwater!" they exclaim—unable in the ordinary language of affection to set free their feelings. To double a clerk's salary is a mere bit of forenoon fun; after dinner, we picture them supplying fraudulent debtors with capital for a new undertaking, or purchasing an estate in Hampshire to be made over forthwith to the widow of some warehouse porter with sixteen children. The harm they must have done, those two jolly old boys! But Dickens would not hear of such a suggestion. He considered, above all, the example of self-forgetfulness, of mercy. And as " people in a book", it is likely enough that Tim Linkinwater's employers are to this day bearing far and wide a true gospel of humanity.

The very heartiness of this benevolence precludes every suspicion of offensive patronage. We know that these men do good because it gives them more pleasure than anything else; and their geniality is a result thereof. Even so in Dickens himself; he is incapable of speaking and thinking of the poor as from a higher place; no man ever pleaded their cause with simpler sincerity. He is always, and naturally, on their side, as against the canter, and the bully, and the snob; even as against a class of rich folk with whom he had otherwise no quarrel. It over-joys him to find good in anyone of lowly station, to show virtues in the uneducated. Those very Cheeryble brothers, do they not *eat with their knives*? We should not have known it, but he goes out of his way to tell us; he insists upon the fact with pride, and to throw scorn upon the fastidious, who would disapprove of this habit. Always it is the heart rather than the head. A man who has been to school and college may, of course, have virtues; but how much fairer do they shine—thinks Dickens—in him who drops his h's and does not know the world is round! In this respect—as in various others—there is a difference between Dickens and that other Radical novelist, Charles Kingsley. The author of *Alton Locke* chooses for his hero a working-man whose intellect is so much above the average that he is nothing less than a true poet. One cannot imagine such a figure in Dickens. Copperfield—by the autobiographic necessity of the case—does not come of the proletariate, and I remember no instance of a person born in that class to whom Dickens gives anything more than mechanical aptitudes. It was reserved for Thackeray to make a great artist of a butler's son, and for Kingsley to show us a tailor writing "The Sands of Dee". I mention this simply as a fact, without implying any adverse criticism; it was the part of Dickens to show the beauty of moral virtues, and to declare that these could be found in all kinds of men, irrespective of birth and education. When sending forth her nephew into the world, Betsy Trotwood gave him this brief counsel: "Never be mean; never be false; never be cruel". Better advice she could not have bestowed; and it was the ideal of conduct held up by Dickens to all his readers, from beginning to end. If he could discover shining examples of such virtue among the poor and the ignorant, their mental dulness seemed to him of but small account.

It does his heart good to play the advocate and the friend to those with whom nature and man have dealt most cruelly. Upon a Smike or a Maggy (in *Little Dorrit*) he lavishes his tenderness simply because they are hapless creatures from whom even ordinary kind people would turn with involuntary dislike. Maggy is a starved and diseased idiot, a very child of the London gutter, moping and mowing to signify her pleasures or her pains. Dickens gives her for protector the brave and large-hearted child of the Marshalsea, whose own sufferings have taught her to compassionate those who suffer still more. Maggy is to be rescued from filth and cold and hunger; is to be made as happy as her nature will allow. It is nobly done, and, undoubtedly, an example of more value to the world than any glorification of triumphant intellect.

At times, he went too far in his championship of the humble. Chapter xxxviii of *The Old Curiosity Shop* contains a paragraph of moralizing in which it is declared that the love of home felt by the poor is "of truer metal" than anything of the kind possible in the wealthy. Twenty years later Dickens would not have spoken so inconsiderately. Sometimes, too, he goes beyond the safe mean in his exhibition of virtuous humility. The lad Kit, who not only "came back to work out the shilling", but repels with a sense of injury an offer of new service at higher wages, comes dangerously near to the kind of thing one meets with in stories written for Sunday School prizes. Many readers, I dare say, are of opinion that Dickens is constantly falling into this error; that it is his besetting sin. Well, that is one way of regarding the matter; on the alternative point of view I have sufficiently insisted.

The enviously discontented poor seldom come forward in his pages; indeed, the discontented in any spirit are not often shown. An interesting exception is his paper on "Tramps", in the *Uncommercial Traveller*, where tramps of every species are discussed with much knowledge and infinite humour, and without a trace of sentimentality. We hear the whining of the rascals, and their curses when they fail to get anything by it; their hopeless brutality is set forth with most refreshing candour. Of characters in the novels, there is no low-class malcontent worth mention except Charley Hexam. He, indeed, makes a very good exception, for he is precisely the one member of his class whom Dickens shows as tolerably educated. The date of *Our Mutual Friend* is 1865; the great scheme of national education was to be established only five years later; and had Dickens been able to foresee every result of 1870, he could not have drawn a more truly prophetic figure than Charley Hexam. This youth has every fault that can attach to a half-taught cub of his particular world. He is a monstrous egotist, to begin with, and "school" has merely put an edge on to the native vice. The world exists solely for his benefit; his "esuriency", to use Carlyle's word, has no bounds. Then he is of course a snob, and with fair opportunity will develop into a petty tyrant with an inclination to active cruelty. Something of resemblance exists between this fellow and Tom Tulliver; it is an odd coincidence, too, that both should have sisters so vastly their superiors, yet alike devoted to them. Tom had the advantage of country air; he is never quite unwholesome, his selfish coarseness of fibre is recognizable as old English. But Hexam's pride is of base metal, through and through. He is capable of swaggering in a bar-room, of lying contemptibly to an audience of commoner lads. Before he was many years older, he became a "secularist"—quite without conviction,—and delivered peculiarly blatant lectures; after that he added "socialism", and pointed to himself as an example of the man of great talents, who had never found a fair chance. Dickens did well in giving him for teacher and friend such a man as Bradley Headstone, whose passionate nature (with which one can sympathize well enough when it comes to the love-story) must needs have an evil influence on Lizzie's brother. But this was not absolutely necessary for the development of a Charley Hexam, whose like, at this moment, may be found throughout London by anyone studying the less happy results of the board-school system.

Of noble discontent, Dickens cannot be said to give us any picture at all. The inventor in *Little Dorrit*, foiled by the Circumlocutionists, is too mild and dreamy to nourish a spirit of revolt; Stephen Blackpool in *Hard Times* would hold rebellion a sin; and as for the rank and file of hungry creatures, they seem never to have heard that there is movement in the land, that voices are raised on their behalf, and even to some purpose. No; their hope is in the Cheeryble brothers; not at all in Chartist or in Radical or in Christian Socialist. Very significant the omission. Dickens, for all his sympathy, could not look with entire approval on the poor grown articulate about their wrongs. He would not have used the phrase, but he thought the thought, that humble folk must know "their station". He was a member of the middle class, and as far from preaching "equality" in its social sense as any man that ever wrote. Essentially a member of the great middle class, and on that very account able to do such work, to strike such blows, for the cause of humanity in his day and generation.

XI

Comparisons

Twenty years ago a familiar topic for debating societies was a comparison of the literary characteristics of Dickens and Thackeray—or of Thackeray and Dickens, I forget which. Not impossibly, the theme is still being discussed in country towns or London suburbs. Of course, it was always an absurdity, the points of difference between these authors being so manifest, and their mutual relations in literature so easy of dismissal, that debate in the proper sense there could be none. As to which of the two was the "greater novelist", the question may be left for answer to those who are capable of seriously propounding it. He will be most positive in judgment whose acquaintance with the novelists' writings is least profound.

It seems to me, however, that we may, without waste of time, suggest comparison in certain points between Dickens and one or two of his foreign contemporaries, writers of fiction who, like the English master, were pre-occupied with social questions, and evinced special knowledge in dealing with the life of the poor. Balzac, Victor Hugo, Dostoieffsky, Daudet—these names readily occur to one, and I shall not err in assuming familiarity with their principal works in those who have cared to read so far in this little book. Of course I have no intention of saying all that might easily be said as to points of contrast: so thorough an Englishman as Dickens must needs differ in particulars innumerable from authors marked on their side by such strong national characteristics. Enough to indicate certain lines of similarity, or divergence, which, pursued in thought, may help to a complete under-standing of our special subject.

Evidently there is a difference on the threshold between Dickens and three of the foreign authors named—a difference which seems to involve the use of that very idle word "realism". Novels such as those of Balzac are said to be remorseless studies of actual life; whereas Dickens, it is plain, never pretends to give us life itself, but a selection, an adaptation. Balzac, calling his work the "human comedy", is supposed to have smiled over this revelation of the littleness of man, his frequent sordidness, his not uncommon bestiality. Dostoieffsky, absorbed in compassionate study of the wretched, the desolate, the oppressed, by no means goes out of his way to spare our feelings; and Daudet, so like to Dickens in one or two aspects, matures into a conception of the novel which would have been intolerable to the author of *David Copperfield*—cultivates a frankness regarding the physical side of life which in England would probably have to be defended before legal authorities with an insular conception of art. Realists, we say; men with an uncompromising method, and utterly heedless as to whether they give pleasure or pain.

The distinction is in no way a censure upon Dickens. As soon as a writer sits down to construct a narrative, to imagine human beings, or adapt those he knows to changed circumstances, he enters a world distinct from the actual, and, call himself what he may, he obeys certain laws, certain conventions, without which the art of fiction could not exist. Be he a true artist, he gives us pictures which represent his own favourite way of looking at life; each is the world in little, and the world as *he* prefers it. So that, whereas execution may be rightly criticised from the common point of view, a master's general conception of the human tragedy or comedy must be accepted as that without which his work could not take form. Dickens has just as much right to his optimism in the world of art, as Balzac to his bitter smile. Moreover, if it comes to invidious comparisons, one may safely take it for granted that "realism" in its aggressive shapes is very far from being purely a matter of art. The writer who shows to us all the sores of humanity, and does so with a certain fury of determination, may think that he is doing it for art's sake; but in very truth he is enjoying an attack upon the order of the universe—always such a tempting form of sport. Well, Dickens was also combative, and enjoyed his palpable hits; only, his quarrel was with certain people, and certain ways of thought, never with human nature or the world at large.

There are orders of imaginative work. A novel is distinct from a romance; so is a fairy tale. But there can be drawn only a misleading, futile distinction between novels realistic and idealistic. It is merely a question of degree and of the author's temperament.

In Balzac's *Cousin Pons* are two figures, amiable, eccentric, such as Dickens might have conceived in other surroundings. Pons, the collector of bric-a-brac, and his friend Schmucke, are good, simple creatures, and Balzac loves them; but so bent is he on showing that life, or at all events Paris, is a vast machine for torturing and crushing the good (and therefore the weak), that these two old men end in the most miserable way, amid baseness and cruelty which triumphs over them. We know how Dickens would have shaped the story. In art he was incapable of such sternness; and he utterly refused to believe that fate was an irresponsible monster. Compare the Maison Vauquer in *Le Père Goriot*, with "Todgers's" in *Martin Chuzzlewit*. No one will for a moment believe that Dickens's picture differs from that of Balzac, because the one is a bit of London, the other of Paris. Nor is it a question of defect of humour; Mme Vauquer (née de Conflans) and her group of boarders in the Rue Neuve-SainteGenevieve, are presented with sufficient suggestion of humorous power. But Balzac delights in showing us how contemptible and hateful such persons can be; whereas Dickens throws all his heart on to the side of the amusing and the good. When sheets are wanted to shroud the dead body of poor old Goriot (a victim of atrocious greed), Mme Vauquer exclaims: "*Prends les draps retournés; par Dieu! c'est toujours assez bon pour un mort*". It is a fierce touch, and Dickens could no more have achieved it in a novel than have uttered the words in his own person. There is a difference of artistic method. We are free to express a preference for this or for that way of presenting life; but such preference involves no judgment. On either side, a host of facts can be brought forward to justify the artist's view; the critic's part is merely to inquire how the work has been executed.

One finds in Balzac a stronger intellect, but by no means a greater genius. Very much wider is his scope in character and circumstance; he sees as clearly and as minutely as Dickens; but I doubt whether he ever imparts his vision with the vividness of Dickens at his best; and assuredly his leagues of description fail in art when compared with the English author's mode of showing us what he wishes. In construction they are both flagrantly defective, though erring in different ways.

Let the critic who dismisses Dickens's figures as types, turn for a moment to Victor Hugo's masterpiece, *Les Misérables*. What are we to call the personages in this story? Put side by side the detective Javert and Inspector Bucket. It is plain at once that in the latter we have an individual, a living man full of peculiarities, some professional, others native to himself; he represents, no doubt, the London police force of his day, but only as any very shrewd, brisk, and conscientious inspector would have done so. Javert, on the other hand, is an incarnation of the penal code; neither more nor less. Never for one instant do we mistake him for a being such as walks the earth. He is altogether superhuman; he talks the language of an embodied Idea; it cannot surprise us however ubiquitous he seems or however marvellous his scent for a criminal. Go through the book, and it is always the same thing. Jean

Valjean might be likened to Prometheus; he is a type of suffering humanity, he represents all the victims of social wrong. Let his adventures go to any length of the heroic, the surprising, we do not protest; he is not one man, but many. Fantine, too; what is she but the spirit of outraged womanhood? Even as Cosette stands for childhood robbed of its natural inheritance, trodden under foot by a greedy and ferocious civilization. *Les Misérables* is not rightly to be called a novel; it belongs to the region of symbolic art. And my only reason for putting it beside Dickens's work is to make manifest at a glance his superior quality as a writer of fiction.

Hugo is concerned with wide historical questions, with great forces in the life of the world; he probes the theory of society, searches into the rights of the individual; he judges man; he seeks to justify the ways of God. He is international; and his vast drama belongs to all modern time. He is in the faithfulest sense of the word a democrat; for him there can be, in the very nature of things, no ruling voice save that of the people; all other potentates and lawgivers are mere usurpers, to be suffered for a time. Dickens, though engaged heart and soul in the cause of the oppressed, fights their battle on a much narrower ground. The laws he combats are local, belonging, for the most part, to certain years of grace. His philosophy is the simplest possible, and all his wisdom is to be read in the Sermon on the Mount. Democrat he is none, but a hearty English Radical. His force is in his intense nationality, enabling him to utter the thoughts of voiceless England. Yet of necessity there are many points at which his work and Hugo's touch together, inviting comparison. Child-life is one of them. I have spoken of Dickens's true pathos; but is there anything in all his stories that springs from so deep a fount of tender pity as that vision of Cosette putting out her wooden shoe at Christmas? For the rest, Dickens's children are generally creatures of flesh and blood; Cosette, save at moments, belongs to the spirit world. An inferiority in the Englishman—if we care to glance at it—becomes plain by a contrast of his wronged women with Fantine. Abstractions these, as we have already noted, and therefore an illustration of what his people for the most part are *not*; as abstractions, how thin and futile and untrue when brought into the light of a fine creation, such as the mother of Cosette! At root, both writers have the same faith in man; they glorify the same virtues. But for Dickens life is so much simpler—and so greatly more amusing. From his point of view, how easily all could be set right, if the wealthy and the powerful were but reasonably good-natured—with an adequate sense of humour!

He is wroth with institutions; never bitter against fate, as is so often the case in "realistic" novels of our time. Something of this, though for the most part unconsciously, appears in the great Russian novelist Dostoieffsky, whose work, in which Dickens would have found much to like and admire, shows so sombre a colouring beside the English novels. It is gloomy, for one reason, because it treats of the empire of the Tzar; for another, because Dostoieffsky, a poor and suffering man, gives us with immense power his own view of penury and wretchedness. Not seldom, in reading him, one is reminded of Dickens, even of Dickens's peculiarities in humour. The note of his books is sympathy; a compassion so intense as often to seem morbid—which indeed it may have been, as a matter of fact. One novel is called *The Idiot*, a study of mental weakness induced by epilepsy. Mark the distance between this and *Barnaby Rudge*; here we have the pathos of saddest truth, and no dallying with half-pleasant fancies. But read the opening of the story called in its French translation *Humiliés et Offensés*; it is not impossible that Dickens's direct influence worked with the writer in those pages describing the hero's kindness to the port little waif who comes under his care; in any case, spiritual kindred is manifest. And in how alien a world as to all things outward!

Dostoieffsky's masterpiece, *Crime and Punishment*, abounds in Dickens-like touches in its lighter passages. Extravagances of character delighted him, and he depicted them with a freer hand than Dickens was permitted or would have cared to use. Suppose the English novelist born in Russia, he might well have been the author of the long scene at the beginning of the book, where Sonia's father, the eccentric drunkard, makes himself known to us in his extraordinary monologue. For that matter, with such change of birth and breeding, Dickens might well have written the whole book, which is a story of a strange murder, of detective ingenuity, of a ruined girl who keeps her soul clean, and of a criminal redeemed by love and faith in Christ; the scene throughout being amid the darkness, squalor, and grotesque ugliness of Russia's capital. Dostoieffsky is invariably pure of tone and even decorous from our own peculiar point of view; his superiority as a "realist" to the author of *David Copperfield* consists merely in his frank recognition of facts which Dickens is obliged to ignore, or to hint with sighing timidity. Sonia could not have been used by the Englishman as a heroine at all; as a subordinate figure he would have turned her to his most stagey purposes, though meaning all the time an infinitude of gentleness and sympathy; instead of a most exceptional girl (by no means, I think, impossible), she would have become a glaring unreality, giving neither pleasure nor solace to any rational reader. The crucial chapter of the story, the magnificent scene in which Raskolnikoff makes confession to Sonia, is beyond Dickens, as we

know him; it would not have been so but for the defects of education and
the social prejudices which forbade his tragic gift to develop. Raskolnikoff
himself, a typical Russian, a man of brains maddened by hunger and by the
sight of others hungry, is the kind of character Dickens never attempted
to portray; his motives, his reasonings, could not be comprehended by an
Englishman of the lower middle class. And the murder itself—Bill Sikes,
Jonas Chuzzlewit, show but feebly after we have watched that lank student,
with the hatchet under his coat, stealing up the stairs; when we have seen
him do his deed of blood, and heard the sound of that awful bell tinkling in
the still chamber. Dostoieffsky's work is indescribably powerful and finely
tragic; the murders in Dickens are too vulgar of motive greatly to impress
us, and lack the touch of high imaginativeness.

Little as he cared for foreign writers, we learn that Dickens found pleasure in a book called *Le Petit Chose*, the first novel of a very young author
named Alphonse Daudet. It would have been strange indeed had he not
done so; for Daudet at that time as closely resembled Dickens himself as
a Frenchman possibly could. To repeated suggestions that he modelled his
early work on that of his great contemporary, Daudet replied with a good-
humoured shake of the head; and as an illustration of how one can seem to
plagiarize without doing anything of the kind, he mentions in his *Memoirs*
that he was about to give to the little lame girl, Desiree Delobelle, the occupation of doll's dressmaker, when a friend made known to him the existence
of just such a figure in *Our Mutual Friend*. If indeed Daudet did not deceive
himself, we can only wonder at the striking resemblance between his mind
and that of Dickens. Not only is it a question of literary manner, and of the
humour which is a leading characteristic in both; the Frenchman is pene-
trated with a delicate sense, a fine enjoyment, of the virtues and happiness of
simple domestic life, and in a measure has done for France what Dickens in
his larger way did for England, shaping examples of sweetness and goodness
among humble folk, which have been taken to their hearts by his readers.
Bélisaire, in *Fromont Jeune*, is a typical instance; and the like may be found
even in his later novels, where, as some think, he has been unhappily led
after false gods by the literary fashion of his time. Real life has frequently
supplied him with an artistic motive precisely such as Dickens rejoiced in
finding; for example, "*le père Joyeuse*" in *Le Nabab*, the clerk who, having
lost his employment, shrinks from letting his family know, and leaves home
each morning as if going to the office as usual—a delightful sketch, done
with perfection of kindliness and humour. Then, there is Daudet's fine
compassion. He says, again in his *Memoirs*: "*Je me sens en cœur l'amour de*

Dickens pour les disgraciés et les pauvres, les enfances mèlées aux misères des grandes villes"; and this is abundantly proved throughout his writings.

Daudet has a great advantage in his mastery of construction. Where, as in *Fromont Jeune*, he constructs too well, that is to say, on the stage model, we see what a gain it was to him to have before his eyes the Paris stage of the Second Empire instead of that of London in the early Victorian time. Moreover, he is free from English fetters; he can give us such a portrait as Sidonie, done with wonderful truth, yet with a delicacy, even a tenderness, which keeps it thoroughly in tone with his pure ideals. I do not speak of the later novels, much as I see to admire and like in them; only of the time when his resemblance to Dickens was most pronounced. Jack's mother, the feather-brained Ida de Barancy, belongs to a very different order of art from anything attained in female portraiture by the English novelist. In his men, too, this advantage is often very noticeable. Delobelle the illustrious, and the mouthing D'Argenton, have points of character which easily suggest persons in Dickens; but they belong to a world which has more colour, more variety, and the writer does not fear to present them completely. These things notwithstanding, Dickens's work is of course beyond comparison wider in scope and richer in significance. We may concede to Daudet all his superiority as a finished artist, and only become the more conscious of Dickens's unapproachable genius.

Telling us of the hapless lad from whom he modelled his Jack, Daudet notes points of difference between the real and the fictitious character; the Jack he knew had not altogether that refinement which heightens our interest in the hero of the novel. "*Il faut dire*", adds the writer, "*que le peuple ignore bien des délicatesses, des susceptibilités morales.*" Could such a remark possibly have fallen from the pen of Dickens, even when not employed upon fiction? Of "the people" he could neither have said nor thought it; was it not to "the people" that he turned when he wanted an example of the finest delicacy of heart, the most sensitive moral susceptibility? Perhaps it was just this lack of faith that held Daudet from fulfilling what seemed the promise of his early time. Such lack of faith in the multitude is not difficult to account for in a very acute observer. It was especially hard to maintain in face of a literary movement which devoted itself to laying bare the worst of popular life. The brothers Goncourt, Flaubert, and M. Zola were not companions likely to fortify a naïve ideal. It is just possible that they inflicted serious injury upon Daudet's work, and robbed France of a precious gift—the books he might have written but for the triumph of "realism". Dickens, who died before the outbreak of the Franco-Prussian war, can barely have suspected the lines that literature was to follow in the next decade; to the end he represented in himself a literary force which had burst upon the world with irresistible charm, had held its way victoriously for five-and-thirty years, and seemed as far as ever from losing its dominion over English readers. The likelihood is that his unwavering consistency will stand him in better stead through the twentieth century than any amount of that artistic perfection which only a small class can appreciate and enjoy.

XII

The Latter Years

It is the privilege of a great writer to put into his work the finest qualities of his heart and brain, to make permanent the best part of himself, and through that to influence the world. In speaking of Dickens's triumphs as an author, I have felt that the most fervent praise could not err by excess; every time I open his books, as the years go on, it is with ever more of wonder, delight, admiration, and love. To point out his shortcomings as a man could give little satisfaction to one who thus thinks of him; merely for the sake of completeness in my view of his life and works, I feel it necessary to glance at those disastrous latter years which show him as a "public entertainer", all true peace and leisure at an end, shortening his life that he might be able to leave a fortune to his family. Carlyle said that the story of Charles Dickens's doings in America "transcended in tragic interest, to a thinking reader, most things one has seen in writing". We see plainly enough what a deplorable mistake it was, and men such as Forster, Dickens's true friends, not only saw it at the time, but did their utmost in the way of protest. He himself had no misgiving—or would confess none. In the words with which he prefaced his first paid reading (1853) he said he had satisfied himself that to adopt this career could involve no possible compromise of the credit and independence of literature, and that whatever brought a public man and his public face to face, on terms of mutual confidence and respect, was of necessity a good thing. Both assertions may be contested. Carlyle, and many another man of letters, saw very grave objections to semi-theatrical "touring" on the score of the credit of literature; and as to the relations between "a public man" and his admirers, it is very doubtful whether a novelist should bear that title at all. But Dickens's intimate relations with the theatre made it impossible for him to give due weight to these objections. Moreover he was a very keen man of business, and could not resist the temptation of enriching himself by means which, in themselves, were thoroughly congenial to him.

For he enjoyed those readings. The first he ever gave—that of his *Christmas Carol* to a little group of friends—was arranged on his own suggestion, and he read several times for charitable purposes before he began to do so for profit. Not without reason he felt that all who knew him in his books were as personal friends to him, and he to them; he delighted in standing before those vast audiences, and moving them to laughter or to tears. Opinions differ as to his merits as a reader, but it is plain that the public thought him unsurpassable. He had always wished to shine as an actor; as a "reader" (it was in truth recitation, and not reading) he came very near to that—especially in such efforts as the murder scene from *Oliver Twist.* The life, too, one of ceaseless travel and excitement, suited him at the time when he was making grave changes in his domestic circumstances; changes which may or may not have been inevitable, but which doubtless helped to urge him along the fatal course. Forster's Biography makes it clear that, from 1857 onwards, Dickens suffered somewhat in character from the effects of this public life; nothing like so much as in health; but he was no longer quite the man of his best literary years. Remember the intensely practical strain in his nature. As a very young man, he allowed himself to be put at a disadvantage with publishers; but this was soon, and energetically, set right; afterwards, he transacted the business of his books with high commercial aptitude. It was the same in everything; subtract his genius, and we have a most capable, upright, vigorous man of business—the very ideal (so much better than all but a few actual examples) of commercial England. It is a surprising combination—such qualities united with those which characterized the author Charles Dickens. To minds of a certain type there appears to be the utmost satisfaction in pointing out that Shakespeare made money, and built "the trimmest house in Stratford town"; but who can seriously suggest that, even *mutatis mutandis,* Shakespeare's business aptitudes and success were comparable with those of Dickens? The author of *Hamlet* indubitably had common sense, but, most happily, business as it is understood among us nowadays had not been dreamt of in Elizabethan England, and one may very safely assert that Shakespeare was no distinguished merchant even in the sense of that day. Dickens might easily have become a great capitalist; and his generosity would have secured him against any self-reproach when treading the ways of capitalism. He reflected with annoyance on the serious loss occasioned him by the lack of American copyright; granted the opportunity, he could have drawn up an international arrangement in this matter which would have been a model of clear-headed justice. After all, what was the financial result of his brilliant and laborious life? He had a large family; his expenses were considerable; he bought himself a country house, which became to him, as an occupation of his leisure, a small Abbotsford. And at his death he leaves an estimated total of £93,000. The merest bagatelle, from a commercial point of view. His readings seem to have brought him, altogether, a matter of some £40,000. What man of business, with a world-wide reputation, would be content to toil to the detriment of his health for such results? I go into these details merely to suggest how a man such as Dickens must have felt regarding the pecuniary question. Save in reference to American copyright, he did not complain; that would have been ignoble, and inconsistent with his habits of mind. But it seemed to him indispensable that he should gain more money than would arrive from his literary work. His sons must go forth into the world as English gentlemen—a term implying so much; his daughters must be made independent; his own mode of life must be on a scale recognized as "respectable" by middle-class England. One need not be much of an optimist to foresee that, as in days gone by, so in a time to come, the spectacle of such a man so beset will be altogether impossible, and the record of such a life will become a matter for wonder and sad smiling.

Restoration House, Rochester

With the utmost precision of punctuality in all details of daily life, he combined a character of sanguine impulsiveness, and as a result thereof could not endure restraints and burdens which ordinary men accept as a matter of course. If he desired a thing, he must at once obtain it; or at all events aim at obtaining it, and with all his energy. He could work day after day—the kind of work which demands a patience, an assiduity, a self-control unintelligible to the mass of mankind; could exhibit in himself, and exact from others, a rare conscientiousness in things small and great; but when it came to any kind of constraint which was not imposed by his own temperament he failed at once. The moralist may remark, in his dry way, that no man can receive so much of the good things of life, and remain unspoilt; that Dickens, moreover, was a very unlikely man to go through the ordeal of world-wide flattery, and draw from it moral benefit. The wonder is that Dickens was spoilt so little. In a day when there exists no writer of supreme acceptance, we are in danger of forgetting what his popularity meant. I suppose that for at least five-and-twenty years of his life, there was not an English-speaking household in the world, above the class which knows nothing of books, where his name was not as familiar as that of any personal acquaintance, and where an allusion to characters of his creating could fail to be understood. When seeking a title for the periodical eventually called *Household Words*—it was in 1849—he seriously suggested "Charles Dickens: Conducted by Himself". It was, he admitted, "a strange idea, but with decided advantages". In any other writer then living, the idea would have been strange indeed, and of anything but decided advantage. Dickens could entertain it without egotism, without ridicule; far and wide, at home and abroad, hands would have clutched eagerly at the magazine bearing such a superscription. He passed it over; but whatever the title of the paper he edited, *Household Words* or *All the Year Round*, the name it bore in all minds was no other than "Charles Dickens".

It is easy to distinguish between the British characteristic of practicality, and the unpleasant attribute of worldliness; but the intensely practical man seldom escapes a tincture of that neighbouring vice. In dismissing as "fanciful" every intrusion of the pure *idea*, the English guard themselves against certain risks, and preserve a pretty even current of national life; but they pay a penalty, understood or not. Dickens is an illustration of it. I cannot do better than copy the words written on this subject by his most intimate friend; they occur in the chapter which tells all that need be told about his domestic troubles. "Not his genius only, but his whole nature, was too exclusively made up of sympathy for, and with, the real in its most intense form, to be sufficiently provided against failure in the realities around him. There was for him no 'city of the mind' against outward ills for inner consolation and shelter. ... By his very attempts to escape the world, he was driven back into the thick of it. But what he would have sought there, it supplies to none; and to get the infinite out of anything so finite, has broken many a stout heart." This, observe, is spoken of a man who was not only "good" in most meanings of the word, but had a profound feeling for the moral significance of the religion he professed. We see the type of nineteenth-century Englishmen; the breed of men who established a commercial supremacy which is (or very lately was) the wonder and the envy of the outer world. You cannot create Lancashire and Yorkshire if at the same time you have to guard a "city of the mind"; much too embarrassing would be the multitude of uneasy questions rushing in at every new step. This typical Englishman has no "detachment". In work or play, he must press onward by the world's high-road. In 1857 Dickens wrote to Forster: "I have now no relief but in action. I am become incapable of rest. I am quite confident I should rust, break, and die, if I spared myself. Much better to die, going. What I am in that way, nature made me first, and my way of life has of late, alas! confirmed." It was a moment of peculiar stress, but that was not needed to explain the letter. As I said in the early pages of this essay, a better education might have done much for Dickens; yet it could hardly have helped him to that "removed ground" where some few men, even in thriving England, were able to possess their souls in peace.

His life was ceaseless activity, mental and physical. After an ailing childhood, he grew into health which perhaps was never robust, but which allowed him to expend the energy of three ordinary mortals. He thought nothing of a twenty-mile walk in the odd hours before dinner, and would not be deterred from it by rain or snow. His position obliged him to give a great deal of time to social and public engagements; yet they never interfered with his literary tasks. He was always ready to take the chair at a meeting for any charitable purpose with which he sympathized, and his speeches on these occasions were masterpieces of their kind. Three of them are worthy of a permanent place among his writings; that spoken on behalf of the Child's Hospital; that in which, at the dinner of the Newspaper Press Fund, he gave his recollections of life as a reporter; that for the Theatrical Fund, in which he sketches, as no other man ever did or could have done, the whole world of the stage, with the drollest humour and the kindliest note of pathos. With a popular audience on such occasions he was most perfectly in touch. Never for a moment did his style or thought rise

above their heads; never was there a suspicion of condescending. He knew
how to bestow pleasant flattery, without ever passing the limits of tact and
taste. If ladies were among his hearers, he always put in a word of jesting
gallantry which was exactly what they liked and expected. Withal, his talk
invariably made appeal to the good and unselfish instincts; it was always
admirable common sense; it was always morally profitable.

The power he had of pursuing his imaginative tasks amid distractions
which most men would find fatal, is especially interesting. Read Forster's
description of the state of things in Dickens's house just before the
Christmas of 1856, whilst *Little Dorrit* was being written. "Preparations
for the private play had gone on incessantly, and in turning the school-
room into a theatre sawing and hammering worthy of Babel continued for
weeks." The novelist became stage-carpenter as well as stage-manager. "All
day long", he writes in a letter, "a labourer heats size over the fire in a great
crucible. We eat it, drink it, breathe it, and smell it. Seventy paint-pots
(which came in a van) adorn the stage." The private play was acted night
after night to overflowing audiences, and not till the 20th of January was
the house clear and quiet. But fiction-writing went on as usual, with never
a hint at difficulty owing to circumstances.

In his letter-writing alone, Dickens did a life's literary work. Nowadays
no one thinks of writing such letters; I mean, letters of such length and
detail, for the quality is Dickens's own. He evidently enjoyed this use of the
pen. Page after page of Forster's "Life" is occupied with transcription from
private correspondence, and never a line of this but is thoroughly worthy of
print and preservation. If he makes a tour in any part of the British isles, he
writes a full description of all he sees, of everything that happens, and writes
it with such gusto, such mirth, such strokes of fine picturing, as appear in no
other private letters ever given to the public. Naturally cheerful beyond the
common wont, a holiday gave him the exhilaration of a school-boy. See how
he writes from Cornwall, when on a trip with two or three friends, in 1843.
"Heavens! if you could have seen the necks of bottles, distracting in their
immense variety of shape, peering out of the carriage pockets! If you could
have witnessed the deep devotion of the post-boys, the maniac glee of the
waiters! If you could have followed us into the earthy old churches we visited, and into the strange caverns on the gloomy sea-shore, and down into
the depths of mines, and up to the tops of giddy heights, where the unspeak-
ably green water was roaring, I don't know how many hundred feet below!
… I never laughed in my life as I did on this journey. It would have done
you good to hear me. I was choking and gasping and bursting the buckle off

the back of my stock, all the way. And Stanfield"—the painter—"got into such apoplectic entanglements that we were obliged to beat him on the back with portmanteaus before we could recover him."

The mention of "bottles, distracting in their immense variety", leads one to speak of the convivial temper so constantly exhibited in Dickens's letters and books. It might be easily imagined that he was a man of large appetite and something of a toper. Nothing of the kind; when it came to actual eating and drinking no man was more habitually moderate. I am not much in the way of attending "temperance" meetings, and cannot say whether the advocates of total abstinence make a point of holding up Dickens's works to reprobation; but I should hardly think they look upon him with great favour. Indeed, it is an odd thing that, writing so much of the London poor, he so seldom refers to the curse of drunkenness. Of drinking there is any amount, but its results serve only for gaiety or comic extravagance. One remembers "Mr Dolls" in *Our Mutual Friend*, a victim to the allurements of gin; he is a pitiful creature, and Jenny, the doll's dressmaker, suffers much from his eccentricities; for all that, we are constrained to laugh at him. A tragedy of drink Dickens never gives us. Criticising Cruikshank's pictured morality, "The Bottle", he points out, truly enough, that the artist had seriously erred in making the habit of drunkenness arise from mere conviviality in persons well-to-do; drink, as a real curse, being commonly the result of overwork, semi-starvation, vile dwellings, and lack of reasonable entertainment. Nowadays he would necessarily have viewed the subject in a graver light. The national habits in this matter have been so greatly changed during the last half-century, that it would now be impossible to glorify the flowing bowl as Dickens does in all his most popular writing. His works must have had a great part in promoting that Christmas joviality which of late years is manifestly on the decline. Whatever the perils of strong drink, his imagination could not dispense with it. One is amused to find him writing to his friend from America: "I wish you drank punch, dear Forster. It's a shabby thing not to be able to picture you with that cool green glass." How it happened that John Forster, after many years of such intimacy, did not make at all events a show of handling the "cool green glass", passes our comprehension. We hear in Dickens's words a note of humorous, yet true, regret; it seemed impossible to him that a man could be in the enjoyment of his fireside if no alcoholic comfort stood at his elbow. Scott, by the by, though as hearty and hospitable a man as ever lived, and in youth no shirker of the bottle, always speaks with grave disapprobation of excessive conviviality. Possibly a difference of rank accounts for this; whilst the upper classes were learning to live with prudence and decency, the lower clung to their old habits. Be that as it may, Dickens could not throw his weight on the side of teetotalism. He held that, if social reforms such as he advocated could only be set in motion, the evils of drink would tend to disappear of themselves. He was right; the tendency showed itself beyond dispute; and if, as some think, drunkenness is again increasing among us, the cause must be sought in the social conditions of a new time—a civilization fraught, perhaps, with quite as many evils as those of the old order.

But not only in holiday time did Dickens live with extraordinary gusto; at his desk he was often in the highest spirits. Behold how he pictured himself, one day at Broadstairs, when he was writing *Chuzzlewit*. "In a bay-window in a one-pair sits, from nine o'clock to one, a gentleman with rather long hair and no neck-cloth, who writes and grins, as if he thought he were very funny indeed. At one he disappears, presently emerges from a bathing-machine, and may be seen, a kind of salmon-colour porpoise, splashing about in the ocean. After that, he may be viewed in another bay-window on the ground-floor eating a strong lunch; and after that, walking a dozen miles or so, or lying on his back on the sand reading a book. Nobody bothers him, unless they know he is disposed to be talked to, and I am told he is very comfortable indeed. He's as brown as a berry, and they *do* say he is as good as a small fortune to the innkeeper, who sells beer and cold punch." Here is the secret of such work as that of Dickens; it is done with delight—done (in a sense) easily, done with the mechanism of mind and body in splendid order. Even so did Scott write, though more rapidly and with less conscious care; his chapter finished before the world had got up to breakfast. Later, Dickens produced novels less excellent with much more of mental strain. The effects of age could not have shown themselves so soon, but for the unfortunate waste of energy involved in his non-literary labours.

Travel was always a great enjoyment to him, and when on the Continent he largely appreciated the spirit of life dissimilar to that of England. His *Pictures from Italy* are not of great value either for style or information; there are better things in his private letters written whilst he travelled than in any volume. For Italy he had no intellectual preparation; he saw everything merely with the eyes of intelligence and good humour. Switzerland and France gave him a better opportunity. Very noticeable is the justice he does to the French character. As a proof of this, and of the fact that his genius did not desert him when he crossed the Channel, nothing could be better than his description of M. Beaucourt, the proprietor of a house he rented at Boulogne. It is a picture—to be put together out of various anecdotes and sketches—really wonderful for its charm. In this little French bourgeois the great novelist had found a man after his own heart—loyal, mirthful, sweet-natured, and made only more likeable by traits especially amusing to an Englishman. "I see little of him now, as, all things being *bien arrangées*, he is delicate of appearing. His wife has been making a trip in the country during the last three weeks, but (as he mentioned to me with his hat in his hand) it was necessary that he should remain here, to be continually at the disposition of the tenant of the property. (The better to do this, he has had roaring dinner parties of fifteen daily; and the old woman who milks the cows has been fainting up the hill, under vast burdens of champagne.)" And what could be more apt, more beautiful, than the words which describe M. Beaucourt as he retires from Dickens's presence, after a little dialogue in which he has shown all the gentle goodness of his heart? "He backed himself down the avenue with his cap in his hand, as if he were going to back himself straight into the evening star, without the ceremony of dying first."

This was at the time of the Anglo-French alliance in the Russian war. How just he could be under less favourable circumstances, and how strongly in contrast with that peculiarly offensive type, the supercilious Englishman abroad, appears in an account of his experiences in leaving Italy by the Austrian frontier. "The Austrian police are very strict, but they really know how to do business, and they do it. And if you treat them like gentlemen they will always respond. ... The thing being done at all, could not be better done, or more politely—though I dare say if I had been sucking a gentish cane all the time, or talking in English to my compatriots, it might not unnaturally have been different." Dickens could always hold his own as a man among men. At all times he was something more than a writer of books; in this respect, as in literary genius, establishing his claim of brotherhood with Fielding and with Scott.

Reading his life, it is with much satisfaction that we come to his last appearance as a public entertainer. The words with which he took leave of his audience at St. James's Hall have frequently been quoted; they breathe a sense of relief and hopefulness very pathetic in the knowledge of what followed. "In but two short weeks from this time I hope that you may enter, in your own homes, on a new series of readings at which my assistance will be indispensable; but from these garish lights I vanish now for evermore, with a heartfelt, grateful, respectful, affectionate farewell." The garish lights had done their work upon him, but he did not recognize it; he imagined that he had but to sit down in his house at Gadshill, and resume the true, the honourable occupation of his life, with assurance that before long all would be

Gad's Hill Place
(As it appeared in Dickens's time)

well with him in mind and body. It was too late, and the book he promised
to his hearers remains in our hands a fragment.

Throughout the pages of *Edwin Drood* there is premonition of the end.
Whether it came of feeble health; whether of the melancholy natural in one
who has just closed a definite epoch of his life, or merely of the theme he
had chosen, there broods over this interrupted writing a shadow of mortal-
ity; not oppressive; a shadow as of the summer eventide, descending with
peaceful hush. We are in and about the old minster of a quiet English town;
among the old graves, to which our attention is constantly directed. It is
touching to read that final chapter, which must have brought back to the
writer's mind the days long past, when, a little boy, he read and dreamt amid
the scenes he was now describing. There is no gloom; he shows us such a
brilliant morning as, after a lifetime, will yet linger in the memory from
days of earliest childhood. He was tired, but not despondent; true to himself, he saw the sunshine above the world's dark places, nourished the hope
of something beyond this present. "Changes of glorious light from moving
boughs, songs of birds, scents from gardens, woods, and fields ... penetrate
into the cathedral, subdue its earthly odour, and preach the Resurrection
and the Life." It was no form of words; what he wrote in that solemn mood

assuredly he believed. Whatever his mistakes and his defects, insincerity had no place among them.

For him, there could be no truer epitaph than the words written by Carlyle on hearing he was dead:

"The good, the gentle, high-gifted, ever-friendly, noble Dickens—every inch of him an honest man".

Dickens-Land

J. A. Nicklin

The central shrine of a literary cult is at least as often its hero's home of adoption as his place of birth. To the Wordsworthian, Cockermouth has but a faint, remote interest in comparison with Grasmere and Rydal Mount. Edinburgh, for all its associations with the life and the genius of Scott, is not as Abbotsford, or as that beloved Border country in which his memory has struck its deepest roots. And so it is with Dickens. The accident of birth attaches his name but slightly to Landport in Southsea. The Dickens pilgrim treads in the most palpable footsteps of "Boz" amongst the landmarks of a Victorian London, too rapidly disappearing, and through the "rich and varied landscape" on either side of the Medway, "covered with cornfields and pastures, with here and there a windmill or a distant church", which Dickens loved from boyhood, peopled with the creatures of his teeming fancy, and chose for his last and most-cherished habitation.

What Abbotsford was to Scott, that, almost, to Dickens in his later years was Gadshill Place. From his study window in the "grave red-brick house" "on his little Kentish freehold"—a house which he had "added to and stuck bits upon in all manner of ways, so that it was as pleasantly irregular and as violently opposed to all architectural ideas as the most hopeful man could possibly desire"—he looked out, so he wrote to a friend, "on as pretty a view as you will find in a long day's English ride. ... Cobham Park and Woods are behind the house; the distant Thames is in front; the Medway, with Rochester and its old castle and cathedral, on one side." On every side he could not fail to reach, in those brisk walks with which he sought, too strenuously, perhaps, health and relaxation, some object redolent of childish dreams or mature achievement, of intimate joys and sorrows, of those phantoms of his brain which to him then, as to hundreds of thousands of his readers since, were not less real than the men and women of everyday encounter. On those seven miles between Rochester and Maidstone, which he discovered to be one of the most beautiful walks in England, he might be tempted to strike off at Aylesford for a short stroll to such a pleasant old Elizabethan mansion as Cobtree Hall, the very type, it may be, of Manor Farm, Dingley Dell or for a longer tramp to Town Mailing, from which he may well have borrowed many strokes for the picture of Muggleton, that town of sturdy Kentish cricket. Sometimes he would walk across the marshes to Gravesend, and returning through the village of Chalk, would pause for a retrospective glance at the house where his honeymoon was spent and a good part of *Pickwick* planned. In the latter end of the year, when he could take a short cut through the stubble fields from Higham to the marshes lying farther down the Thames, he would often visit the desolate churchyard where little Pip was so terribly frightened by the convict. Or, descending the long slope from Gadshill to Strood, and crossing Rochester Bridge—over the balustrades of which Mr Pickwick leaned in agreeable reverie when he was accosted by Dismal Jemmy—the author of *Great Expectations* and *Edwin Drood* would pass from Rochester High Street—where Mr Pumblechook's seed shop looks across the way at Miss Twinkleton's establishment—into the Vines, to compare once more the impression on his unerring "inward eye" with the actual features of that Restoration House which, under another name, he assigned to Miss Havisham, and so round by Fort Pitt to the Chatham lines. And there—who can doubt?—if he seemed to hear the melancholy wind that whistled through the deserted fields as Mr Winkle took his reluctant stand, a wretched and desperate duellist, his thoughts would also stray to the busy dockyard town and "a blessed little room" in a plain-looking plaster-fronted house from which dated all his early readings and imaginings.

Between the "very small and not-over-particularly-taken-care-of boy" and the strong, self-reliant man whose fame had filled two continents, Gadshill Place was an immediate link. Everyone knows the story which Dickens tells of a vision of his former self meeting him on the road to Canterbury.

> "So smooth was the old high road, and so fresh were the horses, and so fast went I, that it was midway between Gravesend and Rochester, and the widening river was bearing the ships, white-sailed or black-smoked, out to sea, when I noticed by the wayside a very queer small boy.
>
> "'Halloa!' said I to the very queer small boy, 'where do you live?'
>
> "'At Chatham,' says he.
>
> "'What do you do there?' said I.

"'I go to school,' says he.

" I took him up in a moment, and we went on. Presently, the very queer small boy says, 'This is Gadshill we are coming to, where Falstaff went out to rob those travellers and ran away.'

"'You know something about Falstaff, eh?' said I.

"'All about him', said the very queer small boy. 'I am old (I am nine), and I read all sorts of books. But *do* let us stop at the top of the hill, and look at the house there, if you please!'

"'You admire that house?' said I.

"'Bless you, sir,' said the very queer small boy, 'when I was not more than half as old as nine, it used to be a treat for me to be brought to look at it. And now I am nine I come by myself to look at it. And ever since I can recollect, my father, seeing me so fond of it, has often said to me, If you were to be very persevering, and were to work hard, you might some day come to live in it. Though that's impossible!' said the very queer small boy, drawing a low breath, and now staring at the house out of window with all his might.

"I was rather amazed to be told this by the very queer small boy; for that house happens to be my house, and I have reason to believe that what he said was true."

As the queer small boy in the *Uncommercial Traveller* said, Gadshill Place is at the very top of Falstaff's hill. It stands on the south side of the Dover road;—on the north side, but a little tower down, is "a delightfully old-fashioned inn of the old coaching days", the "Sir John Falstaff";—surrounded by a high wall and screened by a row of limes. The front view, with its wooden and pillared porch, its bays, its dormer windows let into the roof, and its surmounting bell turret and vane, bears much the same appearance as it did to the queer small boy. But amongst the many additions and alterations which Dickens was constantly making, the drawing-room had been enlarged from a smaller existing one, and the conservatory into which it opens was, as he laughingly told his younger daughter, "positively the last improvement at Gadshill"—a jest to prove sadly prophetic, for it was uttered on the Sunday before his death. The little library, too, on the opposite side of the porch from the drawing-room and conservatory, was a converted bedroom. Its aspect is familiar to most Dickens-lovers from Sir Luke Fildes's famous picture of "The Empty Chair". In summer, however, Dickens used to do his work not in the library but in a Swiss chalet, presented to him by Fechter, the great actor, which stood in a shrubbery lying on the other side of the highroad, and entered by a subway that Dickens had excavated for the purpose. The chalet now must be sought in the terrace garden of Cobham Hall. When Dickens sat at his desk in a room of the chalet, "up among the branches of the trees", the five mirrors which he had put in reflected "the leaves quivering at the windows, and the great fields of waving corn, and the sail-dotted river". The birds and butterflies flew in and out, the green branches shot in at the open windows, and the lights and shadows of the clouds and the scent of flowers and of everything growing for miles had the same free access. No imaginative artist, whether in words or colour, could have desired a more inspiring environment. The back of the house, looking southward, descends by one flight of steps upon a lawn, where one of the balustrades of the old Rochester Bridge had, when this was demolished, been fitted up as a sundial. The lawn, in turn, communicates with flower and vegetable gardens by another flight of steps. Beyond is "the much-coveted meadow" which Dickens obtained, partly by exchange, from the trustees—not of Watts's Charity, as Forster has stated, but of Sir Joseph Williamson's Free School at Rochester. It was in this field that the villagers from neighbouring Higham played cricket matches, and that, just before Dickens went to America for the last time, he held those quaint footraces for all and sundry, described in one of his letters to Forster. Though the landlord of the Falstaff, from over the way, was allowed to erect a drinking booth, and all the prizes were given in money; though, too, the road from Chatham to Gadshill was like a fair all day, and the crowd consisted mainly of rough labouring men, of soldiers, sailors, and navvies, there was no disorder, not a flag, rope, or stake displaced, and no drunkenness whatever. As striking a tribute, if rightly considered, as ever was exacted by a strong and winning personality! One of those oddities in which Dickens delighted was elicited by a hurdle race for strangers. The man who came in second ran 120 yards and leaped over ten hurdles with a pipe in his mouth and smoking it all the time. "If it hadn't been for your pipe," said the Master of Gadshill Place, clapping him on the shoulder at the winning-post, "you would have been first." "I beg your pardon, sir," he answered, "but if it hadn't been for my pipe, I should have been nowhere."

To the hospitable hearth of Gadshill Place were drawn, by the fame of the "Inimitable Boz", a long succession of brilliant men and women, mostly of the Anglo-Saxon race, whether English or American; and if not in the throngs for which at Abbotsford open house was kept, yet with a frequency which would have made literary work almost impossible for the host without remarkable steadiness of purpose and regularity of habits. For Longfellow and his daughters he "turned out", that they might see all of the surrounding country which could be seen in a short stay, "a couple of postilions in the old red jackets of the old red royal Dover road, and it was like a holiday ride in England fifty years ago".

In his study in the late and early months, and his Swiss chalet through the summer, Dickens would write such novels as *Great Expectations*, and the unfinished *Mystery of Edwin Drood*, taking his local colour from spots which lay within the compass of a reasonable walk; and others, such as *A Tale of Two Cities* and *Our Mutual Friend*, to which the circumstances of time and place furnished little or nothing except their influence on his mood. Some of the occasional papers which, in the character of *The Uncommercial Traveller*, he furnished to *All the Year Round*, have as much of the *genius loci* as any of his romances. Even today the rushing swarm of motor cars has not yet driven from the more secluded nooks of Kent all such idylls of open-air vagabondage as this:

> "I have my eyes upon a piece of Kentish road, bordered on either side by a wood, and having on one hand, between the road dust and the trees, a skirting patch of grass. Wild flowers grow in abundance on this spot, and it lies high and airy, with a distant river stealing steadily away to the ocean, like a man's life. To gain the milestone here, which the moss, primroses, violets, bluebells and wild roses would soon render illegible but for peering travellers pushing them aside with their sticks, you must come up a steep hill, come which way you may. So, all the tramps with carts or caravans—the gipsy tramp, the show tramp, the Cheap-Jack—find it impossible to resist the temptations of the place, and all turn the horse loose when they come to it, and boil the pot. Bless the place, I love the ashes of the vagabond fires that have scorched its grass!"

The Kentish road that Dickens thus describes is certainly the Dover Road at Gadshill, from which, of course, there is a steep declivity whether the route is westward to Gravesend or eastwards to Strood and Rochester. In Strood itself Dickens found little to interest him, though the view of Rochester from Strood Hill is an arresting one, with the stately medievalism of Castle and Cathedral emerging from a kind of haze in which it is hard to distinguish what is smoke-wreath and what a mass of crowding roofs. The Medway, which divides Strood from the almost indistinguishably overlapping towns of Rochester, Chatham, and Brompton, is crossed by an iron bridge, superseding the old stone structure commemorated in Pickwick. Mr Pickwick's notes on "the four towns" do not require very much modification to apply to their present state.

"The principal productions", he wrote, "appear to be soldiers, sailors, Jews, chalk, shrimps, officers, and dockyard men. The commodities chiefly exposed for sale in the public streets are marine stores, hard-bake, apples, flat-fish, and oysters. The streets present a lively and animated appearance, occasioned chiefly by the conviviality of the military. ... The consumption of tobacco in these towns must be very great, and the smell which pervades the streets must be exceedingly delicious to those who are extremely fond of smoking. A superficial traveller might object to the dirt, which is their leading characteristic, but to those who view it as an indication of traffic and commercial prosperity, it is truly gratifying."

This description is much less true of Rochester than of its three neighbours, and does no justice to the aspects which Dickens himself presented in the Market Town of *Great Expectations*, and the Cloisterham of *Edwin Drood*. Amid the rather sordid encroachments of a modern industrialism, Rochester still keeps something of the air of an old-world country town, and in the precincts of its Cathedral there still broods a cloistral peace. The dominating feature of the town, from whatever side approached, is the massive ruin of the Norman Keep of Bishop Gundulf, the architect also of London's White Tower. Though the blue sky is its only roof, and on the rugged staircase the dark apertures in the walls, where rafters and floors were once, show like gaping sockets from which the ravens and claws have picked out the eyes, it seems to stand with all the immovable strength of some solid rock on which the waves of rebellion or invasion would have dashed and broken. It is easy to believe the saying of Lambarde, in his *Perambulation of Kent*, that "from time to time it had a part in almost every tragedie". But the grimness of its grey walls is relieved by a green mantle of clinging ivy, and though it can no longer be said of the Castle that it is "bathed, though in ruins, with a flush of flowers", the beautiful single pink grows wild on its ramparts.

From the Castle to the "Bull" in the High Street is a transition which seems almost an anachronism. It is but to follow in the traces of the Pickwick Club. The covered gateway, the staircase almost wide enough for a coach and four, the ballroom on the first floor landing, with card-room adjoining, and the bedroom which Mr Winkle occupied inside Mr Tupman's—all are there, just as when the club entertained Alfred Jingle to a dinner of soles, a broiled fowl and mushrooms, and Mr Tupman took him to the ball in Mr Winkle's coat, borrowed without leave, and Dr Slammer of the 97th sent his challenge next morning to the owner of the coat. The Guildhall, with its gilt ship for a vane, and its old brick front, supported by Doric stone columns, is not so memorable because Hogarth played hopscotch in the colonnade during his *Five Days' Peregrination by Land and Water*, as for the day when Pumblechook bundled Pip off to be bound apprentice to Joe before the Justices in the Hall, "a queer place, with higher pews in it than a church ... and with some shining black portraits on the walls". This was the Town Hall, too, which Dickens has told us that he had set up in his childish mind "as the model on which the genie of the lamp built the palace for Aladdin", only to return and recognize with saddened, grown-up eyes—exaggerating the depreciation a little, for the sake of the contrast—"a mere mean little heap of bricks, like a chapel gone demented". Close by the Guildhall is the Town Clock, "supposed to be the finest clock in the world", which, alas! "turned out to be as moon-faced and weak a clock as a man's eyes ever saw".

On the north side of the High Street, not many yards from the "Bull", is a Tudor two-storied stone-built house, with latticed windows and gables. This is the Charity founded by the will of Richard Watts in 1579, to give lodging and entertainment for one night, and four-pence each, to "six poor travellers, not being rogues or proctors". It furnished the theme to the Christmas cycle of stories, *The Seven Poor Travellers*, the narrator, who treats the waifs and strays harboured one Christmas eve at the Charity to roast turkey, plum pudding, and "wassail", bringing up the number to seven, "being", as he says, "a traveller myself, though an idle one, and being withal as poor as I hope to be".

Farther up the High Street towards Chatham, about a quarter of a mile from Rochester Bridge, are two sixteenth-century houses, with fronts of carved oak and gables, facing each other across the street. One has figured in both *Great Expectations* and *Edwin Drood*, for it is the house of Mr Pumblechook, the pompous and egregious corn and seedsman, and of Mr Sapsea, the auctioneer, still more pompous and egregious. The other— Eastgate House, now converted into a museum—is the " Nun's House", where Miss Twinkleton kept school, and had Rosa Bud and Helena Landless for pupils.

From the hum and traffic of the cheerfully frequented High Street to the calm and hush of the Cathedral precincts entrance is given by Chertsey's or College Yard Gate, which abuts on the High Street about a hundred yards north of the Cathedral. It was this Gate which Sir Luke Fildes sketched, as he has recorded in an interesting letter published in *A Week's Tramp in Dickens-Land*, by W.R. Hughes, for the background of his drawing of "Durdles Cautioning Sapsea". There are, however, two other gatehouses, the "Prior's", a tower over an archway, containing a single room approached by a "postern stair"; and "Deanery Gate", a quaint old house adjoining the Cathedral which has ten rooms, some of them beautifully panelled. Its drawing-room on the upper floor bears a strong resemblance to the room—as depicted by Sir Luke Fildes—in which Jasper entertained his nephew and Neville Landless, but the artist believes that he never saw the interior. It is not unlikely that Dickens took some details from each of the gatehouses to make a composite picture of "Mr Jasper's own gatehouse", which seemed so to stem the tide of life, that while the murmur of the tide was heard beyond, not a wave would pass the archway.

Rochester Cathedral, which overshadows, though in a less insistent and tragic manner, the whole human interest of *Edwin Drood* almost as much as Notre Dame overshadows the human interest in Victor Hugo's romance, preserves some remains of the original Saxon and Norman churches on the site of which it was erected. Its Early English and Decorated Gothic came off lightly from three restorations, but the tower is nineteenth-century vandalism. The Norman west front enshrines in the riches of its sculptured portal, with its five receding arches, figures of the Saviour and His Twelve Apostles, and on two shafts are carved likenesses of Henry I and his Queen. Freeman has pronounced it to be far the finest example of Norman architecture of its kind. The Chapter House Door, a magnificent example of Decorated Gothic, is adorned with effigies representing the Christian and Jewish Churches, which are surrounded by Holy Fathers and Angels who pray for the soul, emblematically represented as a small nude form above them. But it is about the stone-vaulted crypt, where even by daylight "the heavy pillars which support the roof engender masses of black shade", with "lanes of light" between, and about the winding staircase and belfry of the great tower that the spells of the Dickens magic especially cling, and Jasper and Durdles revisit these haunts by the glimpses of the moon as persistently as Quasimodo and the sinister Priest beset with their ghostly presences the belfry of the great Paris minster.

Of the historic imagination Dickens had little or none. He could not evoke, and never had the faintest desire to evoke, a Past that was divided from the Present by an unbridgable chasm. Thus Rochester Castle, though he seldom failed to bring his guests to view it, affected him only with a remote sense of antiquity such as he would have experienced, no more and no less, amongst the Pyramids. But he was keenly sensitive to the influences of a Past which still survived and, by the continuity of a corporate life, made an integral part in the Present. The Cathedral life, in which by virtue of their office canons and dean were living relics of antiquity, and as much the contemporaries as the successors of the ecclesiastics who lay crumbling in the crypt, stirred this sense in him as it had been stirred by the ancient Inns of London. Almost the last words that he wrote were a tribute to the beauty of the venerable fane in which, beneath the monument of the founder of that quaint Charity rendered so famous by his story of *The Seven Poor Travellers*, a simple brass records his birth, death, and burial-place, "To connect his memory with the scenes in which his earliest and his latest years were passed, and with the associations of Rochester Cathedral and its neighbourhood which extended over all his life".

In the old cemetery of St. Nicholas' Church, on the north side of the Cathedral, it was Dickens's desire to be buried, and his family would have carried out his wishes had it not been that the burial-ground had been closed for years and no further interments were allowed. On the south side of the Cathedral is the delightfully old-fashioned terrace known as Minor Canon Row—Dickens's name for it is Minor Canon Corner—where the Reverend Septimus Crisparkle kept house with the "china shepherdess" mother. The "Monks' Vineyard" of *Edwin Drood* exists as "The Vines". Here under a group of elms called "The Seven Sisters" Edwin Drood and Rosa sat when they decided to break their engagement; and opposite "The Seven Sisters" is the "Satis House" of *Great Expectations*, where the lonely and embittered Miss Havisham taught Estella the cruel lessons of a ruined life. It is really Restoration House—Satis House is on the site of the mansion of Master Richard Watts, to whose apologies for no better entertainment of his Sovereign, Queen Elizabeth answered "Satis"—and it takes its name from having received the restored Merry Monarch under its roof on his way to London and the throne. Pepys, who was terrified by the steepness of the castle cliff and had no time to stay to service at the Cathedral, when he had been inspecting the defences at Chatham, found something more to his mind in a stroll by Restoration House, and into the Cherry Garden, where he met a silly shopkeeper with a pretty wife, "and did kiss her".

Dickens would often follow this route of Pepys, but in the reverse direction, that is, through the Vines to Chatham and its lines of fortification, where Mr Pickwick, Mr Winkle, and Mr Snodgrass became so hopelessly entangled in the sham fight which they had gone over from Rochester to see. At No. 11 Ordnance Terrace the little Charles Dickens lived from 1817 to 1821, and at No. 18 St. Mary's Place from 1821 to 1823, the financial troubles, which eventually drove the family into the Marshalsea debtors' prison, and Charles himself into the sordid drudgery of the blacking-shop by Hungerford Stairs, having already enforced a migration to a cheaper and meaner house. In Clover Street (then Clover Lane) the little Dickens went to a school kept by a Mr William Giles, who years afterwards sent to hint, when he was halfway through with *Pickwick*, a silver snuff-box inscribed to the "Inimitable Boz". To the Mitre Inn, in the Chatham High Street, where Nelson had many times put up, Dickens was often brought by his father to recite or sing, standing on a table, for the amusement of parties of friends. He speaks of it in the "Holly Tree Inn" as

> "The inn where friends used to put up, and where we used to go to see parents, and to have salmon and fowls, and be tipped. It had an ecclesiastical sign—the 'mitre'—and a bar that seemed to be the next best thing to a bishopric, it was so snug. I loved the landlord's youngest daughter to distraction—but let that pass. It was in this inn that I was cried over by my little rosy sister, because I had acquired a black eye in a fight."

When the little Charles Dickens was taken away to London inside the stage-coach Commodore—his kind master on the night before having come flitting in among the packing-cases to give him Goldsmith's *Bee* as a keepsake—he was leaving behind for ever, in the playing-field near Clover Lane and the grounds of Rochester Castle and the green drives of Cobham Park, the untroubled dreams of happy childhood. And though he could not know this, yet, as he sat amongst the damp straw piled up round him in the inside of the coach, he "consumed his sandwiches in solitude and dreariness" and thought life sloppier than he had expected to find it. And in *David Copperfield* he has thrown back into those earlier golden days the shadow of his London privations by bringing the little Copperfield, foot-sore and tired, toiling towards dusk into Chatham, "which, in that night's aspect is a mere dream of chalk and drawbridges and mastless ships in a muddy river, roofed like Noah's arks". No doubt the terrible old Jew in the marine-stores shop, who rated and frightened David with his "Oh, my eyes and limbs, what do you want? Oh, my lungs and liver, what do you want? Oh—goroo, goroo!"—until the helpless little fellow was obliged to close with an offer of a few pence instead of half a crown for his waist-coat, is the portrait of some actual Jew dealer whom, in one of the back streets of Chatham, the keen eyes of the precocious child, seeming to look at nothing, had curiously watched hovering like a hideous spider on the pounce behind his grime-encrusted window.

It was old associations that led Dickens so often in his walks from Gadshill Place to Chatham. But the neighbourhood which gave him most pleasure, combining as it did with similar associations an exquisite beauty, was, Forster tells us, the sylvan scenery of Cobham Park. The green woods and green shades of Cobham would recur to his memory even in far-off Lausanne; and the last walk that he ever enjoyed—on the day before his fatal seizure—was through these woods, the charm of which cannot be better defined than in his own description in *Pickwick*.

> "A delightful walk it was; for it was a pleasant afternoon in June, and their way lay through a deep and shady wood, cooled by the light wind which gently rustled the thick foliage, and enlivened by the songs of the birds that perched upon the boughs. The ivy and the moss crept in thick clusters over the old trees, and the soft green turf overspread the ground like a silken mat. They emerged upon an open park, with an ancient hall, displaying the quaint and picturesque architecture of Elizabeth's time. Long vistas of stately oaks and elm trees appeared on every side; large herds of deer were cropping the fresh grass; and occasionally a startled hare scoured along the ground with the speed of the shadows thrown by the light clouds, which swept across a sunny landscape like a passing breath of summer."

The mission on which Mr Pickwick and his two disciples were engaged was, it will be remembered, to convert Mr Tupman from his resolution to forsake the world in a fit of misanthropy, induced by the faithlessness of Rachael Wardle.

> "'If this', said Mr Pickwick, looking about him—'If this were the place to which all who are troubled with our friend's complaint came, I fancy their old attachment to this world would very soon return.'"

Mr Pickwick was right, for when they arrived at the village, and entered that "clean and commodious village alehouse", the "Leather Bottle", they found Mr Tupman set down at a table "well covered with a roast fowl, bacon, ale, and et ceteras", and "looking as unlike a man who had taken leave of the world as possible".

The "ancient hall" of Cobham consists of two Tudor wings, with a central block designed by Inigo Jones. It has a splendid collection of Old Masters, and a music room which the Prince Regent pronounced to be the finest room in England. In the terrace flower garden at the back of the Hall, it may be mentioned again here, is the Swiss chalet from Gadshill Place, which served Dickens for a study in the summer months. The circuit of Cobham

Park is about seven miles, and it is crossed by the "Long Avenue", leading to Rochester, and the "Grand Avenue", which, sloping down from the tenant-less Mausoleum, opens into Cobham village. The inn to which Mr Tupman retired, in disgust with life, still retains the title of the "Leather Bottle", but has mounted for its sign a coloured portrait of Mr Pickwick addressing the Club in characteristic attitude. It was in Cobham village that Mr Pickwick made his notable discovery of the stone with the mysterious inscription—an inscription which the envious Blotton maintained was nothing more than BIL STUMPS HIS MARK. Local tradition suggests that Dickens intended the episode for a skit upon archaeological theories about the dolmens known as Kit's Coty House, and that a Strood antiquary keenly resented the satire. However that may be, Kit's Coty House is not at Cobham, but some miles away, near Aylesford. In Cobham church there is perhaps the finest and most complete series of monumental brasses in this country, most of them commemorating the Lords of Cobham.

Out of the Cobham woods it is not a long walk to the little village of Shorne, where Dickens was fond of sitting on a hot summer afternoon in its pretty, shaded churchyard. This is believed to be the spot which he has described in *Pickwick* as "one of the most peaceful and secluded churchyards in Kent, where wild flowers mingle with the grass, and the soft landscape around forms the fairest spot in the garden of England". A picturesque lane leads into the road from Rochester to Gravesend, on the outskirts of the village of Chalk. Here, in a corner house on the south side of the road, Dickens spent his honeymoon, and many of the earlier chapters of *Pickwick* were written. In February of the following year—1837—Dickens and his wife returned to the same lodgings, shortly after the birth of his eldest son. Chalk church is about a mile from the village. There was formerly above the porch the figure of an old priest in a stooping attitude, holding an upturned jug. Dickens took a strange interest in this quaint carving, and it is said that, whenever he passed it, he took off his hat or gave it a nod, as to an old acquaintance.

Very different to the soft and genial landscapes about Cobham is the grey and desolate aspect of another haunt which Dickens loved to frequent. This was the "meshes" around Cooling. In winter, when it was possible to make a short cut across the stubble fields, he would visit Cooling churchyard not less seldom than in summer he would go to sit in the churchyard of Shorne. First, however, he would have to pass through the village of Higham, where, too, was his nearest railway station, though he often preferred to walk over and entrain at Gravesend or Greenhithe. But the pleasant tinkle of harness bells was a familiar sound in the night to the Higham villagers, as the carriage was sent down from Gadshill Place to meet the master or his friends returning from London by the ten o'clock train. Dickens took a kindly and active interest in the affairs of the village, and the last cheque which he ever drew was for his subscription to the Higham Cricket Club.

The flat levels that stretch away from beyond Higham towards the estuary of the Thames are more akin to the characteristics of Essex than of Kent. The hop gardens are dwarfed and stunted, and presently hops, corn, and pasture give place to fields of turnips, which show up like masses of jade on the chocolate-coloured soil. The bleak churchyard of Cooling, overgrown with nettles, lies amongst these desolate reaches, which resound at evening with the shrill, unearthly notes of sea-gulls, plovers, and herons. Beyond the churchyard are the marshes, "a dark, flat wilderness", as Dickens has described it in *Great Expectations*, "intersected with dykes and mounds and gates, with scattered cattle feeding on it"; still farther away is the "low, leaden line" of the river, and the "distant, savage lair", from which the wind comes rushing, is the sea. It was in this churchyard that the conception of the story sprang into life, and there are actually not five but ten little stone lozenges in one row, with three more at the back of them, which suggested to Dickens the five little prematurely cut off brothers of Pip. The grey ruins of Cooling Castle attracted him no less than the grey and weather-beaten churchyard. Besides some crumbling and broken walls there is a gate tower, with an inscription on fourteen copper plates, the writing in black, the ground of white enamel, with a seal and silk cords in their proper colours which made known to all and sundry the purpose for which Lord Cobham—whose granddaughter married, for one of her five husbands, Sir John Oldcastle, the Lollard martyr—had erected this castle.

> "Knoweth that beth and schul be
> That i am mad in help of the cuntre
> In knowyng of whych thyng
> This is chartre and witnessyng."

No forge stands now on the site of Joe Gargery's smithy, where, as the hammer rang on the anvil to the refrain—

> "Beat it out, beat it out—Old Clem!
> With a clink for the stout—Old Clem!
> Blow the fire, blow the fire—Old Clem!
> Roaring drier, soaring higher—Old Clem!"

Pip would see visions of Estella's face in the glowing fire or at the wooden window of the forge, looking in from the darkness of the night, and flitting away. But though the smithy has gone, the "Three Jolly Bargemen", where Joe would smoke his pipe by the kitchen fire on a Saturday night, still survives as the "Three Horseshoes"—the inn to which the secret-looking man who stirred his rum and water with a file, brought Magwitch's two one-pound notes for Pip, and the redoubtable Jaggers, the autocrat of the Old Bailey, with his burly form, great head, and huge, cross-examining forefinger announced to Pip his Great Expectations. Down the river in the direction of yonder "distant savage lair", from which the wind comes rushing, lie those long reaches, between Kent and Essex, "where the river is broad and solitary, where the waterside inhabitants are very few, and where lone public-houses are scattered here and there"—the lonely riverside on which Pip and Herbert sought a hiding-place for Magwitch until the steamer for Hamburg or the steamer for Rotterdam could be boarded, as she dropped down the tide from the Port of London. Whether on the Kent or the Essex side, the cast of the scenery corresponds with equal closeness to Dickens's description. Slimy stakes stick out of the mud, and slimy stones stick out of the mud, and red landmarks and tidemarks stick out of the mud, and old roofless buildings slip into the mud, and all about is stagnation and mud! The desolate flat marshes look still more weird by reason of the tall pollards that lean over them like spectres. Far away are the rising grounds, between which and the marshes there appears no sign of life except here and there in the foreground a melancholy gull. The course which the boat, bearing the hunted man took from Mill Pond stairs through the crowded shipping of the Pool, past the floating Custom House at Gravesend, and onwards, skirting the little creeks and mudbanks where the Thames widens to the sea—when every sound of the tide flapping heavily at irregular intervals against the shore, and every ripple, were fraught with the terror of pursuit—exemplifies in the most striking way the rapidity and instinctive ease of Dickens's observation. Forster says:

"To make himself sure of the actual course of a boat in such circumstances, and what possible incidents the adventure might have, Dickens hired a steamer for the day from Black wall to Southend. Eight or nine friends, and three or four members of his family, were on board, and he seemed to have no care, the whole of that summer day (22nd of May, 1861), except to enjoy their enjoyment and entertain them with his own in shape of a thousand whims and fancies; but his sleepless observation was at work all the time, and nothing had escaped his keen vision on either side of the river."

Scattered amongst the deserted reaches along the riverside may be seen such lonely farmhouses or taverns as suggest the aspect of the alehouse, "not unknown to smuggling adventurers"—for the "owling", that is, the smuggling industry, had flourished for centuries in these parts—to which the fugitives were led by a twinkling light in the window up a little cobbled causeway, and where Dickens placed that amphibious creature, "as slimy and smeary as if he had been low-water mark too", who exhibited a bloated pair of shoes "as interesting relics that he had taken from the feet of a drowned seaman washed ashore". This type of the gruesome long-shoremen whom Dickens had encountered in his waterside rambles, as he collected the materials for *Great Expectations*, was afterwards elaborated in the Rogue Riderhood of *Our Mutual Friend*.

"Swamp, mist, and mudbank"—if that is the dominant impression made by the view of the Thames off the Cooling marshes, it is not the only and the invariable impression. Even the bleak churchyard, at the foot of the cold, grey tower, is sometimes strewn by the light and flying gust "with beautiful shadows of clouds and trees". And from the Old Battery, where Joe would smoke his pipe with a far more sagacious air than anywhere else, as Pip strove to initiate him into the mysteries of reading and writing by the aid of a broken slate and a short piece of slate pencil, it is "pleasant and quiet" to watch the vessels standing out to sea with their white sails spread, and the light struck aslant, afar off, upon a cloud or sail or green hillside or silvery waterline.

To the west of Cooling Castle, beyond wide fields—turnips or cabbages—of the colour of dark-green jade, the Church of Cliffe, with its lichgate, standing out boldly from its ridge of chalk, overlooks a straggling village of old and weather-boarded houses. It would be into the road from Cliffe to Rochester, at a point about half a mile from Cooling, that Uncle Pumblechook's chaise-cart would debouch when he took Mrs Joe to Rochester market "to assist him in buying such household stuffs and goods as required a woman's judgment".

Between the scenery about Cooling and Cliffe and the scenery of the valley of the Medway from Rochester to Maidstone there is all the difference between a November fog and a brilliant summer's day. At the foot of Rochester Castle, from which the long vista of the valley, lying between two chalk ranges of hills that form the watershed of the Medway, stretches far away to a distant horizon, the Esplanade extends along the east side of the river, and there it was that Edwin Drood and Rosa met for the last time and to speak of their separate plans. For a few miles along the valley the natural beauty of the scene is spoilt by the cement works of Borstal, Cuxton, and Wouldham, and the brickworks of Burham. The piles of clay and chalk, the beehive furnaces, and the chimneys vomiting smoke and flame, almost reproduce the characteristics of the Black Country or of a northern manufacturing district. But, when But-ham has been left behind, the bright emerald pastures, the tender green of springing corn or the gold of waving harvests, and the orchards—a dazzling sight in May with the snowy clouds of pear and plum and cherry blooms, and the delicate pink-and-white of the apple blossom—more than justify the appellation claimed for Kent of the garden of England. Opposite to Cuxton, on the western bank, the village of Snodland stands at the junction of Snodland Brook with the Medway. It has been conjectured that Snodland Weir, a mile or so up the brook, was in Dickens's mind when he described Mr Crisparkle's pilgrimages to Cloisterham Weir in the cold rimy mornings, and his discovery, first of Edwin Drood's watch in a corner of the weir, and then, after diving again and again, of his shirt-pin "sticking in some mud and ooze" at the bottom. The nearest weir on the Medway is at Allington, seven or eight miles above Rochester, and Cloisterham Weir was but "full two miles" away.

Before Allington can be reached, in ascending the Medway, the river is spanned by an ancient stone bridge, of pointed arches and triangular buttresses, at Aylesford. The ancient Norman church, and the red roofs and crowding gables of the picturesque and historic village, are set in a circle of elm trees, with a background of rising chalk downs beyond. Those who have investigated with perhaps "an excess"—as Wordsworth would say— "of scrupulosity" all the details of Pickwickian topography are inclined to believe that the wooden bridge, upon which the chaise hired by the Club to make the journey from Rochester to Dingley Dell came hopelessly to grief, was Aylesford Bridge, transmuted for the nonce from Kentish ragstone into timber. However that may be, there is a matter of genuine history which has signalized in no common way this old-world village. At this ford, the lowest on the Medway, the Jutes under Hengist and Horsa routed the British in a battle which decided the predominating strain of race in future Men of Kent and Kentish Men: natives of Kent, that is, according as they dwell on the right or left bank of the Medway. A farmhouse with the name of Horsted, at the point farther back where the Rochester to Maidstone road is joined by the road from Chatham, stands, it is believed, on the grave of Horsa. And about a mile and a half north of Aylesford, a grey old cairn, set on a green sward in the midst of a cornfield, is also closely associated with the first great victory won by English people on the soil which they were destined to make their own and distinguish with their name. In his *Short History of the English People* J.R. Green says of this cromlech:

"It was from a steep knoll on which the grey weather-beaten stones of this monument are reared that the view of their first battlefield would break on the English warriors; and a lane which still leads down from it through peaceful homesteads, would guide them across the ford which has left its name in the little village of Aylesford. The Chronicle of the conquering people tells nothing of the rush that may have carried the ford, or of the fight that went straggling up through the village. It only tells that Horsa fell in the moment of victory, and the flint heap of Horsted, which has long preserved his name, and was held in after-time to mark his grave, is thus the earliest of those monuments of English valour of which Westminster is the last and noblest shrine. The victory of Aylesford did more than give East Kent to the English; it struck the keynote of the whole English conquest of Britain."

This cromlech, known as Kit's Coty House, consists of three upright dolmens of sandstone, with a fourth, much larger, crossing them above horizontally. In a neighbouring field there is another group of stones, scattered in disarray amongst the brushwood, to which, as also to Stonehenge and other so-called "Druidical" remains, there attaches the local superstition that they cannot be counted. It would be pleasanter to believe that the current story, to which reference has already been made, that Dickens was poking fun at the antiquarian's reverence for this hoary relic in his narrative of Mr Pickwick's "BIL STUMPS" inscription, is altogether erroneous. Certainly it is open to anyone who wishes to be incredulous, for there is as much dissimilarity as possible between the massive cromlech near Aylesford and the small slab that Mr Pickwick discovered at Cobham.

The most salient feature in the Medway valley between Rochester and Maidstone is the height of Blue Bell, or Upper Bell. Here Dickens, who as he said, had come to realize that the Rochester to Maidstone road passed through some of the most beautiful scenery in England, would often picnic with his visitors. Undulating slopes of pasture and cornfields, hop gardens, orchards, and woodlands, with many a deep-sunk lane embowered in overarching trees that rise from hedgerow clusters of dog-rose, ivy, and honeysuckle, and with snugly nestling homesteads and quaintly-cowled "oast-houses" sprinkled here and there, sweep across the valley, through which the river winds in sinuous curves, onwards to a long range of hills upon the skyline.

Somewhere in this district Dickens came across the types of the old-fashioned and jovially comfortable home of the English yeoman, represented by his Manor Farm, Dingley Dell, and of the little country town, represented by the Muggleton of *Pickwick*, in which local enthusiasm for cricket was ardent, if the standard of skill was somewhat low. The most plausible identification of the home of Mr Wardle is with Cobtree Hall, which divides the parishes of Boxley and Allington; and it is probable that the original of Muggleton was Town Malling, which is also known as West Malling.

In the Jubilee Edition of *Pickwick* Mr Charles Dickens the Younger introduced a woodcut of High Street, Town Malling, with a note to the following effect:

> "Muggleton, perhaps, is only to be taken as a fancy sketch of a small country town; but it is generally supposed, and probably with sufficient accuracy, that, if it is in any degree a portrait of any Kentish town, Town Malling, a great place for cricket in Mr Pickwick's time, sat for it."

Town Malling does not correspond with the description of Muggleton in its distance from Rochester. It is only seven and a half, instead of fifteen miles, from Rochester. And it is not a corporate town. But:

> "Everybody whose genius has a topographical bent knows perfectly well that Muggleton is a corporate town, with a mayor, burgesses, and freemen, and anybody who has consulted the addresses of the mayor to the freemen, or the freemen to the mayor, or both to the corporation, or all three to Parliament, will learn from thence what they ought to have known before, that Muggleton is an ancient and loyal borough, mingling a zealous advocacy of Christian principles with a devoted attachment to commercial rights; in demonstration whereof, the mayor, corporation, and other inhabitants have presented, at divers times, no fewer than one thousand four hundred and twenty petitions against the continuance of negro slavery abroad, and an equal number against any interference with the factory system at home; sixty-eight in favour of the sale of livings in the Church, and eighty-six for abolishing Sunday trading in the street."

If Town Malling has not had so distinguished a political history as that which Dickens assigned to Muggleton, it has a pretty cricket ground, not far removed from the High Street, and the reputation of having in past years distinguished itself in the local cricket of this district of Kent. It is not difficult to believe, then, that Dumkins and Podder here made their gallant stand for All-Muggleton against the Dingley Dellers, and that at the Swan—otherwise the Blue Lion—the Pickwick fellowship shared the conviviality of the rival teams, until Mr Snodgrass's notes of the evening's transactions faded away into a blur in which there was an indistinct reference to "broiled bones" and "cold without". The stately ruins of a Benedictine Abbey, founded by Bishop Gundulf, give to the town an attraction of a severer kind.

From Town Mailing to Cobtree Hall, supposing the double identification to be correct, should be a walk of not above two miles "through shady lanes and sequestered footpaths", the delightful scenery of which made Mr Pickwick feel regret to arrive in the main street of "Muggleton". The distance, however, is in fact something more than two miles as the crow flies. Cobtree Hall is a green-muffled Elizabethan mansion, of red brick, faced with stone, and looks out over an undulating country of orchards and hop fields. It has been altered and enlarged since the days of *Pickwick*, but the kitchen is just such another large, old-fashioned kitchen as befits the Christmas games and wassail that had been kept up at Manor Farm, Dingley Dell, "by old Wardle's forefathers from time immemorial". The dining-room, though modernized, has a massive marble mantelpiece not unsuited to that "capacious chimney up which you could have driven one of the new patent cabs, wheels and all", and in which a blazing fire used to roar every evening, not only when its warmth was grateful, but for a symbol, as it were, of old Wardle's attachment to his fireside. This was the kind of antiquity which made the most direct appeal to Dickens's sentiment and imagination—not a remote and historic antiquity, but the furthest extent of a living link between the Present and the Past. In many an old house of Kentish yeoman or squire Dickens would have seen some such long, dark-panelled room as the best sitting-room at Manor Farm, with four-branched, massive silver candlesticks in all sorts of recesses and on all kinds of brackets; with samplers and worsted landscapes of ancient date on the walls; with a very old lady in lofty cap and faded silk gown in the chimney corner, where she had sat on her little stool as a girl more than half a century before, and with a hearty, rubicund host presiding over a mighty bowl of wassail, something smaller than an ordinary washhouse copper, in which the hot apples would "hiss and bubble with a rich look and a jolly sound that were perfectly irresistible". Or when the carpet was up, the candles burning brightly, and family, guests, and servants were all ranged in eager lines, longing for the signal to start an old-fashioned country dance as, from a shady bower of holly and evergreens at the upper end of the room, the two best fiddles and only harp of the nearest market town prepared to strike up, it is no wonder that such a lover of unspoilt, natural manners as Boz declared, "If any of the old English yeomen had turned into fairies when they died, it was just the place in which they would have held their revels".

A triangular piece of ground, with a sprinkling of elms about it, is all that is left of the rookery in which Mr Tupman met with an accident from the unskilful marksmanship of Winkle. At the back of the house is the pond where Mr Winkle's reputation as a sportsman led him into another catastrophe, and his skating exposed itself as of anything but a graceful and "swan-like" style; where, too, Mr Pickwick revived the sliding propensities of his boyhood with infinite zest until the ice gave way with a "sharp, smart crack", and Mr Pickwick's hat, gloves, and handkerchief, floating on the surface, were all of Mr Pickwick that anyone could see.

Cobtree Hall, it has been mentioned, divides the parishes of Boxley and Allington, the initials of which are carved on a beam in the kitchen that suggests Phiz's plate of "Christmas Eve at Mr Wardle's". In Aylesford the tomb of the prototype, according to local tradition, of "Mr Wardle" bears the inscription, "Also to the memory of Mr W. Spong, late of Cobtree, in the Parish of Boxley, who died November 15th, 1839". Boxley village is near the ancient Pilgrims' Road to Canterbury, and here Alfred Tennyson stayed in 1842. Park House, nearer the Medway, was the home of Edward Lushington, who married Tennyson's sister Cecilia, and in its grounds Tennyson found the setting for the prologue to the "Princess". The "happy faces" of "the multitude, a thousand heads", by which the "sloping pasture" was "sown", under "broad ambrosial aisles of lofty lime", had probably come from Maidstone on the annual jaunt of that town's Mechanics' Institute. The village of Allington stands on the other side of the Medway, though the boundaries of the parish extend beyond the right bank of the river. Allington Castle, which the Medway half-encircles with a sweeping bend, was one of the seven chief castles of Kent. It was here that Sir Thomas Wyatt, the elder, diplomatist, poet, and lover of Anne Boleyn, who with the gallant and ill-fated Surrey "preluded", in a more exact sense than it could be said of Chaucer, "those melodious bursts that fill the spacious times of great Elizabeth", was able to proclaim, in an epistle to "Mine own John Poins":

> "I am here in Kent and Christendome,
>   Among the Muses where I read and rhyme".

Hither there comes, in Tennyson's "Queen Mary", to Sir Thomas Wyatt, the younger, his man William, with news of "three thousand men on Penenden heath all calling after you, and your worship's name heard into Maidstone market, and your worship the first man in Kent". And Wyatt sets out to lead a rising which will end on Tower Hill, and setting out, looks back and cries:

> "Ah, grey old castle of Allington, green field
> Beside the brimming Medway, it may chance
> That I shall never look upon you more".

"The brimming Medway"—the epithet is as just as Tennyson's descriptive epithet almost invariably proves to be. For at Allington the Medway, which from Aylesford Bridge to Allington Lock has dwindled to a narrow stream, swells out into a broad expanse, where many boats can easily move abreast. If the Cloisterham Weir of *Edwin Drood* were really the nearest weir on the Medway to Rochester, then Allington Lock would be the place. But it has been pointed out on an earlier page that the distances do not tally in the novel and in actuality, and Dickens may have had in mind the weir on Snodland Brook.

The country round Maidstone abounds in the "happy valleys" portrayed in the epilogue to the "Princess", with "grey halls alone among their massive groves", and "here and there a rustic tower half lost in belts of hop and breadths of wheat". The gyres and loops of the Medway, too, afford through the screen of woodlands and orchards "the shimmering glimpses of a stream". To the credulous enthusiasm of an early eighteenth-century native of Strood, that Anne Pratt who did for English wild flowers what White of Selborne did for English wild birds, "travellers who have beheld in other lands the various scenes of culture—the olive grounds of Spain or Syria, the vineyards of Italy, the cotton plantations of India, or the rose fields of the East—have generally agreed that not one of them all equals in beauty our English hop gardens". To Dickens himself such a panegyric of the Kentish hop gardens would have scarcely seemed exaggeration, but he would have hastened to add the dismal antithesis of the missionary bishop—"Only man is vile". He had barely settled in at Gadshill Place when he wrote:

> "Hop-picking is going on, and people sleep in the garden, and breathe in at the keyhole of the house door. I have been amazed, before this year, by the number of miserable base wretches, hardly able to crawl, who go hop-picking. I find it is a superstition that the dust of the newly picked hop, falling freshly into the throat, is a cure for consumption. So the poor creatures drag themselves along the roads, and sleep under wet hedges, and get cured soon and finally."

The county town of Kent is situated not only on the Medway, but on the pilgrim road to Canterbury, and of a monastic hospital for pilgrims and other poor travellers there still survive some relics. Overlooking the river stand some fine old houses, and the conspicuous grey square tower of All Saints, built by the proud Archbishop Courtenay, the enemy of Wycliffe, in the fourteenth century. Here is the tomb of Grocyn, that "lord of splendid lore Orient from old Hellas' shore", who was appointed master of the collegiate church in 1506. One of the sixteen palaces that the Archbishops of Canterbury could boast in days gone by is preserved as the local school of science and art, a dedication to public use which commemorates the Jubilee of Queen Victoria in 1887. The Corporation Museum is an even more interesting and beautiful structure. It was Chillington Manor House, a seat of the Cobham family, and, though it has had a new wing annexed to it, it is an exceptionally well preserved and beautiful example of Elizabethan domestic architecture, with its latticed windows, jutting gables, elaborately moulded timber, and pillared chimneys. In the panel of an oak fireplace is a carved head of Dickens, by a local carver named Hughes, who was employed at Gadshill Place. To Maidstone Jail Dickens proposed to carry Sir Luke Fildes, in order that he might make a picture of Jasper in the condemned cell, and do something which would surpass Cruikshank's illustration to *Oliver Twist*, in which Fagin's terror-stricken vigil in the murderer's cell is portrayed.

At Maidstone the southern limit may be considered to have been reached of the district of Kent which can be distinguished as "Dickensland" in the most intimate sense, as lying within the radius of the novelist's habitual walks and drives from his residence at Gadshill. It does not enter into the scope of this brief essay to describe topographically other parts of Kent. But it will be excusable to glance very slightly at Dickens's associations with Canterbury, Broadstairs, Deal, Dover, and the famous London-to-Dover road through Rochester, Chatham, and Canterbury.

No one, perhaps, who has ever read *Little Dorrit*, whatever else in the novel may slip the memory, fails to recall the oracular utterance of Mr F.'s aunt that "There's milestones on the Dover road". To the opening of *A Tale of Two Cities* the colour and atmosphere of the time in which it is set, and of the drama which is to be developed, are given at once by the alarm of the passengers of the Dover coach as they walk up Shooter's Hill to ease the horses, when the furious galloping of a horseman is heard behind them—the supposed highwayman proving to be, however, Jerry Cruncher, messenger at Tellson's Bank by day, and at night an "agricooltural character" of ghoulish avocations. David Copperfield trudged the Dover road, footsore and hungry, when he left Murdstone and Grinby's blacking warehouse to throw himself on the compassion of Betsey Trotwood, "and got through twenty-three miles on the straight road" to Rochester and Chatham on a certain Sunday. Afterwards, when he had found a home and a protecting providence with his aunt, he met with his "first fall in life" on the Canterbury coach, being asked by the coachman to resign the box seat to a seedy gentleman, who proclaimed that "'Orses and dogs is some men's fancy. They're wittles and drink to me."

> "I have always considered this as the first fall I had in life. When I booked my place at the coach office, I had had 'Box Seat' written against the entry, and had given the bookkeeper half a crown. I was got up in a special greatcoat and shawl, expressly to do honour to that distinguished eminence; had glorified myself upon it a good deal; and had felt that I was a credit to the coach. And here, in the very first stage, I was supplanted by a shabby man with a squint, who had no other merit than smelling like a livery stables, and being able to walk across me, more like a fly than a human being, while the horses were at a canter."

Pip, in *Great Expectations*, makes many expeditions to and fro on the Dover road, between Rochester and London; and on one of them, riding outside, has the two convicts, bound for the hulks moored off the marshes, as fellow passengers on the back seat.

At Canterbury it is not possible to establish the identity of Dr Strong's house—"a grave building in a courtyard, with a learned air about it that seemed very well suited to the stray rooks and jackdaws who came down from the Cathedral towers, and walked with a clerkly bearing on the grass plot"—but Canon Benham has asserted his conviction that Mr Wickfield's house—where David made the acquaintance of Agnes and of Uriah Heep—is at the corner of Broad Street and Lady Wotton's Green, though it is another residence, by the West Gate, which is represented on the picture postcards.

The Royal Fountain Hotel in St. Margaret's Street (formerly the Watling Street) is recognized as the County Inn at which Mr Dick used to sleep when he went over to Canterbury to visit David Copperfield at Dr Strong's school. All the little bills which he contracted there, it will be remembered, were referred to Miss Trotwood before they were paid; a circumstance which caused David to think "that Mr Dick was only allowed to rattle his money, and not to spend it". A less pretentious establishment, the "little inn" where

Mr Micawber put up on his first visit to Canterbury, and "occupied a little room in it partitioned off from the commercial, and strongly flavoured with tobacco smoke", is probably the Sun Inn in Sun Street. Here Mr and Mrs Micawber entertained David to "a beautiful little dinner"—

> "Quite an elegant dish of fish; the kidney end of a loin of veal roasted; fried sausage meat; a partridge and a pudding. There was wine, and there was strong ale; and after dinner Mrs Micawber made us a bowl of hot punch with her own hands."

Local tradition at Broadstairs used to point to Fort House, on the cliff by the Coastguard Station, as the holiday residence at which Dickens wrote most of *Bleak House*. But though it has been rechristened from the title of the novel, by an owner who demolished Dickens's summer home, and built the existing pseudo-Gothic structure on its foundations, no part of *Bleak House* was written at Broadstairs. Dickens, however, for many summers, visited the little town on the curving bay between Margate and Ramsgate; the Albion Hotel, where he notes that "the landlord has delicious hollands", No. 12 (now 31) High Street, and Lawn. House, near Fort House, receiving him at different times. At Broadstairs he wrote a portion of *Pickwick*, of *Nicholas Nickleby*, and *The Old Curiosity Shop*, and he also stayed there while engaged on the *American Notes*, *Dombey and Son*, and *David Copperfield*. He forsook it at last, because it had become too noisy, but he has left an agreeable picture of it in *Our English Watering Place*; but a passage in a letter to Forster invests it with still gayer colours:

> "It is the brightest day you ever saw. The sun is sparkling on the water so that I can hardly bear to look at it. The tide is in, and the fishing boats are dancing like mad. Upon the green-topped cliffs the corn is cut and piled in shocks; and thousands of butterflies are fluttering about, taking the bright little red flags at the mastheads for flowers, and panting with delight accordingly."

To the characters and the *mise en scène* of his novels, however, Broadstairs appears to have contributed nothing, except that the lady whose aversion to donkeys furnished so strong an idiosyncrasy to Miss Betsey Trotwood's character was a native, not of Dover, as in the novel, but of Broadstairs.

Dover, besides giving a local habitation to David's aunt, is associated with *A Tale of Two Cities*, since it was here that Mr Lorry made the startling revelation to Miss Manette that her father had been "Recalled to Life".

The vignette of eighteenth-century Dover is executed with true Dickensian verve:

"The little narrow, crooked town of Dover hid itself away from the beach, and ran its head into the chalk cliffs like a marine ostrich. The beach was a desert of heaps of sea and stones tumbling wildly about, and the sea did what it liked, and what it liked was destruction. It thundered at the town, and thundered at the cliffs, and brought the coast down, madly. The air among the houses was of so strong a piscatory flavour that one might have supposed sick fish went up to be dipped in it, as sick people went down to be dipped in the sea. A little fishing was done in the port, and a quantity of strolling about by night, and looking seaward: particularly at those times when the tide made, and was near flood. Small tradesmen, who did no business whatever, sometimes unaccountably realized large fortunes, and it was remarkable that nobody in the neighbourhood could endure a lamplighter."

It was to Dover that Dickens went when he was labouring with unusual difficulty over *Bleak House*, and lamenting his inability to "grind sparks out of this dull anvil". At Dover, on his second series of readings, he found "the audience with the greatest sense of humour", and "they laughed with such really cordial enjoyment, when Squeers read the boys' letters, that the contagion" was irresistible even to Dickens himself.

Deal, as it was in 1853, is rapidly but vigorously sketched in chapter xlv of *Bleak House*. Esther Summerson arrives from a night journey by coach, eager and anxious to help, if possible, Richard Carstone, the unhappy victim of the fatal chancery lawsuit:

"At last we came into the narrow streets of Deal; and very gloomy they were, upon a raw misty morning. The long flat beach, with its irregular houses, wooden and brick, and its litter of capstans, and great boats, and sheds, and bare upright poles with tackle and blocks, and loose gravelly waste places overgrown with grass and weeds, wore as dull an appearance as any place I ever saw. The sea was heaving under a thick white fog; and nothing else was moving but a few early rope-makers, who, with the yarn twisted round their bodies, looked as if, tired of their present state of existence, they were twisting themselves into cordage. But when we got into a warm room in an excellent hotel, and sat down, comfortably washed and dressed, to an early breakfast (for it was too late to think of going to bed), Deal began to look more cheerful. ... Then the fog began to rise like a curtain; and numbers of ships, that we had had no idea were near, appeared. I don't know how many sail the waiter told us were then lying in the Downs. Some of these vessels were of grand size: one was a large Indiaman, just come home: and when the sun shone through the clouds, making silvery pools in the dark sea, the way in which these ships brightened, and shadowed, and changed, amid a bustle of boats putting off from the shore to them, and from them to the shore, and a general life and motion in themselves and everything around them, was most beautiful."

That Dickens was essentially a "Kentish Man", in spite of the absence of a birth qualification, in spite, too, of his long residence in London, and of his peculiarly intimate knowledge of the byways and nooks and corners of London, ample proof has by this time been given. To this, however, may be added Forster's significant statement that, "Excepting always the haunts and associations of his childhood, Dickens had no particular sentiment of locality, and any special regard for houses he had lived in was not a thing noticeable in him". This was not surprising. The conditions of life in a modern capital under most circumstances, but especially for anyone who has made many removes, tend to produce the impression that a man's rooftree only represents the transient shelter of a caravanserai rather than an abiding habitation on which memory has stamped indelible traces. Nor can even the most extended associations of maturity take the place of the imperishable links forged in the most susceptible years of fresh and sensitive childhood. For Dickens this vital distinction was emphasized both by natural idiosyncrasy and by the pressure of events which shaped his destiny.

> "If it should appear", he says, speaking of himself under the mask of David Copperfield, "from anything I may set down in this narrative, that I was a child of close observation, or that as a man I have a strong memory of my childhood, I undoubtedly lay claim to both of these characteristics."

The change from Chatham and Rochester to London was indissolubly connected in his mind with a change in the family fortunes that deprived him of the ordinary advantages and pleasures open to any average boy of even the lower middle classes. It ushered in a period of misery and degradation that he could never recall without acute suffering. The few years of happiness which he enjoyed before he was carried away to London in the stage coach "Commodore", at the age of nine, were divided from a strenuous and successful manhood by so dark a gulf as to concentrate all the powers of recollection upon them with a desperate kind of intensity. It was the realization of a childish ambition conceived in that halcyon era which drew him to Gadshill, and he returned again and again to the contemplation of his earliest dreams and imaginings. He wrote from Gadshill of his old nurse—the original, it can hardly be doubted, of Peggotty:

"I feel much as I used to do when I was a small child, a few miles off [i.e. at Ordnance Terrace, Chatham], and somebody—who, I wonder, and which way did she go when she died?—hummed the evening hymn, and I cried on the pillow—either with the remorseful consciousness of having kicked somebody else, or because still somebody else had hurt my feelings in the course of the day."

For the second number of *Household Words*, when he "felt an uneasy sense of there being a want of something tender, which would apply to some universal household knowledge", he composed a little paper about "a child's dream of a star". It was the story of a brother and sister, constant child companions, who used to make friends of a star, watching it together until they knew when and where it would rise, and always bidding it good-night, so that when the sister dies, the lonely brother still connects her with the star, which he then sees opening as a sea of light, and its rays making a shining pathway from earth to heaven. It was his sister Fanny, who had often wandered with him at night in St. Mary's Churchyard, near their home at Chatham, looking up at the stars, and her death, shortly before the paper was written, had revived the fancy of childhood. In *The Uncommercial Traveller* he revisits "Dullborough", and the first discovery he makes is that the station has swallowed up the playing field of the school to which he went during his last two years at Chatham.

"It was gone. The two beautiful hawthorn trees, the hedge, the turf, and all those buttercups and daisies, had given place to the stoniest of jolting roads; while, beyond the station, an ugly dark monster of a tunnel kept its jaws open, as if it had swallowed them and were ravenous for more destruction. The coach that had carried me away, was melodiously called Timpson's Blue-eyed Maid [it was really called the 'Commodore'], and belonged to Timpson, at the coach office up street; the locomotive engine that had brought me back was called severely No. 97, and belonged to S.E.R., and was spitting ashes and hot water over the blighted ground. ... Here, in the haymaking time, had I been delivered from the dungeons of Seringapatam, an immense pile (of haycock), by my countrymen, the victorious British (boy next door and his two cousins), and had been recognized with ecstasy by my affianced one (Miss Green), who had come all the way from England (second house in the terrace) to ransom me and marry me."

In playful vein Dickens professes to record his disappointment at failing to receive any recognition from a "native", in the person of a phlegmatic greengrocer, when he revisits Rochester, and revives the associations of haunts beloved in childhood.

"Nettled by his phlegmatic conduct, I informed him that I had left the town when I was a child. He slowly returned, quite unsoftened, and not without a sarcastic kind of complacency, Had I? Ah! and did I find it had got on tolerably well without me? Such is the difference (I thought when I had left him a few hundred yards behind, and was by so much in a better temper) between going away from a place and remaining in it. I had no right, I reflected, to be angry with the greengrocer for his want of interest; I was nothing to him; whereas he was the town, the cathedral, the bridge, the river, my childhood, and a large slice of my life, to me."

That is one side of the medal, but the other is displayed in *David Copperfield*, when little Mr Chillip, the doctor, welcomes David back to England:

"'We are not ignorant, sir,' said Mr Chillip, slowly shaking his little head again, 'down in our part of the country, of your fame. There must be great excitement here, sir,' said Mr Chillip, tapping himself on the forehead with his forefinger. 'You must find it a trying occupation, sir!'"

A feature of Dickens's literary manner, so insistent that the most superficial reader cannot miss it, is the individual and almost human aspect which a street or a landscape, a house or a room, takes on in his description. A typical example may be selected in Mr Wickfield's house:

"A very old house bulging out over the road; a house with long, low lattice windows bulging out still farther, and beams with carved heads on the ends bulging out too, so that I fancied the whole house was leaning forward, trying to see who was passing on the narrow pavement below."

It was the outcome of an acute nervous sensibility, amounting at times to an almost neurotic irritability, such as peeps out from his confession that the shape of Earl Grey's head, when he was a Parliamentary reporter in the Gallery, "was misery to me and weighed down my youth". This peculiarity of temperament had established itself when, a little delicate and highly strung child, he used to transfer the scenes and happenings of the novels to which he stole away from the other boys at their play, into the setting of his own existence, and "every barn in the neighbourhood, every stone in the church, and every foot of the churchyard, had some association of its own connected with these books, and stood for some locality made famous in them".

There has seldom, perhaps, been such an absence of complexity in genius of a high order as there was in Dickens's character. But though there was no complexity, there were two very different aspects—acute sensibility was not incompatible with a virile and buoyant spirit. And so Dickens's associations with the country which he loved best and knew most intimately were, on the one side, those of a dreamy childhood, on the other, of a lusty zest in out-door life and the rustic jollity of an old-world "Merry England". The sports and revels of Manor Farm, Dingley Dell, have all the exuberance of Lever's Irish novels. Dickens must have often taken part in merrymakings such as he describes, on flying visits that are not recorded in Forster, before he sat down to write about them during his honeymoon at Chalk. As the Master of Gadshill, his lithe, upright figure, clad in loose-fitting garments, and rather dilapidated shoes, was a familiar sight to all the country neighbours, as he swung along the shady lanes, banked high with hedges that were full of violets, purple and white, ferns, and lichens, and mosses. Often he would call at the old-fashioned "Crispin and Crispianus", on the north side of the London road just out of Strood, for a glass of ale, or a little cold brandy and water, and sit in the corner of the settle opposite the fireplace, looking at nothing but seeing everything. In the chapter on "Tramps" in *The Uncommercial Traveller*, he imagines him-self to be the travelling clockmaker, who sees to something wrong with the bell of the turret stable clock up at Cobham Hall, and after being regaled in the enormous servants' hall with beef and bread, and powerful ale, sets off through the woods till the town lights appear right in front, and lies for the night at the ancient sign of Crispin and Crispianus. The floating population of the roads,—the travelling showman, the cheap-jack, the harvest- and hop-ping-tramps, the young fellows who trudge along barefoot, their boots slung over their shoulders, their shabby bundles under their arms, their sticks newly cut from some roadside wood, and the truculently humorous tramp, who tells the Beadle: "Why, blow your little town! who wants to be in it? Wot does your

dirty little town mean by comin' and stickin' itself in the road to anywhere?"—
all are closely scanned and noted, as they mount or descend Strood Hill in
perennial procession. Dickens was himself a sturdy and inveterate pedestrian.
When he suffered from insomnia he would think nothing of rising in the middle of the night and taking a thirty miles' spin before breakfast.

> "Coming in just now," he wrote in his third year at Gadshill, "after twelve
> miles in the rain, I was so wet that I have had to change and get my feet into
> warm water before I could do anything."

In February, 1865, he wrote:

> "I got frost-bitten by walking continually in the snow, and getting wet in
> the feet daily. My boots hardened and softened, hardened and softened, my
> left foot swelled, and I still forced the boot on; sat in it to write, half the day;
> walked in it through the snow, the other half; forced the boot on again next
> morning; sat and walked again; and being accustomed to all sorts of changes
> in my feet, took no heed. At length, going out as usual, I fell lame on the
> walk, and had to limp home dead lame, through the snow, for the last three
> miles—to the remarkable terror, by the way, of the two big dogs."

It is hardly necessary to say that Dickens never so absorbed the local spirit
and genius of that part of rural England which he knew and loved best as
the Brontës absorbed the spirit of the Yorkshire moorlands, or Mr Hardy
the spirit of Wessex, or Mr Eden Phillpotts the spirit of Dartmoor, or Sir A.
Quiller-Couch the spirit of the "Delectable Duchy". He was too busy and
preoccupied a man for this, and had too much of his life and work behind
him, when he made his permanent home in "Dickens-Land". And Gadshill
was too near to the bustle and stir of Chatham to furnish a purely idyl-
lic environment or entirely unsophisticated rusticity. But it is not unduly
fanciful to discover the influence of Kentish scenery, with its bright, clear
atmosphere, its undulating slopes of green woodland and green hop fields,
pink-and-white orchards, and golden harvests—the prettiest though not the
most beautiful scenery in England—upon his conception of a typical

> "English home—grey twilight pour'd
> On dewy pastures, dewy trees,
> Softer than sleep—all things in order stored,
> A haunt of ancient Peace".

Though no local name is attached to it, and no local tradition identifies it with any particular spot, there is no difficulty in fixing in the very heart of "Dickens-Land" the picture upon which the "Battle of Life" is opened: the joyous dance of two girls, "quite unconstrained and careless", "in one little orchard attached to an old stone house with a honeysuckle porch", "while some half-dozen peasant women standing on ladders, gathering apples from the trees, stopped in their work to look down, and shared their enjoyment".

"As they danced among the orchard trees and down the groves of stems and back again, and twirled each other lightly round and round, the influence of their airy motion seemed to spread and spread, in the sun-lighted scene, like an expanding circle in the water. Their streaming hair and fluttering skirts, the elastic grass beneath their feet, the boughs that rustled in the morning air— the flushing leaves, their speckled shadows on the soft green ground—the balmy wind that swept along the landscape, glad to turn the distant windmill, cheerily—everything between the two girls, and the man and team at plough upon the ridge of land, where they showed against the sky as if they were the last things of the world—seemed dancing too."

Something, too, of the love of good cheer, quaint old Christmas customs, of junketings in ancient farmhouse kitchens and the parlours of ancient hostelries, which has made Dickens the early Victorian apostle of Yuletide "wassail", can be derived from his having "powlert up and down" in a county abounding with comfortable manor houses and cosy inns. It is a ripe and mellow tradition of good cheer, that is quite distinct from the bovine stolidity of a harvest home in George Eliot's Loamshire or the crude animalism of Meredith's Gaffer Gammon. For Kent, even from the time of Caesar's Commentaries, has been "the civil'st place of all the isle".

That is the aspect of Dickens's country on the one side—the side which, some years before he established himself at Gadshill, he mapped out, already knowing it intimately, to show to Forster in a brief excursion:

"You will come down booked for Maidstone (I will meet you at Paddockwood), and we will go thither in company over a most beautiful little line of railroad. The eight miles walk from Maidstone to Rochester, and a visit to the Druidical altar on the wayside, are charming. This could be accomplished on the Tuesday; and Wednesday we might look about us at Chatham, coming home by Cobham on Thursday."

The other side—the dreary marshes lying between the Medway and the Thames, a dark, flat wilderness intersected by dykes and mounds and gates—had associations not less intimate. In *David Copperfield* Dickens transferred the dreams and the events of his childhood to an alien setting. In *Great Expectations* he invents a fictitious story in harmony with scenes in which he delighted to retrace his childish memories. Again, the amphibian creatures which he lightly sketches in *Great Expectations*, and more elaborately in *Our Mutual Friend*, had first impressed themselves on his imagination as he rambled, a tiny, eager-eyed boy, about the dockyards and waterside alleys of Chatham, or made trips to Sheerness with "Mr Micawber", that is to say, his father, in the Navy Pay yacht, though he long afterwards pursued his studies of them more exhaustively at Wapping and the Isle of Dogs, and in expeditions with the Thames police. It was from a walk with Leech through Chatham by-streets that he gathered the hint of Charley Hexam and his father, for *Our Mutual Friend*, from the sight of "the uneducated father in fustian and the educated boy in spectacles".

But when Dickens took Rochester once more for the background of a story in *Edwin Drood* there seems, to us in our knowledge of the event, something almost ominous. It suggests Waller's famous simile of the stag that returns to die where it was roused. Dickens's last visit to the town was to stimulate his imagination for the conference between Datchery and the Princess Puffer at the entrance to the "Monks' Vineyard". On the last day of his life he was busy, in the chalet in the garden at Gadshill Place, embodying the fancies which he had gathered and fused on that last visit. On the last page which he was to write he endeavoured to record—for the last time —his sense of the atmosphere of the old city.

> "A brilliant morning shines on the old city. Its antiquities and ruins are surpassingly beautiful, with the lusty ivy gleaming in the sun, and the rich trees waving in the balmy air. Changes of glorious light from moving boughs, songs of birds, scents from gardens, woods, and fields—or, rather, from the one great garden of the whole of the cultivated island in its yielding time—penetrate into the Cathedral, subdue its earthy odour, and preach the Resurrection and the Life. The cold stone tombs of centuries ago grow warm, and flecks of brightness dart into the sternest marble corners of the building, fluttering there like wings."

On the eve of that last day he had more than once expressed his satisfaction at having finally abandoned all intention of exchanging Gadshill for London. He had done this still more impressively a few days before.

"While he lived, he said, he should wish his name to be more and more asso-ciated with the place; and he had a notion that when he died, he should like to lie in the little graveyard belonging to the Cathedral at the foot of the Castle wall."

Half of his wish had to go unfulfilled; the other half has been realized in a different but a profounder sense than that in which it is conceived. While he lives, in the creations of his humour and pathos, airy things of fun and frolic, tenderness and tears, his name is more and more associated "with the scenes"— to borrow the words of the memorial tablet in Rochester Cathedral—"in which his earliest and his latest years were passed", scenes that "from the associations … which extended over all his life" have the best right to be known as "Dickens-Land".

A Dictionary of Characters, Places, etc., in the Novels & Stories of Dickens

The references in this Dictionary are to the pages of the volumes in the Standard Edition. The names of the novels and stories are represented by initials, according to the following list:

Names in Volumes XVIII and XIX, and in *A Child's History of England*, *The Uncommercial Traveller*, and the minor sketches of Volume I, are not included in this Dictionary. As a rule only the first reference to a character is given, but in some cases one or two additional references are given for special reasons.

A

Adams, the head-boy at Dr Strong's, afterwards called to the bar. D. C. 175.

Adams, Captain, Lord Frederick Verisopht's second in the duel with Sir Mulberry Hawk. N. N. 514.

Adams, Jack, a friend of whom Cousin Feenix told an ill-timed story. D. S. 400.

Adams, Mr, cleric in a Life Assurance Office. H. D. 438.

Admiral, a judge in a juvenile court-martial. H. R. 459.

"Admiral Napier", an omnibus. S. B. 357.

Affery Flintwinch, See *Flintwinch, Affery.*

African knife-swallower, a member of Vincent Crummles's company. N. N. 486.

Aged, The, Wemmick's name for his old father. See *Wemmick, Mr*

Agnes, See *Fleming, Agnes; Copperfield, Agnes; Wickfield, Agnes.*

Agnes, Mrs Bloss's maid. S. B.221.

Aix, where Captain Doubledick met the French officer who had caused Major Taunton's death. C. S. 76.

Akerman, Mr, governor of Newgate. B. R. 374

Akershem, Sophronia, who married Mr Lammle for money and found out her mistake; Mr Lammle was similarly deceived in her, and they then agreed to prey upon society. O. M. F. 8, 93.

Albany, where Fledgeby lived. O. M. F. 214.

Alice, youngest of the Five Sisters of York. N. N. 45.

Alice, daughter of a wealthy London bowyer; loved by Hugh Graham, but eloped with a nobleman; returned repentant. M. H. C. 445

Alick, a damp earthy child in red worsted socks. S. B. 77.

Alicumpaine, Mrs H. R. 481.

Allen, Arabella, who eloped with Mr Winkle, against her brother's will that she should marry Bob Sawyer. P. P. 296.

Allen, Benjamin, medical student, friend of Bob Sawyer, and brother of Arabella Allen; ultimately went to India as a surgeon. P. P. 316.

All-Muggleton, a cricket club that played the Dingley Dell club. P. P. 70.

Allonby, visited by the idle apprentices. L. T. 394.

Alphonse, page to Mrs Wititterly. N. N. 207.

Amelia, a client of Mr Jaggers. G. E. 120, 121.

Amelia, daughter of a stout lady at Ramsgate. S. B. 264.

America Square, where the house of Dringworth Brothers was. C. S. 255.

Analytical Chemist, name given to Veneering's butler. O. M. F. 8.

"Angel", an inn at Bury. P. P. 165.

Anglo-Bengalee Disinterested Loan and Life Assurance Company, a fraudulent company promoted by Montague Tigg. M. C. 339.

Anne, Mr Dombey's housemaid, who married Towlinson. D. S. 190.

Anny, an aged pauper. O. T. 134.

Apothecary, who attended Paul Dombey in his illness at Dr Blimber's school. D. S. 190.

Apothecary's Apprentice. O. T. 33.

Apple-woman, Old. N. N. 384.

Apprentice, Bony, of Mr Lobbs. P. P. 180.

Apprentices, Two, to Mr Snagsby. B. H. 102.

Archbishop of Greenwich, name applied to a head waiter. O. M. F. 535.

Artful Dodger. See *Dawkins, John*.

Arthur, half-brother of Miss Havisham; an accomplice of Compeyson. G. E. 133, 254.

Artist, Street, Cheerful. C. S. 329.

Artist, Street, Humble. C. S. 325.

Ashford, Nettie, child bride of William Tinkling. H. R. 457

Assistant to Miss Pupford. C. S. 277.

Astley's, a circus visited by the families of Kit and Barbara, O. C. S. 221; visited by Mr George, B. H. 233; described, S. B. 78.

Atherfield, Mrs, mother of the Golden Lucy. C. S. 121.

Attendant, at railway station. O. M. F. 601.

Attendant, Elderly Female, at the Foundling Hospital. C. S. 507.

Attorney, who bid for David Copperfield's caul. D. C. 1.

Attorney-General, at Darnay's trial for treason. T. T. C. 44.

Attorneys. P. P. 468.

Aunt, of Arabella Allen, who eloped from her house. P. P. 418.

Aunt, of Kate, who understood Florence Dombey's secret sorrow. D. S. 269.

Aunt, of Mrs Lammle. O. M. F. 95

Aunt, of the Emperor of France. H. R. 460.

Aunt, Mr F.'s, a legacy left to Flora Finching by her deceased husband; she disliked Arthur Clennam. L. D. 124.

Austin Friars, where Mr Fips's office was. M. C. 476.

Avenger, The. See *Pepper*.

Avignon, where Captain Doubledick lived for a time. C. S. 75.

"Away with Melancholy", played on the flute by Dick Swiveller, O. C. S. 326; sung by Eugene Wrayburn, O. M. F. 236.

Ayresleigh, Mr, a debtor. P. P. 438.

B

B, Master, a ghost. C. S. 210.

Babley, Richard. See *Dick, Mr*

Baby, in the Pocket family. G. E. 136

Baby, of a juggler's wife. D. S. 188.

Baby, of Jenny. B. H. 82.

Baby, Mrs Veneering's. O. M. F. 95

Baby, Mrs Peerybingle's. C. B. 128.

Baby, Moist, of the landlady of "The Tilted Waggon". E. D. 147.

Baby, Mr Chillip's, with the heavy head and goggle eyes. D. C. 245.

Baby, Spotted. C. S. 191.

Bachelor, The. See *Garland*.

Bachelor friend, of Tulkinghorn. B. H. 236.

Badger, Bayham, a doctor in London, with whom Richard Carstone studied; constantly referred to Mrs Badger's first two eminent husbands; cousin of Mr Kenge. B. H. 133.

Badger, Mrs Bayham, wife of Mr Bayham Badger, who was her third husband. B. H. 133.

Bagman, The One-eyed, whom Mr Pickwick met at Eatanswill and at Bristol; he told "The Bagman's Story" and "The Story of the Bagman's Uncle". P. P. 139, 529.

"Bagman's Story, The." P. P. 140.

Bagnet, Malta, daughter of Mr and Mrs Bagnet. B. H. 296.

Bagnet, Matthew, nicknamed *Lig num Vitae*, an ex -artilleryman; he acknowledged his wife's greater capacity, but not to her, because "discipline must be maintained". B. H.295. Called *Joseph* at B. H. 513.

Bagnet, Mrs, wife of Matthew Bagnet.. B. H. 296.

Bagnet, Quebec, daughter of Mr and Mrs Bagnet. B. H. 296.

Bagnet, Woolwich, son of Mr and Mrs Bagnet. B. H. 296.

Bagstock, Major Joseph, a retired army officer who lived near Miss Tox; he made Mr Dombey's acquaintance, and brought about his second unhappy marriage; constantly referred to himself as J. B., Joey B., &c. D. S. 67.

Bailey, Benjamin, called Bailey Junior, the boots at Todgers's boarding-house; afterwards employed by Montague Tigg; finally became a hairdresser. M. C. 98, 113.

Bailey, Captain, whom David Copperfield cut out at a ball. D. C. 207.

Bailie Mac Something, and four syllables after it. P.P. 532.

Bailie's Grown-up Son. P. P. 532.

Bailie's Three Daughters. P. P. 532.

Bailie's Wife, one of the best creatures that ever lived. P. P. 532.

Baker, cousin of Mr Fezziwig's housemaid. C. B. 23.

Baker, with whom Mrs Bardell kept company. P. P. 376.

Baker, who was angry with Harold Skimpole. B. H. 462.

Balderstone, Thomas, Mrs Gattleton's brother, called Uncle Tom; an ardent Shakespearean. S. B. 320.

"Bald-faced Stag", a public house. M. C. 440.

Ball's Pond, where Mr Perch lived, D. S. 188; where Theodosius Butler and his wife lived, S. B. 252.

Bamber, Jack, a law clerk, P. P. 215; joined Master Humphrey's circle, M. H. C. 493

Banger, Captain, a vestryman. R. P. 474

Bangham, Mrs, charwoman in the Marshalsea. L. D. 48.

Banks, Major, an old East India director, a disguise of Meltham. H. D. 445

Bantam, Angelo Cyrus, Grandmaster at Bath. P. P. 386.

Baps, Mr, the dancing-master at Dr Blimber's establishment; keen on a fiscal argument. D. S. 155.

Baps, Mrs, wife of Mr Baps. D. S. 155.

"Bar", guest of Mr Merdle's. L. D. 196.

Barbara, Mr Garland's servant; married to Kit Nubbles. O. C. S. 128.

Barbary, Miss, godmother and aunt of Esther Summerson; sister of Lady Dedlock. B. H. 12.

Barbary, Mrs Captain, of Cheltenham. L. D. 111.

Barbox Brothers, a name of Mr Jackson (q.v.), in *Mugby Junction*. C. S. 441.

Bardell, Martha, widow of a custom-house officer, Mr Pickwick's landlady, who brought an action for breach of promise against him. P. P. 118.

Bardell, Tommy, son of Mrs Bardell. P. P. 119.

Bargeman, father of Mick Walker. D. C. 119.

Bark, lodging-house keeper and receiver of stolen goods. R. P. 436

Barker, Phil. O. T. 145.

Barker, William, waterman, transported as a convict; afterwards a bus conductor. S. B. 108.

Barkis, Mr, a carrier who married Clara Peggotty. D. C. 49.

Barley, Clara, Herbert Pocket's sweetheart, afterwards his wife. G. E. 275.

Barley, Old Bill, father of Clara Barley; a gouty, drunken, bedridden man. G. E. 274.

Barmaid, at Rochester. P. P. 12.

Barmaid, at the "George and Vulture". P. P. 326.

Barmaid, at the "Saracen's Head". N. N. 429.

Barmaid, at the "Town Arms", Eatanswill, bribed to hocus the brandy of fourteen electors. P. P. 131.

Barmaid, who supplied Captain Cuttle. D. S. 429.

Barnacle, Clarence, also called Barnacle, Junior, son of Tite Barnacle, and employed in the Circumlocution Office; a great ass, but the dearest fellow. L. D. 85, 162.

Barnacle, Ferdinand, a sprightly young barnacle, private secretary to Lord Decimus Barnacle. L. D. 91, 443.

Barnacle, Lord Decinms Tite, head of the Barnacle family, uncle of Tite Barnacle. L. D. 117.

Barnacle, Tite, in the Circumlocution Office. L. D. 84.

Barnacles, Three Miss Tite, daughters of Tite Barnacle. L. D. 84.

Barnard's Inn, where Pip lived with Herbert Pocket. G. E. 125.

Barnet, where Oliver Twist first met the Artful Dodger. O. T. 41.

Barney, a Jewish confederate of Fagin, employed as waiter at the "Three Cripples". O. T. 82.

Barnstaple. C. S. 254.

"Baron of Grogzwig", a story in *Nicholas Nickleby*. N. N. 52.

Barronneau, Henri, landlord at the "Cross of Gold", who had the misfortune to die. L. D. 8.

Barronneau, Madame, who married M. Rigaud, and was murdered by him. L. D. 8.

Barsad, John, assumed name of Solomon Pross (q.v.).

Bartholomew Close. G. E. 120.

Barton, Jacob, a grocer, Mrs Malderton's brother, who was not ashamed of his business. S. B. 273.

Bastille, captured by the French revolutionaries. T. T. C. 154.

Bates, Belinda, a young lady who married Alfred Starling. C. S. 217.

Bates, Charley, one of Fagin's pickpockets; reformed and became a grazier. O. T. 47.

Bath, visited by Mr Pickwick and friends. P. P. 385.

Bayton, Mr, husband of Mrs Bayton. O. T. 28.

Bayton, Mrs, a woman buried by the parish. O. T. 26.

Bazzard, Mr, Mr Grewgious's clerk, who had a thorn of anxiety which he hoped would come out at last. H. D. 80, 100.

Beadle. B. H. 28.

Beadle. P. P. 179.

Beadle, of the church where Paul Dombey was christened. D. S. 44.

Beadle, of the church where Walter Gay and Florence Dombey were married. D. S. 616.

Beadle, who watched Captain Cuttle. D. S. 542.

Beadle, Harriet. See *Tattycoram*.

Bear-leader, in a procession. T. T. C. 112.

Beau, who gave away a bride. D. S. 45.

"Beauty, The", Captain Boldheart's ship. H. R. 471.

Beauvais, to which Dr Manette belonged. T. T. C. 179.

Beaver, Nat, a sea captain. C. S. 218.

Bebelle, pet form of Gabrielle (q.v.).

Beckwith, Alfred, a disguise assumed by Meltham to prove Slinkton's guilt. H. D. 443, 448

Becky, barmaid in a public-house at Hampton. O. T. 121.

Bedwin, Mrs, housekeeper to Mr Brownlow. O. T. 60.

Beggar. B. R. 155.

Beggar woman, on whom Dr Strong bestowed his gaiters. D. C. 183.

"Begone dull Care", referred to by Dick Swiveller. O. C. S. 40.

Belinda, a correspondent of Master Humphrey. M. H. C. 467.

Belize. C. S. 145.

"Bell, The", at Berkeley Heath, where Mr Picklviek and party lunched. P. P. 545.

Bell Yard, where the Necketts lived. B. H. 160.

Bella, a young girl prisoner, sister or Emily. S. B. 203.

Bella, Miss Pupford's housemaid. C. S. 277, 281.

Bellamy's Kitchen, frequented by Members or Parliament. S. B. 114.

Belle, Scrooge's old sweetheart. C. B. 25, 27

Belle Savage, where Mr Weller stopped. P. P. 96.

Beller, Henry, toast-master, a convert to temperance. P. P. 358.

Belling, one of Squeers's pupils, a Taunton boy. N. N. 25, 27.

Bellows, Brother, guest of Mr Merdle. L. D. 197.

Bellringer, in the church where Walter Gay and Florence Dombey were married. D. S. 616.

Belltott, Mrs, maid to Miss Maryon; widow of a non-commissioned officer. C. S. 150.

Belvawney, Miss, a member of Vincent Crummles's theatrical company. N. N. 228.

Ben, a servant at "The Two Robins". L. T. 384.

Ben, a waiter. C. S. 62.

Ben, guard of a coach. O. T. 282.

"Bench", a guest of Mr Merdle. L. D. 197.

Benjamin. B. R. 49.

Benjamin, Mr Pell's clerk P. P. 476.

Benton, Miss, housekeeper to Master Humphrey. M. H. C. 503, 468.

Berinthia, called Berry, niece of Mrs Pipchin. D. S. 79.

Bet or Betsy, a Female thief in Fagin's gang. O. T. 49.

Bethnal Green, where Bill Sikes stayed. O. T. 105, 145.

Betley, Mr, a lodger with Mrs Lirriper. C. S. 343.

Betsey, a servant with Benjamin Britain. C. B. 232.

Betsey Jane, a child of Mrs Wickam's uncle referred to by Mrs Wickam. D. S. 83.

Betsy. See *Bet.*

Betsy, Mrs Raddle's servant. P. P. 345

Bevan, Mr, an American who befriended Martin Chuzzlewit and Mark Tapley; he advanced money to enable them to return to Britain. M. C. 217.

Bevan, Mrs, referred to by Mrs Nickleby. N. N. 410.

Beverley, Mr, otherwise Loggins. S. B. 92

Bevis Marks, where Sampson Brass carried on his legal business. O. C. S. 65, 184.

Bib, Julius Washington Merryweather, an American, in the lumber line. M. C. 423.

Biddy, a second cousin or Mr Wopsle, at first an assistant in her grandmother's school, afterwards nurse to Mrs Gargery; became Joe Gargery's second wife; had loved Pip, but was neglected by him. G. E. 31.

Biffin, Miss, referred to by Mrs Nickleby. N. N. 373.

Bigby. Mrs, mother of Mrs Meek. R. P. 363.

Bigwig Family. C. S. 51.

Biler, nickname of Robin Toodle. See *Toodle.*

Bill, a coach guard. M. C. 441.

Bill, a gravedigger. O. T. 30

Bill, a turnkey. P. P. 449

Billickin, Mrs, a candid lady who let lodgings to Rosa Bud and Miss Twinkleton. E. D. 215.

Billsmethi, Master, son of Signor Billsmethi. S. B. 193.

Billsmethi, Miss, daughter of Signor Billsmethi. S. B. 192.

Billsmethi, Signor, who kept a dancing academy. S. B. 191.

Bilson and Slum, a city firm. P. P. 530

Bintrey, Mr, lawyer to Walter Wilding. C. S. 509.

Bird, Little Nell's, a linnet, kept for her by Kit. O. C. S. 73, 81.

Birmingham, where Mr Winkle senior lived. P. P. 549.

Bishop. P. P. 179.

"Bishop", guest of Mr Merdle. L. D. 196.

Bishopsgate Street Without, where Brogley the broker lived. D. S. 90.

Bitherstone, Bill, of Bengal, a former friend of Major Bagstock. D. S. 98.

Bitherstone, Master, son of Bill

Bitherstone, a child in Mrs Pipchin's establishment at Brighton. D. S. 79.

Bitzer, a light-haired light porter; general spy and informer at Mr Bounderby's Bank. H. T. 247.

"Black Badger", a public-house frequented by the Game Chicken. D. S. 245.

"Black Boy", an inn at Chelmsford. P. P. 212.

"Black Lion", inn in Whitechapel. B. R. 79.

Blackey, a street beggar. R. P. 433

Blackheath, where the Rokesmiths lived, O. M. F. 534; where Salem House was, D. C. 56.

Blackmore, Mr, an entertainer in Vauxhall Gardens. S. B. 95.

Blackpool, Mrs, Stephen Blackpool's drunken wife. H. T. 302.

Blackpool, Stephen, who had known a peck of trouble; he was unjustly suspected of robbing the Bank, but was cleared after his death. H. T. 298.

"Bladud, Prince, The True Legend of", MS. found by Mr Pickwick. P. P. 395.

Blandois, M. See Rigaud, M.

Blathers, a Bow Street officer. O. T. 171.

Blazo, Colonel Sir Thomas, with whom Jingle said he once played cricket. P. P. 72.

Bleak House, Mr Jarndyce's house in Hertfordshire. B. H. 24, 51. Also the name of the house given to Allan Woodcourt and Esther Summerson by Mr Jarndyce. B. H. 662.

Bleeding Heart Yard, where Doyce & Clennam's works were, and where

Mr Casby's house property was. L. D. 78.

Blight, Young, boy and clerk to Mortimer Lightwood. O. M. F. 68.

Blimber, Cornelia, daughter of Dr Blimber and a teacher in his school; afterwards married to Mr Feeder. D. S. 112.

Blimber, Doctor, head of a private school in Brighton where Paul Dombey received his education. Original, Dr Everard. D. S. 111.

Blimber, Mrs, wife of Dr Blimber, who would have liked to know Cicero. D. S. 112.

Blinder, Mrs, a friend of the Neckett family. B. H. 160.

Blockitt, Mrs, nurse to Mrs Dombey at Paul's birth. D. S. 3.

Blockson, Mrs, a charwoman employed by Miss Knag. N. N. 172.

Blogg, Mr, a beadle. O. M. F. 159.

"Blood-drinker's Burial", Miss Petowker's recitation. N. N. 131, 246.

Bloss, Mrs, boarder of Mrs Tibbs. S. B. 223.

Blossom, Little, Betsey Trotwood's name for Dora Copperfield. D. C. 462.

Blotton, Mr, a member of the Pickwick Club. P. P. 4.

Blowers, Mr, an eminent counsel, B. H. 4.

"Blue Boar", an inn in the village where Pip was brought up. G.E. 76.

"Blue Boar", at Leadenhall Market. P. P. 349

"Blue Boar" or "Blue Bull", an inn in Whitechapel where David

Copperfield was left to be called for. D. C. 55.

"**Blue Dragon**", an inn near Salisbury. M. C. 7, 21.

"**Blue Lion**", an inn at Muggleton. P. P. 73.

"**Blue Lion and Stomach-warmer**", an inn at Great Winglebury. S. B. 307.

Bluffy, a familiar name of Mr George. B. H. 296.

Blunderstone, a village in Suffolk, where David Copperfield was born. Original, Blundeston, in Suffolk. D. C. 2.

Boarders, Thirty, at Westgate House. P. P. 174.

Boat-builder, for whom Ham Peggotty worked. D. C. 606.

Boatmen, at Dover. D. C. 144.

Boatmen, Three, who permitted Nell and her grandfather to travel in their canal boat.

Bob. S. B. 319.

Bob, guard of a coach. S. B. 101.

Bob, turnkey in the Marshalsea, and godfather of Little Dorrit. L. D. 45

Bobbo, a schoolboy. C. S. 371.

Bobster, Cecilia, the young lady whom Newman Noggs mistook for Madeline Bray. N. N. 404, 408.

Bobster, Mr, father of Cecilia Bobster. N. N. 408.

Bocker, Tom, referred to by Frank Milvey. O. M. F. 83.

Boffer, a stockbroker, who was expelled from the Exchange. P. P. 606.

Boffin, Henrietta, wife of Nicodemus Boffin, the Golden Dustman. O. M. F. 44.

Boffin, Nicodemus, called The Golden Dustman, an unlettered but good-hearted and honourable man; servant of John Harmon, the elder, whose property fell to him on the supposed death of the son, John Harmon; unspoiled by prosperity, but pretended to become miserly to test Wegg and Bella Wilfer. O. M. F. 37

Boffin's Bower, where Mr Boffin lived before going to his large house. O. M. F. 44.

Bogsby, James George, landlord of the "Sol's Arms". B. H. 352.

Bokum, Mrs, bridesmaid to Mrs MacStinger at her marriage with Captain Bunsby. D. S. 664.

Bolder, one of Squeers's pupils. N. N. 72.

Boldheart, Captain. H. R. 471.

Boldwig, Captain, on whose ground Mr Pickwick trespassed. P. P. 194.

Bolo, Miss, a lady of ancient and whist-like appearance. P. P. 391.

Bolter, Morris, assumed name of Noah Claypole. O. T. 251.

Bonnet, a young man. C. S. 193.

Bonney, Mr, a business friend of Ralph Nickleby. N. N. 8.

Boodle, Lord, a friend of Sir Leicester Dedlock. B. H. 123.

Book-pedlar, one of the poor travellers in Rochester. C. S. 63.

Bookseller, in Groombridge Wells. Bookstall Keeper. O. T. 58.

"**Boot, The**", a tavern. B. R. 225.

Bootmaker, one of Mr Micawber's creditors. D. C. 122.

Boots, of the "Bull Inn". P. P. 18.

Boots, Mr, one of Mr Veneering's friends. O. M. F. 6.

Boots, The, at the "Holly-Tree Inn". See *Cobbs*.

Boots, Top and Under, at the "Winglebury Arms". S. B. 308.

Boozey, Bill, captain of the foretop. H. R. 472.

Boroughbridge, near which Nicholas Nickleby found Smike when walking to London. N. N. 123.

Borrioboola-Gha, a Nigerian district where Mrs Jellyby sought to educate the natives and promote the cultivation of coffee. B. H. 29.

Borum, Augustus, son of Mr Borum. N. N. 243.

Borum, Charlotte, daughter of Mr Borum. N. N. 243.

Borum, Emma, daughter of Mr Borum. N. N. 243.

Borum, Mr, a patron of Mr Crummles's theatrical company.

Borum, Mrs, wife of Mr Borum. N. N. 243.

Bottles, a deaf stableman. C. S. 214.

Bouclet, Madame, who let lodgings. C. S. 304.

Bounderby, Josiah, a self-made man, the bully of humility; he married Louisa Gradgrind, who left him, and he was pitied and despised by Mrs Sparsit. H. T. 255.

Bounderby, Louisa, daughter of Mr Gradgrind, and brought up on his system; she married Mr Bounderby, but left him and returned to her father. H. T. 254.

Bow, where the Nicklebys lived in a house provided by the Cheerybles. N. N. 355.

Bow Street, where the Artful Dodger was tried. O. T. 256.

Bowley, Lady, wife of Sir Joseph Bowley. C. B. 81.

Bowley, Master, son of Sir Joseph Rowley. C. B. 100.

Bowley, Sir Joseph, a member of Parliament, the Poor Man's Friend. C. B. 80.

Bowley Hall, the residence of Sir Joseph Bowley. C. B. 100.

Bowyer, a wealthy London money-lender. M. H. C. 445.

Bowyer, Sam'l, who died in the workhouse. R. P. 449

Boxer, Mr Peerybingle's dog. C. B. 130.

Boy. M. C. 423.

Boy, a customer of Mr Venus. O. M. F. 64

Boy, a degraded, found by Redlaw. C. B. 267.

Boy, a friend of Little Nell. O. C. S. 310.

Boy, a messenger. N. N. 367.

Boy, an apprentice to dancing. B. H. 441.

Boy, assistant to Mrs Jellyby. B. H. 323.

Boy, attended in his death by Dr Manette. T. T. C. 234.

Boy, at the Fezziwigs' ball. C. B. 23.

Boy, employed by Mr Nupkins. P. P. 272.

Boy, employed by Mr Pickles, the fishmonger. H. R. 464.

Boy, employed by Mr Trabb, the tailor. G. E. 110.

Boy, half-booted, leather-leggined. P. P. 193.

Boy, in a crowd. C. S. 325.

Boy, in hospital. O. M. F. 264.

Boy, in Namby's house. P. P. 438.

Boy, murdered by his uncle. M. H. C. 461.

Boy, servant of Captain Bunsby. D. S. 261, 429.

Boy, Sir Geoffrey Manning's. P. P. 194.

Boy, to whom Dick Swiveller gave moral advice. O. C. S. 215.

Boy, who drove a chaise-cart. C. B. 230.

Boy, who gave Neckett's address. B. H. 160.

Boy, whom Nell met in the churchyard. O. C. S. 297.

Boy, who performed at Mrs Leo Hunter's. P. P. 160.

Boy, who succeeded Walter Gay in Donlhey's counting-house. D. S. 365.

Boy, who wanted a pound and knew a dog. D. C. 429.

Boy, with a blue bag. P. P. 471.

Boy, with a comforter. D. C. 270.

Boy, Beer, who supplied Dick Swiveller. O. C. S. 192.

Boy, Brown-faced, at Mugby Junction. C. S. 452.

Boy, Cripple, befriended by Tim Linkinwater. N. N. 399.

Boy, Deaf and Dumb, charged with theft. O. C. S. 255.

Boy, Monotonous. L. D. 135.

Boy, Post. O. C. S. 267.

Boy, Post. O. C. S. 393,

Boy, Post. O. T. 193.

Boy, Post, discharged from the "Blue Boar". G. E. 204.

Boy, Sailor, one of the poor travellers in Rochester. C. S. 63.

Boy, Sharp, employed by Mr Traddles. D. C. 231.

Boy, Small.   P. P. 489.

Boy, Surgeon's. S. B. 230.

Boy, Tall, a companion of Oliver Twist in the workhouse. O. T. 10.

Boy, Town-made Little. N. N. 354.

Boy, Young, of about three feet high,

from the "Blue Boar", Leadenhall Market. P. P. 349.

Boys, Coketown. H. T. 340.

Boys, Hideous Small. E. D. 42.

Boys, Several. D. C. 159.

Boys, Six Small, who represented the "men of Eatanswill". P. P. 132.

Boys, Three, stepsons of Mr Stryver. T. T. C. 152.

Boys, Two, concerned in the Gordon riots. B. R. 394.

Boys, Two, in Turveydrop's Academy. B. H. 415.

Boys, Two Ragged, who assisted the Pickwickians in their shooting. P. P. 66.

Boythorn, Lawrence, a friend of Mr Jarndyce, very jovial and fond of superlatives; he had a standing feud with Sir Leicester Dedlock, whose property adjoined his. Original, Walter Savage Landor. B. H. 89.

Brandley, Miss, daughter of Mrs Brandley. G. E. 220.

Brandley, Mrs, a lady with whom Estella lived at Richmond. G. E. 220.

Brass, Sally (Sarah), sister of Sampson Brass, and partner in his villainies; came to a bad end. O. C. S. 155.

Brass, Sampson, a disreputable attorney in league with Quilp; he tried to ruin Kit Nubbles by a false charge of theft, but failed, and was himself condemned to imprisonment with hard labour. O. C. S. 65.

Bravassa, Miss, a member of Mr Crummles's theatrical company. N. N. 228.

Bray, Madeline, a young lady saved by Nicholas Nickleby from a forced marriage with Gride; married Nicholas. N. N. 146, 400, 464.

Bray, Walter, father of Madeline Bray; a selfish debaucher, willing to sacrifice his daughter for money. N. N. 470.

"Break of Day", an inn at Chalons. L. D. 99.

Break-Neck-Stairs. C. S. 508.

Brentford, where Betty Higdon lived. O. M. F. 155.

Brewer, Mr, a friend of Mr Veneering. O. M. F. 6.

Brick, Jefferson, an American war correspondent, on the staff of the "New York Rowdy Journal". M. C. 207.

Brick, Mrs Jefferson, wife of Jefferson Brick. M. C. 214.

Brickmaker, husband of Jenny. B. H. 82.

Bride, mentioned incidentally. D. S. 44.

Bride, who wouldn't shame her bridegroom. B. H. 390.

Bridegroom, mentioned incidentally. D. S. 44.

Bridegroom, who couldn't write. B. H. 390.

Bridesmaid, at Mr Dombey's second marriage. D. S. 346.

Bridesmaid,   Mr and Mrs Lammle's. O. M. F. 94.

Bridesmaids, Louisa Gradgrind's. H. T. 336.

Brieg, where Marguerite married George Vendale. C. S. 611.

Brig Place, where Captain Cuttle lodged with Mrs MacStinger. D. S. 92.

Briggs, one of Dr Humber's pupils. D. S. 121.

Briggs, Alexander, articled to his brother. S. B. 291.

Briggs, Kate, daughter of Mrs Briggs. S. B. 297.

Briggs, Mrs, a widow. S. B. 291.

Briggs, Samuel, an attorney, of Furnival's Inn. S. B. 291.

Briggses, The Miss, rivals of the Miss Tauntons. S. B. 291.

Brighton, where Mrs Pipchin's boarding-house and Dr Blimber's school were; also where Mrs Skewton died. D. S. 77, 111, 446.

Brimer, Mr, fifth mate of the "Halsewell". R. P. 324.

Bristol, where Mr Winkle fled, and where he found Miss Arabella Allen. P. P. 413.

Britain, Benjamin, called also **Little Britain**, servant of Dr Jeddler; afterwards landlord of the "Nutmeg Grater"; married Clemency Newcome. C. B.194.

Britain, Clem, child of Benjamin Britain and Clemency Newcome. C. B. 232.

Britains, Master, Two, sons of Benjamin Britain and Clemency Newcome. C. B. 232.

Brittles, a servant of Mrs Maylie. O. T. 157.

Broadway, in New York. M. C. 209.

Brobity, Miss. See *Sapsea, Mrs*

Brogley, Mr, a broker. D.S. 90.

Brogson, guest of Mr Budden. S. B. 240.

Brook Street, where Mrs Skewton and her daughter lived before the latter's marriage. D. S. 331.

Brooker, a former employee of Ralph Nickleby; a returned convict. N. N. 443

Brooks, one of Squeers's pupils. N. N. 64.

Brooks, Mr, a pieman, a fellowlodger of Sam Weller's. P. P. 199.

Brooks of Sheffield, name given to David Copperfield by Mr Murdstone. D. C. 18.

Brother, of James Harthouse. H. T. 352.

Browdie, John, a Yorkshire farmer who befriended Nicholas Nickleby; married Matilda Price. N. N. 83.

Brown, of Muggleton, maker of Miss Rachael Wardle's shoes. P. P. 99.

Brown, Alice, otherwise Alice Marwood, the unfortunate daughter of Good Mrs Brown and cousin of Edith Granger; cast off by James Carker. D. S. 375.

Brown, Emily, who married Horace Hunter. S. B. 307.

Brown, Good Mrs, mother of Alice Brown; she robbed Florence Dombey of her clothes. D. S. 55.

Brown, Henry. S. B. 30.

Brown, Mr, a violoncellist. S. B. 322.

Brown, Mr, passenger on a Thames boat. S. B. 77.

Browndock, Miss, referred to by Mrs Nickleby. N. N. 166.

Brownlow, Mr, an old gentleman who befriended Oliver Twist and ultimately adopted him as his son. O. T. 51.

Browns, The Three Miss. S. B. 7.

Brussels, where Captain Doubledick was in hospital. C. S. 73.

Bryanstone Square, near which Mr Dombey lived. D. S. 17.

Bucket, Inspector, a detective employed on the Tulkinghorn murder; also found Lady Dedlock after her flight. B. H. 237.

Bucket, Mrs, wife of Inspector Bucket. B. H. 549.

Bud, Rosa, a charming young lady betrothed as a child to Edwin Drood and loved by Jasper; she and Edwin Drood agreed to become merely friends; she fell in love with Lieutenant Tartar. E. D. 19.

Budden, Alexander Augustus, son of Octavius Budden. S. B. 236.

Budden, Amelia, wife of Octavius Budden. S. B. 236.

Budden, Octavius, a retired corn-chandler, cousin of Augustus Minns. S. B. 236.

Budger, Mrs, a widow who caused the quarrel between Dr Slammer and Mr Winkle. P. P. 16.

Buffers, Two, friends of Mr Veneering. O. M. F. 9.

Buffle, Miss Robina, daughter of Mr and Mrs Buffle. C. S. 382.

Buffle, Mr, a tax-collector. C. S. 379.

Buffle, Mrs, wife of Mr Buffle. C. S. 382.

Buffum, Oscar, an American. M. C. 423.

Buffy, Right Hon. William, a member of Parliament, friend of Sir Leicester Dedlock. B. H. 124.

Bulder, Colonel, head of the garrison at Rochester. P. P. 16.

Bulder, Miss, daughter of Colonel Bulder. P. P. 16.

Bulder, Mrs, wife of Colonel Bulder. P. P. 16.

Bule, Miss, a pupil of Miss Griffin. C. S. 224.

Bull, Prince, in a political allegory. R. P. 450.

"Bull, The", an inn in Holborn, where Mrs Gamp attended Mr Lewsome. M. C. 321.

"**Bull Inn**", Rochester, where Mr Pickwick and his friends stayed. P. P. 11.

"**Bull Inn**", Whitechapel, from which Mr Pickwick started for Ipswich. P. P. 230.

Bullamy, porter to the Anglo-Bengalee Company. M. C. 341.

Bullman, who has a lawsuit with Ramsey. P. P. 205.

Bullock, a church warden who got involved in a scuffle. D. C. 329.

Bull's-Eye, Bill Sikes's dog. O. T. 67, 84, 301.

Bulph, Mr, parish beadle, afterwards married to Mrs Corney, matron of the workhouse; both became inmates of the workhouse latterly. O. T. 5.

Bumple, Michael, a plaintiff at Doctor's Commons. S. B. 66.

Bung, successful candidate for beadleship. S. B. 16.

Buskin, Mrs, which clear-starched; a neighbour of Mrs Barden. P. P. 376.

Bunsby, Captain John, a friend of Captain Cuttle, who regarded him as a man of profound wisdom; forcibly married to Mrs MacStinger. D. S. 261.

Burgess and Co., Mr Toots's tailors. D. S. 122.

Burton, Thomas, purveyor of cat's meat; a convert to temperance. P. P. 358.

Bury, George, of West Bromwich. R. P. 390.

Bury St. Edmunds, where Mr Pickwick followed Mr Jingle. P. P. 165.

"**Bush, The**", an inn at Bristol, where Mr Winkle put up. P. P. 413.

Butcher, with whom David Copperfield fought. D. C. 205.

Butcher, William, a Chartist. R. P. 390.

Butcher's Boy. O. T. 83.

Butler, Dr Blimber's. D. S. 123.

Butler, Mr Dombey's. D. S. 350.

Butler, Mr Merdle's, whose eye was a basilisk to Mr Merdle. L. D. 197.

Butler, Theodosius, who eloped with Miss Brook Dingwall. S. B. 247.

Button, William, a part played by Signor Jupe. H. T. 254.

Buzfuz, Serjeant, counsel for plaintiff in Bardell *v.* Pickwick. P. P. 363.

C

Cabbery, an old suitor of Mrs Nickleby. N. N. 412.

Cabman, who drove the Raddles and Mrs Cluppins to Mrs Bardell's. P. P. 502.

Cadogan Place, where Mrs Wititterly lived. N. N. 206.

Caen Wood, where Lord Mansfield's country seat was. B. R. 391.

Callow, a physician. R. P. 481.

Calton, Mr, bonder of Mrs Tibbs, a superannuated beau. S. B. 210.

Camberwell, where Ruth Pinch was a governess. M. C. 107.

Camden Town, where the Toodles lived, D. S. 50; where Bob Cratchit lived, C. B. 9.

Camilla, Mr J., or Raymond, husband of Mrs Camilla. G. E. 58.

Camilla, Mrs, sister of Matthew Pocket, and a fawning relative of Miss Havisham. G. E. 58, 149.

Campbell, Mr, a name given to Magwitch in hiding. G. E. 278.

Canary, belonging to Lawrence Boythorn. B. H. 91.

Canterbury, where David Copperfield went to school and where Agnes Wickfield lived. D. C. 173.

Cape, Mr, a violinist. S. B. 322.

Captain, of the Screw, the ship in which Martin Chuzzlewit sailed for America. M. C. 204.

Carker, Harriet, sister of John and James Carker; stood by the former in his disgrace; afterwards married Mr Morfin. D. S. 234.

Carker, James, Dombey & Son's manager, who brought the business to ruin; he eloped with Edith Dombey, but was cast off by her immediately; killed on a railway when escaping from Mr Dombey; his white teeth were a prominent feature. D. S.134.

Carker, John, elder brother of James Carker, occupying a very humble position in the firm of Dombey & Son; he had robbed the firm at one time, but was kept on in a junior post, and lived a repentant life; after his brother's death he inherited his wealth, but made over the interest to Mr Dombey on his ruin. D. S. 60.

Carlo, one of Jerry's performing dogs. O. C. S. 107.

Caroline, a harassed mother, who was relieved at the thought of Scrooge's death. C. B. 50.

Carol-singer, chased off by Scrooge. C. B. 8.

Carpenter, in a crowd. C. S. 326.

Carpenter, who officiated at Mrs Gargery's funeral. G. R. 205.

Carpenter, Sleepy-faced, in a crowd. O. T. 84.

Carrier, who took Kit's box to Finchley. O. C. S. 125.

Carrock, a hill ascended by Idle and Goodchild. L. T. 363.

Carstone, Richard, a ward in Chancery whose career was rendered aimless and unprofitable by the interminable Chancery suit of Jarndyce and Jarndyce; tried successively medicine, law, and the army, but latterly became absorbed in watching the Chancery suit, ruined his health, and died young; married Ada Clare, a distant cousin and fellow ward. B. H. 23.

Carstone, Richard, posthumous child of the preceding. B. H. 675.

Cart Driver, who gave a lift to Nell and her grandfather. O. C. S. 92.

Carter. G. E. 114.

Carter, in a smock-frock, who was disposed to enlist. B. R. 181.

Carter, Half-drunken, with whom Rogue Riderhood travelled. U. M. F. 444.

Carton, Captain (afterward Admiral Sir) George, who married Miss Marion Maryon. C. S.155.

Carton, Sydney, a lawyer of dissipated habits who devilled for Stryver; helped to get Darnay acquitted of treason through his close resemblance to Darnay; through love for Lucie Manette he voluntarily suffered death by the guillotine in place of Darnay, Lucie's husband, who had been condemned by the Paris Revolutionists. T. T. C. 43.

Casby, Christopher, the "Last of the Patriarchs", landlord of Bleeding Heart Yard; his mask of benevolence was finally torn off by Pancks, his agent. L. D. 110.

Castle, the Poor Relation's. C. S. 34.

Cat, in Mrs Pipchin's establishment. D. S. 83.

"Cautious Clara", Captain Bunsby's ship. D. S. 261.

Cavalier. M. H. C. 481.

Cavalier, with whom Alice eloped; slain by Hugh Graham. M. H. C. 447, 450.

Cavalletto, John Baptist, fellow prisoner with Rigaud, and later employed by Doyce & Clennam. L. D. 3.

Cavendish Square, near which Silas Wegg had his stall, and near which Boffin went to live, O. M. F.35, near which Madame Mantalini lived, N. N. 94.

Certainpersonio, Prince. H. K. 470.

Chadband, Mrs, wife of the Rev. Mr Chadband, formerly, as Mrs Rachael, servant to Miss Barbary. B. H. 12, 202.

Chadband, Rev. Mr, a canting, hypocritical minister, who assisted Smallweed in an attempt to blackmail Sir Leicester Dedlock; a very oily person. B. H. 201.

Chairman, of a harmonic meeting. S. B. 45.

Chairman, of many Boards. O. M. F. 500.

Chairman, Long Thin, who brought Mrs Dowler home in a Sedan chain P. P. 399

Chairman, Short Fat, who brought Mrs Dowler home in a Sedan chair. P. P. 399

Chairmen, who carried Mr Chester to Clerkenwell. B. R. 156.

Chalons. L. D. 98.

Chamberlain, at the Hummums. G. E. 268.

Chambermaid, at an inn in Salisbury. M. C. 397

Chambermaid, at the "Bull", Holborn. M. C. 322.

Chambermaid, at the "Golden Cross". D. C. 218.

Chambermaid, at the "Great White Horse", in Ipswich. P. P. 238.

Chambermaid, at "White Hart Inn", in Southwark. P. P. 94.

Chambermaid, Assistant, at the "Bull", Holborn. M. C. 325.

Chambermaid, Unlimited Head, at Furnival's Inn. E. D. 199.

Chancery, Court of. B. H. 2.

Chancery Prisoner, The, in the Fleet, from whom Mr Pickwick rented an apartment. P. P. 462.

Chap, Lanky, with a red nose, an assistant of the Rev. Mr Stiggins. P. P. 231.

Chaplain, Drunken, in the Fleet. P. P. 460.

Charitable Grinders, an educational establishment to which Robin Toodle was sent by Mr Dombey. D. S. 47.

Charker, Harry, a corporal of marines. C. S. 144.

Charles, Old, a waiter. C. S. 296.

Charley. See *Neckett, Charlotte*.

Charley, a dealer, to whom David Copperfield sold his jacket. D.C. 141, 142.

Charley, narrator of *The Holly Tree Inn*. C. S. 83, 113.

Charley, shambling, red-headed potboy, of "Magpie and Stump". P. P. 215.

Charlotte, daughter of John, the smith. R. P. 389.

Charlotte, school friend of Miss Wade. L. D. 525.

Charlotte, servant of Mrs Sowerberry; ran off to London with Noah Claypole. O. T. 22.

Charwoman, in one of Scrooge's visions. C. B. 47.

Charwoman, Occasional, who officiated as Bob Sawyer's housekeeper. P. P. 418.

Chatham, where David Copperfield slept near a cannon, and where the sold his jacket, D. C. 140; where Richard Doubledick enlisted, C. S. 65.

Cheeryble, Charles, a merchant in London, in partnership with his brother Edwin (Ned); very charitable; their business passed to Frank Cheeryble and Nicholas Nickleby; originals of Cheeryble Brothers, Daniel & William Grant, calico printers in Manchester. N. N. 348.

Cheeryble, Edwin (Ned), brother of Charles Cheeryble. N. N. 351.

Cheeryble, Frank, nephew of the Cheeryble brothers; succeeded to the business along with Nicholas Nickleby; married Kate Nickleby. N. N. 432.

Cheeryble Brothers. See *Cheeryble, Charles*.

Cheeseman, Old, a Latin master, who married Jane Pitt. C. S. 41.

Cheeseman, Young, son of Old Cheeseman and Jane Pitt. C. S. 50.

Cheesemonger, who married Emma Gordon. H. T. 486.

Cheggs, Alexander, a market-gardener who ousted Dick Swiveller from the affections of Sophy Wackles. O. C. S. 48.

Cheggs, Miss, sister of Mr Cheggs. O. C. S. 48.

Chelsea, where the Wackles family lived. O. C. S. 47.

Chemist, who sold a drug to Sydney Carton. T. T. C. 226.

Chertsey, the scene of the burglary in *Oliver Twist*. O. T. 125.

Cherub, The, a name of Reginald Willer (q.v.).

Chesney Wold, the seat of Sir Leicester Matlock., in Lincolnshire. Original, Rockingham Castle. B. H. 63.

Chester, Edward, son of Sir John Chester, in love with Emma Haredale, whom he at length married. B. R. 3.

Chester, Sir John, father of Edward Chester, whose marriage with Emma Haredale he tried to prevent; he was killed by Mr Haredale. B. R. 33.

Chestle, Mr, a hop-grower who married Miss Larkins and upset David Copperfield's pleasant dream. D. C. 208.

Chib, Mr, father of a vestry. R. P. 475.

Chick, John, husband of Louisa Chick, given to humming tunes. D. S. 9.

Chick, Louisa, sister of Mr Dombey, fond of urging people to make an effort. D. S. 5.

Chickenstalker, Mrs Anne, shopkeeper; married Mr Tugby in Trotty Veck's vision. C. B. 85, 109, 110.

Chicksey, Veneering, and Stobbles, Mr Veneering's firm, in which

Reginald Wilfer was employed as a clerk. O. M. F. 26.

Chickweed, Conkey, a burglar. O. T. 175.

Chiggle, a supposed American sculptor. M. C. 425.

Chigwell. B. R. 4.

Child, killed by the Marquis St. Evremonde's carriage. T. T. C. 78.

Child, of a keeper at Chesney Wold. B. H. 7.

Child, of John and Mary Heyling. P. P. 222.

Child, of Margaret Raybrock. C. S. 240.

Child, of Mrs Fisher, killed by the pirates. C. S. 154.

Child, who pitied Esther Summerson. B. H. 390.

Childers, E. W. B., one of Mr Sleary's troupe. H. T. 269.

Children, of Mrs Joram. D. C. 232.

Children, of tollman, who greeted Tom Pinch. M. C. 52.

Children, Three, of cottager. O. C. S. 90.

Children, Three, whom Mark Tapley looked after on board ship. M. C. 197.

Children, Two, of Kidderminster. H. T. 486.

Children, Two, of Plornish. L. D. 107.

Children in Arms, Six, for election purposes. P. P. 133.

Children's Hospital, where Johnny died. O. M. F. 263.

Chill, the miserly uncle of Mr Michael, the Poor Relation. C. S. 26.

Chillip, Mr, a doctor who attended at David Copperfield's birth; the meekest of little men. D. C. 8.

Chillip, Mrs, the first, associated in David Copperfield's remembrance with a pale tortoise-shell cat. D. C. 115.

Chillip, Mrs, the second. D. C. 245

Chimney-sweep, in funeral procession. T. T. C. 112.

Chimney-sweeper, in Staggs's Gardens. D. S. 51, 172.

Chinaman, in an opium den. E. D. 4.

Chinaman, Jack, who kept an opium den. E. D. 4.

Chinks's Basin, near which Clara Barley lived. G. E. 273.

Chitling, Tom, one of Fagin's pupils. O. T. 104.

Chivery, John, turnkey in the Marshalsea, and a man of few words. L. D. 167.

Chivery, Mrs, mother of Young John. L. D. 167.

Chivery, Young John, the devoted admirer of Little Dorrit; he relieved his feelings of unrequited love by composing his own epitaphs. L. D. 166.

Choke, General Cyrus, an American. M. C. 272.

Chollop, Major Hannibal, an American. M. C. 407.

Chopkins, Laura, daughter of a neighbour of the Kenwigses. N. N. 530.

Chopper, Great-uncle. H. R. 461.

Chopski, a corruption of Tpschoffki (q.v.). C. S. 190.

Chowser, Colonel, a guest of Ralph Nickleby at dinner. N. N. 185.

Christiana, former sweetheart of Mr Michael. C. S. 26.

Christiana, daughter of the preceding Christiana. C. S. 32.

Christians, Wandering. C. S. 344.

"Christmas Carol, A", sung by Mr Wardle. P. P. 306.

Christopher, Mr, the waiter who narrates *Somebody's Luggage*. C. S. 291, 298

Chuckster, Mr, clerk to Mr Witherden, the notary, and a boon companion of Dick Swiveller; an enemy of Kit Nubbles. O. C. S. 85.

Chuffey, Mr, Anthony Chuzzlewit's old clerk; faithful to Anthony, but distrustful of Jonas. M. C. 141.

Church Street, where Lizzie Hexam lived. O. M. F. 176.

Chuzzlewit, Anthony, father of Jonas Chuzzlewit, and brother of Martin Chuzzlewit, senior; died suddenly; Jonas suspected of poisoning him. M. C. 42.

Chuzzlewit, Anthony, & Son, a firm of Manchester warehousemen. M. C. 139.

Chuzzlewit, George, a gay bachelor cousin of Martin Chuzzlewit, senior. M. C. 44.

Chuzzlewit, Jonas, son of Anthony Chuzzlewit, whom he tried to poison; married Mercy Pecksniff and treated her cruelly; came into the clutches of Montague Tigg, who levied blackmail on him, and whom he murdered; arrested for the murder, but poisoned himself on the way to prison. M. C. 42.

Chuzzlewit, Martin, Junior, grandson of Martin Chuzzlewit, senior; turned out by his grandfather, and apprenticed himself to Pecksniff as an architect, but discharged at Old Martin's instance; went to America with

Mark Tapley, was disillusioned, and returned; ultimately reconciled to his grandfather, and married Mary Graham. M. C. 58.

Chuzzlewit, Martin, Senior, grandfather of Martin Chuzzlewit, junior; alienated from his grandson; lived with Pecksniff, whom he found out and exposed; dealt out justice at the end. M. C. 21.

Chuzzlewit, Misses, Three, daughters of Mrs Ned Chuzzlewit. M. C. 44.

Chuzzlewit, Mrs Ned, sister-in-law of Martin Chuzzlewit, senior. M. C. 43, 48.

Cicero, a negro who had bought his freedom, and who was saving up to buy his daughter's freedom. M. C. 222.

Circumlocution Office, a Government department that showed in all its methods "How not to do it". L. D. 82.

City Square, where Cheeryble Brothers' business was. N. N. 363.

Clapham Road, where Mr Michael, the Poor Relation, lived. C. S. 26.

Clare, Ada, a ward in Chancery; companion of Esther Summerson; married her distant cousin and fellow-ward, Richard Carstone. B. H. 23.

Clark, Betsy, a servant girl. S. B. 40.

Clark, Mr, in the employment of Dombey & Son. D. S. 59.

Clark, Mrs, a client of the General Agency Office. N. N. 147.

Clarke, Susan, widow, afterwards Mrs Weller. P. P. 96.

Clarriker, Mr, of Clarriker & Co., who employed Herbert Pocket G. E. 219, 305.

Claypole, Noah, a charity boy, apprentice to Sowerberry the undertaker; robbed his employer and went with Charlotte to London, where he became a thief; turned queen's evidence against Fagin; made a living afterwards as informer; alias Morris Bolter. O. T. 24.

Cleaver, Fanny, more often called Jenny Wren, a doll's dressmaker, a deformed child with whom Lizzie Hexam lived; greatly troubled by her drunken father, whom she called her "bad child". O. M. F. 176, 186.

Cleaver, Mr, Fanny Cleaver's drunken father, who betrayed the secret of Lizzie Hexam's whereabouts for drink; he met his death in the street through drink. O. M. F. 191.

Clennam, Arthur, who befriended Little Dorrit and was loved by her; in business with Doyce, but was imprisoned in the Marshalsea for debt; married Little Dorrit on his release by his partner Doyce. L. D. 14.

Clennam, Mrs, stepmother of Arthur Clennam; she had abstracted a will in favour of Little Dorrit, who forgave her, and kept the truth from Arthur. L. D. 27.

Cleopatra, a name applied to the Hon. Mrs Skewton (q.v.).

Clergyman, in the church where Walter Gay was married to Florence Dombey. D. S. 616.

Clergyman, officiating at Mrs Bayton's funeral. O. T. 30.

Clergyman, who married Mr Dombey to Edith Granger. D. S. 346.

Clergyman, who officiated at the burial of Hugh. B. R. 470.

Clergyman, The, in the village where Little Nell settled. O. C. S. 293.

Clergyman, The Old, at Dingley Dell. P. P. 53.

Clerk. M. C. 515.

Clerk, at Bow Street. O. T. 259.

Clerk, at Tellson's Bank. T. T. C. 41.

Clerk, at the "Blue Bull". D. C. 55.

Clerk, in a Government office, who killed himself on principle, of whom Sam Weller told the story. P. P. 479

Clerk, in Dombey & Son's, who presided at a dinner. D. S. 560.

Clerk, in Mr Fang's court. O. T. 57.

Clerk, in spectacles. P. P. 442.

Clerk, to Mr Tulkinghorn. B. H. 300.

Clerk, to Mr Tulkinghorn. B. H 372.

Clerk, Articled, in the Temple. P. P. 325.

Clerk, Attorney's. L. D. 50.

Clerk, Common-law, with a bass voice. P. P. 443.

Clerk, Copying, in the Six Clerks' Office at the Chancery Court. B. H. 4.

Clerk, Middle-aged Copying, in the Temple. P. P. 325.

Clerk, Officiating. P. P. 608.

Clerk, Parish, at Mrs Bayton's funeral. O. T. 29.

Clerk, Parish, at the christening of Little Paul Dombey. D. S. 45.

Clerk, Parish, at the marriage of Walter Gay and Florence Dombey. D. S. 616.   •

Clerk, Parish, at the marriage of Mr Dombey and Edith Granger. D. S. 346.

Clerk, Salaried, in the Temple. P. P. 325.

Clerk, Superannuated Bank, a friend of Tim Linkinwater. N. N. 368.

Clerkenwell, where the Dodger picked Mr Brownlow's pocket, O. T. 51; where Gabriel Varden lived, B. R. 24; also T. T. C. 73.

Clerks, of Spenlow & Jorkins. D. C. 296.

Clerks, Four, of Dodson & Fogg. P. P. 204.

Clerks, Out-door. E. D. 103.

Clerks, Three, with Mr Jaggers. G. E. 145-6.

Clerks, Two Spare, in a Bank at Venice. L. D. 387.

Click, Mr R. P. 429.

Click, Mr, a gasfitter. C. S. 324.

Clickett, "a Orfling", servant to the Micawbers, and addicted to snorting. D. C. 121, 126.

Client, Queer. See *Heyling*.

Clifford's Inn, where John Rakesmith offered himself to Mr Boffin as secretary. O. M. F. 76.

Clissold, Lawrence, a cleric guilty of forgery; afterwards a supercargo; shipwrecked with Hugh Raybrock. C. S. 253.

Clive, Mr, in the Circumlocution Office. L. D. 90.

Clock Room, in the Haunted House. C. S. 217.

Clocker, Mr, a grocer. R. P. 385.

Cloisterham, a cathedral city, where Jasper lived, and where Edwin Drood disappeared. Original, Rochester. E. D. 17.

Clown, New. H. T. 485.

Clubber, Lady, wife of Sir Thomas Clubber. P. P. 15.

Clubber, Sir Thomas, head of the dockyard at Chatham. P. P. 15.

Clubber, Two Misses, daughters of Sir Thomas Clubber. P. P. 15.

Cluppins, Betsey, friend of Mrs Bardell. P. P. 278.

Cly, Roger, servant to Charles Darnay, and a spy; he gave evidence against Darnay at the treason trial. T. T. C. 47.

"Coach and Horses", a public house passed by Sikes and Oliver Twist. O. T. 120.

Coachmaker, Young, in love with Dolly Varden. B. H 109.

Coachman, hired by Squeers. N. N. 386.

Coachman, of the London mail. O. T. 282.

Coachman, of the "Muggleton Telegraph". P. P. 292, 294.

Coachman, on the stage-coach from London. G. E. 166.

Coachman, who drove Bella Rokesmith to her new house. O. M. F. 614.

Coachman, who drove Casket in his flight. D. S. 599

Coachman, who drove Grandfather Smallweed. B. H. 358.

Coachman, who drove Jonas Chuzzlewit home drunk. M. C. 358

Coachman, who drove Jonas Chuzzlewit on his murderous errand. M. C. 564.

Coachman, who drove Nicholas Nickleby to London. N. N. 316.

Coachman, who drove Pip to Mr Jaggers's office. G. E. 118.

Coachman, who drove Susan Nipper into the country. D. S. 484

Coachman, who drove Tom Pinch to London. M. C. 438.

Coachman, who drove the single

gentleman to Brass's house. O. C.
S. 194.

Coachman, who drove to the "Holly-Tree Inn". C. S. 87.

Coachman, who received a flower intended for Mercy Pecksnill. M. C. 151.

Coachman, who tried to take Susan Nipper to Staggs's Gardens. D. S. 170.

Coachman, with whom Mrs Gump had an altercation. M. C. 368.

Coachman, Mr Dombey's. D. S. 516.

Coachmen, Eight Stout, who escorted Sam Weller to prison. P. P. 476.

Coalheaver, who was refused a shave. N. N. 531.

Coavinses. See *Neckett*.

Cobb, Tom, a general chandler and post-office keeper. B. R. 4.

Cobbey, a pupil of Squeers. N. N. 73, 580.

Cobbler, who refused to mend Mr Melt's boots any more. D. C. 59.

Cobbler, Bald-headed, of whom Mr Pickwick rented lodgings in the Fleet. P. P. 480.

Cobbs, boots at the "Holly-Tree Inn"; formerly under gardener to Mr Walmers. C. S. 102.

Cobham, to which the Pickwickians followed Mr Tupman. P. P. 105.

Codger, Miss, a literary American lady. M. C. 426.

Codlin, Tom, a Punch-and-Judy showman, companion of Short, with whom Nell and her grandfather became acquainted; told Nell that "Codlin's the friend, not Short". O. C. S. 93.

Coffin Lane. P. V 309.

Coiler, Mrs, a neighbour of the Pockets. G. E. 139.

Coketown, the scene of action in *Hard Times*. H. T. 252.

Coleshaw, Miss, a passenger on the "Golden Mary". C. S. 120, 121.

Collegian, The Lean Clerk, in buttonless black. L. D. 178.

Collegian, The Stout Greengrocer. L. D. 178.

Collegian in the Dressing-gown. L. D. 178.

Collegian in the Seaside Slippers. L. D. 178.

Colonel, in Newgate for coining. G. E. 192.

Comedian, Low, who "mugged" at Frederick Dorrit. L. D. 186.

"Commodore, The", the Rochester coach. P. P. 8.

Compeyson, Miss Havisham's deceitful lover, in league with Magwitch; brought about the recapture of Magwitch, but met his death in the struggle. G. E. 12, 154.

Compeyson, Sally, wife of Compeyson. G. E. 255.

Constable, who arrested Kit Nubbles. O. C. S. 335

Constable, who made Jo move on. B.H. 205.

Constable, Special, who laughed at the wrong time before Mr Nupkins. P. P. 264.

Constable, Special, who laughed at the wrong time before Mr Nupkins, denied he was drunk, and was dismissed. P. P. 264.

Contractor, a friend of Veneering. O. M. F. 500.

Convict, on a stage-coach. G. E. 166.

"Convict's Return, The", tale told by

the old clergyman at Dingley Dell. P. P. 58.

Conway, General, who defended the House of Commons against the Gordon rioters with their petition. B. R. 289.

Cook, at the Haunted House. C. S. 211.

Cook, at Westgate House. P. P. 174

Cook, in a hotel near Hyde Park.

Cook, Buxom-looking, who had designs upon Mr Weller, senior. P. P. 571.

Cook, Miss Pupford's. C. S. 277.

Cook, Mr Dombey's. D. S. 387.

Cook, Mr Fezziwig's. C. B. 23.

Cook, Mr Toots's. D. S. 484.

Cook, Mrs Maylie's. O. T. 160.

Cook, Mrs Nupkins's. P. P. 272.

Cook, Pastry. D. S. 341.

Cook, Ship's, a mulatto who married Willing Sephy. C. S. 345

Cook, Ship's, who offered to marry Mrs Gummidge. D. C. 668.

Cook and Housemaid of John Willet. B. R. 317.

Cook's Court, where Mr Snagsby's place was. B. H. 98.

Cooper, Augustus, in the oil-andcolour line, who attended Signor Billsmeth is dancing academy. S. B. 191.

Copperfield, Agnes, David Copperfield's oldest child. D. C. 665.

Copperfield, Clara, mother of David Copperfield; her unfortunate second marriage with Mr Murdstone was terminated by an early death. D. C. 3.

Copperfield, David, son of Clara and David Copperfield; his early days were made miserable by his stepfather, M,. Murdstone, and his stepfather's sister; he went to school at Mr Creakle's, and afterwards at Dr Strong's, living with Mr Wick field and his daughter Agnes; he married first a "child-wife" Dora, but found perfect happiness after her death in his marriage with Agnes Wickfield. Original, largely Dickens himself. D. C. throughout.

Copperfield, Dora, daughter of Mr Spenlow, David Copperfield's master; after Mr Spenlow's death she lived with two aunts; she married David Copperfield, but did not live long; was called by him his "child-wife". Original, an early love of Dickens, Maria Beadnell. D. C. 298.

Coram, originator of an institution for foundlings, after whom Tattycoram was named. See *Tattycoram*.

Corner Room, in the Haunted House. C. S. 218.

Corney, Mrs, workhouse matron, afterwards married to Mr Bumble, and became with him an inmate of the workhouse. O. T. 128.

Coroner, at inquest on Captain Hawdon. B. H. 112.

Corresponding Society of the Pickwick Club, consisting of Pickwick, Tupman, Snodgrass, and Winkle. P. P. 2.

"Cosy", a room in the "Six Jolly Fellowship-Porters". O. M. F. 49.

Cottager. P. P. 292.

Cottager, who befriended Little Nell on her wanderings. O. C. S. 90.

Cottager, Old. O. C. S. 90.

Counsel. B. H. 5.

Counsel, Two, at Kit's trial. O. C. S. 353

Counsel for Defence, in a murder trial. C. S. 432.

Count, French, at Mrs Merdle's dinner. L. D. 512.

Countryman, whom Sikes came across in his flight. O. T. 281.

Couple, New-married, lodgers with Mrs Lirriper. C. S. 346.

Courier. T. T. C. 81.

Courier, Mr Dorrit's. L. D. 343.

Cousin, of Mary Anne Paragon, in the Life Guards. D. C. 486.

Cousin, of old Martin Chuzzlewit, deaf. M. C. 44.

Covent Garden Market. O. C. S. 2.

Crackit, Toby, a housebreaker associated with Fagin; took part in the burglary expedition to Chertsey. O. T. 123.

Craddock, Mrs, Mr Picicwick's landlady at Bath. P. P. 394.

Craggs, Mrs, wife of Mr Craggs. C. B. 207.

Craggs, Thomas, a lawyer friend of Dr Jeddler; a partner of Mr Snitchey. C. B. 196, 197.

Cratchit, Belinda, second daughter of Bob Cratchit. C. B. 33.

Cratchit, Bob, Scrooge's poorly paid but contented clerk, who benefited materially by the change in Scrooge's nature. C. B. 5, 33

Cratchit, Martha, oldest daughter of Bob Cratchit. C. 13. 33.

Cratchit, Master, younger son of Bob Cratchit. C. 13. 33.

Cratchit, Miss, youngest daughter of Bob Cratchit. C. B. 33.

Cratchit, Mrs, Bob Cratchit's wife. C. B. 33.

Cratchit, Peter, son of Bob Cratchit. C. B. 33.

Cratchit, Tim. See *Tiny Tim*.

Craven Street, where Mr Brownlow stayed. O. T. 238.

Crawley, Mr, a visitor at Bath. P. P. 392.

Creakle, Miss, daughter of Mr Creakle, a young lady of extraordinary attractions. D. C. 62.

Creakle, Mr, master of Salem House, where David Copperfield was for a time; a Tartar; ultimately became a Middlesex magistrate. Original, Mr Jones of Wellington House Academy. D. C. 62.

Creakle, Mrs, wife of Mr Creakle; she broke to David Copperfield the news of his mother's death. D. C. 62.

Creevy. See *La Creevy*.

Crewler, Caroline, the Beauty, eldest sister of Sophy. D. C. 377.

Crewler, Louisa, sister of Sophy. D. C. 377.

Crewler, Margaret, sister of Sophy. D. C. 378.

Crewler, Mrs, mother of Sophy, to whom Sophy was a mother. D. C. 378

Crewler, Rev. Horace, father of Sophy, and an exemplary man. D. C. 453

Crewler, Sarah, Sophy's second sister, a charming girl with a great deal of feeling. D. C. 377

Crewler, Sophy, fourth daughter of the Rev. Horace Crewler; "the dearest girl", whom Traddles married. D. C. 310.

Criminal. See also *Vagrant*.

Criminal, condemned for hawking

tin saucepans without a licence. O. T. 71.

Criminal, Shoeless, convicted for playing the flute. O. T. 70.

Crimp, original name of David Crimple (q.v.). M. C. 340.

Crimple, David, a pawnbroker who afterwards became secretary of Montague Tigg's Anglo-Bengalee Company. M. C. 174, 337.

Cripple Corner, where the business of Wilding & Co. had its offices. C. S. 508, 509.

Cripples, Master, son of Mr Cripples of the Dancing Academy. L. D. 73.

Cripples, Mr, owner of Mr Cripples's Academy. L. D. 73.

"Cripples, The". See *"Three Cripples"*.

Cripples, Two, boys hanged in Bloomsbury Square for their share in the Gordon riots. B. R. 459.

Cripps, Mrs, mother of Bob Sawyer's boy. P. P. 418.

Crisparkle, Mrs, mother of Mr Crisparkle, compared to a China shepherdess. E. D. 43.

Crisparkle, Rev. Septimus, minor canon of Cloisterham, tutor of Neville Landless, and a specimen of muscular Christianity. E. D. 7.

Crocodile Book, from which David Copperfield read to Peggotty. D. C. 12.

"Crooked Billet", in lower Street, where Joe Willet was to enlist. B. R. 182.

Crookey, attendant at Mr Namby's. P. P. 439.

Cropley, Miss, referred to by Mrs Nickleby. N. N. 328.

"Cross Keys", an inn in Wood Street, Cheapside, London. G. E. 118.

Crowl, Mr, a fellow lodger of Newman Noggs. N. N. 125.

"Crown, The", where Newman Noggs lived. N. N. 65.

"Crown and Anchor", a temporary ballroom at Greenwich Fair. S. B. 88.

"Crozier, The", a hotel in Cloisterham. E. D. 179.

Crummles, Master, elder son of Vincent Crummles. N. N. 219.

Crummles, Mrs, wife of Vincent Crummles. N. N. 224.

Crummles, Ninetta, "The Infant Phenomenon", daughter of Vincent Crummles. N. N. 224.

Crummles, Percy, younger son of Vincent Crummles. N. N. 223.

Crummles, Vincent, head of a travelling theatrical company which Nicholas Nickleby and Smike joined at Portsmouth; went to America. N. N. 216.

Crompton, Miss Amelia, one of the heads of Minerva House, a finishing establishment for young ladies. S. B. 244.

Crumpton, Miss Maria, one of the heads of Minerva House, a finishing establishment for young ladies. S. B. 244.

Cruncher, Jerry, a messenger for Tellson's Bank, and a resurrectionist; gave up his ghoulish occupation. T. T. C. 5.

Cruncher, Jerry, Jun., son of Jerry Cruncher. T. T. C. 38.

Cruncher, Mrs Jerry, wife of Jerry Cruncher, who annoyed her husband by praying. T. T. C. 38.

Crupp, Mrs, David Copperfield's landlady, afflicted with the spazzums, but a mother to her lodger. D. C. 271.

Crushton, Hon. Mr, a visitor to Bath, bosom friend of Lord Mutanhed. P. P. 391.

Cummins, Tom, referred to by one of Dodson & Fogg's clerks. P. P. 205.

Cupboard Room, in the Haunted House. C. S. 218.

Curate, at Little Paul Dombey's christening. D. S. 45.

Curate, Our. S. B. 7.

Curdle, Mr, a Shakespearean critic. N. N. 241.

Curdle, Mrs, wife of Mr Curdle. N. N. 241.

Cursitor Street, where Mr Snagsby had his business. B. H. 98.

Curzon, Thomas, hosier, employer of Mark Gilbert. B. R. 50.

Cute, Alderman, who wanted to put things down. Original, Sir Peter Laurie. C. B. 73, 74.

Cutler, Mr and Mrs, a newly-married couple who visited the Kenwigses. N. N. 127.

Cuttle, Captain Edward, a retired seaman, friend of Solomon Gills and Walter Gay; uncouth and unpolished, but kind-hearted. D. S. 33.

D

Dabber, Sir Dingleby, a poet in a rosy vision of Mrs Nickleby's. N. N. 265.

Dadson, Mr, writing-master at Minerva House, finishing-school for young ladies. S. B. 248.

Dadson, Mrs, wife of Mr Dadson. S. B. 248.

Daisy, Solomon, parish clerk and bellringer of Chigwell. B. R. 3, 4, 9.

Dame Darden, a name given to Esther Summerson (q.v.). Dancing-master, who taught Fanny Dorrit. L. D. 57.

Dando, head man at Searle's yard on the Thames. S. B. 74.

Danton, Mr, an impudent young man, a friend of Mr Kitterbell. S. B. 362.

Daph, one of Sir Geoffrey Manning's dogs. P. P. 193.

Darby, a constable, who accompanied Inspector Bucket to Tom-all-alone's. B. H. 240.

Darnay, Charles, a French *émigré* who renounced his fortune in favour of his tenants; became Marquis of St. Evremonde; acquitted of treason in London; condemned in Paris at the Revolution, but saved in spite of himself by Sydney Carton, who died in his place for love of Darnay's wife, Lucie Manette. T. T. C. 43.

Darnay, Lucie, daughter of Charles Darnay and Lucie Manette. T. T. C. 151.

Dartle, Rosa, Mrs Steerforth's companion, who detested Little Emily and insulted her in her desolation. D. C. 224.

Datchery, Dick, who took Mrs Tope's lodgings opposite Jasper's house; he has been supposed to be another of the characters in disguise, watching John Jasper. E. D. 179.

Daughter, of brickmaker. B. H. 82.

Daughter, of Mrs Rachael. B. H. 14.

Daughter, of physician, seller of patent medicines. C. S. 308.

Daughter, of Scrooge's old sweetheart. C. B. 26.

Daughter, of Sophy. C. S. 439.

Daughter, of the jailer at Marseilles, who called the prisoners "my birds". L. D. 5.

Daughter, Decidedly Grown-up, of a deaf old English mother. L. D. 18.

Daughter, Married, of Mr Porker's laundress. P. P. 510.

Daughters, of matchmaking mammas. P. P. 390.

Daughters, Three, of a landlady. B. H. 603.

Daughters, Three Growing-up, of a majestic English mamma and papa. L. D. 18.

Daughters, Two, of robe-maker. B. H. 102.

D'Aulnais, the name of Darnay's mother; the original of his adopted English name Darnay. T. T. C. 132.

David, a deaf gravedigger, who was pitied by the sexton. O. C. S. 303.

David, butler to the Cheeryble brothers. N. N. 368, 369.

Davis, Gilt, a brave private of marines; cherished a hopeless love for Miss Maryon. C. S. 143.

Dawes, nurse of Miss Wade's pupils. L. D. 527.

Dawkins, John, called the Artful Dodger, one of Fagin's pickpockets; led Oliver Twist into Fagin's clutches; ultimately transported for thieving. O. T. 41.

Dawlish, from near which the Nicklebys originally came. N. N. 2.

Daws, Mary, a kitchen-maid in Mr Dombey's service. D. S. 644.

Dawson, Mr, the surgeon who attended Mrs Robinson at her confinement. S. B. 14.

Deal, where Esther Summerson visited Richard Carstone. B. H. 476.

Dean, The, of Cloisterham. E. D. 7.

Debtor, who shared a room with Mr Micawber in the Kings' Bench Prison D. C. 127.

Dedlock, Lady Honoria, wife of Sir Leicester Dedlock; proved to be mother of Esther Summerson by Captain Hawdon before her marriage. B. H. 6.

Dedlock, Sir Leicester, Baronet, a proud gentlemen of ancient descent, with all the prejudices and virtues of his class. B. H. 7.

Dedlock, Sir Morbury, an ancestor of Sir Leicester Dedlock. B. H. 69.

Dedlock, Velomnia, a cousin of Sir Leicester Dedlock. B. H. 301.

"Dedlock Arms", a tavern near Chesney Wold. B. H. 400.

Deedles, a banker who shot himself. C. B. 83, 101.

Demple, George, one of the boys atSalem House. D. C. 61.

Dennis, Ned, the hangman, who was a ringleader in the riots; hanged for his part in them. B. R. 211.

Deptford, where the House to Let was. C. S. 189.

Deputy, a hideous small boy who attended Durdles, and whose animosity Jasper excited. E. D. 37.

Derrick, John, a valet. C. S. 425, 426.

Derrick, Mrs, wife of John Derrick. C., S. 425, 426.

Detective, who along with Tom arrested William Warden. S. B. 371.

Devasseur, M. Loyal, a landlord at a French watering-place. R. P. 348.

Devil's Punch Bowl, passed by Nicholas Nickleby and Smike on their way to Portsmouth. N. N. 214.

Dibabs, Jane, referred to by Mrs Nickleby. N. N. 560.

Dick, an hostler at Salisbury. M. C. 61.

Dick, a young workhouse playmate of Oliver Twist, whose blessing was the first Oliver ever received. O. T. 38, 94, 310.

Dick, guard of the coach to Yorkshire. N. N. 39.

Dick, Joram's youngest 'prentice. D. C. 562.

Dick, Mr Christopher's father, a waiter. C. S. 292, 293.

Dick, Tim Linkinwater's blind blackbird. N. N. 364.

Dick, Mr, a weak-minded man who lived with Betsey Trotwood; his real name was Richard Babley; he was writing a Memorial, but couldn't keep King Charles the First's head out of it. D. C. 147.

Digby, Smike's theatrical name. N. N. 299.

Dijon, where James Carker and Edith Dombey met—and parted. D. S. 586.

Dilber, Mrs, a laundress in one of Scrooge's visions. C. 13. 47.

Dingley Dell, a cricket club that played the All-Muggleton. P. P. 70.

Dingley Dell, near which Mr Wardle lived. P. P. 51.

Dingo, Professor, a former husband of Mrs Badger; of European reputation. B. H. 134.

Dingwall, Cornelius Brook, MP. S. B. 245.

Dingwall, Frederick Brook, son of Cornelius Brook Dingwall, M.P. S. B. 245.

Dingwall, Lavinia Brook, daughter of Cornelius Brook Dingwall, MP., placed at Minerva House under the Misses Crumpton. S. B. 244.

Dingwall, Mrs Brook, wife of Cornelius Brook Dingwall, MP. S. B. 245.

Diogenes, familiarly called Di, a dog at Dr Blimber's school, afterwards given to Florence Dombey by Mr Toots. D. S. 153, 197.

Director, Bank, at dinner with Mr Podsnap. O. M. F. 106.

Director, Bank, who dined with Mr Dombey. D. S. 398.

Director, East India, who dined with Mr Dombey. D. S. 398.

Dismal Jemmy, same as Jem Hutley (q.v.).

Diver, Colonel, editor of the "New York Rowdy Journal". M. C. 204.

Dobble, Mr, who gave a New-Year party. S. B. 169, 171.

Dobble, Mr, Junior, son of Mr Dobble. S. B. 171.

Dobble, Mrs, wife of Mr Dobble. S. B. 171.

Dobbleton, Dowager Duchess of. S. 13. 256.

Doctor. C. S. 425.

Doctor, in a story told by Sam Weller. P. P. 479.

Doctor, in the Children's Hospital. O. M. F. 265.

Doctor, who attended Mrs Marigold at the birth of Doctor Marigold. C. S. 403.

Doctor, who attended Nell at an inn. O. C. S. 257.

Doctor, who attended Oliver Twist at Mr Brownlow's. O. T. 61.

Doctor, who attended Rogue Riderhood when he was almost drowned. O. M. F. 355

Doctors, Two, who attended to Mr Toots. D. S. 616.

Doctors' Commons. S. B. 65; D. C. 267.

Dodger, Artful. See Dawkins, John.

Dodson, Mr, partner in the legal firm of Dodson & Fogg. P. P. 207.

Dodson & Fogg, attorneys of the plaintiff in Bardell *v.* Pickwick. P. P. 204.

Dog, defied by Quilp. O. C. S. 125.

Dog, great black-haired, like Mr Murdstone. D. C. 33.

Dogginson, a vestryman. R. P. 472.

Dolloby, Mr, the dealer to whom David Copperfield sold his waistcoat. D. C. 138.

Dolls, Mr, a name given to Mr Cleaver by Eugene Wrayburn. O. M. F. 431.

Dolly, of Esther Summerson. B. H. 11.

"Dolphin, The", an inn. D. C. 231.

Dombey, Edith. See *Granger*.

Dombey, Fanny, first wife of Mr Dombey, mother of Florence and Paul; she died at Paul's birth. D. S. 1.

Dombey, Florence, daughter of Mr Dombey, who repelled her love and ultimately drove her to flight; she was befriended by Captain Cuttle and married Walter Gay; her father, after his material ruin, lived with her repentant. D. S. 2.

Dombey, Paul, head of Dombey & Son, a proud man who neglected his daughter Florence; he made a loveless second marriage with Edith Granger, who ran away from him; his business failed, and he passed his last days with his daughter in her home. D. S. throughout.

Dombey, Paul, son of Paul Dombey, senior, who hoped that he would continue the greatness of Dombey & Son; he was taken to Brighton for his health, and educated there, but getting weaker he went home to die. Original, Harry Burnett, nephew of Dickens. D. S. 1.

Dombey & Son, a merchant firm in London, brought to ruin by James Carker. D. S. 1.

Domestic, to the Baron of Grogzwig. N. N. 56.

Doncaster, visited by Idle and Goodchild. L. T. 377, 421.

Donkey, Fair-complexioned. C. S. 325.

Donkey-boy, who brought Miss Murdstone to Betsey Trotwood's house. D. C. 159.

Donkeys, the excitement of Betsey Trotwood's life. D. C. 149.

Donny, Misses, Two, who kept a boarding-school at Reading, which Esther Summerson attended. B. H. 19.

Doodle, Lord, at Tulkinghorn's funeral. B. H. 549

Doorkeeper. T. T. C. 43.

Dor, Madame, in the employ of Jules Obenreizer; chaperon of Marguerite. C. S. 534

Dora. See *Copperfield, Dora*.

Dorker, a pupil of Mr Squeers. N. N. 29.

Dorking, whore Mrs Weller lived. P. P. 283.

Dornton, Sergeant, a detective. R. P. 407.

Dorrit, Amy, called Little Dorrit, the devoted drudge of her family, and their support; she nursed Arthur Clennam in the Marshalsea and afterwards married him. L. D. 32.

Dorrit, Edward, called Tip, Little Dorrit's spendthrift brother. L. D. 59.

Dorrit, Fanny, sister of Little Dorrit; she became a dancer and married Edmund Sparkler, Mrs Merdle's son. L. D. 58.

Dorrit, Frederick, brother of William Dorrit, a clarionet player in an orchestra; devoted to his younger niece, Little Dorrit. L. D. 62.

Dorrit, Little. See *Dorrit, Amy*.

Dorrit, Mrs, mother of Little Dorrit; she died when Little Dorrit was eight years old. L. D. 46, 51.

Dorrit, William, the Father of the Marshalsea, and of Little Dorrit; he came into a fortune, which was lost in the ruin of Mr Merdle. L. D. 45.

Dotheboys Hall, Mr Squeers's academy in Yorkshire, where boys were starved and ill-treated. N. N. 21, 60.

Double Room, in the Haunted House. C. S. 217.

Doubledick, Richard, a wild soldier who reformed; he married his old love, Mary Marshall. C. S. 65.

Dounce, John, a widower who was disappointed in a love affair; ultimately married his cook. S. B. 182.

Dover, where Betsey Trotwood lived. D. C. 144; also T. T. C. 10.

Dowdles, Two Miss, referred to by

Mrs Nickleby. N. N. 263.

Dowler, Captain, irascible husband of Mrs Dowler, whom the Pickwickians met at Bath. P. P. 382.

Dowler, Mrs, wife of Mr Dowler. P. P. 383.

Doyce, Daniel, a victim of the Circumlocution Office who became Clennam's partner, and made his fortune abroad. L. D. 92.

Doylance, a schoolmaster. C. S. 222.

Dragon, Mrs Lupin's horse. M. C. 439.

Drawers, Two, at "Royal George Hotel", Dover. T. T. C. 10, 11.

Draymen, Two, incidentally introduced. M. C. 638.

Dressmaker, to Mrs Kenwigs. N. N. 127.

Dressmaker, who seemed never to take her thimble off. D. C. 481.

Dringworth Brothers, a London firm. C. S. 255.

Driver, engaged by Grandfather Smallweed. B. H. 285.

Driver, of a carriage that contained Jonas Chuzzlewit and Montague Tigg. M. C. 505.

Driver, of a coach, whom Jonas Chuzzlewit treated at Pecksniff's expense. M. C. 259.

Driver, of a hearse. T. T. C. 112.

Driver, who drove Alfred Heathfield to Dr Jeddler's. C. B. 227.

Driver, who drove Harriet Carker to Alice Brown's deathbed. D. S. 638.

Driver, who drove Inspector Bucket and Esther Summerson in search of Lady Dedlock. B. H. 594

Driver, who drove Mr Garland and Kit to Little Nell's village. O. C. S. 398.

Drooce, Sergeant, one of the marines. C. S. 146.

Drood, Edwin, nephew of John Jasper, betrothed as a child to Rosa Bud; they agreed to become merely brother and sister; mysteriously disappeared and supposed to be murdered. E. D. 10.

Drowvey, Misses, Two, schoolmistresses. H. R. 458.

Drowvey and Grimmer, schoolmistresses. H. R. 457

Drum, The, in a band, who gave a New-Year greeting to Trotty Veda and his daughter. C. B. 121.

Drummer, Conscientious, who never left off. M. C. 433.

Drummle, Bentley, a boarder at Matthew Pocket's; married Estella, and ill-treated her; accidentally killed at last; called "The Spider". G. E. 138.

Drury Lane, near which Dick Swiveller lodged. O. C. S. 40.

Dubbley, an officer of Mr Nupkins. P. P. 259.

Duff, a Bow Street officer, who along with Blathers investigated the burglary at Mrs Maylie's house. O. T. 171.

Duke Street, St. James's, where Twemlow lived. O. M. F. 5.

Dulwich, where Mr Pickwick settled. P. P. 619.

Dumkins, Mr, a distinguished cricketer in the All-Muggleton team. P. P. 71.

Dumps, Nicodemus, a child-hating, miserable bachelor, nephew of Charles Kitterbell. S. B. 353.

Dunkle, Doctor Ginery, an American. M. C. 423.

Durdles, a stonemason at Cloisterham, in the monument way. E. D. 33

Dustman. D. C. 487.

Dustman, The Golden. See *Boffin, Nicodemus.*

E

"Eagle, The", a place of amusement. S. B. 172.

Eatanswill, where a parliamentary election in the old style took place, the two parties being Blue and Buff. Original most probably Sudbury. P. P. 123.

"Eatanswill Gazette", the organ of the Blue party, edited by Mr Pott. P. P. 124.

"Eatanswill Independent", organ of the Buff party. P. P. 124.

Eden, a pestilential swamp in the United States, to which Martin Chuzzlewit and Mark Tapley went to make their fortune. M. C. 296.

Edgware Road, near which the Bobsters lived. N. N. 406.

Edkins, Mr, a passenger on the steam excursion. S. B. 292, 303.

Edmunds, father of John Edmunds, the convict. P. P. 58.

Edmunds, John, a convict, who returned a penitent to his native village. P. P. 59.

Edmunds, Mrs, mother of John Edmunds, the convict. P. P. 59.

Edson, Mr, a lodger with Mrs Lirriper, father of Jenny Jackman Lirriper. C. S. 350, 394.

Edson, Mrs (Peggy), supposed wife of Mr Edson, who deserted her; her

child was adopted by Mrs Lirriper.
C. S. 350.

Edward, a donkey. O. M. F. 43.

Edwards, Miss, a pupil at Miss
Monflathers's school. O. C. S. 178.

Edwin. C. S. 83.

Egham Races. C. S. 192.

Ellen, a bride married for money and
made to die. L. T. 410, 411.

Ellis, Mr, in a bar-parlour. S. B. 176,
177.

Emanuel, Mr Stiggins's chapel. P. P.
575

Emilia, Mrs Orange's baby. H. R. 479

Emily, a hardened prisoner. S. B. 203.

Emily, Little, niece of Mr Peggotty,
engaged to Ham; betrayed and
abandoned by Steerforth, but rescued
by her uncle and accompanied him
to Australia. D. C. 24.

Emma, a waitress. C. S. 99.

Emma, maid at Mr Wardle's. P. P. 51.

Emmeline. C. S. 114.

Emperor of France, president of a
juvenile court martial H. R. 459.

"Endeavour, The", hired for the
steam excursion. S. B. 291.

Endell, Martha, a poor girl who
befriended Little Em'ly. D. C. 249

Engine-driver, on an American
railway. M. C. 268.

Engine-driver, who told how the
signalman met his death. C. S. 501.

Englishman, Mr The, a corruption
of Mr Langley (q.v.), through
L'Anglais. C. S. 305.

"Esau Slodge", a steamer that called
at Eden. M. C. 414.

Estella, heroine of G. E.; brought up
by Miss Havisham and educated as
a lady; married Bentley Drummle
and was ill-treated; afterwards

married Pip; proved to be daughter
of Abel Magwitch and Molly. G. E.
throughout.

Eton Slocomb, where Nicholas
Nickleby dined on his coach
journey to Yorkshire. N. N. 40.

Evans, Jemima, called also J'mima
Ivins, beloved of Mr Samuel
Wilkins, who took her to the
"Eagle". S. B. 172.

Evans, Mr, a friend of the Cattletons.
S. B. 318.

Evans, Richard, a pupil of Mr
Marton. O. C. S. 296.

Evenson, John, boarder of Mrs Tibbs,
a thorough Radical. S. B. 224.

"Exchange or Barter", boy at Salem
House. D. C. 67.

Ezekiel, the boy at Mugby Junction.
C. S. 480, 485.

F

Fagin, a villainous old Jew who
trained up thieves in Saffron Hill;
got Oliver Twist into his clutches;
hanged for complicity in Nancy's
murder; name from a companion
of Dickens at the blacking
warehouse where he was employed
for a time. O. T. 44.

"Family, The", a ship. H. R. 476.

Family Pet, a burglar. O. T. 175.

Fang, Mr, an overbearing, harsh
police magistrate; original, Mr
Laing of Hatton Garden. O. T. 55.

Fanny, a young lady engaged to be
married. C. S. 38.

Fareway, Adelina, daughter of Lady
Fareway, married to Mr Granville
Wharton. G. S. E. 503.

Fareway, Lady, mother of Adelina Fareway. G. S. E. 501.

Fareway, Mr, second son of Sir Gaston and Lady Fareway. G. S. E. 500.

Farm Labourer, with whom Mrs Gargery spoke just before she was attacked. G. E. 87.

Farmer, at Hoghton Towers. G. S. E. 493

Farmers, Three, who forced Pip and Bentley Drummle from the inn fire. G. E. 261.

Farrier, who declined to face the witches. M. H. C. 475.

Farrier, who denounced Darnay at Beauvais. T. T. C. 179.

Fat Boy. See, *Joe*.

Father, of children opposite Dombey's house. D. S. 194.

Father, of George Silverman. G. S. E. 488.

Father, of Mrs Peerybingle. C. B. 183.

Feeder, Mr, BA, an assistant in Dr Blimber's school; he married Cornelia Blimber, and became head of the school. D. S. 112.

Feeder, Rev. Alfred, MA, who married his brother, Mr Feeder, BA, to Cornelia Blimber. D. S. 659.

Feenix, Cousin, cousin of Edith Dombey, garrulous but goodhearted; fond of referring to his parliamentary days. D. S. 346.

Fellow, Lubberly, who helped to catch Oliver Twist. O. T. 53.

Fellow, Simpering, with weak legs, who took Agnes Wickfield down to dinner. D. C. 286.

Fellow, Tall, who attacked Gabriel Varden. B. R. 376.

Fellow, Uncommonly Ill-looking, in "The Story of the Bagman's Uncle". P. P. 536.

Fellow, Young, who was going to burn down Varden's door. B. R. 369.

Fellows, three or four stout, bushy eye-browed, canty old Scotch, in "The Story of the Bagman's Uncle". P. P. 532.

Female, Dilapidated, a servant of Mr Chester. B. R. 153.

Female, Genteel, a client of the General Agency Office. N. N. 145.

Female, Singularly Tall, in a black veil, mother of a criminal. S. B. 280.

Fendall, Sergeant, a detective. R. P. 407.

Ferdinand, Miss, schoolfellow of Rosa Bud at the Nuns' House. E. D. 73.

Fern, Lilian, Will Fern's little niece. C. B. 86, 88.

Fern, Will, "put down" by Alderman Cute. C. B. 83, 86.

Fezziwig, Mr, to whom Scrooge was apprenticed; seen by Scrooge in one of his visions as giving a Christmas ball. C. B. 22.

Fezziwig, Mrs, wife of Mr Fezziwig. C. B. 23.

Fezziwigs, Miss, Three, daughters of Mr Fezziwig. C. B. 23.

Fibbitson, Mrs, an old woman in an almshouse. D. C. 57.

Fiddler, at Fezziwig's ball. C. B. 23.

Field, Inspector. R. P. 427.

Field Lane, near which was Fagin's den. O. T. 44, 142.

Fielding, May, sweetheart of Edward Plummer; almost forced into a marriage with Tackleton, but saved in time by Edward's return from South America. C. B. 155.

Fielding, Mrs, mother of May Fielding. C. B. I55.

Fielding, Sir John, a magistrate. B. R. 341.

Fikey, a forger. R. P. 413•

Filer, Mr, a very statistical gentleman, who lacked human feeling for the poor. C. B. 73, 74.

Filletoville, Only Son of the Marquess of, in "The Story of the Bagman's Uncle". P. P. 536, 541.

"Finches of the Groves", a club joined by Pip. G. E. 200.

Finching, Flora, daughter of Mr Casby, and widow of Mr Finching; an early love of Arthur Clennam. Original, same as original of Dora Copperfield. L. D. 118.

Finchley, where the Garland family lived. O. C. S. 110.

Fips, Mr, a lawyer who acted on behalf of old Martin Chuzzlewit in befriending Tom Pinch. M. C. 477.

Fireman, on an American railway. M. C. 269.

Fireman, who was also a waterman, father of Mealy Potatoes. D. C. 119.

Fireman-waterman, Old, who took Percy Noakes out to the "Endeavour". S. B. 295.

Fish, Mr, secretary to Sir Joseph Bowley. C. B. 8.

Fisher, Mr, husband of Mrs Fisher. C. S. 172.

Fisher, Mrs Fanny, daughter of Mrs Yenning; her child was killed by the pirates. C. S. 154.

Fitz-Marshall, Charles, a disguise of Alfred Jingle (q.v.).

"Five Sisters of York", a story in *Nicholas Nickleby*. N. N. 45.

Fixem, Mr Bung's master, the broker,

who acted very considerately to an old gentleman. S. B. 22.

Fizkin, Horatio, Buff candidate at the Eatanswill election, defeated by the Hon. Samuel Slumkey. P. P. 124.

Fizzgig, Don Bolaro, father of Donna Christina Fizzgig. P, P. 10.

Fizzgig, Donna Christina, an imaginary Spanish conquest of Alfred Jingle. P. P. 10.

Fladdock, General, an American who crossed the Atlantic in the same ship as Martin Chuzzlewit. M. C. 200, 229.

Flair, Honourable Augustus, a friend of Lord Peter. S. B. 310.

Flamwell, Mr, a gentleman who pretended to remarkably extensive information. S. B. 273.

Flasher, Wilkins, a stockbroker. P. P. 604.

Fledgeby, Fascination, a young dandy who carried on a moneylending business under the name of Pubsey & Co., but tried to hide his connection with it; Lammle tried to marry him to Georgiana Podsnap, in order to gain some money for himself, but the scheme failed; he was soundly thrashed by Lammle. O. M. F. 209.

Fledgeby, Mr, father of Fascination Fledgeby. O. M. F. 214.

Fledgeby, Mrs, mother of Fascination Fledgeby. O. M. F. 214.

Fleet, The, a debtors' prison, in which Mr Pickwick was incarcerated. P. P. 443.

Fleetwood, Master, son of Mr and Mrs Fleetwood, one of the steam excursion party. S. B. 297.

Fleetwood, Mr, one of the steam excursion party. S. B. 297.

Fleetwood, Mrs, wife of Mr Fleetwood, one of the steam excursion party. S. B. 297.

Fleming, Agnes, mother of Oliver Twist and sister of Rose Maylie; betrayed by Monks's father; died in the workhouse at Oliver's birth. O. T. 2, 303, 319.

Flintwinch, Affery, wife of Jeremiah Flintwinch; in terror of the two clever ones, her husband and Mrs Clennam. L. D. 27.

Flintwinch, Ephraim, twin brother of Jeremiah Flintwinch; the custodian of the papers Jeremiah stole from Mrs Clennam, L. D. 619.

Flintwinch, Jeremiah, partner of Mrs Clennam; stole valuable papers, and placed them in his brother's keeping. L. D. 30.

Flite, Miss, a suitor in Chancery, good-hearted but crazy. B. H. 3.

Flopson, a nurse in Matthew Pocket's family. G. E. 136.

Flowers, maid to Mrs Skewton. D. S. 307.

Fluggers, who did the heavy business in Vincent Crummles's theatrical company. N. N. 300.

Fly-drivers, at Dover.   D. C. 144

Fogg, Mr, partner of Mr Dodson in Dodson & Fogg. P. P. 207.

Fogo, Frosty-faced. E. D. 165.

Folair, Thomas, a member of VincentCrummles's company. N. N. 226.

Followers, Six, of the Miss Fezziwigs. C. B. 23.

Folly Ditch, in Southwark, surrounding Jacob's Island. O. T. 293.

Foodle, Duke of, at Mr Tulkinghorn's funeral. B. H. 549.

Footman, in a light-blue suit. P. P. 407.

Footman, in a yellow waistcoat, with a coach-trimming border. P. P. 405.

Footman, in green-foil smalls. P. P. 405.

Footman, in purple cloth, with a great extent of stocking. P. P. 406.

Footman, in the family where Ruth Pinch was governess. M. C. 107, 446.

Footman, who interrupted Trotty Veck's dinner. C. B. 73.

Footman, Mr Dorrit's. L. D. 362.

Footman, Mr Merdle's. L. D: 188.

Footman, Sir Leicester Dedlock's, along with Mercury. B. H. 562.

Foreigner, at Mugby Junction. C. S. 482.

Foreigner, one of the poor travellers at Rochester. C. S. 63.

Foreigner, who accompanied Mr and Mrs Dombey to Paris. D. S. 341.

Fort Pitt, at Chatham, where Mr Winkle's affair of honour with Dr Slammer came off. P. P. 20.

Foulon, put to death by the Paris mob. T. T. C. 160.

Foundling Hospital. C. S. 503.

Fountain Court, where Tom Pinch and his sister often met. M. C. 537.

Foxey, Old, father of Sampson and Sally Brass. O. C. S. 203.

Frank, Little, the Poor Relation's companion. C. S. 27.

Fred, Scrooge's nephew. C. B. 5, 39

Freeman's Court, Cornhill, where Dodson & Fogg's office was. P. P. 191.

Frenchman, who dined with Mr
   Podsnap, and was patronized by
   him. O. M. F. 104.

Friar, in "The Five Sisters of York". N.
   N. 46.

Friend, of Dr Haggage. L. D. 47

Friend, of Jules Obenreizer. C. S 555

Frome, where Captain Taunton's
   mother lived. C. S. 71.

Frost, Miss, a pupil at Our School. R.
   P. 466.

Fruiterer, who was sheriff of the City
   of London and Lord Mayor elect.
   M. H. C. 438.

Fulham, where Sir Barnet Skettles
   lived. D. S. 266.

Functionary, at Beauvais, who placed
   an escort in charge of Darnay. T. T.
   C. 178.

Furnaceman, who befriended Little
   Nell. O. C S. 248.

Furnaceman, Another. O. C. S. 249.

Furnival's Inn, where John Westlock
   lodged, M. C. 442; where Samuel
   Briggs was an attorney, S. B. 291;
   where Rosa Bud lived, E. D. 203.

G

G, Miss Pupford's supposed lover. C.
   S. 278.

Gabelle, Theophile, a postmaster
   and taxing functionary, in the
   village near the Marquis St.
   Evremonde's seat; imprisoned
   during the Revolution. T. T. C.
   82.

Gabrielle, usually called Bebelle, the
   child friend of Corporal Theophile.
   C. S. 313.

Gallanbile, Mr, a member of
   Parliament, a client of the General
   Agency Office. N. N. 146.

Game Chicken, The, a pugilist
   engaged by Mr Toots. D. S. 245.

Gamekeeper, at Hatfield post-office,
   whom Bill Sikes came across in his
   flight. O. T. 282.

Gamfield, Mr, a chimney-sweeper in
   Oliver Twist's native town; a cruel
   man. O. T. 12, 16, 302.

Gamp, Sairey, a nurse addicted to
   strong drink; fond of referring to
   her friend Mrs Harris. M. C. 244.

Gander, Mr, one of Mrs Todgers's
   boarders. M. C. 114.

Gaoler, in charge of two convicts. G.
   E. 166.

Garden Court, where Pip and
   Herbert Pocket lived. G. E. 229.

Garden Room, in the Haunted
   House. C. S. 218.

Gardener, at Chesney Wold. B. H. 68.

Gardener, at Miss Donny's boarding
   school, who showed his liking for
   Esther Summerson. B. H. 21.

Gardener, suspected of murdering
   Reuben Haredale, but was
   murdered himself by Mr Rudge. B.
   R. 12.

Gargery, Georgiana Maria, sister of
   Pip and wife of Joe Gargery; of
   a harsh disposition; permanently
   incapacitated by a blow from
   Orlick, and died from its effects.
   G. E. 4, 349.

Gargery, Joe, a blacksmith, husband
   of Pip's sister, afterwards of Biddy;
   a simple, unlettered, true-hearted
   man. G. E. 5.

Gargery, Pip, a son of Joe Gargery
   and Biddy. G. E. 353

Garland, Abel, son of Mr and Mrs

Garland, articled to Mr Witherden, the notary. O. C. S. 84.

Garland, Mr, a kind old gentleman who took Kit Nubbles into his service. O. C. S. 83.

Garland, Mr, called The Bachelor, an old bachelor who lived with the clergyman in the village where Little Nell settled; proved to be brother of Mr Garland, Kit's master. O. C. S. 294, 389.

Garland, Mrs, wife of Mr Garland. O. C. S. 83.

Garraway's Coffee House. C. S. 26.

Gashford, Mr, secretary to Lord George Gm-don; an unprincipled villain; sold his master's secrets and became a Government spy; finally committed suicide by poison. B. R. 202.

Gaspard, who killed the Marquis St. Evremonde for running over his child, and was hanged for it. T. T. C. 21.

Gate-porter, at Furnival's Inn.

Gattleton, Caroline, a daughter of Mrs Gattleton. S. B. 320.

Gattleton, Lucina, a daughter of Mrs Gattleton. S. B. 318.

Gattleton, Mr, a stockbroker, whose family went in for private theatricals. S. B. 318.

Gattleton, Mrs, wife of Mr Gattleton. S. B. 319.

Gattleton, Sempronius, son of Mr Gattleton. S. B. 318.

Gay, Florence, daughter of Walter Gay and Florence Dombey. D. S. 682.

Gay, Paul, son of Walter Gay and Florence Dombey. D. S. 682.

Gay, Walter, nephew of Sol Gills, employed as a cleric with Dombey & Son; sent on business to the West Indies, and believed drowned; turned up and married Florence Dombey when she fled from home. D. S. 27.

Gazingi, Miss, a member of Vincent Crummles's company. N. N. 228.

General, Mrs, daughter of a clerical dignitary in a cathedral town, engaged by Mr Dorrit in his prosperity as chaperon of Amy and Fanny Dorrit; supposed to have designs on Mr Dorrit. L. D. 343

General Agency Office, at which Nicholas Nickleby twice sought for a situation. N. N. 145, 347.

General Officer, at dinner with Mr Podsnap. O. M. F. 106.

Genius of Despair and Suicide, that appeared to the Baron of Grogzwig. N. N. 57.

Gentleman. C. B. 111.

Gentleman. M. H. C. 482.

Gentleman. O. M. F. 9.

Gentleman, a brass and copper founder, who employed Ruth Pinch as a governess. M. C. 448.

Gentleman, a prisoner of the Revolution. T. T. C. 184.

Gentleman, at Caddy Jellyby's marriage. B. H. 326.

Gentleman, at Deaf and Dumb Institution. C. S. 418.

Gentleman, at Podsnap's dinner. O. M. F. 105.

Gentleman, at Podsnap's dinner. O. M. F. 111.

Gentleman, from French Consul. C. S. 387.

Gentleman, in a checked shirt and mosaic studs, one of Mr Lowten's convivial party. P. P. 216.

Gentleman, in an embroidered coat. P. P. 409.

Gentleman, in a shirt emblazoned with pink anchors, at Bob Sawyer's. P. P. 343

Gentleman, in black, an official in a law court. P. P. 363.

Gentleman, in black, who did not convict a deaf and dumb boy. O. C. S. 255.

Gentleman, in black calico sleeves, in a crowd. P. P. 6.

Gentleman, in the mail coach from London to Hatfield. O. T. 282.

Gentleman, to whom smoking was board and lodging, at Mr Lowten's convivial gathering. P. P. 216.

Gentleman, who called at Dombey's house in connection with the sale. D. S. 644.

Gentleman, who "did" the review department in the Latan-nazil Gazelle. P. P. 157.

Gentleman, who drove a donkey. O. M. F. 43

Gentleman, who employed Richard. C. B. 113.

Gentleman, who examined children. H. T. 248.

Gentleman, who had been at Crockford's all night (an MP). N. N. 8, 13.

Gentleman, who looked after Mr Pecksniff. M. C. 432.

Gentleman, who praised the good old times. C. 13.74. 75.

Gentleman, who taught dancing at Miss Twinkleton's. E. D. 77.

Gentleman, who visited the Monument. M. C. 454

Gentleman, who was a dirty feeder. M. C. 421.

Gentleman, who was polishing a gun-barrel in the Circumlocution Office. L. D. 90.

Gentleman, whose daughter was taught by Esther Summerson. B. H. 21.

Gentleman, whose pocket had been picked by the Dodger. O. T. 258.

Gentleman, with a double chin. N. N. 10.

Gentleman, with an uncombed head, who kept a whistlingshop in the Fleet. P. P. 501

Gentleman, American. M. C. 289.

Gentleman, American, at Mugby Junction. C. S. 482.

Gentleman, Business, trustee of Miss Akersham. O. M. F. 95.

Gentleman, Catholic, in fear of the Gordon rioters. B. H 357.

Gentleman, Choleric, who objected to travelling beside convicts. G. E. 66.

Gentleman, Convivial, at Todgers's. M. C. 115.

Gentleman, Deaf, a friend of Master Humphrey. M. H. C. 437, 457.

Gentleman, Deaf Old, before whom a will suit was tried. P. P. 482.

Gentleman, Debating, at Todgers's. M. C. 114.

Gentleman, Elderly, at a cricket match. P. P. 72.

Gentleman, Elderly, who helped a street artist. C. S. 326.

Gentleman, Elderly American. M. C 289.

Gentleman, Elderly Country, in a street crowd. C. S. 325.

Gentleman, English, going to the United States. M. C. 201.

Gentleman, Fat Old, one of Mr Wardle's guests at Dingley Dell. P. P. 53.

Gentleman, Feeble Old, at a party in the Wackles's house. O. C. S. 51.

Gentleman, Fox-hunting, brother of Mrs Ralph Nickleby. N. N. 610.

Gentleman, Goggle-eyed, a spiritualist. C. S. 204.

Gentleman, Hearty-looking, a fellow-passenger of Nicholas Nickleby on the Yorkshire coach. N. N. 38.

Gentleman, Husky-voiced, who ate and drank a great deal. D. C. 54

Gentleman, Inside, whose head was broken in the coach accident. N. N. 44

Gentleman, Irascible Old, referred to in a story by Sam Weller. P. P. 479

Gentleman, Literary, at Todgers's. M. C. 114.

Gentleman, Literary, with whom Nicholas Nickleby had a warm passage. N. N. 491.

Gentleman, Little Thin Old, in a story told by Sam Weller. P. P. 330.

Gentleman, Lunatic, who occupied Copperfield's old home. D. C. 244.

Gentleman, Meek, who disturbed Mr Podsnap's company with unpleasant facts. O. M. F. 111.

Gentleman, Mottle-faced, in a blue shawl. P. P. 475

Gentleman, Old, a retired conveyancer who dined at Gray's Inn Collee House. D. C. 631.

Gentleman, Old, inside a coach. P. P. 292.

Gentleman, Old, who died at Chigwell Row. B. R. 10.

Gentleman, Old, who looked into Sol Gills's shop. D. S. 89.

Gentleman, Old, with a bald head, on the steam excursion. S. B. 301.

Gentleman, Professional, at the piano in the "Cripples". O. T. 144.

Gentleman, Red-faced. M. H. C. 476.

Gentleman, Red-faced, on 'Change. C. B. 45.

Gentleman, Sallow, engaged at a theatre. M. C. 57.

Gentleman, Scientific, whom Sam Weller stunned. P. P. 433.

Gentleman, Short, at the marriage of Bunsby and MacStinger. D. S. 663.

Gentleman, Slim, at a cricket match. P. P. 72.

Gentleman, Smoking, at Todgers's M. C. 115.

Gentleman, Sporting, at Todgers's M. C. 114.

Gentleman, Sprightly, engaged at a theatre. L. D. 185.

Gentleman, Stout, at a cricket match. P. P. 70.

Gentleman, Tall French, at breakfast with the Meagleses and Mr Clennam. L. D. 18.

Gentleman, Tall Thin, who nominated Horatio Fizkin for Eatanswill. P. P. 135.

Gentleman, Theatrical, at Todgers's. M. C. 114.

Gentleman, Vocal, at Todgers's. M. C. 115.

Gentleman, Weazen Old, who ogled a nursery-maid. B. R 88.

Gentleman, White-headed Old, who taught Oliver Twist at Chertsey. O. T. 184.

Gentleman, Young, attached to the stable department. P. P. 166.

Gentleman, Young, grand-nephew of old Martin Chuzzlewit M. C. 44.

Gentleman, Young, in an India-rubber cloak. P. P. 385.

Gentleman, Young, in a parody upon a greatcoat. P. P. 385.

Gentleman, Young, on stilts, one of Mr Grinder's show party. O. C. S. 101.

Gentleman in Small Clothes, a madman who made love to Mrs Nickleby. N. N. 373.

Gentleman in White Waistcoat, one of the parochial board. O. T. 8.

Gentlemen, Some Half-dozen Close-shaved, at a theatre. L. D. 184.

Gentlemen, Three Military. B. R. 186.

Gentlemen, Three or Four very Sleepy, who heard a will suit on appeal. P. P. 483.

Gentlemen, Two, who brought Miss Twinlcleton to Mrs Billickin's. E. D. 221.

Gentlemen, Two, who called on Scrooge for a subscription in aid of the poor. C. B. 6, 57.

Gentlemen, Two, who examined Mr Jellyby in bankruptcy. B. H. 255.

George. See *Rouncewell, George*.

George, a bachelor friend of Mr Kenwigs. N. N. 127.

George, a coachman, friend of Mr Weller. P. P. 469.

George, a lad at Astley's. S. B. 79.

George, an articled clerk, lover of Miss Buffle. C. S. 383, 384.

George, a waiter. C. S. 336.

George, caravan-driver to Mrs Jarley, whom he ultimately married. O. C. S. 149.

George, guard of a coach. C. S. 87.

George, guard of the coach that took David Copperfield from Yarmouth to London. D. C. 53.

George, Aunt, who gave a Christmas party. S. B. 166.

George, Mrs, a visitor at Mrs Quilp's. O. C. S. 25.

"George, The", an inn near Chertsey. O. T. 188.

George, Uncle, who gave a Christmas party. S. B. 165.

"George and Gridiron, The", where Mr Christopher began waitering. C. S. 293.

"George and New Inn", at Greta Bridge, where Nicholas Nickleby's coach journey ended. N. N. 59.

"George and Vulture Tavern", Lombard Street, where Mr Pickwick lived after leaving Mrs Bardell's. P. P. 278.

George's Shooting Gallery, kept by George Rouncewell. B. H. 234.

Georgiana, a cousin of Matthew Pocket. G. E. 149.

Gerrard Street, Soho, where Mr Jaggers lived. G. E. 154.

Ghost, that haunted Mr Redlaw. C. B. 262.

Ghost, Marley's. See *Marley*.

Ghost of Christmas Past, which appeared to Scrooge. C. B. 17, 18.

Ghost of Christmas Present, which appeared to Scrooge. C. B. 29.

Ghost of Christmas Yet to Come, which appeared to Scrooge. C. B. 44.

Ghost's Walk, at Chesney Wold. B. H. 63, 69.

Giant, shown by Mr Vuffin. O. C. S. 108.

Giggles, Miss, schoolfellow of Rosa Bud. E. D. 73.

Gilbert, Mark, apprentice to Thomas Curzon, admitted as one of the 'Prentice Knights. B. R. 50.

Giles, Jeremie, and Giles. C. S. 542, 543.

Giles, Mr, Mrs Maylie's butler and steward. O. T. 157.

Gills, Solomon, uncle of Waller Gay, and keeper of a shop for the sale of nautical instruments; he went in search of his missing nephew. D. S. 26.

Gimblet, Brother. G. S. E. 495

Gipsy, at Greenwich Fair. S. B. 85.

Gipsy, condemned to be hanged. B. R. 445

Gipsy, who helped to lead Nell's grandfather astray. O. C. S.

Girl, a pupil of Prince Turveydrop. B. H. 252.

Girl, a pupil of Prince Turveydrop. B. H. 415.

Girl, a servant in "The Valiant Soldier". O. C. S. 171.

Girl, carried across the street by Sydney Carton. T. T. C. 227.

Girl, employed by Mr Nupkins. P. P. 272.

Girl, engaged by Captain Cattle to attend on Florence Dombey. D. S. 533

Girl, executed along with Sydney Carton, and comforted by him in her last hours. T. T. C. 257, 272.

Girl, servant at Harold Skimpole's house. B. H. 458.

Girl, servant of Mr Brownlow. O. T. 78.

Girl, servant to Scrooge's nephew. C. B. 57.

Girl, sweetheart of Edmund Longford. C. B. 316.

Girl, who looked after Mrs Kenwigs's baby. N. N. 141.

Girl, whose ears had been pulled by her mistress. C. B. 23.

Girl, Beautiful Jewish, who attended on Lord George Gordon in Newgate. B. R. 484.

Girl, Irish, a servant at Pawkins's. M. C. 209.

Girl, Odd, a servant in the Haunted House. C. S. 211.

Girl, Pretty, who was frightened by David Copperfield. D. C. 607.

Girl, Smartly Dressed, an inn servant, in "The Bagman's Story". P. P. 142.

Girl Domestic, in Lamps's house. C. S. 461.

Girls, Four, who lived opposite Florence Dombey. D. S. 188, 194.

Girls, Little, of Mrs Leo Hunter. P. P. 158.

Girls, Three or Four Romping. P. P. 181.

Girls, Two, day scholars. O. C. S. 51.

Glamour, Bob, a customer of the "Six Jolly Fellowship Porters" O. M. F. 52.

Glibbery, Bob, potboy at the "Six Jolly Fellowship Porters". O. M. F. 52.

"Glorious Apollos", a club to which Dick Swiveller belonged. O. C. S. 79.

Glubb, Old, who drew Paul Dombey's coach at Brighton. D. S. 85, 119.

Glumper, Sir Thomas, present at the Gattletons' performance of Othello. S. B. 322.

Gobler, Mr, boarder of Mrs Tibbs, with a weak digestion; he married Mrs Bloss. S. B. 221.

Goblin of the Bell, that spoke to Trotty Veck. C. B. 96.

Goblins, that carried off Gabriel Grub. P. P. 310.

Godalming, where Nicholas Nickleby and Smike spent a night on their way to Portsmouth. N. N. 214.

Gog, one of the giants of the Guildhall. M. H. C. 443

"**Golden Cross**", an inn visited by Mr Pickwick. P. P. 5.

"**Golden Cross, The**", an inn at Charing Cross where David Copperfield stayed. D. C. 218.

Golden Dustman. See *Boffin, Nicodemus*.

"**Golden Head**", a hotel at Dijon, where James Carker and Edith Dombey met by arrangement, and where Edith spurned Canker. D. S. 588.

"**Golden Key**", Gabriel Varden's house. B. R. 25.

Golden Lion Court, where Miss Miggs's sister lived. B. R. 56.

Golden Lucy, child of Mrs Atherfield; died on board the boat of the Golden Mary. C. S. 121.

"**Golden Mary**", a ship that is wrecked. C. S. 118.

Golden Square, where Ralph Nickleby lived, and also Newman Noggs. N. N. 5, 65.

Golding, Mary, bathing at Ramsgate. S. 13. 260.

Goldstraw, Dick, husband of Mrs Goldstraw. C. S. 505.

Goldstraw, Mrs Sarah, housekeeper to Mr Wilding; formerly a nurse at the Foundling Hospital. C. S. 504, 517.

Gondoliers, Mr Corrit's. L. D. 394.

Goodchild, Francis, one of the idle apprentices. Original, Dickens himself. L. T. 359

Goodwin, Mrs Pott's bodyguard. P. P. 187.

Goody, Mrs, referred to by Frank Milvey. O. M. F. 83.

Gordon, Colonel, a relative of Lord George Gordon, who barred his access to Parliament. B. R. 289.

Gordon, Emma, one of Sleary's troupe, who would have been a mother to Sissy Jupe. H. T. 275.

Gordon, Lord George, the central figure of the Gordon riots; died in prison as a convert to Judaism. B. R. 201.

Goswell Street, where Mr Pickwick lodged with Mrs Barden. P. P. 5, 118.

Governor, of a prison. G. E. 337.

Governor, Jack, a sailor; married Patty, sister of the tenant of the Haunted House. C. S. 218.

Governor of the Bastille, who was guillotined. T. T. C. 158.

Gowan, Henry, an artist, who found good in most men, but lowered it where it was, and set it up where it was not; he married Minnie Meagles, and was supported by his father-in-law. L. D. 159.

Gowan, Mrs, mother of Henry, living at Hampton Court. L. D. 161.

Gradgrind, Adam Smith, one of the younger Gradgrinds. H. T. 261.

Gradgrind, Jane, younger sister of Louisa. H. T. 261.

Gradgrind, Louisa. See *Bounderby, Louisa*.

Gradgrind, Malthus, one of the younger Gradgrinds. H. T. 261.

Gradgrind, Mrs, a lady of surpassing feebleness. H. T. 257.

Gradgrind, Thomas, a square man, father of Louisa and Thomas; afterwards rounded and softened by misfortune. H. T. 248.

Gradgrind, Thomas, son of the elder Thomas Gradgrind, spoiled by his father's training; a cleric in Bounderby's Bank, which he robbed; Sleary helped him to leave the country. H. T. 254.

Graham, Hugh, a London apprentice of Queen Elizabeth's time. M. H. C. 445

Graham, Mary, companion of old Martin Chuzzlewit; married Martin Chuzzlewit, junior. M. C. 21.

Grainger, a friend of Steerforth's. D. C. 275.

Grandfather of Little Nell, an old curiosity dealer who tried unsuccessfully to gain wealth by gambling in order to provide for Nell, to whom he was passionately devoted; got into Quilp's clutches and was ejected from his house and shop; wandered aimlessly with Nell and endured privations; settled at length in a quiet village, where after the death of Nell he died heart-broken. O. C. S. 4.

Grandmarina, a good fairy. H. R. 464.

Granger, Edith, a young widow, daughter of Mrs Skewton ; married to Mr Dombey, but eloped with Carker, whom she did not live with; befriended Florence, and bade her a pathetic farewell. D. S. 224.

Grannett, Mr, an overseer. O. T. 129.

Grave-digger. B. R. 10.

Graymarsh, a pupil of Squeers. N. N. 73.

Grayper, Mr and Mrs, neighbours of David Copperfield at the Rookery. D. C. 100.

Gray's Inn, where Mr Perker's office was situated, P. P. 213; where Traddles had his chambers. D. C. 631.

Gray's Inn Coffee-house, where David Copperfield inquired about Traddles. D. C. 630.

Gray's Inn Square, where Percy Noakes had chambers. S. 13. 288.

Great Place. C. S. 306.

"Great White Horse", an inn at Ipswich, where Mr Pickwick put up. P. P. 235.

Great Winglebury. See *Winglebury*.

Green, Miss, an elderly lady at the Kenwigses. N. N. 127, 129.

Green, Mr, an aeronaut. S. 13. 96.

Green, Tom, alias of Joe Willet. B. R. 341.

Greengrocer, hired by the Kitterbells to wait at a christening party. S. B. 361.

"Greenleaf", a boarding-school at Reading, where Esther Summerson was educated. B. H. 19.

Greenwich, where Bella Wilfer entertained her father, and where she was married to John Rokesmith. O. M. F. 257, 532.

Greenwich Fair. S. B. 83.

Greenwich Park. C. S. 81.

Greenwood, *alias* Joby, a tramp. C. S. 208.

Gregory, foreman at Murdstone & Grinby's. D. C. 124.

Gregsbury, Mr, a member of Parliament in search of a private secretary, to whom Nicholas Nickleby made unsuccessful application. N. N. 147.

Greta Bridge, near which was Squeers's Academy. N. N. 21.

Grewgious, Hiram, guardian of Rosa Bud, an angular man, but not such a dry chip as he looked. E. D. 74.

Gride, Arthur, an old money-lender, friend of Ralph Nickleby, whom her father tried to force Madeline Bray to marry; he was murdered. N. N. 473.

Gridley, Mr, the "man from Shropshire", ruined by a Chancery suit. B. H. 3, 164.

Griffin, Miss, a schoolmistress. C. S. 224.

Griggses, friends of the Nupkinses. P. P. 271.

Grimble, Sir Thomas, referred to by Mrs Nickleby. N. N. 346.

Grimwig, Mr, a friend of Mr Brownlow, who had no confidence in Oliver Twist; always threatening to eat his head. O. T. 75.

Grimwood, Eliza, a murdered woman. R. P. 420.

Grinder, Mr, a showman. O. C. S. 101.

Grip, Barnaby Rudge's raven, whose frequent cry was "I'm a devil, I'm a devil". B. R. 39.

Grizzled Velveteen, properly Toby Magsman (q.v.). C. S. 189.

Grocer, who dealt with Mrs Pipchin. D. S. 107.

Groffin, Thomas, chemist, one of the jury in Bardell versus Pickwick. P. P. 364.

Grogus, a great ironmonger. S. B. 238.

Grogzwig, an imaginary place in Germany. N. N. 52.

Grompus, Mr, a guest at Mr Podsnap's. O. M. F. 109.

Groombridge Wells. C. S. 542.

Groper, Colonel, an American. M. C. 423.

"Grosvenor", a wrecked East Indiaman. R. P. 326.

Grosvenor Place. C. S. 328.

Grosvenor Square, where Tite Barnacle lived. L. D. 78.

Groves, James (Jem), landlord of "The Valiant Soldier", professedly honest but really in league with card-sharpers. O. C. S. 165, 417.

Growlery, The, at Bleak House, to which Mr Jarndyce retired when he was out of humour. B. H. 73.

Grub, Gabriel, a sexton carried off by goblins. P. P. 308.

Grabble, W., landlord of the "Dedlock Arms". B. H. 400.

Grudden, Mrs, a member of Crummles's company. N. N. 228.

Grueby, John, devoted servant of Lord George Gordon. B. R. 202.

Gruff and Glum, a pensioner who witnessed the marriage of John Rokesmith and Bella Wilfer. O. M. F. 532.

Gruff & Tackleton, a toymaking firm, represented only by Tackleton. C. B. 132.

Grummer, Daniel, officer of Mr Nupkins. P. P. 257.

Grundy, Mr, a gentleman at the "Magpie and Stump" who refused to sing. P. P. 216.

Guard, at Mugby Junction. C. S. 441.

Guard, of a coach. M. C. 93.

Guard, of a coach. M. C. 564.

Guard, of the "Muggleton Telegraph". P. P. 291.

Guard, Mail. P. P. 535.

Gubbins, Mr, an ex-churchwarden. S. B. 8.

Gulpidge, Mr, a guest of MrWaterbrook; connected at second-hand with the law business of the Bank. D. C. 286.

Gulpidge, Mrs, wife of Mr Gulpidge D. C. 186.

Gummidge, Mrs, "a lone lorn creetur", always thinking of "the old un", but who turned over a new leaf and became a comfort to Mr Peggotty. D. C. 26.

Gunter, Mr, guest of Bob Sawyer. P. P. 343

Guppy, Mrs, mother of William Guppy; furious at the rejection of her son by Esther Summerson. B. H. 417.

Guppy, William, clerk to Kenge & Carboy, who twice proposed to Esther Summerson. B. H. 22, 27.

Gusher, Mr, a friend of Mrs Pardiggle. B. H. 80.

Guster, servant in Snagsby's house. B. H. 102.

Gwynn, Miss, the writing and ciphering governess at Westgate House. P. P. 176.

H

Haggage, Doctor, doctor in the Marshalsea. L. D. 47.

"Half Moon and Seven Stars", an inn where Anthony and Jonas Chuzzlewit put up. M. C. 42.

"Halsewell", a wrecked East Indiaman. R. P. 322.

Hamlet's Aunt, a name applied to Mrs Henry Spiker. D. C. 284.

Hammersmith, where Matthew Pocket lived. G. E. 135.

Hampstead Heath, where Sikes wandered in his flight. O. T. 280.

Hampstead Ponds, on which Mr Pickwick wrote a paper. P. P. 1.

Hampton, Racecourse at, N. N. 506; where Oliver Twist and Sikes entered a public-house, O. T. 120; where Mortimer Lightwood and Eugene Wrayburn lived, O. M. F. 114.

Handel, name given to Pip by Herbert Pocket. G. E. 130.

Handford, Julius. See *Harmon John*.

Handmaidens, of Miss Twinkleton. E. D. 125.

Hannah, servant to Miss La Creevy. N. N. 15, 16.

Hardy, Mr, a funny gentleman, one of the steam excursion party. S. B. 289, 291.

Haredale, Emma, niece of Geoffrey and daughter of Reuben Haredale; in love with Edward Chester, whom she at length married. B. R. 5.

Haredale, Geoffrey, brother of Reuben, and uncle of Emma Haredale; a Catholic whose house was destroyed by the Gordon rioters; he brought Rudge, the murderer of his brother, to justice, and killed Sir John Chester in a duel; left the country and died in a monastery. B. R. 5.

Haredale, Reuben, brother of Geoffrey, and father of Emma Haredale; murdered by Rudge. B. R. 9.

Harker, Mr, officer in charge of a jury. C. S. 429.

Harker, Rev. John. C. S. 542.

Harleigh, Mr, an amateur singer. S. B. 319.

Harmon, John, alias Julius Handford, alias John Rokesmith; heir to his father's wealth on condition of marrying Bella Wilfer, but let himself be supposed drowned, and as Rokesmith became private secretary to Mr Boffin, who then obtained the fortune; he lodged for a time with the Wilfers; his secret was forced out when he was about to be arrested for the murder of himself; married Bella Wilfer and entered into his fortune. O. M. F. throughout.

Harmony Jail, another name for Boffin's Bower (q.v.). O. M. F. 43.

Haroun Alraschid. C. S. 223.

Harris, a greengrocer, who waited at the footmen's swarry. P. P. 406.

Harris, Mr, real name of Mr Codlin's fellow Punch-and-Judy showman, usually called Short Trotters, or Trotters, or Short. O. C. S. 99.

Harris, Mr, the law-stationer, a friend of John Dounce. S. B. 183.

Harris, Mrs, a friend to whom Mrs Gamp made constant reference; her existence was denied by Betsey Prig. M. C. 247.

Harrison, Master, referred to by Frank Milvey. O. M. F. 83.

Harry, a pedlar in Hatfield. O. T. 281.

Harry, a young man in a lock-up house. S. B. 339, 342.

Harry, coachman of an early coach. S. B. 101.

Harry, grandson of Dame West, a favourite pupil of Mr Marton; died young. O. C. S. 145.

Harthouse, James, a gentleman of excessive gentility; the immediate cause of Louisa Bounderby's leaving her husband. H. T. 347.

Hatfield, visited by Sikes in his flight. O. T. 280.

Haunted Man. See *Redlaw*.

Havisham, Arthur, half-brother of Miss Havisham (in G. E.). See *Arthur*.

Havisham, Miss, an heiress who was deceived by Compeyson, and afterwards lived in a strange seclusion; she adopted Estella, and trained her to break men's hearts; she befriended Pip. G.E. 41.

Hamden, Captain, father of Esther Summerson by Lady Dedlock before the latter's marriage; lived as a law-writer by name of Nemo over Krook's shop, and died there; Lady Dedlock, after her flight, was found dead at his grave. B. H. 44.

Hawk, Sir Mulberry, a profligate man about town, thrashed by Nicholas Nickleby for insulting his sister; killed Lord Frederick Verisopht in a duel; latterly imprisoned for debt, and died in jail. N. N. 182.

Hawkins, a baker from whom Miss Rugg recovered damages for breach of promise of marriage. L. D. 237.

Hawkyard, Verity, a drysalter, who preached to a narrow sect. G. S. E. 489.

Headstone, Bradley, Charley Hexam's schoolmaster, who fell in love with Lizzie Hexam, and made a murderous attack on Eugene Wrayburn, whom she favoured; he was drowned in a struggle with

Rogue Riderhood. O. M. F. 171, 172.

Heathfield, Alfred, a young doctor, pupil of Dr Jeddler, engaged to Marion Jeddler; he went abroad, and on the night of his return Marion disappeared; the married Grace Jeddler. C. B. 196.

Heathfield, Marion, child of Alfred Heathfield and Grace Jeddler. C. B. 241.

Heep, Mrs, mother of Uriah Heep, and also very 'umble. D. C. 196.

Heep, Uriah, clerk and afterwards partner of Mr Wickfield, over whom, though very 'umble, he gained an evil ascendancy; by the agency of Mr Micawber his nefarious designs on Agnes were frustrated, and his last appearance was as a convict. D. C. 168.

Helpers, Two Sleepy, who harnessed horses wrongly. P. P. 90.

Helves, Captain, a member of the steam excursion party. S. B. 296.

Hendon, visited by Sikes in his flight. O. T. 280.

Henri, a murdered man. C. S. 94.

Henrietta, sweetheart of Thomas, the artist. C. S. 327.

Henry, a son of a drunkard. S. B. 370.

Henry, brother of Kate, cousin of Maria Lobbs, whom he married. P. P. 182.

Henry, Mr, pawnbroker. S. B.140.

Herbert, Mr, a member of Parliament. B. R. 429.

Heroes, Four, among Joe Willet s fellow-soldiers. B. R. 186.

Hexam, Charley, brother of Lizzie Hexam; spoiled by his scholastic success; tried to advance Bradley

Headstone's suit for his sister's hand. O. M. F. 14.

Hexam, Jesse, or Gaffer, father of Charley and Lizzie Hexam; a longshoreman who found the body supposed to be John Harmon's; falsely accused of the murder, and found drowned. O. M. F. 1.

Hexam, Lizzie, daughter of Jesse Hexam; helped her brother to acquire learning; left home after her father's death to earn her living; Eugene Wrayburn and Bradley Headstone both fell in love with her; she eluded them and obtained employment in a factory up the Thames; saved Wrayburn's life after Headstone's attack, and married Wrayburn. O. M. F. 1.

Heyling, George, the Queer Client; his wife and child died in a debtors' prison through the heartlessness of his father-in-law; he exacted a terrible revenge. P. P. 222.

Heyling, Mary, wife of George Heyling. P. P. 222.

Hicks, Septimus, boarder of Mrs Tibbs, a walker of the hospitals, given to quoting Don Juan. S. B. 209.

Higden, Betty, a poor old woman who kept a minding-school at Brentford; abhorred the workhouse; set out on a tramp, but her strength failed, and Lizzie Hexam found her dying. O.M.F. 156.

High Street, Rochester. C. S. 58.

Highgate, where David Copperfield visited. D. C. 223.

Hilton, Mr, a young man at the

Minerva House ball, very popular with the ladies. S. B. 248.

Hoghton Towers, a farmhouse near Preston. G. S. E. 491.

Holliday, Arthur, a well-to-do young man who went to Doncaster races, and saved the life of Mr Loan. L. T. 377.

Holliday, Mrs Arthur, formerly engaged to Mr Lorn. L. T. 391.

"Holly-tree Inn". C. S. 83.

Hominy, Miss, an American lady. M. C. 295.

Hominy, Mrs, an American literary lady. M. C. 289.

Honeythunder, Luke, a philanthropist who was always denouncing someone; guardian of Helena and Neville Landless. E. D. 45.

"Hop Pole, The", an inn at Tewkesbury, where Mr Pickwick and his friends dined. P. P. 549

Hopkins, candidate for beadleship. S. B. 16.

Hopkins, Captain, an acquaintance of Mr Micawber in King's Bench Prison. D. C. 127.

Hopkins, Heaven-born, a witchfinder. M. H. C. 485.

Hopkins, Jack, friend and fellow student of Bob Sawyer. P. P. 341

"Horn Coffee-house", in Doctors' Commons. P. P. 486.

"Horse Guards", guest of Mr Merdle. L. D. 196.

Horseman. M. H. C. 475.

Hortense, Mademoiselle, Lady Dedlock's French maid, who murdered Mr Tulkinghorn. B. H. 122.

Hostler. O. C. S. 365.

Hostler. P. P. 90.

Hostler, at Coventry. P. P. 556.

Hostler, at the "Bull Inn", Rochester. P. P. 47.

Hostler, at the "Bull Inn", Whitechapel. P. P. 233.

Hot-pieman, in a crowd. P. P. 7.

Hounslow, to which Martin Chuzzlewit was driven by a vanman. M. C. 173.

House-agent, in Groombridge Wells. C. S. 543

Housekeeper, to the Checryble brothers. N. N. 367.

Housemaid, at Westgate House P. P. 174.

Housemaid, Assistant, at the "White Hart". P. P. 123.

Housemaid, Mr Fezziwig's. C. B. 23.

Housemaid, Mr Parsons's. S. B. 333.

Housemaid, Mrs Maylie's. O. T. 160.

Housemaids, of Miss Twinkleton. E. D. 124.

Howler, Rev. Melchisedech, minister of the Ranters, to whom Mrs MacStinger belonged. D. S. 163.

Hubble, Mr, a wheelwright, friend of the Gargerys. G. E. 16.

Hubble, Mrs, wife of Mr Hubble. G. E. 16.

Hugh, servant of John Willet and son of Sir John Chester; he became a leader of the Gordon rioters and was hanged; Sir John refused to intercede for him. B. R. 59.

Humm, Anthony, president of a Temperance Association. P. P. 357.

"Hummums", an inn in Covent Garden. C. E. 268.

Humphrey, Master, an old man who is the central figure of Master Humphrey's Clock. M. H. C. 433.

Hunt, Captain Boldwig's gardener. P. P. 201.

Hunter, Horace, who challenged Alexander Trott to a duel; he married Emily Brown at Gretna Green. S. B. 307.

Hunter, Leo, husband of Mrs Leo Hunter. P. P. 152.

Hunter, Mrs Leo, who sought the society of celebrities; writer of the "Ode to an Expiring Frog". P. P. 158.

Husband, of Caroline. C. B. 50.

Husband, of Scrooge's old sweetheart. C. B. 27.

Husband, of young woman, in the Fleet prison. P. P. 451.

Husband, Clerical English. L. D. 18.

Husband of Miss Hominy. M. C. 295.

Hutley, Jem, known as Dismal Jemmy, a brother of Job Trotter. P. P. 26.

I

I, a narrator in *Doctor Marigold's Prescriptions.*

Idle, Thomas, one of the idle apprentices. Original, Wilkie Collins. L. T. 359.

Ignorance, a boy seen by Scrooge in his vision. C. B. 43.

Ikey, a stableman of an inn. C. S. 207.

Ikey, factotum at Solomon Jacobs's. S. B. 336, 341.

Imperial Bulgraderian Brigade. C. S. 190.

Infant Phenomenon. See *Crummles, Ninetta.*

Innkeeper, in Hesket-Newmarket, Cumberland. L. T. 363.

Inspector, Police. O. M. F. 611.

Inspector, Police, at the inquest on the body supposed to be that of John Harmon. O. M. F. 19.

Irish Family, who begged from Mr Pickwick and his friends. P. P. 546.

Irish Member of Parliament. N. N. 10, 13.

Irishwoman, a servant of Harold Skimpole. B. H. 637.

Isaac, who accompanied Mr Jackson from Dodson & Fogg. P. P. 507, 508.

Islington, where Tool and Ruth Pinch lodged. M. C. 452.

Ivins, J'mima. See *Evans, Jemima.*

"Ivy Green, The", song composed by the old clergyman. P. P. 57.

Izzard, Mr, an American. M. C. 423.

J

Jack, a police officer. M. C. 619.

Jack, clerk of Dodson & Fogg. P. P. 205.

Jack, The, of the "Ship", a little public-house down the Thames. G. E. 323.

Jackman, Major Jemmy, a fixed lodger with Mrs Lirriper. C. S. 348

Jackson, Michael, referred to by Inspector Bucket. B. H. 599.

Jackson, Mr, clerk of Dodson & Fogg. P. P. 205.

Jackson, Young, otherwise Barbox Brothers, a reserved, disappointed man, wandering aimlessly. C. S. 446.

Jacobs, Solomon, who kept a lock-up house. S. B. 337.

Jacob's Island, in Southwark, where Sikes met his death. O. T. 293.

Jaggers, Mr, a lawyer who acted for Miss Havisham and Abel Magwitch; he announced to Pip his great expectations. G. E. 60, 97, 118.

Jailer, at Newgate. O. T. 314.

Jailers, Two, at the Old Bailey. T. T. C. 43.

James, a servant of Mr Badger. B. H. 135.

James, son of John, the smith. R. P. 389.

Jane, a servant of Mr Wardle. P. P. 52.

Jane, a servant to Mr Pecksniff. M. C. 389.

Jane, Mr Pott's maid. P. P. 129.

Jane, Aunt, at a Christmas dinner. S. B. 166.

Jane's Sister, a visitor with Jane at Madame Mantalini's. N. N. 174.

Janet, Betsey Trotwood's maid. D. C. 146.

Jarber. C. S. 199.

Jarley, Mrs, proprietor of a waxwork show, who employed Nell for a time. O. C. S. 147.

Jarndyce, John, a party in the case of Jarndyce and Jarndyce, guardian of Richard Carstone and Ada Clare; he took Esther Summerson under his protection and afterwards became engaged to her, but gave her up to Allan Woodcourt when he found out that they loved each other. B. H. 18, 49.

Jarndyce, Tom. B. H. 4.

Jarndyce and Jarndyce, a long-drawn-out Chancery suit. B. H. 3.

Jarvis, clerk to Mr Wilding. C. S. 516.

Jasper, John, uncle of Edwin Drood; choirmaster in Cloisterham cathedral, and musicmaster of Rosa Bud; a frequenter of opium dens; he was suspected of the murder of his nephew, and was being watched by Datchery. E. D. 1.

Jeddler, Doctor Anthony, a great philosopher, who looked upon the world as a gigantic practical joke. C. B. 192, 245.

Jeddler, Grace, daughter of Dr Jeddler; married to Alfred Heathfield, who had been betrothed to her sister. C. B. 192.

Jeddler, Marion, daughter of Dr Jeddler; betrothed to Alfred Heathfield, but ran from home on the night of his return from abroad, in order that her sister might win him; married Michael Warden. C. B. 192.

Jeddler, Martha, spinster sister of Dr Jeddler, who received Marion in her flight. C. B. 200, 244.

Jellyby, Caroline (or Caddy), daughter of Mrs Jellyby, whose mission she detested; befriended by Esther Summerson; married Prince Turveydrop. B. H. 29.

Jellyby, Mr, husband of Mrs Jellyby. B. H. 32.

Jellyby, Mrs, a woman who neglected her household and devoted herself to promoting the cultivation of coffee and the improvement of the natives in Borrioboola-Gha. B. H. 28.

Jellyby, Peepy, son of Mrs Jellyby. B. H. 28, 30.

Jem, a servant of Solomon Jacobs. S. B. 338.

Jem, servant of Mr Wardle. P. P. 307.

Jemima, sister of Polly Toodles. D. S. 12.

Jenkins, Miss, who had a talent for the piano. S. B. 322.

Jenkinson, mashed potatoes messenger in the Circumlocution Office. L. D. 89.

Jennings, a pupil of Squeers. N.N. 64.

Jennings, Miss, schoolfellow of Rosa Bud. E. D. 73.

Jennings, Mr, a robe-maker, one of John Dounce's jolly companions. S. B. 183.

Jenny, a brickmaker's wife, who assisted Lady Dedlock in her flight. B. H. 82.

Jerry, a showman with performing dogs, whom Little Nell and her grandfather fell in with. O. C. S. 106.

Jerusalem Buildings, where Mr Denham lived, and where the Tetterbys' shop was. C. B. 260, 270.

Jeweller, who put Edwin Drood's watch right E. D. 139.

Jews, Two. G. E. 120-1.

Jilkins, a physician. R. P. 481.

Jingle, Alfred, alias Charles FitzMarshall, a strolling player who befooled Mr Pickwick, and was afterwards rescued by him from the Fleet; notable for a staccato, disconnected style of conversation. P. P. 7.

Jiniwin, Mrs, who lived with her daughter, Mrs Quilp; hated and feared Quilp. O. C. S. 22.

Jinkins, a drunken brute in a pawnshop. S. B. 141.

Jinkins, Mr, a boarder at Todgers's. M. C. 101.

Jinkins, Mr, rival of Tom Smart, in the "Bagman's Story". P. P. 143.

Jinkinson, a barber referred to by Sam Weller. M. H. C. 496.

Jinks, Mr, clerk of Mr Nupkins. P. P. 256.

Jip, Dora Copperfield's pet dog. D. C. 301.

Jo, a crossing-sweeper who knew nothing of his parentage; from him Esther Summerson caught smallpox through her maid; he died attended by Allan Woodcourt; "knows a broom's a broom, and knows it's wicked to tell a lie". B. H. 114.

Jobling, Dr John, medical officer of the Anglo-Bengalee Company. M. C. 341.

Jobling, Tony, a friend of William Guppy, who entered Snagsby's employment under the name of Weevle. B. H. 211.

Joby, alias Greenwood. C. S. 208.

Jock, a boy. L. T. 374

Jodd, Mr, an American. M. C. 423.

Joe, a dealer in rags and bones. C. B. 46.

Joe, a hotel servant. O. T. 231.

Joe, a labourer. D. S. 59.

Joe, driver of the omnibus at Cloisterham. E. D. 48.

Joe, guard of a coach. T. T. C. 4.

Joe, the Fat Boy, servant of Mr Wardle; his whole existence consisted in eating and sleeping. P. P. 40.

Joey, Captain, a customer at the "Six Jolly Fellowship-Porters". O. M. F. 52.

John, a drunkard's son. S. B. 370.

John, a host. C. S. 25.

John, a smith. R. P. 389.

John, father of Martha, with whom he bore patiently. D. S. 272.

John, Mr Malderton's servant. S. B. 274.

John, subject of the "Stroller's Tale". P. P. 27.

John, tenant of the Haunted House. C. S. 214.

John, waiter at the "Saracen's Head". P. P. 558.

Johnny, grandson of Betty Higden, who died in hospital when the Boffins were going to adopt him. O. M. F. 157.

Johnson, a name given to Nicholas Nickleby by Newman Noggs, and used by him on the stage. N. N. 157, 224.

Johnson, a pupil of Dr Blimber. D. S. 123.

"Jolly Sandboys", an inn where Nell and her grandfather put up. O. C. S. 102.

Jonathan, a customer at the "Six Jolly Fellowship Porters". O. M. F. 52.

Jones, the barrister's clerk, a jolly companion of John Dounce. S. B. 183.

Jones, George, a customer at the "Six Jolly Fellowship Porters". O. M. F. 52.

Jones, Mary, hanged at Tyburn. B. R. 220.

Jones, Master, a rival of David Copperfield in Miss Shepherd's affections. D. C. 204.

Jones, Mr, friend of the Buddens. S. B. 241.

Jones, Spruggins, & Smith, linen drapers. S. B. 278.

Joram, Joe, son of Mr and Mrs Joram. D. C. 232.

Joram, Mr, son-in-law of Mr Orner. D. C. 97.

Jorgan, Silas Jonas, an American sea captain. C. S. 233.

Jorkins, Mr, partner of Mr Spenlow; he was a mild man, but was kept in the background and represented as harsh and unbending. D. C. 269.

Joseph, waiter at the Slamjam Coffee-house. C. S. 291.

Journeymen, Two. E. D. 115.

Jowl, Mat, a gambler who tempted Little Nell's grandfather. O. C. S. 167.

Joy, Thomas, a London carpenter. R. P. 391.

Judge, at Magwitch's trial. G. E. 335.

Judge, in a murder trial. C. S. 432.

Judge, in the Court of Arches. D. C. 270.

Judge, who tried Darnay for treason. T. T. C. 43.

Juggler. D. S. 188.

Jupe, Cecilia, known as Sissy; she was daughter of one of Sleary's troupe and was brought up by Mr Gradgrind, whose good genius she became. H. T. 247.

Jupe, Signor, one of Sleary's troupe; he disappeared, leaving his daughter alone. H. T. 253.

Justice. O. C. S. 378.

Justice of the Peace. B. R. 273.

K

Kags, a returned transport. O. T. 294.

Kate, an orphan who visited the Skettleses at Fulham. D. S. 269.

Kate, a young lady in a lock-up house. S. B. 339, 342.

Kate, cousin of Maria Lobbs, in the story of "The Parish Cleric". P. P. 180.

Kedgick, Captain, landlord of the "National Hotel". M. C. 287.

Keeper, at Chesney Wold. B. H. 7.

Keeper, at Chesney Wold. B. H. 196.

Keeper, of a chandler's shop in the Marshalsea, with a grievance against the Marshal. L. D. 69.

Keeper, of the mad gentleman in the small clothes who made love to Mrs Nickleby. N. N. 417.

Kenge, Conversation, a solicitor, of Kenge & Carboy, who acted for Mr Jarndyce. B. H. 14, 15.

Kenge & Carboy, a firm of solicitors. B. H. 15.

Kenwigs, Lillyvick, Mrs Kenwigs's baby. N. N. 141.

Kenwigs, Morleena, daughter of Mrs Kenwigs, taught to be deferential to Mr Lillyvick. N. N. 138.

Kenwigs, Mr, an ivory-turner in whose family Nicholas Nickleby became a tutor. N. N. 126.

Kenwigs, Mrs, wife of Mr Kenwigs. N. N. 126.

Kettle, La Fayette, an American. M. C. 272.

Kibble, Jacob, a fellow-passenger of John Harmon from the Cape. O. M. F. 295.

Kidderminster, Master, of the Turf, turfy; one of Sleary's troupe. H. T. 269.

Kidgerbury, Mrs, a charwoman employed by Dora Copperfield. D. C. 490.

Kimmeens, Kitty, a pupil of Miss Pupford. C. S. 276, 280.

King, Christian George, a treacherous Sambo. C. S. 146.

King, Tom, and Seven Dials. S. B. D.

"King Arthur's Arms", an inn at Lanrean, in Cornwall, where Hugh Raybrock was discovered. C. S. 252.

King of the Bill-stickers. R. P. 356.

King's Bench Prison, where David Copperfield visited Mr Micawber. D. C. 127.

King's Bench Prison, Rules of, within which Walter Bray lived. N. N. 468.

Kingsgate Street, where Mrs Gamp lived. M. C. 244.

Kingston, terrified by supposed witch revels. M. H. C. 475

Kit. See *Nubbles, Christopher*.

Kitt, Miss, who was with David Copperfield and Dora on a picnic party. D. C. 370, 373.

Kitt, Mrs, mother of Miss Kitt. D. C. 370.

Kitten, Mr, vice-commissioner of Silver-store. C. S. 152.

Kitterbell, Charles, nephew of Nicodemus Dumps. S. B. 354.

Kitterbell, Frederick Charles William, infant son of Mr and Mrs Kitterbell. S. B. 356.

Kitterbell, Mrs Charles. S. B. 354.

Knag, Miss, Madame Mantalini's forewoman; at first friendly to Kate Nickleby, afterwards her enemy; she took over the business. N. N. 163.

Knag, Mortimer, Miss Knag's brother, a stationer. N. N. 172.

Knuckleboy, Mrs Squeers's variant of Nickleby. N. N. 63.

Koeldwethout, Baron Von, in the story of "The Baron of Grogzwig". N. N. 52.

Koeldwethout, Baroness Von, in the story of "The Baron of Grogswig". N. N. 54.

Krook, Mr, a brother of Mrs Smallweed; a rag and bone merchant, and collector of miscellaneous stuff; called the "Lord Chancellor"; died of spontaneous combustion. B. H. 39.

L

La Creevy, John, brother of Miss La Creevy. N. N. 313.

La Creevy, Miss, a miniature painter who befriended the Nicklebys; married Tim Linkinwater. N. N. 15.

La Force, a Parisian prison, where Charles Darnay was confined. T. T. C. 182.

Labourers, Half-a-dozen, who helped at the Old Hell Shaft accident. H. T. 475

Labourers, Two, bricklayers who saw Saucers carrying off Smike. N. N. 384.

Lad, grandson of Old Glubb. D. S. 85.

Lad, referred to by Fagin. O. T. 99.

Lad, who bought a turkey for Scrooge. C. B. 55.

Lad, Office, of fourteen, with a tenor voice. P. P. 443

Ladies, Eight or Ten Young, who went to Manor Farm for Isabella Wardle's wedding to Mr Trundle. P. P. 290.

Ladies, Three, neighbours of Mrs Gamp. M. C. 245.

Ladies, Two, at dinner in Mr Dombey's. D. S. 404.

Ladies, Two, friends of Mrs Brick. M. C. 23X.

Ladies, Two, visitors at Mrs Quilp's. O. C. S. 25.

Ladies, Young, engaged as dancers in a theatre. L. D. 185.

Ladies, Young, who urged Mr Winkle to skate. P. P. 319.

Ladies' Seminary, kept by the Misses Wackles. O. C. S. 47.

Ladle, Joey, cellar-man to Wilding & Co. C. S. 514.

Lads, Office, in the Temple. P. P. 325.

Lady, at Caddy Jellyby's marriage. B. H. 326.

Lady, at Mr Dombey's dinnerparty. D. S. 399

Lady, at Mrs MacStinger's marriage. D. S. 663.

Lady, who bought flowers from Nell at the races. O. C. S. 114.

Lady, who employed Ruth Pinch as governess. M. C. 448.

Lady, who visited the Monument. M. C. 454.

Lady, whose daughter was taught by Esther Summerson. B. H. 21.

Lady, with a roll of music, who helped Little Dorrit to find her sister at the theatre. L. D. 184.

Lady, Benevolent Old, who helped Oliver Twist on his way to London. O. T. 41.

Lady, Fastidious, who joined a coach. N. N. 41.

Lady, Fat, at a show. C. S. 191.

Lady, Fat, proprietress of the General Agency Office. N. N. 145.

Lady, Fractious, whom Little Emily kept company. D. C. 234.

Lady, Little, without legs or arms, one of Vuffin's show-party. O. C. S. 108.

Lady, Old, a respected parishioner. S. B. 8.

Lady, Old, at Prince Turveydrop's. B. H. 147.

Lady, Old, who disapproved of meandering. D. C. 2.

Lady, Old, who played cards at Manor Farm. P. P. 56.

Lady, Old, who was a mother to Captain Ravender. C. S. 116.

Lady, Red Velvet, with Traddles at Mr Waterbrook's dinner. D. C. 286.

Lady, Rich, and daughter, customers of Madame Mantalini. N. N. 166.

Lady, Stout, at a Ramsgate library with her daughters. S. 13. 264.

Lady, Veiled, mother of Walter Wilding. C. S. 503.

Lady, Young, at the "Blue Boar". P. P. 350.

Lady, Young, attired in an old-fashioned green velvet dress, in the "Story of the Bagman's Uncle". P. P. 536.

Lady, Young, on stilts, one of Grinder's show party. O. C. S. 101.

Lady, Young, peeling potatoes, to whom Sam Weller winked. P. P. 489.

Lady, Young, sweetheart to Will Marks. M. H. C. 474

Lady, Young, who became Abel Garland's wife. O. C. S. 415.

Lady, Young, who "did" the poetry in the *Eatanswill Gazette*. P. P. 157.

Lady, Young, who sang at the "Cripples". O. T. 144.

Lady from the Minories, a visitor aL Mrs Quilp's. O. C. S. 25.

Lady Jane, Krook's cat. B. H. 41.

Lagnier. See *Rigaud*.

Lammle, Alfred, an adventurer who married Miss Akershem in the belief that she was wealthy; she thought the same of him; they jointly tried to prey upon others, but without much success. O. M. F. 9, 90.

Lammle, Mrs See *Akershem*.

Lamplighter. F. D. 114.

Lamplighter. L. D. 25.

Lamps, a railway servant at Mugby Junction. C. S. 443

Lancaster, visited by Dr Marigold. C. S. 434

Lancaster, visited by the idle apprentices. L. T. 404.

Landlady, at Yarmouth. D. C. 50.

Landlady, of an inn where Nell lay ill. O. C. S. 257.

Landlady, of an inn where Nell stayed with Codlin and Short. O. C. S. 95.

Landlady, of "Magpie and Stump". P. P. 214.

Landlady, of "Royal George Hotel", Dover. T. T. C. 11.

Landlady, of the "Break of Day". L. D. 99.

Landlady, of the "Bull", Holborn. M. C. 322.

Landlady, of the "Ship". G. E. 323.

Landlady, of the "Tilted Waggon". E. D. 147.

Landlady, of Tom and Ruth Pinch. M. C. 471. See *Nadgett*.

Landlady, of "White Hart Inn". P. P. 95.

Landlady, with pretty daughters; she helped Esther Summerson on the drive in chase of her mother. B. H. 603.

Landless, Helena, sister of Neville Landless, and friend of Rosa Bud. E. D. 46.

Landless, Neville, pupil of the Rev.
Mr Crisparkle, and suspected of
the murder of Edwin Drood, with
whom he had had a violent quarrel.
E. D. 46.

Landlord, of a cheap tavern. M. C.
432.

Landlord, of an inn where Nell lay ill.
O. C. S. 259.

Landlord, of an inn where Nell stayed
with Codlin and Short. O. C. S. 95

Landlord, of a public-house where
Martin Chuzzlewit put up. M. C.
173.

Landlord, of a public-house where
Mr Dombey was taken after an
accident. D. S. 467.

Landlord, of hotel in Brook Street. L.
D. 486.

Landlord, of the "Peal of Bells" C. S.
265.

Landlord, of the "Saracen's Head". P.
P. 558.

Landlord, of the "Ship". G. E. 323.

Landlord, of "The Two Robins". L.
T. 379.

Landlord, who told of the Haunted
House. C. S. 207.

Lane, Miss, governess in Mr Borum's
family. N. N. 243.

Langdale, Mr, a vintner whose
warehouse was burnt down by the
Gordon rioters. B. R. 76, 358, 398

Langley, Mr, a lodger of Madame
Bouclet, usually called Mr The
Englishman. C. S. 306.

Lanrean, in Cornwall, where Hugh
Raybrock was found. C. S. 246.

Lant Street, in the Borough, where
Bob Sawyer lived. P. P. 337

Larkins, Miss, the eldest, admired by
David Copperfield; she married Mr

Chestle. D. C. 206.

Larkins, Miss, the youngest. D. C.
206.

Larkins, Mr, a gruff old gentleman.
D. C. 206.

Lascar, A, in a London opium den.
E. D. 4.

Laundress, Mr Perlcer's. P. P. 213.

Lawyer, at Barnstaple. C. S. 255.

Lawyer, in the Court of Chancery. B.
H. 24.

Leamington, where Mr Dombey met
Edith Granger. D. S. 223.

Leath, Angela. C. S. 83, 114.

"Leather Bottle", an ale-house at
Cobham, to which Mr Tupman
retired from the world after his
disappointment. P. P. 107.

Ledrook, Miss, a member of Mr
Crummles's company. N. N. 228.

Leeford, Edward, real name of
Monks (q.v.) in O. T.

Legion. C. S. 55.

Leicester Square, near which was
George's Shooting Gallery. B. H.
280.

Lemon, Mrs H. R. 479.

Lenville, Mr, a member of Mr
Crummles's company. N. N. 227.

Lenville, Mrs, a member of Mr
Crummles's company. N. N. 228.

Lewsome, Mr, a doctor's assistant
who sold to Jonas Chuzzlewit the
poison intended for his father. M.
C. 324, 366.

Lightwood, Mortimer, a solicitor
with but little practice; close friend
of Eugene Wrayburn. O. M. F. 9.

Lignum Vitae, a nickname of Mr
Bagnet (q.v.) in B. H.

Lillerton, Miss, whom Mr Watkins
Tottle believed to have accepted

him, but whose marriage with the Rev. Mr Timson he had actually hastened. S. B. 330.

Lilliputian College, Miss Pupford's school. C. S. 277.

Lillyvick, Mr, uncle of Mrs Kenwigs, a collector of water rates; married Miss Petowker, who afterwards ran away from him with a half-pay captain. N. N 128.

Limbkins, Mr, chairman of the parochial board. O. T. 8, 13.

Limehouse Hole, where Rogue Riderhood lived. O. M. F. 280.

Lime-tree Lodge. C. S. 543

Lincoln's Inn Fields, where Mr Tulkinghorn lived. B. H. 101.

Lincoln's Inn Hall. B. H. 1.

Linderwood, a lieutenant of marines. C. S. 146.

Link-boy. P. P. 399

Linkinwater, Miss, sister of Tim Linkinwater. N. N. 367.

Linkinwater, Timothy (Tim), cleric to Cheeryble Brothers; married Miss La Creevy. N. N. 351, 364.

Linx, Miss, a pupil of Miss Pupford. C. S. 278.

Lion, Henry Gowan's dog, poisoned by Rigaud. L. D. 159.

Lirriper, Jemmy Jackman, son of Mr Edson, adopted by Mrs Lirriper on his mother's death. C. S. 359.

Lirriper, Joshua, Mrs Lirriper's brother-in-law, called "The Doctor"; always in trouble. C. S. 377

Lirriper, Mr, Mrs Lirriper's late husband, a free liver, smashed to atoms in a gig when the horse bolted. C. S. 342.

Lirriper, Mrs Emma, keeper of a lodging-house; the central figure of two of the Christmas stories. C. S. 341.

List, Isaac, a gambler who won from Nell's grandfather at "The Valiant Soldier"; ultimately brought to justice. O. C. S. 167, 417.

Littimer, servant of Steerforth, whom he aided in his villainy, and who finally was companion of Uriah Heep in prison. D. C. 228.

Little Bethel, a chapel attended by Mrs Nubbles. O. C. S. 230.

Little Britain, where Mr Jaggers's office was. G. E. 118.

Little Wonder of Scholastic Equitation, E. W. B. Childers' boy. H. T. 486.

Lively, Mr, a receiver of stolen goods in Field Lane. O. T. 142.

Liz, wife of a brickmaker, friend of Jenny. B. H. 85.

Lobbs, Maria, in the story of "The Parish Clerk", beloved of Nathaniel Pipkin, but who married her cousin Henry. P. P. 179

Lobbs, Old, father of Maria Lobbs. P. P. 179.

Lobley, Mr, Mr Tartar's man. E. D. 219.

Lobskini, Signor, the singing master at Minerva House. S. B. 248.

Lodger, with Mrs Lirriper. C. S. 345.

Loggins, Mr, a solicitor. S. B. 291.

Lombard Street, of which Little Frank was very fond. C. S. 27.

Lombard Street, where Miss Snevellicci lived in Portsmouth. N. N. 238.

"Lombards' Arms", an inn. M. C. 337

London, in fog. B. H. 1.

London Bridge, where Nancy met

Mr Brownlow and Rose Maylie. O. T. 267.

London Tavern, where a jury was housed, C. S. 429; where Ralph Nickleby attended a meeting, N. N. 8.

Longford, Edmund, real name of Mr Denham (q.v.). C. B. 282, 284.

Longford, Mr, father of Edmund Longford. C. B. 312.

Looker-on. O. T. 84.

Lord, Old, who came with his young fiancee to Madame Mantalini s. N. N. 174.

Lord Chancellor. B. H. 2.

Lord Mayor, of London. B. R. 358.

Lorn, Mr, assistant to Doctor Speddie. L. T. 376.

Lorry, Jarvis, confidential agent of Tellson's Bank; a friend of Dr and Lucie Marlette and Charles Darnay, whom he helped in their flight from France. T. T. C. 3.

Losberne, Mr, surgeon to the Maylie family; helped to save Oliver Twist from the police officers. O. T. 164.

Louis, a murderer. C. S. 94.

Love Lane. C. S. 109.

Lovely, the name of a dog. L. D. 90.

"Lovely Peg", a favourite air of Captain Cuttle. D. S. 87.

Lovers, Pair of, in Temple Gardens. B. R. 88.

Lowestoft, where Mr Murdstone took David Copperfield. D. C. 17.

Lowten, Mr, clerk of Mr Perker, and a very convivial person. P. P. 215.

Loyal, M., also called M. Loyal Devasseur (q.v.).

Lucas, Solomon, the Jew who provided costumes for Mrs Leo Hunter's fete. P. P. 153.

Lud Hudibras, a king of Britain, in "The True Legend of Prince Bladud". P. P. 395

Luffey, Mr, a leading member of the Dingley Dell cricket team. P. P. 71.

Lukin, an old suitor of Mrs Nickleby. N. N. 412.

Lumbey, Mr, Mrs Kenwigs's doctor. N. N. 357

Lummy Ned, a guard who went to the United States. M. C. 172.

Lupin, Mrs, landlady of the "Blue Dragon" who married Mark Tapley. M. C. 22.

Luth, a dog belonging to Sleary. H. T. 494.

M

Macey, Mr, husband of Mrs Macey. C. S. 163.

Macey, Mrs, sister of Miss Maryon. C. S. 163.

Mackin, Mrs, in a pawn-shop. S. B. 141, 142.

Macklin, Mrs, a typical London housewife. S. B.43.

Macmanus, Mr, a midshipman of the "Halsewell". R. P. 325.

MacStinger, Alexander, a son of Mrs MacStinger. D. S. 257.

MacStinger, Charles, called Chowley, a son of Mrs MacStinger. D. S. 432.

MacStinger, Juliana, daughter of Mrs MacStinger. D. S. 281.

MacStinger, Mrs, a widow, landlady of Captain Cuttle, who ran away from her; she married Captain Bunsby by force. D. S. 93

Madgers, Winifred, a Plymouth Sister, servant to Mrs Lirriper. C. S. 387.

"**Madman's Manuscript, A**", given by the Old Clergyman to Mr Pickwick. P. P. 110.

Magg, Mr, a vestry orator. R. P. 472

Maggy, granddaughter of Mrs Bangham, a half-witted woman, devoted to Little Dorrit; afterwards assistant to Mrs Plornish. L. D. 79.

Magistrate, who read the Riot Act at the Gordon Riots. B. R. 290.

Magistrates, before whom Oliver Twist was taken. O. T. 15.

Magnus, Peter, enamoured of Miss Witherfield, whose bedroom Mr Pickwick took possession of. P. P. 232.

Magog, one of the giants of the Guildhall. M. H. C. 443

"**Magpie and Stump**", a tavern where Mr Lowten passed jolly evenings. P. P. 214.

Magsman, Toby, a showman. C. S. 189.

Magwitch, Abel, a convict who escaped from the hulks and was supplied with food by Pip; he was recaptured and transported to New South Wales, whence after making a fortune at sheep farming he returned to Britain under the alias Provis; he was concealed by Pip, whom he had endowed with wealth through Jaggers, but was recaptured in an attempt to escape; he died in prison before the day of his execution arrived; proved to be father of Estella by Molly. G. E. 2.

Maid, at Bleak House. B. H. 53.

Maid, at Satis House. G. E. 177

Maid, Bella Rokesmith's. O. M. F. 534.

Maid, Fanny Dorrit's. L. D. 367.

Maid, Little Dorrit's. L. D. 367.

Maid, Miss Mills's. D. C. 425.

Maid, Miss Twinkleton's. E. D. 189.

Maid, Miss Twinkleton's Last New. E. D. 20.

Maid, Volumnia Dedlock's. B. H. 614.

Malderton, Frederick, the family authority on taste. S. B. 270.

Malderton, Marianne, younger daughter of Mr Malderton. S. B. 268.

Malderton, Mr, a successful speculator. S. B. 268.

Malderton, Mrs, wife of Mr Malderton. S. B. 268.

Malderton, Teresa, elder daughter of Mr Malderton. S. B. 268.

Malderton, Thomas, who resembled George Barnwell. S. B. 270.

Maldon, Jack, an idle, dissolute chap; in love with Mrs Strong, his cousin. D. C. 173.

Males, Couple of Large-headed, Circular-visaged, at Manor Farm. P. P. 52.

Mallard, Mr, cleric of Sergeant Snubbin. P. P. 333.

Mamma, Majestic English. L. D. 18.

Man. H. D. 445.

Man. L. T. 379

Man. M. H. C. 476.

Man. M. H. C. 480.

Man, a fellow-passenger of Martin Chuzzlewit and Mark Tapley. M. C. 195.

Man, a lodge-keeper who showed sympathy to Barnaby Rudge and his mother. B. R. 273.

Man, a police officer. M. C. 615.

Man, a resident in Eden. M. C. 297.

Man, a servant of Mr Dombey. D. S. 516.

Man, assistant to Mrs Jarley. O. C.
S. 159.

Man, at Veneering's house. O. M. F.
500.

Man, from Mr Cower's, the solicitor's,
who announced the Tuggses' good
fortune. S. B. 253.

Man, from whom Sydney Carton
feared discovery in his disguise. T.
T. C. 257.

Man, husband of Ellen; hanged at
Lancaster for murder; appeared to
Goodchild. L. T. 410.

Man, in a crowd. C. S. 330.

Man, in a pigeon-hole place,
employed at a theatre. D. C. 277.

Man, in gaiters. D. C. 55.

Man, in the crowd at Sydney Carton's
execution. T. T. C. 270.

Man, in the Old Bailey. T. T. C. 42.

Man, in want of airing, employed at a
theatre. L. D. 184.

Man, on "the Skylark". D. C. 19.

Man, servant of a murderer. L. T. 415.

Man, servant of Mr Wardle. P. P. 87.

Man, servant to Mortimer Lightwood.
O. M. F. 95.

Man, **Sir Mulberry Hawk's**. N. N.
379.

Man, valet of Sir Leicester Dedlock.
B. H. 118.

Man, who carried off Dr Manette to
the Bastille. T. T. C. 240.

Man, who carried Tom Pinch's box.
M. C. 394

Man, who gave Pip a tract. G. E. 76.

Man, who handed Inspector Bucket a
dark lantern. B. H. 594

Man, who hired a coach to Carker. D.
S. 597

Man, who lived by holding horses. B.
H. 285.

Man, who looked in at the wedding
of Walter Gay and Florence
Dombey. D. S. 627.

Man, who met Sir Mulberry Hawk at
the races. N. N. 510.

Man, who proved to be a murderer.
C. S. 425, 428.

Man, who sold slippers and dogs'
collars. D. S. 133.

Man, who told of the signalman's
death. C. S. 501.

Man, who wanted Betty Higden to
see the parish doctor. O. M. F. 407

Man, who was charged to wake
Sydney Carton. T. T. C. 61.

Man, whom Jonas Chuzzlewit came
across. M. C. 567.

Man, with a blue bag, who called on
Dora Spenlow. D. C. 429.

Man, with his wife, and a whole
crowd of children. P. P. 448.

Man, **Black**, in John Harmon's story.
O. M. F. 296.

Man, **Busy Little**, a supporter of Mr
Slumkey at the Eatanswill election.
P. P. 125.

Man, **Corpulent**, a waiter at the
"Great White Horse", Ipswich. P.
P. 236.

Man, **Drunk**, in the Fleet. P. P. 451.

Man, **Fat**, on 'Change. C. B. 45.

Man, **Gaunt**, who is out of work. O.
C. S. 254.

Man, **Handy Young**, to wait at David
Copperfield's dinner. D. C. 274.

Man, **Highly Respectable Young**. D.
C. 481.

Man, **Hoarse**, who spoke on behalf
of Mr Slumkey at the Eatanswill
election. P. P. 125.

Man, **Humpbacked**, whom Doctor
Losberne disturbed. O. T. 180.

Man, Humpbacked, whom Ralph Nickleby saw dancing. N. N. 622.

Man, Lame, at Serjeant's Inn, who acted as a bail. P. P. 441.

Man, Little, with a yellow face. M. H. C. 476.

Man, Little Choleric Pink-faced. who proposed Samuel Slumkey for the representation of Eatanswill in Parliament. P. P. 136.

Man, Little Dirty-faced, in the brown coat, who learned to like the Fleet. P. P. 448.

Man, Little Timid-looking, Nervous, in the Fleet. P. P. 454.

Man, Long-legged Young, who ran off with David Copperfield's box and money. D. C. 136.

Man, Mild, at dinner with Mr Dombey. D. S. 399

Man, Murdered. C. S. 425.

Man, Old, familiar with farming. P. P. 385.

Man, Old, in the story of "The Convict's Return". P. P. 62.

Man, Old, who lost his life in the Gordon riots. B. R. 324.

Man, Old, who told Barnaby Rudge's mother of the Gordon association. B. R. 279.

Man, Prowling Young, who showed Mrs Lirriper round Paris. C. S. 391.

Man, Shabby, with a squint, to whom "orses and dorgs" were "wittles and drink". D. C. 217.

Man, Shabby-genteel. S. B. 196.

Man, Shabby-genteel, in a law court. D. C. 270.

Man, Stout. P. P. 436.

Man, Strange Young, who married Sophy Marigold. C. S. 435,

Man, Tall Ill-favoured. S. B. 285.

Man, Tall, on Horseback, who collected gold for the Gordon rioters. B. R. 394.

Man, Very Red-faced. P. P. 470.

Man, Young, at Major Bagstock's club. D. S. 352.

Man, Young, attendant at Mrs Pipchin's establishment. D. S. 113.

Man, Young, driver of Mrs Boffin's equipage. O. M. F. 81.

Man, Young, murdered by Ellen's husband. L. T. 414.

Man, Young, son of a brick-maker. B. H. 82.

Man, Young, who carried luggage for Miss Twinkleton. E. D. 221.

Man, Young, who married Martha Endell. D. C. 667.

Man, Young, who married Mrs Quilp after the dwarf's death. O. C. S. 415.

Man, Young, who wished to be learned in cattle. P. P. 385.

Man, Young, with a whisker, a squint, and an open shirt collar (dirty). P. P. 216.

Man, Young, Large-headed, one of Bob Sawyer's party. P. P. 343.

Man in the Monument. M. C. 454.

Manchester Buildings, where Mr Gregsbury, MP, lived. N. N. 147, 148

Manette, Alexandre, a French doctor imprisoned in the Bastille for eighteen years at the instance of the Marquis of St. Evremonde; came to London when released; made to be an accuser of his son-in-law. T. T. C. 27.

Marlette, Lucie, daughter of Doctor Marlette; married Charles Darnay. T. T. C. 13.

Mann, Mrs, matron of a branch workhouse. O. T. 3, 5.

Manners, Julia, who married Mr Trott at Gretna Green. S. B. 306.

Manning, Sir Geoffrey, who gave Mr Pickwick a day's shooting. P. P. 192.

Manor Farm, Mr Wardle's house at Dingley Dell. P. P. 51.

Manor House, another name of Satis House. G. E. 40.

Mansfield, Lord, whose house was burned down by the Gordon rioters. B. R. 390.

Mantalini, Alfred, properly Mr Mantle, husband of Madame Mantalini; a fashionable spendthrift; fond of the words "demd", "demmit", "demnition"; came down in the world. N. N. 96.

Mantalini, Madame, a fashionable dressmaker and milliner, who employed Kate Nickleby; her business was ruined by her husband. N. N. 97.

Maplesone, Julia, daughter of Mrs Maplesone, with a good figure; she married Mr Simpson, and deserted him. S. B. 210.

Maplesone, Matilda, daughter of Mrs Maplesone; she married Septimus Hicks, and was deserted by him. S. B. 211.

Maplesone, Mrs, boarder with Mrs Tibbs; obtained damages for breach of promise from Mr Calton. S. B. 208.

Marchioness, The, girl servant to Sampson and Sally Brass, probably daughter of Sally Brass and Daniel Quilp; befriended by Dick Swiveller, whom she nursed through an illness, and to whom she was afterwards married. O. C. S. 193.

Margaret, child of Margaret Veck in Trotty's vision. C. B. 113, 115.

Margaret, smart servant girl at Mr Winkle's. P. P. 551.

Margaret, Aunt, at a Christmas dinner. S. B. 167.

Margate. H. R. 477.

Marguerite, niece and ward of Jules Obenreizer; married George Vendale, after saving his life. C. S. 534

Marigold, Doctor, a cheap-jack. C. S. 403.

Marigold, Mrs, mother of Doctor Marigold, who went off her head. C. S. 403.

Marigold, Mrs, wife of Doctor Marigold, who had a bad temper and beat her daughter; she committed suicide. C. S. 408.

Marigold, Willum, a cheap-jack, father of Doctor Marigold; he went off his head. C. S. 403.

Marker, Mrs N. N. 145.

Markham, a friend of Steerforth. D. C. 275.

Markleham, Mrs, mother of Mrs Strong, and known as the Old Soldier. D. C. 183.

Marks, Will, nephew of John Podgers. M. H. C. 474

Marlborough Downs, in "The Bagman's Story". P. P. 142.

Marley, Jacob, late partner of Scrooge, who saw his ghost. C. B. 3, 11.

Maroon, Captain. L. D. 111.

"Marquis of Granby", public-house at Dorking, kept by Mrs Weller. P. P. 283.

Marseilles, prison at. L. D. 1.

Marshall, Mary, the betrothed of

Captain Richard Doubledick, who married her after his reformation. C. S. 66.

Marshalsea Prison, a debtors' prison in which Little Dorrit was born, where for years she tended her father, and where she nursed Arthur Clennam. L. D. 45.

Martha, a servant in the Parsons family. S. B. 345.

Martha, an old pauper. O. T. 135.

Martha, daughter of John. D. S. 272.

Martin, servant of Arabella Allen's aunt. P. P. 425.

Martin, tall raw-boned gamekeeper of Sir Geoffrey Manning. P. P. 193.

Martin, Amelia, the mistaken milliner. S. B. 186.

Martin, Betsy, widow, a convert to temperance. P. P. 358.

Martin, Captain, a former inmate of the Marshalsea. L. D. 179.

Martin, Jack, uncle of the Bagman. P. P. 140, 530, 535.

Martin, Miss, a bar lady. C. S. 298.

Martin, Tom, a butcher, prisoner in the Fleet. P. P. 458.

Marton, Mr, the schoolmaster who befriended Nell and her grandfather. O. C. S. 137.

Marwood, Alice and Mrs, otherwise Brown (q.v.).

Mary, a drunkard's daughter. S. B. 368.

Mary, Captain Ravender's dead sweetheart. C. S. 118.

Mary, daughter of John, the smith. R. P. 389.

Mary, maid at the "Peacock", with whom the Bagman flirted. P. P. 139.

Mary, Mr Nupkins's maid, whom Sam Weller married. P. P. 263.

Mary, of Seven Dials. S. B. 54.

Mary, servant of Mr Wardle. P. P. 52.

Mary Ann, at a Ramsgate library. S. B. 264.

Mary Anne, one of Miss Peecher's pupils. O. M. F. 174.

Mary Anne, Wemmick's servant girl. G. E. 153, 269.

Maryon, Captain, captain of the "Christopher Columbus". C. S. 150.

Maryon, Marion, the heroic sister of Captain Maryon; married Captain Carton. C. S. 150.

Master. C. S. 54.

Master of the Workhouse. S. B. 5.

Matinter, The Two Misses, single and singular, visitors to Bath. P. P. 393

Matron, John Westlock's landlady. M. C. 540.

Matron, of Watts's Charity. C. S. 58.

Matthews, Mr Gregsbury's servant. N. N. 148, 156.

Mawls, Master, a pupil in our school. R. P. 466.

Maxby, a boy at our school, whose sister was favoured by the usher. R. P. 469.

Maxey, Caroline, a servant of Mrs Lirriper. C. S. 346.

Maxwell, Mrs, a guest at the Kitterbells' christening party. S. B. 364.

Maylie, Harry, son of Mrs Maylie; became a clergyman and the husband of Rose Maylie. O. T. 192.

Maylie, Mrs, a lady whose house, near Chertsey, Sikes attempted to burgle; she adopted Rose. O. T. 163.

Maylie, Rose, adopted niece of Mrs Maylie; proved to be sister of Oliver's mother; married Harry

Maylie; original, Mary Hogarth, Dickens's sister-inlaw. O. T. 163.

Mayor, of Eatanswill. P. P. 135.

Mayor, of Margate. H. R. 477.

"Maypole, The", an inn near Chigwell kept by John Willet. B. R. 1.

M 'Choakumchild, Mr, schoolmaster in Mr Gradgrind's school. H. T. 246.

Meagles, Minnie, called Pet, daughter of Mr and Mrs Meagles; married Henry Gowan. L. D. 13.

Meagles, Mr, a retired banker, father of Minnie Meagles, and friend of Arthur Clennam. L. D. 13.

Meagles, Mrs, mother of Minnie Meagles. L. D 13.

Mealy Potatoes, one of the boys at Murdstone & Grinby's. D. C. 119.

Meek, Augustus George, infant son of Mr Meek. R. P. 365.

Meek, George. R. P. 364.

Meek, Maria Jane, wife of Mr Meek. R. P. 363.

'Melia, servant at Dr Blimber's school. D. S. 126.

Melt, Charles, an under-master at Salem House; afterwards in Australia as Dr Mell. Original, Mr Taylor, English master at Wellington House Academy. D. C. 56.

Melt, Helena, fourth daughter of Dr Melt. D. C. 669.

Melt, Mrs, mother of Mr Melt, who lived in an almshouse. D. C. 57.

Melluka, Miss, Polly Tresham's doll. C. S. 478.

Meltham, Mr, an actuary. H. D. 440.

Melvilleson, Miss M., one of the singers at the "Sol's Arms" Harmonic Meetings. B. H. 342.

Member of Parliament for the Gentlemanly Interest. M. C. 433

Men, at the "Break of Day".

Men, in a crowd. C. S. 329.

Men, searching for Edwin Drood. E. D. 152.

Men, Couple of, whom Sam Weller saw playing at rackets. P. P. 489

Men, Five. M. H. C. 484.

Men, Four, in a crowd. C. S. 325.

Men, Four, who arrested Darnay. T. T. C. 210.

Men, Four, who carried Mr Cleaver on a stretcher. O. M. F. 585.

Men, Six, near Mr Jaggers's office. G. E. 120.

Men, Tall Young (Two), who wait at dinner. D. S. 333

Men, Three, in a crowd. T. T. C. 111.

Men, Twenty Washed, for electoral purposes. P. P. 133.

Men, Two. B. H. 83.

Men, Two. B. H. 605.

Men, Two. H. T. 474.

Men, Two, accomplices of Jerry Cruncher in resurrectionism. T. T. C. 114.

Men, Two, business friends of Scrooge. C. B. 45.

Men, Two, in a hotel at Dijon. D. S. 588.

Men, Two, in the Alpine hospice. C. S. 598.

Men, Two, in the lighthouse. C. B. 38.

Men, Two, on 'Change. C. B. 45

Men, Two, turning the grindstone for sharpening weapons at the French Revolution. T. T. C. 189.

Men, Two, who arrested Pip for debt. G. E. 339

Men, Two, who waited on John Westlocki M. C. 541.

Men, Two, whose footsteps alarmed Jonas Chuzzlewit. M. C. 562.

Men, Two Dingy, engaged by Mr Meagles for a dinner party. L. D. 164.

Men, Waterside, Two, who dragged the river for the body of Quilp, who was supposed to be drowned. O. C. S. 276.

Mephistopheles. C. S. 252.

Merchant. FL D. 439

Mercury, a name applied to a footman in Sir Leicester Dedlock's service. B. H. 8.

Merdle, Mr, a wealthy City man, in whose bankruptcy Mr Dorrit's money was lost; he committed suicide. L. D. 194.

Merdle, Mrs, wife of Mr Merdle, mother of Edmund Sparkler, who married Fanny Dorrit. L. D. 188.

Meriton, Henry, second mate of the "Halsewell". R. P. 323.

Merrylegs, dog belonging to Signor Jupe. H. T. 267.

Mesheck, a Jewish bill-stealer. R. P. 418.

Mesrour. C. S. 225.

Micawber, Emma, wife of Mr Micawber, and determined not to desert him. D. C. 121.

Micawber, Emma, daughter of Mr Micawber; afterwards Mrs Ridger Begs. D. C. 121, 669.

Micawber, Wilkins, with whom David Copperfield lodged: he was always on the look-out for something to turn up; eventually he was the means of exposing Uriah Heep and freeing the Wickfields from his domination; last seen as a district magistrate in Australia. Original, largely John Dickens, father of the novelist. D. C. 119, 669.

Micawber, Wilkins, Junior, son of Mr Micawber; became a gifted singer. D. C. 121, 669.

Michael, Mr, the poor relation. C. S. 25, 30.

Miff, Mrs, a pew-opener. D. S. 45, 340.

Miggs, Miss, Mrs Varden's servant, afterwards female turnkey at Bridewell; she had designs on Simon Tappertit. B. R. 43.

Mike, a client of Jaggers. G. E. 122, 304.

Miles, Bob. R. P. 428.

Miles, Owen, a friend of Master Humphrey. M. H. C. 460.

Milkman. B. H. 28.

Milkman, at Traddles's lodgings. D. C. 307.

Milkman, friend of Mr Fezziwig's cook. C. B. 21.

Mill Pond, former name of Folly Ditch (q.v.).

Miller, married to Charlotte Neckett. B. H. 676.

Miller, Mr, guest of Mr Wardle. P. P. 53

Miller, Mrs Jane Ann. C. S. 542.

Millers, a nurse at Matthew Pocket's. G. E. 136.

Milliner, who taught Little Dorrit to sew. L. D. 57.

Mills, Julia, friend and confidante of Dora Spenlow. D. C. 368.

Mills, Julia, who annotated the books of a library. R. P. 338.

Mills, Mr, father of Julia Mills. D. C. 373.

Milvey, Margaretta, wife of Rev. Frank Milvey. O. M. F. 82.

Milvey, Rev. Frank, a clergyman who helped Mr Boffin when he was looking for a boy to adopt. O. M. F. 82.

Mim, master of Pickleson, the Giant. C. S. 415.

Mincing Lane, near which was the business of Chicksey, Veneering, and Stobbles. O. M. F. 252.

Miner, Old. C. B. 38.

Minns, Augustus, a bachelor of forty, upon whom his cousin had designs. S. B. 235.

Minor Canon Corner, where Mr Crisparkle lived. E. D. 44.

Missis, Our, at the Mugby station refreshment room. C. S. 481.

Mistress, Miss Wade's. L. D. 527.

Mistress, of Mr Christopher, the waiter. C. S. 301.

Mith, Sergeant, a detective. R. P 407.

Mithers, Lady, a client of Miss Mowcher. D. C. 251.

Mithers, Lord, husband of Lady Mithers. D. C. 251.

"Mitre Inn". C. S. 92.

Mivins, Mr, prisoner in the Fleet. P. P. 451, 453.

Mobbs, one of Squeers's pupils. N. N. 73.

Meddle, Augustus, a boarder at Todgers's; engaged to marry Charity Pecksniff, but failed to turn up on the wedding-day. M. C. 117, 400.

Mogley, an old suitor of Mrs Nickleby. N. N. 412.

Molly, Jaggers's housekeeper; proved to be Estella's mother. G. E. 147.

Monflathers, Miss, keeper of a boarding-school for young ladies. O. C. S. 176.

Monks, properly Edward Leeford, half-brother of Oliver Twist, whom he tried to ruin with the aid of Fagin; died in prison. O. T. 147, 303.

Monks' Vineyard, in Rochester. E. D. 115.

Monmouth Street. S. B. 57.

Montague, Tigg, same as Montague Tigg (q.v.). M. C. 337

Monument, The. C. S. 27.

Moon, a physician. R. P. 481.

Mooney, a beadle. B. H. 113.

Mopes, Mr, the hermit of Tom Tiddler's ground. C. S. 266.

Mordlin, Brother, a member of the Committee of the Brick Lane Branch of the United Grand Junction Ebenezer Temperance Association. P. P. 358.

Morfin, Mr, chief clerk to Dombey and Son; a player on the 'cello; he married Harriet Corker. D. S. 134.

Morgan, Becky, an old lady who was buried in the churchyard of the village where Nell settled. O. C. S. 303.

Mother, of Barbara. O. C. S. 219.

Mother, of Captain Taunton. C. S. 71.

Mother, of Christiana. C. S. 28.

Mother, of Ellen. L. T. 410.

Mother, of George Silverman. G. S. E. 488.

Mother, of Hugh. B. R. 67.

Mother, of Master Humphrey. M. H. C. 435

Mother, of Mr Christopher. C. S. 292.

Mother, of Mrs Bayton. O. T. 28.

Mother, of Mrs Peerybingle. C. B. 183.

Mother, Deaf Old English. L. D. 18.

Mould, Misses, Two, daughters of Mr Mould. M. C. 316.

Mould, Mr, an undertaker. M. C. 252.

Mould, Mrs, wife of Mr Mould. M. C. 315.

Mourner. T. T. C. 111.

"Mourning Coach-horse", a house of call for undertakers. M. C. 462.

Mowchcr, Miss, a dwarf; a beauty doctor. D. C. 250.

Mudberry, Mrs, who kept a mangle; a neighbour of Mrs Barden. P. P. 376.

Mudge, Jonas, a chandler's shopkeeper, secretary of the Brick Lane Branch of the United Grand Junction Ebenezer Temperance Association. P. P. 356.

Mugby Junction. C. S. 441.

Muggleton, a town with a noted cricket team. Original doubtful. P. P. 69.

Mullins, Jack, a customer of the "Six Jolly Fellowship Porters". O. M. F. 52.

Mullion, John, one of the crew of the "Golden Mary". C. S. 127.

Mullit, Professor, an American professor of education. M. C. 215.

Muntle, Mantalini's proper name. N. N. 97.

Murderer. M. H. C. 460.

Murdstone, Edward, second husband of Mrs Copperfield, and David's stepfather; a harsh man. D. C. 14.

Murdstone, Jane, sister of Edward Murdstone; harsher even than he. D. C. 36.

Murdstone & Grinby, a wine business in which David Copperlield found very humble

and uncongenial employment. D. C. 117.

Mutanhed, Lord, the richest young man in Bath. P. P. 391.

Mutuel, Monsieur. C. S. 304.

Muzzle, Mr, Mr Nupkins's footman. P. P. 255.

N

Nadgett, Mr, a private detective who watched Jonas Chuzzlewit closely and brought him to justice; landlord of Tom Pinch. M. C. 351.

Namby, Mr, a sheriff's officer who arrested Mr Pickwick. P. P. 436.

Nancy, an unfortunate woman, mistress of Bill Sikes, who murdered her. O. T. 49.

Nandy, John Edward, father of Mrs Plornish. L. D. 288.

Narrator. O. C. S. 1.

Nathan, Mr, a dresser at a private theatre. S. B. 92.

"National Hotel", an American hotel at which Marlin Chuzzlewit put up. M. C. 275.

Native, The, a black servant of Major Bagstock. D. S. 67.

Native Gentleman, in a suit of grease. L. D. 517.

Neckett, Charlotte, called Charley, daughter of Neckett, the sheriff's officer; became maid to Esther Summerson; married a miner. B. H. 161

Neckett, Emma, Charlotte Neckett's sister; became maid to Esther Summerson after Charlotte's marriage. B. H. 161.

Neckett, Mr, called Coavinses by

Harold Skimpole, a sheriff's officer, who died and left a young family. B. H. 57.

Neckett, Tom, brother of Charlotte Neckett; afterwards in the service of her husband. B. H. 161.

Ned, a chimney-sweeper referred to by Bill Sikes. O. T. 108.

Ned, Lummy, See *Lummy, Ned.*

Neddy, turnkey in the Fleet. P. P. 458

Neighbour, of man called John. D. S. 273.

Neighbour, Our Next-door. S. B. 32.

Neighbours, of Mrs Billiekin. E. D. 225.

Nell, Little. See *Trent, Nell.*

Nemo. See *Hawdon.*

Nephew, of Miggs. B. R 473, 474

Nephew, of Miss Wade's employers. L. D. 528.

Neptune, a dog. O. T. 157.

Nettingall, The Misses, at whose school Miss Shepherd was a boarder. D. C. 204.

Newcome, Clemency (Clementina), servant of Dr Jeddler; married Benjamin Britain. C. B. 194.

Newgate, visited by Pip, G. B. 191; where Fagin was imprisoned, O. T. 314; visited, S. B. 147.

Newman Street, where Turveydrop's Academy was situated. B. H. 144.

Nicholas, butler of Bellamy's. S. B. 117.

Nickits, whose estate Mr Bounderby came into. H. T. 388.

Nickleby, Godfrey, grandfather of Nicholas Nickleby. N. N. 1.

Nickleby, Kate, sister of Nicholas Nickleby; employed for a time in Madame Mantalini's dressmaking establishment; afterwards a

companion to Mrs Wititterly; married Frank Cheeryble. N. N. 4, 18.

Nickleby, Mrs, mother of Nicholas Nickleby; a very garrulous, rambling lady. Original, Dickens's mother. N. N. 4.

Nickleby, Mrs, wife of Godfrey Nickleby. N. N. 1.

Nickleby, Mrs Ralph, secretly married to Ralph Nickleby. N. N. 610.

Nickleby, Nicholas, hero of N. N.; fought his way from poverty to a partnership in Cheeryble Brothers; at one time master in Squeers's school, at another a member of Crummles's theatrical company; defeated Ralph Nickleby's designs and married Madeline Bray.

Nickleby, Nicholas, the elder, father of foregoing. N. N. 2.

Nickleby, Ralph, uncle of Godfrey Nickleby. N. N. 2.

Nickleby, Ralph, uncle of Nicholas Nickleby, whom he hated; a miserly money-lender; ultimately hanged himself. N. N. 2.

Niner, Margaret, niece of Julius Slinkton, who was slowly poisoning her. H. D. 444

Nipper, Susan, Florence Dombey's maid; married Mr Toots. D. S. 20.

Noakes, Percy, law student, one of the steam excursion party. S. B. 288.

Nobleman, Poor, whose children Miss Wade taught. L. D. 527.

Noddy, Mr, a scorbutic youth, friend of Bob Sawyer. P. P. 343

Noggs, Newman, cleric to Ralph Nickleby, who had come down in the world; befriended Nicholas Nickleby. N. N. 7.

Nondescript. L. D. 72.

Norah, Harry Walmers's child sweetheart. C. S. 103.

Norfolk Street, where Mrs Lirriper's lodgings were. C. S. 341.

Normandy, alleged name of the Bonnet at a gaining-booth. C. S. 193.

Norris, Misses, Two, daughters of Mr Norris. M. C. 226.

Norris, Mr, a New York gentleman. M. C. 226.

Norris, Mr, Junior, son of Mr Norris. M. C. 226.

Norris, Mrs, Senior, mother of Mr Norris. M. C. 226.

Norris, Mrs, wife of Mr Norris. M. C. 226.

Norwood, where James Carker lived. D. S. 367.

Nubbles, Baby. O. C. S. 61.

Nubbles, Christopher, generally called Kit, a friend of Little Nell, employed by her grandfather; afterwards a servant to the Garlands; falsely accused of theft by Sampson Brass, but proved innocent; married Barbara. O. C. S. 6.

Nubbles, Jacob, younger brother of Kit. O. C. S. 61.

Nubbles, Mrs, Kit's mother. O. C. S. 60.

Nuns' House, in Cloisterham, where Miss Twinkleton's Seminary was. E. D. 18.

Nupkins, George, mayor of principal magistrate of Ipswich. P. P. 255.

Nupkins, Henrietta, daughter of Mr Nupkins, upon whom Alfred Jingle

had matrimonial designs. P. P. 269.

Nupkins, Mrs, wife of Mr Nupkins. P. P. 269.

Nurse, at David Copperfield's birth. D. C. 1.

Nurse, of Mr Willet in his last illness. B. R. 487.

Nurse, of the children opposite Dombey's house. D. S. 188.

Nurse, to Mrs Kenwigs. N. N. 361.

Nurse, with whom Miss Edwards's sister lodged. O. C. S. 182.

Nursery-maid, Dark-eyed, in Temple Gardens. B. R. 88.

O

Obelisk, or Obstacle, in South London. C. S. 323.

Obenreizer, Jules, London agent of Defresnier & Co.; guilty of forgery; attempted to murder George Vendale. C. S. 530.

O'Bleary, Frederick, an Irishman who boarded with Mrs Tibbs. S. B. 225.

O'Brien, Mr, passenger on the boat to Gravesend. S. B. 77.

Obstacle. See *Obelisk*.

Officer. B. R. 410.

Officer, T. T. C. 34.

Officer, in pursuit of Magwitch. G. E. 327.

Officer, who identified Magwitch. G. E. 328, 329.

Officer, Commanding. B. R. 290.

Officer, Court. C. S. 430.

Officer, French. C. S. 77.

Officer, Police. B. H. 620.

Officer, Police. C. S. 361.

Officer, Police. O. C. S. 341.

Officer, Police, kind to Oliver Twist O. T. 53.

Officer, Prison. G. E. 337.

Officer, Prison. O. C. S. 345

Officers, of the 19th. P. P. 16.

Officers, Police, Three. B. H. 593.

Officers, Police, Two. C. S. 378.

Old Bailey, where Charles Darnay stood his trial for treason, T. T. C. 41; scene of a murder trial, C. S. 427.

"Old Clem", a song hummed by Joe Gargery. G. E. 69.

Old Hell Shaft, a disused pit, down which Stephen Blackpool fell, receiving fatal injuries. H. T. 475.

"Old Man's Tale about the Queer Client." P. P. 221.

"Old Royal Hotel", Birmingham, visited by Mr Pickwick. P. P. 549

"Old Uri", Mrs Gummidge's late husband. D. C. 108.

Omer, Minnie. See *Joram, Mrs*

Omer, Mr, the undertaker who buried David Copperfield's mother, and for whom Little Em'ly worked. D. C. 95.

Orange, James. H. R. 481.

Orange, Mrs H. R. 479.

Ordinary of Newgate. B. R. 455.

Orfling, The, a servant of the Micawber family. D. C. 121.

Organist's Assistant, friend of Tom Pinch. M. C. 57, 437

Orlick, Dolge, a blacksmith employed by Joe Gargery; he was the cause of Mrs Gargery's death, and afterwards tried to kill Pip. G. E. 81.

Ostler, Attesting, who could swear only profane oaths. P. P. 603.

Overton, Joseph, mayor of Great Winglebury. S. B. 309.

Owen, John, one of Mr Marton's pupils. O. C. S. 295.

P

P.J.T. 1747, inscription over Mr Grewgious's door. E. D. 98.

Packer, Tom, a private of marines. C. S. 155.

Packlemerton, Jasper, one of Mrs Jarley's wax figures. O. C. S. 161.

Page, at Mr Pocket's. G. E. 141.

Page Boy, to David Copperfield; transported for theft. D. C. 530.

Pall Mall. C. S. 194.

Palmer, a pupil of Squeers. N. N. 581.

Pancks, Mr Casby's agent in squeezing the tenants of Bleeding Heart Yard; he exposed Mr Casby in the end; instrumental in restoring Mr Dorrit to fortune. L. D. 11.

Pankey, Miss, a child at Mrs Pipchin's establishment. D. S. 80.

Papa, Majestic English. L. D. 18.

Paragon, Mary Anne, David and Dora Copperlield's first servant. D. C. 486.

Pardiggle, Alfred, a son of Mrs Pardiggle. B. H. 78.

Pardiggle, Egbert, a son of Mrs Pardiggle. B. H. 78.

Pardiggle, Felix, a son of Mrs Pardiggle. B. H. 78.

Pardiggle, Francis, a son of Mrs Pardiggle. B. H. 78.

Pardiggle, Mrs, an ostentatious and interferingly benevolent woman. B. H. 78.

Pardiggle, O. A., F.R.S., husband of Mrs Pardiggle. B. H. 79.

Pardiggle, Oswald, a son of Mrs Pardiggle. B. H. 78.

Parent, Aged. See *Wemmick, Mr, Sen.*

Paris, visited by Mrs Lirriper. C. S. 391.

"**Parish Clerk, The**", a tale of true love. P. P. 178.

Parker, a policeman. R. P. 432.

Parker, Mrs Johnson, president of a ladies' bible and prayer-book distribution society. S. B. 28.

Parkers, The Miss Johnson, daughters of Mrs Johnson Parker. S. B.28.

Parkes, Phil, a ranger. B. R. 4.

Parkins, Mr, a porter. R. P. 375

Parkins, Mrs, a laundress. R. P. 375.

Parksop, Brother, grandfather of George Silverman. G. S. E. 496.

Parlour-maid in Chief; Miss Twinkleton's. E. D. 20.

Parlour-maids, Two, at Mr Meagles's. L. D. 156.

Parochial Parasites, Two, in a jury. C. S. 430.

Parrot, Mrs Merdle's. L. D. 188.

Parsons, Gabriel, a rich sugar baker, who tried to marry Watkins Tottle. S. B. 326.

Parsons, Letitia, a pianist at the Minerva House ball. S. B. 249.

Parsons, Mrs Gabriel, wife of Gabriel Parsons. S. B. 330.

Parts, Arson. C. S. 251.

Passnidge, Mr, a friend of Mr Murdstone, a gay, careless fellow. D. C. 18, 19.

Patriots, Five. T. T. C. 178.

Patty, sister of the tenant of the Haunted House. C. S. 213.

Pavilionstone, a seaside place, probably Folkestone. R. P. 378.

Pawkins, Major, an American whose wife kept a boarding-house. M. C. 211.

Pawkins, Mrs, who kept a boarding-house in New York. M. C. 212.

Pawnbroker, at Cloisterham. E. D. 18.

Payne, Doctor, combative friend of Dr Slammer. P. P. 23.

Peacoat. R. P. 438.

"**Peacock Inn**", at Eatanswill. P. P. 128.

Peak, Sir John Chester's man. B. R. 134.

Peaks, The, former name of Bleak House. B. H. 74.

"**Peal of Bells**", a village alehouse. C. S. 266.

Peasant Woman, with whom Miss Wade lodged. L. D. 518.

Pebbleson Nephew, original name of Wilding & Co. C. S. 511.

Pecksniff, Charity, elder daughter of Seth Pecksniff; engaged to Mr Moddle, who ran off on the wedding-day. M. C. 8.

Pecksniff, Mercy (Merry), younger daughter of Seth Pecksniff; married to Jonas Chuzzlewit and cruelly treated. M. C. 9.

Pecksniff, Seth, an architect and land surveyor in a town near Salisbury; an unctuous hypocrite, cousin of old Martin Chuzzlewit; ultimately exposed. M. C. 8.

Peddle & Pool, solicitors for Edward Dorrit. L. D. 335

Pedro, one of Jerry's performing dogs. O. C. S. 106.

Peecher, Emma, a teacher in the same school as Bradley Headstone, with whom she was in love. O. M. F. 174.

Peepy, Honourable Miss, a former beauty of an English wateringplace. R. P. 337

Peerybingle, John, a carrier. C. B. 128.

Peerybingle, Mary (Dot), wife of Mr Peerybingle. C. B. 125.

Peffer & Snagsby, the name of Mr Snagsby's firm. 13. H. 98.

"Pegasus's Arms", public-house where Sleary's troupe stayed. H. T. 267.

Peggotty, Clara, David Copperfield's faithful nurse, the sister of Mr Peggotty; she married Mr Barkis. D. C. 5.

Peggotty, Daniel, uncle of Hans and of Little Em'ly, and brother of Clara Peggotty; he left home in search of Little Em'ly, and on her return went with her to Australia. D. C. 24.

Peggotty, Ham, nephew of Mr Peggotty, and betrothed to Little Em'ly; he died attempting to save the life of Steerforth, Little Em'ly's betrayer. D. C. 7.

Peggy, a servant. C. S. 200.

Pegler, Mrs, mother of Mr Bounderby, who was ashamed to own her. H. T. 310.

Pell, Mrs, Mr Pell's late wife. P. P. 602.

Pell, Solomon, an attorney who did business for the Wellers. P. P. 468.

Peltirogus, Horatio, referred to by Mrs Nickleby as an old suitor for Kale Nickleby's hand. N. N. 564.

Penrewen, Unchris'en. C. S. 251.

Penrith, birthplace of Captain Ravender. C. S. 251.

Pentonville, near which Mr Brownlow stayed. O. T. 59, 71.

Peplow, Master, son of Mrs Peplow; fond of muffins. S. B. 43.

Peplow, Mrs, a typical London housewife. S. B. 43.

Pepper, Pip's servant, called "The Avenger". G. E. 160.

Peps, Doctor Parker, who attended Mrs Dombey at Paul's birth. D. S. 3.

Perch, Mr, employed with Dombey & Son as messenger. D. S. 133.

Perch, Mrs, wife of Mr Perch; apparently always in an interesting condition. D. S. 142.

Perker, Mr, election agent for Slumkey at Eatanswill; solicitor for Mr Pickwick in the breach of promise case. P. P. 97.

Perkins, a general dealer. C. S. 208.

Perkins, Mrs, a neighbour of Mr Krook. B. H. 111.

Perkins, Young, son of Mrs Perkins. B. H. 111.

Perkinsop, Mary Anne, a servant of Mrs Lirriper. C. S. 345

Person, Amiable, with a bald head, at dinner in Mr Spenlow's. D. C. 299.

Person, Elderly, in Miss Wozenham s. C. S. 385.

Person, Young, one of David Copperfield's troublesome servants. D. C. 491.

Personage, Elderly, with a dirty face, at the "Peacock", Eatanswill. P. P. 139.

Personage, Prim, in clean linen and cloth boots, one of Bob Sawyer's party. P. P. 343

Personage, Shabby-genteel, one of the poor travellers. C. S. 63.

Peter, Lord, a weak-minded lord, for whom Alexander Trott was mistaken. S. B. 310.

Petowker, Henrietta, an actress who married Mr Lillyvick and then ran off with a half-pay captain. N. N. 129.

Pettifer, Tom, steward to Captain Jorgan. C. S. 235.

Pew-opener, at the Lammles's marriage. O. M. F. 93.

Pew-opener, at the marriage of David Copperfield and Dora. D. C. 484.

Pew-opener, in the church where the banns of Walter Gay and Florence Dombey were proclaimed. D. S. 616.

Pew-opener, who acted as bridesmaid to Miss Skiffins. G. E. 333

Phib. See *Phoebe* (second entry).

Phibbs, Mr, a haberdasher. R. P. 422.

Philanthropist, Stipendiary, a servant of Luke Honeythunder. E. D. 165.

Philips, a constable. B. R. 359.

Phoebe, cripple daughter of Lamps. C. S. 450.

Phoebe, maid to Fanny Squeers. N. N. 104.

Phunky, Mr, barrister, and junior counsel for Pickwick. P. P. 336.

Physician, Mr Merdle's. L. D. 200.

Pianist, at Podsnap's. O. M. F. 109.

Piccadilly. C. S. 328, 424.

Pickles, Mr, a fishmonger. H. R. 464.

Pickleson, a giant. C. S. 415.

Pickwick, Samuel, founder of the Pickwick Club; as a result of losing the breach of promise case brought against him by Mrs Barden, he was imprisoned in the Fleet, but ultimately was released, and settled at Dulwich, P. P. 1; visited Master Humphrey, M. H. C. 469.

Pickwick Club, founded by Mr Pickwick. P. P. 1.

Picture Room, in the Haunted House. C. S. 277.

Pidger, Mr, said to have been formerly enamoured of Miss Lavinia Spenlow. D. C. 455

Pieman. B. H. 112.

Pieman, in a procession. T. T. C 112.

Pierce, Captain, of the "Halsewell". R. P. 323.

Pierce, Mary, younger daughter of Captain Pierce. R. P. 325.

Pierce, Miss, elder daughter of Captain Pierce. R. P. 324.

Piff, Miss, a servant at Mugby station refreshment room. C. S. 483

Pigeon, Thomas, an alias of Tallyho Thompson. R. P. 410.

Pilkins, Mr, physician to Mr Dombey's family. D. S. 3.

Pimkin & Thomas's out-of-door cleric. P. P. 215.

Pinch, Ruth, sister of Tom Pinch; at first a governess; afterwards kept house for her brother; married John Westlock. M. C. 107.

Pinch, Tom, assistant to Mr Pecksniff, in whom he had unlimited faith; he afterwards found him out and was discharged; went to London, where he was befriended anonymously by old Martin Chuzzlewit. M. C. 14.

Pincher, a dog. O. T. 157.

Pip, more fully Philip Pirrip, hero of G. E.; brought up by his sister and her husband, Joe Gargery; apprenticed to Joe as a blacksmith; befriended by Miss Havisham and met Estella at her house; came into "great expectations", and went to London; learned that his fortune was conferred by Magwitch, a convict, who came to him on his return from transportation; his fortune forfeited on Magwitch's recapture and conviction; married Estella after her first husband's death.

Pip, Mr, a theatrical man, friend of Montague Tigg. M. C. 354.

Pipchin, Mr, late husband of Mrs Pipchin, who broke his heart in the Peruvian mines. D. S. 77.

Pipchin, Mrs, keeper of an infantine boarding establishment at Brighton, where Paul and Florence Dombey spent some time; afterwards housekeeper to Mr Dombey. D. S. 78.

Piper, Anastasia, a neighbour of Mr Brook. B. H. III, 113.

Piper, Professor, an American. M. C. 423.

Piper, Young, son of Mrs Piper. B. H. 113.

Pipkin, Nathaniel, hero of the tale of "The Parish Clerk"; failed in his suit for the hand of Maria Lobbs. P. P. 178.

Pipson, Miss, one of Miss Griffin's pupils. C. S. 224.

Pirate Captain, Portuguese. C. S. 169.

Pirrip, Georgiana, Pip's mother. G. E. 1.

Pirrip, Philip. See *Pip*.

Pirrip, Philip, father of Pip. G. E.1.

Pitcher, a pupil of Squeers. N. N. 61, 580.

Pitt, Jane, married to Old Cheeseman. C. S. 44, 49.

Plashwater Weir Mill Lock, where Rogue Riderhood was employed. O. M. F. 441.

Plornish, Sally, wife of Mr Plornish, and interpreter to Cavalletto; fond of using the phrase "not to deceive you". L. D. 107.

Plornish, Thomas, plasterer, to whom Clennam was kind; a tenant of Mr Casby in Bleeding Heart Yard; found great difficulty in getting employment. L. D. 52, 109.

Pluck, Mr, one of Sir Mulberry Hawk's friends. N. N. 183.

Plummer, Bertha, blind daughter of Caleb Plummer, who concealed from her the poverty of their surroundings and the real nature of Tackleton, their employer. C. B. 143, 147

Plummer, Caleb, an old toy-maker, in the service of Tackleton. C. B. 135.

Plummer, Edward, son of Caleb Plummer, who returned from South America, and lodged with John Peerybingle in the disguise of a deaf old man; he was in time to marry May Fielding, his former sweetheart, when she was on the eve of being forced into a marriage with Tackleton. C. B. 134, 178.

Pocket, Mick, son of Matthew Pocket. G. E. 136.

Pocket, Belinda, daughter of a deceased knight, and wife of Matthew Pocket; negligent of her household. G. E. 136, 141.

Pocket, Fanny, daughter of Matthew Pocket. G. E. 142.

Pocket, Herbert, son of Matthew Pocket, and Pip's friend; married Clara Barley. G. E 126, 65.

Pocket, Jane, daughter of Matthew Pocket. G. E. 141.

Pocket, Joe, son of Matthew Pocket. G. E. 142.

Pocket, Matthew, a cousin of Miss Havisham, with whom Pip read for a time. G. E. 137.

Pocket, Sarah, one of Miss Havisham's self-seeking relatives.

Fodder, Mr, a leading member of the All-Muggleton cricket team. P. P. 71.

Poddles, a girl kept by Betty Higden. O. M. F. 157.

Podgers, Sir John, in Mr Pickwick's tale; knighted for getting his housekeeper burned as a witch. M. H. C. 472, 485.

Pod's End. H. T. 265.

Podsnap, Georgiana, daughter of Mr and Mrs Podsnap; the Lammles unsuccessfully tried to marry her to Fledgeby. O. M. F. 107.

Podsnap, John, a gentleman in the marine insurance way; well satisfied with himself and everything; considered foreign countries a mistake. O. M. F. 6, 101.

Podsnap, Mrs, wife of Mr Podsnap. O. M. F. 6.

Pogrom, Hon. Elijah, an American politician. M. C. 418.

Policeman. B. H. 111.

Policeman. G. S. E. 489.

Policeman. T. T. C. 126.

Policeman, witness against the Artful Dodger. O. T. 258.

Polly. See *Tresham*

Polly, a waitress in the "Slapbang" dining-house. B. H. 212, 213.

Polreath, David. C. S. 251.

Pony, belonging to Vincent Crummles. N. N. 222.

Poor Relation. C. S. 25.

Poplar, where Captain Ravender had his house. C. S. 116.

"Poplars, The", the Haunted House. C. S. 208.

Pordage, Commissioner, of the Island of Silver-store; an incompetent red-tape official. C. S. 150.

Pordage, Mrs, wife of Commissioner Pordage. C. S. 152.

Porkenham, Mrs, Misses, and Mr Sidney, friends of Mr Nupkins; Sidney Porkenham was in love with Miss Nupkins. P. P. 269.

Porkin & Snob. P. P. 443

Port Middlebay, the place in Australia of which Mr Micawber became district magistrate. D. C. 668.

Porter. C. B. 27.

Porter. C. B. 196.

Porter. D. C. 424.

Porter. D. S. 204.

Porter. T. T. C. 176.

Porter, at the house where Ruth Pinch was governess. M. C. 446.

Porter, at the Mansion House. B. R. 358.

Porter, Mr Dorrit's. L. D. 505.

Porter, Emma, daughter of Mrs Joseph Porter. S. B. 320.

Porter, Mrs Joseph, who helped to spoil the Gattletons' amateur theatricals. S. B. 319.

Porter, Night, at the Middle Temple. B. R. 232.

Porters, Foolish Mr, an old lover of Miss Twinkleton. F. D. 19.

Porters, Two, at "Royal George Hotel", Dover. T. T. C. 11.

Portland Place, near which Mr Dombey lived. D. S. 17.

Portman Square, near which the Podsnaps lived. O. M. F. 103.

Portsmouth, where Nicholas Nickleby acted in Mr Crummles's company. N. N. 223.

Postboy. See also under *Boy*.

Postboy. B. R. 356.

Postboy. C. B. 22.

Postboy, at Coventry. P. P. 556.

Postboy, Grinning. P. P. 48.

Postilion. D. S. 597.

Postilion. T. T. C. 34.

Postilion, Savage Old. H. T. 484.

Postman. M. C. 652.

Postmaster, at Beauvais. T. T. C. 179.

Potboy. B. H. 111.

Potboy. B. H. 353

Potboy, at the Fleet. P. P. 459.

Potkins, William, a wailer at the "Blue Boar". G. E. 349.

Potman, in Newgate. G. E. 191.

Pott, Mr, editor of the *Eatanswill Gazette*. P. P. 127.

Pott, Mrs, wife of Mr Pott. P. P. 128.

Potter, Thomas, a clerk who made a night of it. S. B. 198.

Potterson, Abigail (Abbey), proprietor of the "Six Jolly Fellowship Porters". O. M. F. 50

Potterson, Job, brother of Miss Abbey Potterson, steward on the ship that brought John Harmon from Africa. O. M. F. 24, 295.

Poulterer's Man. C. B. 56.

Powlers, the family of the late Mr Sparsit. H. T. 280.

Pratchett, Mrs, a chambermaid. C. S. 298.

Preacher, at Little Bethel. O.C. S. 230.

'Prentice Knights, a secret society of apprentices of which Simon Tappertit was captain; took part in the Gordon riots under the name of United Bull-Dogs. B. R. 50.

President of the United States, a judge in a juvenile courtmartial. H. R. 459.

Preston, where George Silverman belonged to. G. S. E. 487.

Price, Matilda ('Tilda), a miller's daughter, friend of Miss Squeers; she married John Browdie. N. N. 81.

Price, Mr, a coarse vulgar young man. P. P. 438, 439.

Priest, a mild old man. B. R. 357.

Priest, Ugly. L. D. 505.

Prig, Betsey, a nurse, friend of Mrs Gamp. M. C. 323.

Princess's Place, where Miss Tox and Major Bagstock lived. D. S. 66.

Priscilla, Mrs Jellyby's servant. B. R. 35.

Prisoner. B. H. 3.

Prisoner. G. E. 147.

Prisoner, a woman. O. M. F. 19.

Prisoner, Chancery, from whom Mr Pickwick rented a room in the Fleet. P. P. 462.

Prisoners, Four Condemned. B. R. 378

Prodgit, Mrs, a nurse. R. P. 363.

Proprietor of a Gambling Booth. N. N. 508..

Press, Miss, maid to Lucie Manette; assisted the escape of Darnay and Lucie, and in doing so killed Madame Defarge unintentionally. T. T. C. 18.

Pross, Solomon, brother of Miss Pross; as John Barsad gave evidence against Darnay, and acted as a spy in Paris; afterwards, as a turnkey in the Conciergerie, aided Carton in carrying out his plan of self-sacrifice. T. T. C. 47.

Provis, an alias of Magwitch (q.v.).

Pruffle, servant of a scientific gentleman. P. P. 434

Publican, a second of the butcher in the fight with David Copperfield. D. C. 205.

Pubsey & Co., the name of Fledgeby's money-lending firm. O. M. F. 337.

Puffer, Princess, a woman from an opium den. E. D. 264.

Pugstyles, Mr, one of Mr Gregsbury's constituents. N. N. 150.

Pumblechook, Uncle, a corn chandler, uncle of Joe Gargery. fawned on Pip in his prosperity, but offensively patronizing when his fortune was lost. G. E. 17.

Pupford, Euphemia, head of the Lilliputian College. C. S. 277.

Pupils, Mr Cripples's. L. D. 73.

Pupils, of Mr Marton. O. C. S. 141, 296.

Pupker, Sir Matthew, a member of Parliament. N. N. 8.

Purday, Captain, a naval officer on half-pay. S. B. 10, 15.

Putney, M. H. C. 481.

Pyegrave, Charley, a client of Miss Mowcher. D. C. 253.

Pyke, Mr, a friend of Sir Mulberry Hawk. N. N. 182.

Q

Quale, Mr, a friend of Mrs Jellyby, who wished to marry Caddy. B. H. 32.

Quanko Samba, referred to by Jingle. P. P. 73.

Queen Square, where Richard Carstone lodged. B. H. 187.

Quilp, Betsy, wife of Quilp, the dwarf, living in constant terror of her husband; after Quilp's death, she married more happily. O. C. S. 22.

Quilp, Daniel, a wicked dwarf who drove Nell and her grandfather from their home, and with the aid of Sampson Brass plotted against Kit Nubbles; he was accidentally drowned in the Thames when being pursued by the police. O. C. S. 16.

Quilp's Wharf, a yard beside the Thames. O. C. S. 22.

Quinion, Mr, manager of Murdstone & Grinby's. D. C. 18.

R

Rachael, beloved by Stephen Blackpool, but unable to marry him because he had a dissolute wife alive; she believed in Stephen and helped to vindicate him. H. T. 299.

Rachael, Mrs See *Chadband, Mrs*

Raddle, Mary Ann, landlady of Bob Sawyer. P. P. 338.

Raddle, Mr, husband of Mrs Raddle. P. P. 340.

Radfoot, George, third mate on the ship that brought John Harmon home from Africa; the murdered man whose drowned body was taken for that of Harmon. O. M. F. 287, 294.

Rainbird, Alice, child bride of Robin Redforth. H. R. 457

Rairyganoo, Sally, a servant of Mrs Lirriper. C. S. 384.

Rames, William, second mate of the "Golden Mary". C. S. 125.

Ramsey, client of Dodson & Fogg. P. P. 205.

Ramsgate, visited by the Tuggses in their prosperity. S. B. 254.

Rarx, Mr, a passenger on the "Golden Mary". C. S. 111.

Rats' Castle. R. P. 428.

Ravender, William George, captain of the "Golden Mary". C. S. 115.

Raybrock, Alfred, a young fisherman; married Kitty Tregarthen. C. S. 239.

Raybrock, Hugh, brother of Alfred Raybrock; lost at sea, but turned up again. C. S. 239.

Raybrock, Jorgan, son of Alfred Raybrock and Kitty Tregarthen. C. S. 264.

Raybrock, Margaret, wife of Hugh Raybrock. C. S. 240.

Raybrock, Mrs, mother of Alfred and Hugh Raybrock. C. S. 236.

Reading, where Esther Summerson attended Miss Donny's boarding-school. B. H. 17.

Red Whisker, a man at a picnic party. D. C. 370.

Redburn, Jack, a friend of Master Humphrey. M. H. C. 458.

Redforth, Robin, cousin of William Tinkling; child bridegroom of Alice Rainbird. H. R. 457

Redlaw, Mr, a lecturer on chemistry at an endowment for students; at his own request he lost the memory of sorrow, wrong, and trouble, but blighted others by imparting the gift in spite of himself; got the gift reversed. C. B. 251, 254.

Regent Street, where Lord Frederick Verisopht lived. N. N. 256.

Registrar, in the Court of Chancery. B. H. 3.

Relations, Couple of Poor, of Mr Wardle's, present at the wedding of Trundle and Isabella Wardle. P. P. 300.

Retainers, Four, employed by Mr Veneering. O. M. F. 6.

Reverend, The, head of a school. C. S. 41.

Reynolds, Miss, school-fellow of Rosa Bud. E. D. 73.

Riah, Mr, an old Jew who was employed by Fledgeby in the money-lending business; he befriended Lizzie Hexam and Jenny Wren. O. M. F. 220.

Richard, a waiter at the "Saracen's Head". N. N. 25.

Richard, Margaret Veck's lover, a smith. C. B. 73.

Richards, Mrs, a name given by Mr Dombey to Polly Toodle (q. v.).

Richmond, where Mr Tupman settled down in lodgings, P. P. 623; where Estella lived with Mrs Brandley, G. E. 198.

Rickitts, Little, school-fellow of Rosa Bud. E. D. 124.

Riderhood, Pleasant, daughter of Rogue Riderhood; an unlicensed pawnbroker; afterwards wife of Mr Venus. O. M. F. 281.

Riderhood, Roger (Rogue), a Thames waterside man who was concerned in the unsuccessful attempt on John Harmon's life; drowned by Bradley Headstone. O. M. F. 50.

Rigaud, *alias* Lagnier, *alias* Blandois, a villain and murderer; killed by collapse of a building. L. D. 2.

Rinaldo di Velasco, show name of the giant Pickleson. C. S. 415.

Road-mender, same as Jacques Five

and the Sawyer. T. T. C. 81, 118, 199.

Roadside Inn. C. S. 91.

Rob the Grinder. See *Toodle, Robin*.

Robert, Uncle, at a Christmas dinner. S. B. 166.

Robinson, an employee of Dombey & Son. D. S. 561.

Robinson, Mrs Tibbs's servant. S. B. 210.

Robinson, Mr, who married the youngest Miss Willis. S. B. 12.

Rochester, visited by the Pickwickians, P. P. 10; and the Poor Travellers, C. S. 57. See also *Cloisterham*.

Rodolph, Mr and Mrs Jennings, musical entertainers. S. B. 188.

Rogers, a policeman. R. P. 428.

Rogers, Johnny, who died in the workhouse. R. P. 449

Rogers, Mr, in a bar parlour. S. B. 176.

Rogers, Mr, third mate of the "Halsewell". R. P. 324.

Rogers, Mrs, Mrs Bardell's lodger. P. P. 504.

Roker, Tom, turnkey at the Fleet, from whom Mr Pickwick hired a room. P. P. 445

Rokesmith, Bella, child of John Rokesmith and Bella Wilfer. O. M. F. 604.

Rokesmith, John. See *Harmon, John*.

Rookery, The, home of David Copperfield. D. C. 4.

Rosa, maid to Lady Dedlock; engaged to Watt Rouncewell. B. H. 66.

Rose, loved by a young surgeon. S. B. 280.

Ross, Frank, a partner in a game of whist at the Parsons's. S. B. 329.

Rouge-et-noir Man, at the races. N. N. 508.

Rouncewell, George, a son of Mrs Rouncewell, who ran away and joined the army; turned up again as Mr George, keeper of a shooting-gallery in London; became a servant to Sir Leicester Dedlock. B. H. 65, 227.

Rouncewell, Mr, a son of Mrs Rouncewell, a prosperous iron-master. B. H. 65, 304.

Rouncewell, Mrs, Sir Leicester Dedlock's housekeeper. B. H. 64.

Rouncewell, Watt, son of Mr Rouncewell, engaged to Rosa, pretty maid of Lady Dedlock. B. H. 66.

"Royal George Hotel", at Dover. T. T. C. 10.

"Royal Hotel", where Dombey and Major Bagstock stayed, at Leamington. D. S. 223.

Royal Humane Society. N. N. 2.

"Royal Old Dust-bin", where Mr Christopher's father was headwaiter. C. S. 293.

Rudge, Barnaby, a half-wit, who was condemned to death for participation in the Gordon riots, but was reprieved. B. R. 22.

Rudge, Mary, wife of Rudge the murderer, and mother of Barnaby Rudge. B. R. 32.

Rudge, Mr, father of Barnaby Rudge; murderer of Reuben Haredale; captured by Geoffrey Haredale and hanged. B. R. 12.

Rugg, Anastasia, daughter of Mr Rugg, who had recovered damages from a baker for breach of promise. L. D. 234.

Rugg, Mr, a general agent and accountant; Pancks's landlord. L. D. 234.

S

Sackville Street, where the Lammles stayed. O. M. F. 204.

Saffron Hill, where Fagin and his gang lived. O. T. 43, 142.

St. Albans, near which Bleak House was. B. H. 48.

St. Antoine, a district of Paris, where Defarge had his wine shop. T. T. C. 20.

St. Dunstan's, a church in London, where Will Marks made a secret burial. M. H. C. 481.

St. Evremonde, Marquis, Charles Darnay's uncle; murdered by Gaspard, whose child had been killed by his carriage. T. T. C. 73.

St. Evremonde, Marquis, twin brother of the preceding, and father of Charles Darnay. T.T.C. 231.

St. Evremonde, Marquise, mother of Charles Darnay. T. T. C. 239.

St. Germain, the quarter of Paris where Tellson's Bank had its office. T. T. C. 186.

St. Thomas's Street, where Mr Crummles lived in Portsmouth. N. N. 230.

Saint Julien, Horatio, alias Jem Larkins, in a private theatre. S. B. 91.

Saint Mary Axe, where Pubsey & Co. was situated. O. M. F. 337.

Salem, in Massachusetts, to which Captain Jorgan belonged. C. S. 251.

Salem House, Mr Creakle's school, where David Copperfield was sent by Mr Murdstone. D. C. 140.

Salisbury, near which Pecksniff and Tom Pinch lived. M. C. 55.

Sally, Uncle Bill's niece, at an outing in a Tea Gardens. S. B. 72.

Sally, Old, a workhouse inmate who nursed Oliver Twist's mother on her deathbed, and robbed her. O. T. 2, 132, 136.

Sam, a cabman, who quarrelled with Mr Pickwick. P. P. 5.

Sam, an hostler. M. C. 51.

Samkin & Green's managing clerk. P. P. 215.

Sampson, George, an old sweetheart of Bella Willer; afterwards sweetheart of her sister Lavinia. O. M. F. 85.

Sampson., Mr, manager of a Life Assurance Office. H. D. 439.

Sanders, Susannah, friend of Mrs Bardell. P. P. 279.

Sapsea, Ethelinda, née Brobity, reverential wife of Mr Sapsea. E. D. 31.

Sapsea, Thomas, auctioneer and mayor of Cloisterham. E. D. 28.

"Saracen's Head", an inn in London where Mr Squeers stayed. N. N. 21, 23-24.

"Saracen's Head", Towcester, where Mr Pickwick put up. P. P. 557

Sarah, maid of an old lady in Our Parish. S. B. 9.

Sarah, servant at Westgate House. P. P. 173.

Satellite, of a police inspector. O. M. F. 19.

Satis House, Miss Havisham's house. G. E. 40.

Savage Chief. H. R. 475.

Sawyer, same as the road-mender and Jacques Five in T. T. C. (199).

Sawyer, Bob, an impecunious medical student, friend of Benjamin Allen and a rival of Mr Winkle for the affections of Arabella Allen; ultimately settled in the East Indies as a surgeon. P. P. 317.

Scadder, Zephaniah, agent of the Eden Land Corporation, who tricked Martin Chuzzlewit. M. C. 278.

Scadgers, Lady, great-aunt of Mrs Sparsit. H. T. 280.

Scaley, Mr, a sheriff's officer. N. N. 201.

Scarborough. H. D. 444

Scholars, at the High School in Cloisterham. E. D. 135.

Schoolmaster, Scrooge's. C. B. 21.

Schoolmaster, Our. S. B. 6.

Schutz, Mr, a passenger on the "Halsewell". R. P. 325.

"Scorpion, The", the Latin-grammar master's bark. H. R. 473.

Scotch Member. N. N. 10, 13.

Scotland Yard. S. B. 50.

Scott, Tom, Quilp's boy, who became a processional tumbler, under an Italian name, after Quilp's death. O. C. S. 31.

Scout. B. R. 353.

"Screw", the ship that took Martin Chuzzlewit and Mark Tapley to the United States. M. C. 196.

Scrooge, Ebenezer, a miserly old man who acquired the spirit of Christmas. C. B. 3.

Scrooge, Fan, Scrooge's sister. C. B. 21.

Scrooge and Marley, Scrooge's firm. C. B. 3.

Seamstress, put to death by the guillotine, and comforted in her last hours by Sydney Carton. T. T. C. 257, 271

Sens, visited by Mrs Lirriper. C. S. 392.

Sentry. B. H. 192.

Seraphina. C. S. 371.

Sergeant. B. R. 341.

Sergeant. G. E. 21.

Sergeant, Police. C. S. 361.

Sergeant, Recruiting. B. R. 180.

Servant G. E. 289.

Servant, of a Justice of the Peace. B. R. 277.

Servant, to Scrooge's schoolmaster. C. B. 22.

Servant, Female. B. R. 85.

Servant, Hotel. L. D. 490.

Servant, Irish. M. C. 224.

Servant, Madeline Bray's. N. N. 146.

Servant, Mr Laramie's. O. M. F. 209, 445

Servant, Mrs Gowan's. L. D. 247.

Servant, Mrs Henry Gowan's. L. D. 388.

Servant, Mrs Rogers's. P. P. 504.

Servant Girl, at Dick Swiveller's lodgings. O. C. S. 44.

Servant Girl, at the inn where Nell lay ill. O. C. S. 257.

Servant Girl, at the "Jolly Sandboys". O. C. S. 107.

Servant Girl, at the Wilfers'. O. M. F. 30.

Servant Girl, at Westgate House. P. P. 173.

Servant Girl, Youthful. D. C. 307.

Servants, Buxom, of Mr Wardle. P. P. 76.

Servants, Five Female, at Westgate House. P. P. 174.

Serving-maid, of Mr Sapsea. E. D. 33.

Serving-woman, **Deaf**. H. T. 342.

"Seven Bells", an inn. C. S. 48.

Seven Dials. S. B. 53.

Sexton, at the church where Mr Dombey was married. D. S. 340

Sexton, in the village where Nell settled. O. C. S. 297.

Sexton, successor to Gabriel Grub. P. P. 315.

Sexton, who befriended Little Dorrit. L. D. 139.

Shanklin, in the Isle of Wight, where the Lammles spent their honeymoon. O. M. F. 97.

Sharp, **Mr**, first master at Salem House, D. C. 64.

Shepherd. C. S. 93.

Shepherd, **Miss**, beloved of David Copperfield, but who preferred Master Jones. D. C. 204.

"Ship, The", a public-house on the lower Thames. G. E. 324.

Ship-broker, at Mr Podsnap's house. O. M. F. 106.

Shooter's Hill, where Mr Weller, senior, kept a public-house in his retirement. P. P. 623.

Shopman, in an oyster-shop. O. C. S. 222.

Shopman, in Defarge's wine-shop. T. T. C. 127.

Short, usual name of Mr Harris, a Punch-and-Judy showman. See *Harris*.

Signalman, at Mugby Junction. C. S. 489.

Sikes, **Bill**, a thief and burglar; chief spirit in the attempted burglary at Mrs Maylie's house; murdered his mistress, Nancy, and fled from justice; accidentally hanged from a chimney-stack when attempting to escape imminent capture. O. T. 67.

Silver-Store, an island near Belize, attacked by pirates. C. S. 145.

Silverman, **George**, brought up in a Preston slum, and became a clergyman. G. S. E. 487.

Simmery, **Frank**, who betted with Wilkins Flasher. P. P. 606.

Simmonds, **Miss**, an employee of Madame Mantalini. N. N. 164.

Simmons, the parish beadle. S. B.3.

Simmons, **Henrietta**, a visitor at Mrs Quilp's. O. C. S. 25.

Simmons, **William**, a van driver M. C. 171.

Simon, servant of a Justice of the Peace. B. R. 275, 277.

Simplon Pass. C. S. 590.

Simpson, prisoner in the Fleet. P. P. 458.

Simpson, **Mr,** boarder of Mrs Tibbs; married Miss Julia Maplesone, who deserted him; became a hairdresser and wrote fashionable novels. S. B. 208.

Simson, **Mr**, one of the steam excursion party. S. B. 293.

Singers, **Four Something-ean**, at Mrs Leo Hunter's. P. P. 158.

Single Gentleman, The, brother of Nell's grandfather, who searched for the wanderers and found them; he lodged with the Brasses. O. C. S. 193.

Sister, of Miss Edwards. O. C. S. 182.

Sister, of Mrs Crisparkle, also like a China shepherdess. E. D. 47.

Sister, of Mrs Kenwigs. N. N. 127.

Sister, of Scrooge's niece. C. B. 40.

Sister, **Married**, of Miss Miggs. B. R. 56. Also called sister-inlaw, 130.

Six Clerks' Office. B. H. 4.

"Six Jolly Fellowship Porters", a public-house kept by Miss Abbey Potterson. O. M. F. 22, 48.

Skettles, Barnet, Junior, son of Sir Barnet and Lady Skettles. D. S. 156.

Skettles, Lady, wife of Sir Barnet Skettles. D. S. 156.

Skettles, Sir Barnet, a member of Parliament. D. S. 156.

Skewton, Hon. Mrs, mother of Edith Granger; called Cleopatra. D. S. 224.

Skiffins, Miss, who married Mr Wemmick. G. E. 216.

Skimpin, Mr, junior counsel for Mrs Barden. P. P. 363.

Skimpole, Arethusa, Harold Skimpole's Beauty daughter. B. H. 460.

Skimpole, Harold, a friend of Mr Jarndyce, professing absolute ignorance of the value of money, and therefore living selfishly on others. Partly based on Leigh Hunt. B. H. 53.

Skimpole, Kitty, Harold Skimpole's Comedy daughter. B. H. 460.

Skimpole, Laura, Harold Skimpole's Sentiment daughter. B. H. 460:

Skimpole, Mrs, wife of Harold Skimpole. B. H. 460.

Skipper, who joined Captain Cottle in a song. D. S. 166.

"Skylark, The", a ship with one of whose crew David Copperfield was left. D. C. 19.

"Skylark, The", a ship. H. R. 478.

Slackbridge, a demagogue. H. T. 363, 365.

"Slamjam Coffee-house". C. S. 291.

Slammer, Dr, surgeon to the 97th, who challenged Mr Winkle for cutting him out at a ball. P. P. 16.

"Slap-Bang", a dining-house visited by young Smallweed and Guppy. B. H. 212.

Slasher, an eminent surgeon referred to by Jack Hopkins. P. P. 342.

Slaughter, Lieutenant. S. B. 266.

Sleary, Josephine, daughter of Sleary, and a member of his troupe. H. T. 253.

Sleary, Mr, owner of the troupe of which Signor Jape was a member; he aided Tom Gradgrind to escape. H. T. 253.

Sliderskew, Peg, housekeeper to Arthur Gride, from whom she stole documents. N. N. 519.

Slingo, a horse dealer with whom Little Dorrit's brother found a job for a time. L. D. 60.

Slinkton, Julius, of the Middle Temple; a murderer; original, T. G. Wainewright. H. D. 438.

Slithers, Mr, a barber. M. H. C. 496, 468.

Sloppy, a boy brought up by Betty Higden and befriended by the Boffins. O. M. F. 157.

Stout, Mr, workhouse master, succeeded by Mr Bumble. O. T. 153.

Slowboy, Tilly, a servant to Mrs Peerybingle. C. B. 129, 130.

Sludberry, Thomas, defendant in an action at Doctors' Commons. S. B. 66.

Slum, Mr, a puff poet, who did business with Mrs Jarley. O. C. S. 159.

Slumkey, Hon. Samuel, successful "Blue" candidate for Eatanswill. P. P. 124.

Slummintowkens, friends of the Nupkinses. P. P. 271.

Slurk, Mr, editor of the *Eatanswill Independent*, violently opposed to Mr Pott and the *Eatanswill Gazette*. P. P. 562.

Slyme, Chevy, a relative of old Martin Chuzzlewit, and a friend of Montague Tigg; as a police officer he helped to arrest Jonas Chuzzlewit. M. C. 36.

Smallweed, Bartholomew, grandson of Mr and Mrs Smallweed, a friend of Guppy. B. H. 211.

Smallweed, Grandmother, wife of Joshua Smallweed; in her dotage. B. H. 221.

Smallweed, Joshua, an old usurer; tried to blackmail Sir Leicester Dedlock. B. H. 222, 364.

Smallweed, Judy, brother of Bartholomew Smallweed. B. H. 222.

Smangle, Mr, a prisoner in the Fleet. P. P. 451.

Smart, Tom, traveller for Bilson and Slum; hero of "The Bagman's Story". P. P. 140, 141.

Smacker, John, Mr Bantam's footman, who introduced Sam Weller to the footmen's swarry. P. P. 388, 403.

Smif, Putnam, an ambitious young American, who wrote to Martin Chuzzlewit. M. C. 286.

Smifser, an old suitor of Mrs Nickleby. N. N. 412.

Smiggers, Joseph, Perpetual Vicepresident of the Pickwick Club. P. P. 1.

Smike, a lad at Squeers's academy who was befriended by Nicholas Nickleby, and went with him to London; proved to be son of Ralph Nickleby; cherished a hopeless love for Kate Nickleby. N. N. 60, 62.

Smith, Mr, a cleric. S. B. 161, 162.

Smith, Payne, and Smith. P. P. 608.

Smith, Samuel, junior partner in Jones, Spruggins, and Smith. See also *Sparkins, Horatio*. S. B. 279.

Smith, The, on the "Golden Mary". C. S. 133.

Smith Square, where Jenny Wren lived. O. M. F. 176.

Smithers, Emily, belle of Minerva House. S. B. 247.

Smithers, Miss, a boarder at Westgate House. P. P. 174.

Smithers, Robert, who joined Thomas Potter in making a night of it. S. B. 199.

Smithers & Price's Chancery clerk. P. P. 215.

Smithfield, on market morning. O. T. 119.

Smithick and Watersby, a Liverpool merchant firm. C. S. 116.

Smithie, Mr, guest at the ball at Rochester. P. P. 16.

Smithie, Mrs, wife of Mr Smithie, guest at the ball at Rochester. P. P. 16.

Smithie, The Misses, daughters of Mr and Mrs Smithie, guests at the ball at Rochester. P. P. 16.

Smiths, Two. B. R. 456.

Smivey, Chicken, the name by which Montague Tigg introduced Martin Chuzzlewit at the pawnbroker's. M. C. 175.

Smorltork, Count, guest of Mrs Leo Hunter. P. P. 159.

Smouch, Mr, attending on Mr Namby. P. P. 436.

Smuggins, Mr, who sang a song at a harmonic meeting. S. B. 46.

Snagsby, Mr, a law stationer. B. H. 98.

Snagsby, Mrs, wife of Mr Snagsby, jealous of her husband; a follower of the Rev. Mr Chadband. B. H. 99.

Snap, Betsy, a domestic. C. S. 29.

Snawley, Mr, who placed two stepsons with Mr Squeers; afterwards induced by Ralph Nickleby to aid him in his schemes by personating Smike's father. N. N. 26, 386.

Snawley, Mr, Stepsons of, placed at Squeers's Academy. N. N. 26.

Snawley, Mrs, wife of Mr Snawley. N. N. 386.

Snevellicci, Miss, a member of Crummles's company who was in love with Nicholas Nickleby; married a wax chandler. N. N. 228, 488.

Snevellicci, Mr, father of Miss Snevellicci. N. N. 302.

Snevellicci, Mrs, mother of Miss Snevellicci. N. N. 302.

Snewkes, Mr, a friend of the Kenwigses. N. N. 129.

Snicks, Mr, a Life Office Secretary. P. P. 511.

Sniff, Mr, a servant in Mugby station refreshment room. C. S. 483

Sniff, Mrs, employed in Mugby station refreshment room. C. S. 483

Sniggle & Blink. P. P. 443.

Snigsworth, Lord, cousin of Mr Twemlow. O. M. F. 5.

Snipe, Hon. Wilmot, guest at the ball at Rochester. P. P. 15.

Snitchey, Jonathan, a lawyer friend of Dr Jeddler. C. B. 195, 197.

Snitchey, Mrs, wife of Mr Snitchey. C. B. 206.

Snitchey & Craggs, a firm of lawyers. C. B. 195, 206.

Snobb, Honourable Mr, a friend of Ralph Nickleby. N. N. 183.

Snodgrass, Augustus, companion of Mr Pickwick; he was a poet, and married Emily Wardle. P. P. 2.

Snorridge Bottom. C. S. 143.

Snow, Tom, black steward of Captain Ravender. C. S. 121.

Snow Hill, where the "Saracen's Head" was situated. N. N. 21, 23.

Snubbin, Serjeant, counsel for Mr Pickwick in the breach of promise case. P. P. 331.

Snuffim, Sir Tumley, doctor to Mrs Wititterly. N. N. 208.

Snugglewood, a physician. R. P. 481.

Snuphanuph, Lady, a visitor at Bath. P. P. 390.

Soho Square, where Doctor Manette lodged, T. T. C. 64; where Jules Obenreizer stayed, C. S. 530; where Esther Summerson met Caddy Jellyby, B. H. 250.

Soldier. B. R. 291.

Soldiers, Six. T. T. C. 120.

Solicitor, engaged in defending Darnay. T. T. C. 55.

"Sol's Arms", a tavern where Harmonic Meetings were held. B. H. 112.

Somebody. C. S. 298, 334.

Somers Town, where Harold Skimpole lived. B. H. 457.

"Son and Heir", the ship in which Walter Gay was wrecked on his way to the West Indies. D. S. 181.

Sons, Two, of doomed prisoner. B. R. 369.

Sophia, Mr Pocket's housemaid. G. E. 143.

Sophia, pupil of Ruth Pinch. M. C. 107, 448.

Sophy, adopted deaf-and-dumb daughter of Doctor Marigold. C. S. 415.

Sophy, daughter of Doctor Marigold, ill-treated by her mother; died young. C. S. 410.

Sophy, Willing, servant of Mrs Lirriper. C. S. 345.

Southwark, where Sikes met his death. O. T. 293.

Sowerberry, Mr, an undertaker to whom Oliver Twist was apprenticed. O. T. 18.

Sowerberry, Mrs, wife of Mr Sowerberry. O. T. 21.

Sownds, Mr, a beadle. D. S. 44, 342

"Spaniard, The", at Hampstead, where Mrs Barden was arrested. P. P. 505.

Sparkins, Horatio, alias of Mr Samuel Smith. S. B. 268, 279.

Sparkler, Edmund, son of Mrs Merdle by her first husband; not so much a young man as a swelled boy; always offering marriage to someone; he married Fanny Dorrit. L. D. 196.

Sparsit, Mrs, Mr Bounderby's housekeeper. H. T. 280.

Spatter, John, clerk to the poor relation. C. S. 28.

Speddie, Doctor, who attended Thomas Idle. L. T. 374.

Spendthrift, Broken-down. P. P. 448.

Spenlow, Clarissa, sister of Mr Spenlow. D. C. 455.

Spenlow, Dora. See *Copperfield, Dora*.

Spenlow, Francis, father of Dora Copperfield; his generous impulses were represented by him as being always thwarted by his partner, Mr Jorkins. D. C. 268.

Spenlow, Lavinia, sister of Mr Spenlow and an authority in affairs of the heart. D. C. 455.

Sphynx, Sophronia, the name under which Dick Swiveller sent the Marchioness to school. O. C. S 416.

Spider, The, a nickname of Bentley Drummle (q.v.).

Spiker, Henry, solicitor to something or somebody remotely connected with the Treasury. D. C. 284.

Spiker, Mrs Henry, wife of Henry Spiker; called Hamlet's aunt. D. C. 284.

Spinster, Ancient. B. R. 88.

Spottletoe, Mr, husband of a niece of old Martin Chuzzlewit. M. C. 43

Spottletoe, Mrs, niece of old Martin Chuzzlewit. M. C. 43.

Sprodgkin, Mrs, one of the Rev. Frank Milvey's parishioners. O. M. F. 598.

Sprouter, a pupil of Squeers. N. N. 580.

Spruggins, a defeated candidate for beadleship. S. B. 16.

Spyers, Jem. O. T. 175.

Squeers, Fanny, daughter of Mr Squeers; in love with Nicholas Nickleby, and afterwards his enemy. N. N. 79.

Squeers, Master Wackford, son of Mr Squeers. N. N. 69.

Squeers, Mrs, wife of Mr Squeers. N. N. 61.

Squeers, Wackford, the brutal and ignorant master of Dotheboys Hall;

thrashed by Nicholas Nickleby; ultimately transported. N. N. 24.

Squires, landlord of the "Blue Boar". G. E. 349

Squod, Phil, employed by George Rouncewell at his shooting gallery. B. H. 234.

Stables, Honourable Bob, a cousin of Sir Leicester Dedlock. B. H. 302.

Stagg, a blind man, who kept an underground cellar. B. R. 48.

Staggs's' Gardens, where the Toodles lived. D. S. 49, 51, 171.

Stakes, original name of Major Tpschoffki. C. S. 191.

Stalker, Inspector, a detective. R. P. 406.

Staple, Mr, a Dingley Deller. P. P. 74.

Staple Inn, where Mr Grewgious and Neville Landless lived. E. D. 97.

Stareleigh, Justice, judge in Mr Pickwick's case. P. P. 363.

Starling, Alfred, one of those in the Haunted House; married Belinda Bates. C. S. 217.

Startop, Mr, a boarder at Matthew Pocket's; helped in the attempt to get Magwitch out of the country. G. E. 138.

Statuary. D. S. 189.

Steadiman, John, chief mate of the "Golden Mary". C. S. 118.

Steel, Mr, a name assumed by George Rouncewell in presenting himself to his brother, the iron-master. B. H. 653.

Steepways, a village in Devonshire. C. S. 237.

Steerforth, James, friend of David Copperfield's; he betrayed Little Em'ly, and was drowned at Yarmouth. D. C. 223.

Steerforth, Mrs, mother of James Steerforth. D. C. 223.

Stevens, Billy, in the workhouse. R. P. 449.

Stiggins, Rev. Mr, a drunken shepherd of the flock to which Mrs Weller belonged; Mr Weller, senior, took revenge on him. P. P. 285.

Stiltstalking, Lord Lancaster, a retired diplomat. L. D. 247.

Stone Lodge, Mr Gradgrind's house. H. T. 252.

"Story of the Bagman's Uncle, The". P. P. 530.

Strand, where Miss La Creevy lived. N. N. 15.

Straw, Sergeant, a detective. R. P. 407.

Streaker, housemaid in the Haunted House. C. S. 211.

"Stroller's Tale, The". P. P. 27

Strong, Annie, wife of Dr Strong, on whom suspicion fell with regard to her cousin, Jack Maldon; from this however she was cleared. D. C. 173.

Strong, Dr, to whose school David Copperfield was sent by his aunt; engaged in the preparation of a monumental Greek dictionary, never likely to be completed. D. C. 173.

Struggles, Mr, a Dingley Dell bowler. P. P. 71.

Stryver, Mr, counsel for Darnay in the treason trial. T. T. C. 52.

Stryver, Mrs T. T. C. 152.

Stubbs, a pony at Mr Boythorn's place. B. H. 389.

Stubbs, Mrs, Percy Noakes' laundress. S. B. 289.

Stumps, Bill, whose mark Mr Pickwick took for an ancient inscription. P. P. 108.

Stumpy & Deacon. P. P. 443.

Sulliwin, Sarah. S. B. 54

Summerson, Esther, heroine of B. H.; taken to Bleak House by Mr Jarndyce to be companion to Ada Clare; became engaged to John Jarndyce, but released by him when he discovered her love for Allan Woodcourt, whom she married; she proved to be daughter of Captain Hawdon and Lady Dedlock. B. H. throughout.

Surgeon, employer of Jerry Cruncher. T. T. C. 112.

Surgeon, ready to succour Stephen Blackpool. H. T. 475

Surgeon, who attended Anthony Chuzzlewit at his death. M. C. 242.

Surgeon, who attended Bailey, Junior. M. C. 510.

Surgeon, who attended Miss Havisham after the burning

Surgeon, who attended Mrs Gargery after Orlick's attack. G. E. 87.

Surgeon, Parish. O. T. 1.

Surgeon, Young. S. B. 280.

Surgeons, Three, who examined Mr Dombey after his accident. D. S. 467.

Surgeons, Two, who attended Eugene Wrayburn. O. M. F. 562.

Susan, Mrs Mann's servant. O. T. 5, 93.

Sweedlepipe, Paul (Poll), a barber and bird fancier, landlord of Mrs Camp. M. C. 328.

Sweep, who supported the butcher in his fight with David Copperfield. D. C. 205.

Sweet William, a showman. O. C. S. 108.

Swidger, George, the profligate son of Philip Swidger. C. B. 292.

Swidger, Milly, wife of William Swidger. C. B. 256, 257.

Swidger, Philip, father of William Swidger. C. B. 256, 257.

Swidger, William, lodge-keeper in an endowment for students. C. B. 254, 255.

Swillenhausen, Baron von, in the story of "The Baron of Grogzwig". N. N. 53.

Swillenhausen, Baroness von, in the story of "The Baron of Grogzwig". N. N. 55.

Swills, Little, a comic singer. B. H. 112.

Swiss, Tall. L. D. 100.

Swiveller, Dick, a good-hearted, jovial fellow associated at first with Little Nell's profligate brother Frederick; he became cleric to Sampson Brass, and there met the little servant whom he called the Marchioness; she nursed him through an illness, and he ultimately married her, after he came into an annuity. O. C. S. 13.

Swiveller, Rebecca, of Cheselbourne, in Dorsetshire, aunt of Dick Swiveller; she left Dick an annuity. O. C. S. 378.

Swoshle, Mrs Henry George Alfred, née Tapkins. O. M. F. 166.

Swosser, Captain, a former husband of Mrs Badger. B. H. 134

Swubble, a name on Mr Bumble's list. O. T. 6.

Sylvia, a girl at Hoghton Towers. G. S. E. 492, 493.

Symond's Inn, where Mr Vholes had his office. B. H. 421.

T

Tabby, a serving drudge. C. S. 224.

Tacker, assistant to Mr Mould. M. C. 253.

Tackleton, Mr, sole partner of Gruff & Tackleton, toy merchants; his marriage with May Fielding was frustrated. C. B. 137.

Tadger, Brother, of the United Grand Junction Ebenezer Temperance Association. P. P. 357, 359.

Tailor. M. C. 514.

Tamaroo, an old woman who succeeded Bailey at Todgers's. M. C. 399

Tangle, Mr, a lawyer. B. H. 4.

Tapkins, Antonina. O. M. F. 166.

Tapkins, Euphemia. O. M. F. 166.

Tapkins, Frederica. O. M. F. 166.

Tapkins, Malvina. O. M. F. 166.

Tapkins, Miss. O. M. F. 166.

Tapkins, Mrs, who called on the Boffins. O. M. F. 166.

Tapley, Mark, hostler at the "Blue Dragon" inn; went with Martin Chuzzlewit to America; married Mrs Lupin and became landlord of the "Blue Dragon"; always longing for enough adversity to give him credit in being jolly. M. C. 52.

Tappertit, Simon, apprentice of Gabriel Varden, and captain of the United Bulldogs, an organization of apprentices; in love with Dolly Varden, and loved by Miss Miggs; took part in the Gordon riots and lost his legs; set up as a shoe-black and married. B. R. 25.

Tappleton, Lieutenant, Dr Slammeats second in the duel with Winkle. P. P. 19.

Tartar, Lieutenant, Neville Landless's neighbour at Staple Inn; in love with Rosa Bud, who also was in love with him. E. D. 176.

Tarter, Bob, the first boy at a school. C. S. 43.

Tatham, Mrs, in a pawnshop. S. B. 100.

Tatt, Mr, an amateur detective. R. P. 424.

Tattycoram, Minnie Meagles's maid. L. D. 14.

Taunton, Captain, a soldier, killed at Badajos. C. S. 66.

Taunton, Emily, daughter of Mrs Taunton. S. B. 290.

Taunton, Mrs, good-looking widow of fifty, a rival of Mrs Briggs; one of the steam excursion party. S. B. 289.

Taunton, Sophia, daughter of Mrs Taunton. S. B. 290.

Tavern-keeper, who married Janet. D. C. 642.

Teacher, cheered by mistake. M. C. 433

Teachers, Three, at Westgate House. P. P. 174.

Teachers, Two, at Miss Monflathers's school. O. C. S. 177.

Tellson & Co., bankers at Temple Bar, with business in Paris. T. T. C. 8, 36.

Temple, The. B. R. 87.

Temple Bar, where Tellson's bank was. T. T. C. 36.

Temple Gate, where Toni Pinch met Mr Fips. M. C. 479

Penant, Solitary, in the Fleet. P. P. 448.

Tetterby, Adolphus, eldest son of Mr Tetterby; a newsboy. C. B. 273.

Tetterby, Adolphus, Senior, who kept a newspaper shop. C. B. 269.

Tetterby, Johnny, son of Mr Tetterby. C. B. 269.

Tetterby, Sally, baby daughter of Mr Tetterby. C. B. 269, 272.

Tetterby, Sophia, wife of Mr Tetterby. C. B. 272, 274.

Tetterby and Co., A., the name over Mr Tetterby's newspaper shop. C. B. 270.

Tetterbys, Master, Five. C. B. 269.

Thames. O. C. S. 31.

Thames Street, where Ralph Nickleby provided a house for Mrs Nickleby and Kate. N. N. 102.

Thavies Inn. B. H. 27.

Theophile, Corporal, a French soldier. C. S. 310.

Thomas, an artist, who did work for street artists. C. S. 322.

Thomas, Sir Leicester Dedlock's groom. B. H. 136.

Thomas, the pastry-cook who supplied the Gattletons. S. B. 320.

Thomas, waiter at the "Winglebury Arms". S. B. 306.

Thompson, Bill. S. B. 44.

Thompson, Harry, seen bathing at Ramsgate. S. B. 260.

Thompson, Tally-ho, a horsestealer, couper, and magsman R. P. 409.

"Three Cripples", an inn in Saffron Hill, where Fagin and his friends gathered. O. T. 143.

"Three Jolly Bargemen", a public-house. G. E. 53.

"Three Magpies", an inn in Brentford. O. M. F. 156.

Tibbs, Mr, husband of Mrs Tibbs; often began a story about his days in the volunteers which he was never allowed to finish. S. B. 207.

Tibbs, Mrs, who kept a boarding-house. S. B. 207.

Ticket-porter. D. C. 279.

Ticket-porter. D. S. 133.

Ticket-porter. P. P. 477

Tickit, Mrs, Mr Meagles's housekeeper. L. D. 156.

Tickler, a cane used by Mrs Gargery in beating Pip. G. E. 5.

Tiddypot, Mr, a vestryman. R. P. 474.

Tiffey, Mr, Mr Spenlow's old clerk. D. C. 296.

Tigg, Montague, alias Tigg Montague, a thorough rascal; started a fraudulent company and got Jonas Chuzzlewit into his clutches; murdered by Chuzzlewit. M. C. 35

Tiggin & Welps, in the calico and waistcoat piece line. P. P. 530.

"Tilted Waggon, The", an inn visited by Neville Landless. L. D. 147.

Timberry, Snittle, a member of Crummles's company. N. N. 489

Timkins, candidate for beadleship. S. B. 16.

Timson, Rev. Mr, who married Miss Lillerton. S. B. 330.

Tinker. O. T. 158.

Tinker, at Tom Tiddler's ground. C. S. 269.

Tinker, in Phil Squod's story. B. H. 283.

Tinker, who assaulted and robbed David Copperfield. D. C. 143.

Tinkler, Mr Dorrit's valet. L. D. 367.

Tinkling, William, a schoolboy who narrates the first part of the Holiday Romance. H. R. 457

Tiny Tim, youngest child of Bob Cratchit; a cripple. C. B. 33.

Tip. See *Dorrit, Edward.*

Tipkinson, a politician. R. P. 463

Tipp, carman at Murdstone & Grinby's. D. C. 125.

Tippin, Master. S. B. 264.

Tippin, Miss. S. B. 264.

Tippin, Mr, a fat man in black tights, who sang at Ramsgate. S. B. 264.

Tippin, Mrs, of the London theatres, who sang at Ramsgate. S. B. 264.

Tippins, Lady, a friend of the Veneerings. O. M. F. 9.

Tipslark, an old suitor of Mrs Nickleby. N. N. 412.

Tipstaff, to whom Mr Pickwick was handed over. P. P. 443

Tipstaff, Little White-headed Applefaced, in the Insolvent Court. P. P. 468.

Tisher, Mrs, Miss Twinkleton's companion. E. D. 19.

Tix, Tom, a broker. N. N. 202.

Toby, Gabriel Varden's brown jug. B. R. 28.

Toby, one of Jerry's dogs. O. C. S. 106.

Toddles, a boy kept by Betty Higdcn. O. M. F. 157.

Todd's, Mr, Young Man. S. B. 40.

Toddyhigh, Joe, who had been a poor boy with a Lord Mayor elect. M. H. C. 440.

Todgers, Mrs M., who kept a commercial boarding-house near the Monument in London. M. C. 99

Toll-keeper. B. R. 328

Tollman. M. C. 52.

Tom, a coach driver. T. T. C. 4.

Tom, a detective. S. B. 371.

Tom, a police officer. M. C. 619.

Tom, an assistant of Mr Mould. M. C. 253.

Tom, at the "George and Vulture". P. P. 326.

Tom, Bob Sawyer's boy in grey livery. P. P. 416.

Tom, clerk at the General Agency Office. N. N. 145, 432.

Tom, cousin of Captain Boldheart. H. R. 477

Tom, driver of Mr Wardle's carriage. P. P. 44.

Tom, Mr Gattleton's man. S. B. 319.

Tom, Mr Parsons's gardener. S. B. 336.

Tom, omnibus cad. S. B. 357.

Tom, rowing on the Thames. S. B. 74.

Tom, stout country lad at the "Leather Bottle". P. P. 107.

Tom-all-alone's, where Jo lived. B. H. 170.

Tomkinley, Mr, referred to by Mr Garland. O. C. S. 84.

Tomkins, one of Squeers's pupils. N. N. 114.

Tomkins, Alfred, clerk in a wine-house; a boarder with Mrs Tibbs. S. B. 225.

Tomkins, Miss, head of the Westgate House boarding-school. P. P. 174, 175.

Tomlinson, Miss, a post-office keeper. P. P. 16.

Tommy, a greengrocer, in a bar parlour. S. B. 177, 178.

Tommy, a waterman. P. P. 5.

Toodle, John, son of Mr and Mrs Toodle. D. S. 11.

Toodle, Mr, employed on the railway. D. S. 11.

Toodle, Polly, also called Richards, wife of Mr Toodle, employed as wet nurse to Paul Dombey. D. S. 11.

Toodle, Robin, also called Biler and

Rob the Grinder, eldest son of Mr and Mrs Toodle; educated at the Charitable Grinders' establishment; entered the service of Solomon Gills as a spy of Carker's; afterwards in Carker's service. D. S. 11, 54.

Tootle, Tom, a customer of the "Six Jolly Fellowship Porters". O. M. F. 52.

Tootleum-boots, Mrs Lemon's baby. H. R. 479.

Toots, P., a pupil of Dr Blimber, with ample means and a good heart but little brains; cherished a hopeless affection for Florence Dombey; married Susan Nipper. D. S. 111.

Tope, Mr, the verger of Cloisterham Cathedral. E. D. 7.

Tope, Mrs, wife of Mr Tope, who attended on Mr Jasper, and let her rooms to Mr Datchery. E. D.11.

Topper, in love with a sister of Scrooge's niece. C. B. 40.

Toppit, Miss, an American literary lady. M. C. 426.

Topsawyer, a stout gentleman who fell dead after drinking ale. D. C. 51.

Tottenham Court Road, near which was Mortimer Knag's shop. N. N. 172.

Tottle, Watkins, who wished to be married; failed to win Miss Lillerton, and committed suicide. S. B. 326.

Toughey, another name for Jo (q.v.).

Towcester, where Mr Pickwick put up. P. P. 557.

Tower Hill, where Quilp lived. O. C. S. 22.

Towlinson, Thomas, a servant in Mr Dombey's house; married Anne, the housemaid. D. S. 40.

"Town Arras Inn", Eatanswill. P. P. 125.

Town-beadle. P. P. 203.

Tox, Lucretia, a friend of Mrs Chick; she aspired to Mr Dombey's hand. D. S. 5.

Tozer, a pupil of Dr Blimber. D. S. 121.

Tozer, Mrs, mother of Tozer. D. S. 142.

Tpschoffki, Major, a show dwarf. C. S. 190.

Trabb, Mr, tailor and undertaker. G. E. 110.

Traddles, Tommy, friend of David Copperfield; became a barrister; after a long engagement he married Sophy Crewler. D. C. 61.

Tradesman, Respectable, in a story by Sam Weller. P. P. 329.

Traveller. C. S. 265.

Traveller. D. C. 667.

"Travellers' Twopenny", a publichouse in which Deputy was employed. E. D. 38.

Treasure, A, one of David Copperfield's servants. D. C. 490.

Treasurer, of the Foundling Hospital. C. S. 542.

"Treasury", guest of Mr Merdle. L. D. 196.

Tredgear, John. C. S. 251.

Tregarthen, Kitty, sweetheart of Alfred Raybrock. C. S. 240.

Tregarthen, Mr, father of Kitty Tregarthen; he had suffered at Lawrence Clissold's hands. C. S. 256.

Trent, Frederick, Little Nell's profligate brother; fell in with gamblers; drowned in Paris. O. C. S. 12.

Trent, Nell, or Little Nell, the heroine of O. C. S.; when her grandfather was turned out of his shop, she wandered with him from place to place, and after varied hardships settled in a quiet village, where she died soon after. O. C. S. throughout.

Tresham, Beatrice, old sweetheart of Barbox Brothers. C. S. 472.

Tresham, Mr, husband of Beatrice Tresham. C. S. 478.

Tresham, Polly, child of Beatrice Tresham C. S. 467.

Trimmers, Mr, a friend of the Cheeryble brothers, who helped them in their charitable work. N. N. 351.

Trinkle, Mr, an upholsterer. R. P. 422.

Trip, a dog. O. T. 22.

Trott, Alexander, mistaken for Lord Peter; married Julia Manners at Gretna Green. S. B. 307.

Trotter, Jem. See *Hutley, Jem*.

Trotter, Job, sanctimonious servant of Jingle. P. P. 166.

Trotters, Short, a showman in O. C. S. See *Harris*.

Trottle. C. S. 199.

Trotwood, Betsey, aunt of David Copperfield; she adopted him in spite of her disappointment that he was not a girl. D. C. 2.

Trotwood, Betsey, Husband of. D. C. 2.

Trundle, Mr, who married Isabella Wardle. P. P. 39.

Tuckle, a footman. P. P. 405.

Tugby, Mr, porter to Sir Joseph Bowley; married Mrs Chickenstalker in Trotty Veck's vision. C. B. 80, 109, 110.

Tugby, Mrs See *Chickenstalker*.

Tuggs, Charlotte, daughter of Mr and Mrs Tuggs. S. B. 252.

Tuggs, Joseph, a grocer who came into a fortune. S. B. 252.

Tuggs, Mrs, wife of Joseph Tuggs. S. B. 252.

Tuggs, Simon (or Cymon), son of Mr and Mrs Tuggs, whose Platonic love affair involved his family in difficulties. S. B. 252.

Tulkinghorn, Mr, solicitor to Sir Leicester Dedlock; he gradually learned Lady Dedlock's secret and meant to inform Sir Leicester; murdered by Mademoiselle Hortense. B. H. 8.

Tungay, the porter at Salem House. D. C. 59.

Tupman, Tracy, romantic companion of Mr Pickwick, enamoured of Rachael Wardle. P. P. 2.

Tupple, Mr, at Dobble's New Year party. S. B. 169.

Turk, a bloodhound. C. S. 210.

Turnkey. D. C. 127.

Turnkey. G. E. 193.

Turnkey, long thin man. P. P 444.

Turnkey, rather surly-looking gentleman. P. P. 445.

Turnkey, Stout, of the Fleet. P. P. 444

Turnkeys, Three. O. C. S. 343, 345.

Turnkeys, Three, in La Force prison. T. T. C. 183.

Turnpike-man, who helped Oliver Twist on his way to London. O. T. 41.

Turpin, Romance of, sung by Sam Weller P. P. 475.

Turveydrop, Mr, father of Prince

Turveydrop, who exhibited himself as a model of deportment. B. H. 147.

Turveydrop, Prince, who ran a dancing academy; married Caddy Jellyby. B. H. 146.

Twemlow, Melvin, a friend of the Veneerings. O. M. F. 5.

Twickenham, where the Meagleses lived. L. D. 148.

Twinkleton, Miss, who kept the Seminary for Young Ladies in which Rosa Bud was educated. E. D. 18.

Twist, Oliver, an orphan boy, born in a workhouse, hero of O. T. He fell into the power of thieves, but remained unspoiled, and escaped from them. He ultimately obtained a fortune that had been left to him, and lived with Rose Maylie, who proved to be his aunt, and her husband. O. T. throughout.

"Two Robins, The", an inn at Doncaster. L. T. 379.

U

Uncle, of Tozer. D. S. 143

Undertaker's Man. C. B. 47.

Undery, Mr, solicitor to the tenant of the Haunted House. C. S. 219.

United Bull-Dogs, the name under which the 'Prentice Knights took part in the Gordon riots. B. R. 211.

United Grand Junction Ebenezer Temperance Association. P. P. 356.

United Metropolitan Improved Hot Muffin and Crumpet Baking and Punctual Delivery Company. N. N. 9.

Unwin, one of the names on Bumble's list. O. T. 6.

Upper-boots, at the "Winglebury Arms". S. B. 308.

Upwitch, Richard, greengrocer; a juryman in Bardell versus Pickwick. P. P. 364.

Urchin, in "The Parish Cleric". P. P. 179.

Urchin, Young, who annoyed Gabriel Grub with a Christmas song. P. P. 309.

V

Vagrant, a criminal in the police office. O. T. 71.

Valet, of the Marquis St. Evremonde. T. T. C. 89.

"Valiant Soldier, The", an inn where Nell and her grandfather took shelter, and in which the old man was tempted to gamble. O. C. S. 165.

Varden, Dolly, the charming daughter of a locksmith, loved by Joe Willet, whom she at length married. B. R. 20.

Varden, Gabriel, a locksmith, father of Dolly Varden. B. R. 14.

Varden, Martha, wife of Gabriel Varden; a lady of uncertain temper, but greatly improved by experience. B. R. 25.

Vauxhall Gardens. S. B. 94.

Veck, Margaret, daughter of Toby Veck. C. B. 68.

Veck, Toby (or Trotty), a ticket porter. C. B. 64.

Vendale, George, a partner in Wilding & Co.; proved to be the real Walter Wilding; married Marguerite. C. S. 326.

Veneering, Anastasia, wife of Mr Veneering. O. M. F. 5.

Veneering, & Stobbles; entered Parliament. O. M. F. 5.

Vengeance, The, a woman of the French Revolution, wife of a grocer. T. T. C. 159.

Venning, Mrs, killed by pirates. C. S. 154.

Venus, Mr, a preserver of animals; for a time in league with Silas Wegg against Boffin, but turned against Wegg; married Pleasant Riderhood. O. M. F. 62.

Verger. M. C. 58.

Verisopht, Lord Frederick, a weak aristocrat fleeced by Sir Mulberry Hawk and ultimately killed by him in a duel. N. N. 182.

Vestry-clerk. S. B. 5.

Vestryman, an idiotic juryman. C. S. 430.

Vholes, Mr, a lawyer who acted for Richard Carstone. B. H. 410.

Vilkins, one of the names on Bumble's list. O. T. 6.

Vines, The, a green in Rochester. C. S. 80.

Voigt, Maître, a Swiss lawyer. C. S. 602.

Vuffin, Mr, a showman. O. C. S. 108.

W

Wackles, Jane, youngest daughter of Mrs Wackles. O. C. S. 47.

Wackles, Melissa, oldest daughter of Mrs Wackles. O. C. S. 47.

Wackles, Mrs, who kept a day-school for young ladies at Chelsea. O. C. S. 47.

Wackles, Sophy, second daughter of Mrs Wackles, whom Dick Swiveller loved and lost; she married Mr Cheggs. O. C. S. 47.

Wade, Miss, an embittered woman who influenced Tattycoram. L. D. 18.

Waggoner. B. H. 47.

Waiter. B. R. 477.

Waiter. D. S. 602.

Waiter. G. H. 194.

Waiter. G. E. 260.

Waiter. H. T. 362.

Waiter. M. C. 643.

Waiter. O. C. S. 269.

Waiter, at coffee house on Ludgate Hill. L. D. 24.

Waiter, at the "Bull Inn". P. P. 12.

Waiter, at the "Crozier". E. D. 179

Waiter, at the "Golden Cross". D. C. 218.

Waiter, at the "Gray's Inn Coffeehouse". D. C. 630.

Waiter, at the "Holly-Tree Inn" C. S. 80.

Waiter, at the "Old Royal Hotel", Birmingham. P. P. 550.

Waiter, at " White Horse Cellar". P. P. 382.

Waiter, from a coffee-house, who attended on Lightwood and Wrayburn. O. M. F. 115.

Waiter, of noted coffee-house in Covent Garden. B. R. 163.

Waiter, who served Dick Swiveller, O. C. S. 46.

Waiter, Flying. E. D. 103.

Waiter, Immovable. E. D. 103.

Waiter, Non-resident, married to Mr Perker's laundress's daughter. P. P. 510.

Waiters, Two, at Greenwich. O. M. F. 535.

Wakefield, Miss, one of the steam excursion party. S. B. 297.

Wakefield, Mr, one of the steam excursion party. S. B. 297.

Wakefield, Mrs, one of the steam excursion party. S. B. 297.

Walcot Square, in Lambeth, where Mr Guppy proposed to set up for himself. B. H. 664.

Waldengarver, Mr, the stage name of Mr Wopsle. G. E. 187.

Walker, H., tailor, a convert to temperance. P. P. 357.

Walker, Mick, a boy at Murdstone & Grinby's. D. C. 119.

Walker, Mr, prisoner in a lock-up house. S. B. 339

Walker, Mrs, a London housewife. S. B. 43.

Walmers, Harry, young son of Mr Walmers; eloped with Norah. C. S. 102.

Walmers, Mr C. S. 102.

Walters, Charley, who died in the workhouse. R. P. 449.

Walworth, where Mr Wemmick lived and uttered his "Walworth sentiments". G. E. 150.

Want, a girl seen by Scrooge in his vision. C. B. 43.

Wapping. C. S. 260.

Warden, a drunkard. S. B. 366.

Warden, Michael, proprietor of an estate, who got into financial difficulties; became an inmate of Dr Jeddler's house, and was supposed to have run off with Marion; married Marion Jeddler. C. B. 207.

Wardle, Emily, daughter of Mr Wardle, who married Mr Snodgrass. P. P. 39.

Wardle, Isabella, daughter of Mr Wardle; married Mr Trundle. P. P. 39.

Wardle, Mr, friend of Mr Pickwick. P. P. 39.

Wardle, Mrs, deaf old lady, mother of Mr Wardle. P. P. 53.

Wardle, Rachael, sister of Mr Wardle, in love with Mr Tupman; she eloped with Mr Jingle, but was pursued and brought back by her brother. P. P. 39.

Warren, an acrostic on, referred to. O. C. S. 160.

Warren, The, home of Mr Haredale and Emma; burned down by the Gordon rioters. B. R. 5.

Warwick Castle, visited by Mr Dombey and Edith Granger. D. S. 303.

Watchman. G. E. 239.

Watchman, at the Temple. O. M. F. 438.

Waterbrook, Mr, husband of Mrs Waterbrook; agent of Mr Wickfield. D. C. 284.

Waterbrook, Mrs, with whom Agnes Wickfield stayed, and at whose house David Copperfield dined. D. C. 283.

Waterman. D. C. 119.

Waterman. D S. 211.

Waters, Belinda, wife of Captain Waters; she flirted with Simon Tuggs to entrap him and get money. S. B. 255.

Waters, Captain Walter. S. B. 255.

"Watertoast Gazette", an American newspaper. M. C. 286.

"Watertoast Sympathizers", an American society. M. C. 282.

Whitefriars, where Jerry Crutcher lived. T. T. C. 38.

Wickam, Mrs, wife of a waiter, who acted as nurse to Paul Dombey. D. S. 71.

Wickfield, Agnes, daughter of Mr Wickfield; she was David Copperlield's good angel, was the object of Uriah Heep's designs, but eventually became the second wife of Copperfield. D. C. 171.

Wickfield, Mr, father of Agnes Wickfield; he fell into the power of his clerk Uriah Heep, but was released through the agency of Mr Micawber. D. C. 167.

Wicks, Mr, clerk of Dodson & Fogg. P. P. 205.

Widow. H. T. 486.

Widow, a visitor at Mrs Quilp's. O. C. S. 24.

Widow, one of the Seven Poor Travellers. C. S. 63.

Widow, who married Simon Tappertit. B. R. 485.

Widow, whom Nell met in the churchyard. O. C. S. 98.

Widow, Buxom, whom Tom Smart married. P. P. 142.

Widower, County, whose daughter Mrs General "formed". L. D. 355.

Wield, Inspector, a detective. R. P. 406.

Wife, of a clerical English husband. L. D. 18.

Wife, of a dead forester. T. T. C. 33.

Wife, of a carrier. O. C. S. 127.

Wife, of a cottager. O. C. S. 90.

Wife, of a juggler. D. S. 188.

Wife, of a tinker. D. C. 143.

Wife, of keeper at Chesney Wold. B. H. 7.

Wife, of respectable tradesman ; a most audacious vixen ; in a story by Sam Weller. P. P. 329.

Wife, of Scrooge's nephew. C. B. 39

Wife, of the clergyman at Dingley Dell. P. P. 53.

Wife, of the jailer at La Force. T. T. C. 183.

Wife, of tollman. M. C. 52.

Wigsby, Mr, a vestry orator. R. P. 472.

Wigton, visited by the idle apprentices. L. T. 372.

Wilderness, Mr Quilp's summerhouse by the Thames. O. C. S. 123, 129.

Wilding, Walter, partner in Wilding & Co.; originally a foundling. C. S. 506.

Wilding & Co., a firm of wine merchants in London. C. S. 508.

Wildspark, Tom, referred to by Mr Weller. P. P. 355.

Wilfer, Bella, daughter of Reginald Wilfer; became an inmate of the Boffins' house; married John Rokesmith. O. M. F. 27.

Wilfer, Cecilia, a married sister of Bella Wilfer. O. M. F. 29.

Wilfer, Lavinia, a sister of Bella Wilfer. O. M. F. 27.

Wilfer, Mrs, wife of Reginald Wilfer. O. M. F. 27.

Wilfer, Reginald, a clerk in the office of Chicksey, Veneering, & Stobbles; called "The Cherub" and "Rumty"; father of Bella Wilfer. O. M. F. 25.

Wilkins, Captain Boldwig's sub-gardener. P. P. 201.

Wilkins, Dick, Scrooge's fellow apprentice. C. B. 22.

Wilkins, Samuel, carpenter, who took Jemima Evans to the "Eagle". S. B. 172.

Willet, Joe, who was in love with Dolly Vanden; enlisted as a soldier, and returned in time to save her during the riots; married Dolly. B. R. 5.

Willet, John, landlord of the "Maypole", and father of Joe Willet. B. R. 2.

William, a boy at Astley's. S. B. 79.

William, a coachman who drove David Copperfield. D. C. 217.

William, a groom. N. N. 323.

William, a waiter at the "Saracen's Head". N. N. 35.

William, son of a drunkard. S. B. 369.

William, son of a widow; he wore his life out in hopeless toil. S. B. 34.

William, Shiny, deputy hostler at the "Bull Inn". P. P. 47.

Williams, a policeman. R. P. 434.

Williams, William, a customer of the "Six Jolly Fellowship Porters". O. M. F. 52.

Williamson, Mrs, landlady of the "Winglebury Arms". S. B. 306.

"Willing Mind, The", public-house frequented by Mr Peggotty. D. C. 29.

Willis, Mr, a prisoner in a lock-up house. S. B. 339.

Willises, The Four Miss. S. B. 11.

Wilson, Caroline, a boarder at Minerva House. S. B. 247.

Winchester, where Richard Carstone came from. B. H. 27.

Windsor, where Esther Summerson was brought up, B. H. 17; where John Podgers lived, M. H. C. 472.

Winglebury, Great, scene of the Great Winglebury duel. Original, Rochester. S. B. 305.

"Winglebury Arms", an inn. S. B. 305.

Winkle, Mr, Sen., a wharfinger at Birmingham; father of Mr Winkle, friend of Pickwick. P. P. 518.

Winkle, Nathaniel, companion of Mr Pickwick, reputed a sportsman; he got into many troubles, and finally eloped with Arabella Allen. P. P. 2.

Winks, otherwise Deputy (q.v.). E. D. 238.

Wisbottle, Mr, boarder of Mrs Tibbs; a high Tory. S. B. 224.

Wisk, Miss, a friend of Mrs Jellyby. B. H. 326.

Witcham, Sergeant, a detective. R. P. 407.

Witherden, Mr, a notary, to whom Abel Garland was articled. O. C. S. 83.

Witherfield, Miss, the lady into whose room Mr Pickwick wandered; she was the object of Mr Peter Magnus's devotion.

Withers, page to Mrs Skewton. D. S. 225.

Wititterly, Henry, Mrs Wititterly's husband. N. N. 208.

Wititterly, Julia, a lady to whom Kate Nickleby was companion for a time. N. N. 206.

Witness. G. E. 123.

Wizzle, Mr, one of the steam excursion party. S. B. 293.

Wobbler, Mr, an official in the Circumlocution Office. L. D. 90.

Wolf, Mr, a friend of Montague Tigg, a literary character. M. C. 354.

Woman. B. H. 390.

Woman. B. H. 595.

Woman. C. B. 47.

Woman. G. E. 120.

Woman. G. E. 342.

Woman. O. M. F. 482.

Woman, a witness in a murder trial. C. S. 431.

Woman, befriended by Mark Tapley. M. C. 197.

Woman, from whom Captain Cuttle bought a nosegay. D. S. 169.

Woman, in witness-box. G. E. 147

Woman, the owner of Bray's house. N. N. 557.

Woman, who befriended Betty Higden. O. M. F. 406.

Woman, who pitied Little Dorrit. L. D. 138.

Woman, whose little girl was carried by Sydney Carton. T. T. C. 227.

Woman, wronged by the brother of the Marquis St. Evremonde. T. T. C. 232.

Woman, Dirty Old. L. D. 579.

Woman, Fat Old, who sat up with Oliver Twist. O. T. 61.

Woman, Old. O. C. S. 144.

Woman, Old, where Miss Wade lived. L. D. 259.

Woman, Sprightly Little. L. D. 503.

Woman, Unfortunate. C. B. 290.

Woman, Young. D. S. 155.

Woman, Young, a visitor at Mrs Quilp's. O. C. S. 25.

Woman, Young, at a private hotel. O. T. 231.

Woman, Young, with a child, in the Fleet prison. P. P. 451.

Woman Servant, employed by Jules Obenreizer. C. S. 557.

Women, Three Young. D. C. 96.

Women, Two. M. H. C. 479.

Women, Two. O. C. S. 255.

Women, Two. O. T. 83.

Women, Two, in a crowd. C. S. 325.

Women, Two or Three Young. D. C. 62.

Wood Street, Cheapside. G. E. 190.

Woodcourt, Allan, a surgeon, who attended Captain Hawdon on his deathbed; married Esther Summerson. B. H. 107.

Woodcourt, Mrs, mother of Allan Woodcourt. B. H. 184.

Woolford, Miss, at Astley's. S. B. 80.

Wopsle, Mr, parish clerk, and afterwards an actor. G. E. 16.

Wopsle's Great-aunt, Mr, whose school Pip attended. G. E. 31.

Workman. B. H. 652.

Workman. D. S. 151.

Workmen, of Doyce & Clennam. L. D. 534

Wosky, Dr, Mrs Bloss's medical attendant. S. B. 222.

Wozenham, Miss, a rival of Mrs Lirriper as a lodging-house keeper, but befriended by her in her misfortune. C. S. 342.

Wrayburn, Eugene, a barrister of small practice; fell in love with Lizzie Hexam; murderously attacked by Bradley Headstone, but saved by Lizzie, whom he married on his sick-bed; recovered. O. M. F. 9.

Wren, Jenny, a name given to Fanny Cleaver, the doll's dressmaker. See *Cleaver*.

Wrymug, Mrs, a client of the General Agency Office. N. N. 145.

Wugsby, Jane, daughter of Mrs Colonel Wugsby. P. P. 392.

Wugsby, Mrs Colonel, a lady of ancient and whist-like appearance, at Bath. P. P. 391.

Wugsby, The Elder Miss, daughter of Mrs Colonel Wugsby. P. P, 392.

Y, Z

Yarmouth, where the Peggottys lived. D. C. 22.

Yawler, friend of Traddles. D. C. 309.

York. N. N. 45.

Young Columbians, Two. M. C. 282.

"**Young Gal**", to wash up at a dinner given by David Copperfield. D. C. 274.

Youth, who helped Susan Nipper to buy books for Florence Dombey. D. S. 129.

Youth, Pale, with a plated watch-guard; a visitor at Bob Sawyer's. P. P. 343

Zhoé-Ladelle, M., Joe Ladle's name in Switzerland. C. S. 619.

Zobeide. C. S. 223.

Notes on the Illustrations

F. G. Kitton

The "Bull" Inn, Rochester

Immortalized in *Pickwick* as the scene of the "ball for the benefit of a charity", which led to the memorable quarrel on the staircase between Dr Slammer and Jingle. There yet remains a marked Dickens flavour about the "Bull", where may be seen the actual ball-room as described by the novelist, with its "glass chandeliers" and the "elevated den" for the musicians, just as they appeared in Mr Pickwick's time. The bedrooms, too, which were occupied by Mr Pickwick and Mr Winkle are pointed out to visitors, Nos. 13 and 19. The "Bull" still justifies Jingle's recommendation of "good house—nice beds". In 1836 her late Majesty the Queen (then Princess Victoria) stayed here when on her way to Dover—hence the more pretentious name subsequently bestowed upon the inn, the "Royal Victoria and Bull Hotel". It is rumoured that the old-fashioned hostelry, so reminiscent of Dickens and his immortal *Pickwick Papers*, is about to share the fate which has befallen so many places associated with the novelist, and that a new building, intended to meet the more exacting requirements of present-day travellers, will be erected on the site.

The Old "White Hart" Inn, Southwark

Of the several coaching-inns formerly abounding in this part of the Metropolis but few remain even in a fragmentary condition. To lovers of Dickens the most interesting was undoubtedly the "White Hart", entirely demolished in 1889. It will be remembered that the tenth chapter of *Pickwick* opens with a delightful reference to the old coaching-inns of

London, and to the "White Hart" as the scene of Mr Pickwick's first meeting with Sam Weller. Ugly red brick buildings—the premises of a firm of hop merchants—now mark the site of this vanished hostelry, the name only being perpetuated in a modern luncheon-bar.

Cooling church

It was in the churchyard at Cooling, amidst the dreary marshes of Kent, that Pip encountered the escaped convict, Magwitch, as forcibly narrated in the opening chapter of *Great Expectations*. Near the church porch are the curious coffin-shaped gravestones to which Pip alludes, these marking the resting-places of the family of "Comport of Cowling Court, 1771". The tower of Cooling church stands out like a beacon in the flat landscape. Forster tells us that the weird character of the locality fascinated Dickens, who, when living at Gadshill, frequently selected it for his walks in late autumn and winter. Certainly no pen could describe more faithfully or more suggestively the peculiar aspect of the Kentish marshes, apropos of which Forster observes: "It is strange as I transcribe the words, with what wonderful vividness they bring back the very spot on which we stood when he said he meant to make it the scene of the opening of this story—Cooling castle ruins and the desolate church, lying out among the marshes seven miles from Gadshill!"

No. 48 Doughty Street, Mecklenburgh Square

Dickens's residence, 1837 to 1839, removing thence from Furnival's Inn, Holborn, in the early part of the former year. Here he completed *Pickwick*, and wrote *Oliver Twist*, *Memoirs of Joseph Grimaldi*, *Sketches of Young Gentlemen*, and *Nicholas Nickleby*. The novelist's eldest daughter, "Mamie" Dickens, was born in this house, where also occurred the sudden death of his favourite sister-in-law, Mary Hogarth, at the early age of seventeen—a bereavement which so unnerved him that the writing of Pickwick and Oliver Twist (parts of both stories being composed concurrently) was temporarily suspended. Number 48 is on the east side of Doughty Street, and a small room on the ground floor at the rear is believed to have been the novelist's study.

The Market-Cross, Salisbury

"The fair old town of Salisbury", as Dickens describes it in *Martin Chuzzlewit*, plays a somewhat important part in that story. One of the duties customarily imposed upon honest Tom Pinch was to meet Mr Pecksniff's new pupils and escort them to the august presence of the great architect, Tom driving to the city in Mr Pecksniff's trap and putting up at one of the old inns near the market-place. Dickens's description of Salisbury Market, with its shops and stalls and crowd of country folks buying and selling, applies with equal exactitude today. Although no mention is made of the ornate stone structure in the market-place, called the "Poultry Cross", it must have been a perfectly familiar object to the novelist, who knew Salisbury well.

The "George" Inn, Greta Brigde

"Mr Squeers, and the little boys, and their united luggage, were all put down together at the George and New Inn, Greta Bridge." Thus concludes the sixth chapter of *Nicholas Nickleby*; but be it observed that Dickens here bestows upon one establishment the names of two distinct hostels, the "George" and the "New" Inns being about half a mile from each other. The former, as depicted in the illustration, stands in close proximity to Rokeby Park, near the bridge spanning the river Granta; that part of the house formerly comprising the inn has been converted into a dwelling-house, the remainder being used as a granary. The "New" Inn has also undergone transformation, and is now a farmhouse. It is conjectured that Dickens stopped here in the winter of 1838, when travelling by coach to Bowes for the purpose of instituting enquiries concerning the cheap boarding-schools in the locality; writing to his wife, he said that at eleven p.m. the mail reached "a bare place with a house, standing alone in the midst of a dreary moor" [dreary then, no doubt, after a heavy snowstorm], "which the guard informed us was Greta Bridge. I was in a perfect apprehension, for it was fearfully cold, and there were no outward signs of anybody being up in the house. But to our great joy we discovered a comfortable room, with drawn curtains and a most blazing fire."

No. 146 High Street, Rochester

In The Mystery of Edwin Drood we read that "Mr Sapsea's premises are in the High Street over against the Nuns' House. They are of about the period of the Nuns' House, irregularly modernized here and there." The Nuns' House of the story is really "Eastgate House", and has been adapted for the purposes of a Museum; nearly opposite there still stand three old gabled houses, timber-framed and with plaster fronts, one of which (it is fair to assume) was the home of Mr Thomas Sapsea, Mayor of Rochester, according to the story. Dating from about the end of the sixteenth century, these picturesque remains of ancient Rochester are in excellent preservation, and one of the rooms contains old oak panelling and handsome plaster enrichments.

No. 1 Devonshie Terrace, Regent's Park

Dickens's residence, 1839 to 1851, during which period he wrote Master Humphrey's Clock (i.e. The Old Curiosity Shop and Barnaby Rudge), American Notes, Martin Chuzzlewit, Dombey and Son, David Copperfield, and the Christmas Books. The novelist had a great affection for this house, occupying it for a longer period than any other of his London homes. He described it as "a house of great promise (and great premium), undeniable situation, and excessive splendour". In his day it contained thirteen rooms, one of them on the ground floor being the study, which Miss Dickens recalled as "a pretty room, with steps leading directly into the garden from it, and with an extra baize door to keep out all sounds and noise". It was at Devonshire Terrace that the pet ravens were kept, to be immortalized in the single embodiment of "Grip" in Barnaby Rudge. The house eventually proving too small for his growing family, Dickens was reluctantly compelled to relinquish his tenancy and to take up his abode in Tavistock House, Tavistock Square. Writing to Forster at this time he said: "I seem as if I had plucked myself out of my proper soil when I left Devonshire Terrace, and could take root no more until I return to it".

This was also the first English home which received Du Maurier, the famous Punch artist. Several years ago the house underwent considerable structural alteration, the owner raising the building by inserting another story between the ground floor apartments and the upper story.

Tong church

Sufficient evidence is forthcoming to prove that the scene of Little Nell's death was the pleasant little village of Tong, on the eastern side of Shropshire. The church, dating from 1411, was thoroughly restored in 1892; when *The Old Curiosity Shop* was written (1840) its condition was that of picturesque decay, presenting the appearance which is so well described in the story. This fine specimen of Gothic architecture owes to its beautiful monuments the title of "The Westminster Abbey of the Midlands". There are still extant the original oak choir-stalls with the miserere seats and carved poppy-heads; the old oak roof and sculptured bosses; the wood screens in the aisles, of very rich workmanship, and the colouring well preserved. The Vernon Chantry. with its remarkable fan-traceried vaulting, once entirely gilt, is perhaps the most striking feature of the church; it is known as "The Golden Chapel" (called the "baronial chapel" in the story) owing to its costly ornamentation. Here, as well as in the church itself, are recumbent effigies of "warriors … cased in armour as they lived"—memorials of members of the Vernon family.

The "Sir John Falstaff" and Westgate, Canterbury

This quaint hostelry almost adjoins the western side of the sturdy old battlemented West Gate, one of the surviving entrance-gates to the ancient and historical city of Canterbury. It has been conjectured that this house, with its projecting sign displaying the rotund proportions of Shakespeare's fat knight, was the "little Inn" where Mr Micawber put up on his first visit to Canterbury, and where he subsequently exposed with considerable dramatic effect the base machinations of that vile schemer, Uriah Heep. That this establishment was familial to Dickens there can be no doubt, as the drive to Canterbury from Gadshill or Broadstairs was one of his favourite excursions. The "Sun" Hotel and the "Queen's Head" have each been considered as the possible original of the "little Inn"; but as the story affords no real clue, its identification becomes very much a matter of conjecture.

RESTORATION HOUSE, ROCHESTER

The "Satis House" of *Great Expectations*. This picturesque Elizabethan structure (overlooking "The Vines") had a great attraction for Dickens; three days before his death he walked from Gadshill Place to Rochester, and was observed by several persons as he stood leaning against the wooden railing (which then existed near the house), contemplating the beautiful old-world residence.

Charles II lodged at Restoration House in 1660, and subsequently presented to his host, Sir Francis Clarke, several large tapestries, which are still preserved in the building. It should be mentioned that there is a veritable Satis House in Rochester—a modern structure occupying the site of one dating back a considerable period,—but Dickens's description really applies to Restoration House. With regard to the origin of the name "Satis", it is said that when Queen Elizabeth visited Rochester in 1573 she was the guest of Richard Watts (founder of the local charity bearing his cognomen), and, on expressing to the Queen his regret that he could offer her no better accommodation, her Majesty graciously replied, "Satis" (enough), by which designation the house was afterwards known.

GADSHILL PLACE

On the main road to Dover, at a point about three miles on the London side of Rochester, stands a red-brick building which, by reason of its homely appearance and picturesque surroundings, cannot fail to attract the attention of passers-by. Erected in 1780, the house (familiar as Gadshill Place), with its bay-windows overlooking a shady lawn, and its roof surmounted by dormers and quaint bell-turret, constitutes a striking object in the landscape. The main interest of Gadshill Place is, of course, that it was the last home of Dickens; here he lived from 1860 until that memorable day in June, 1870, when his spirit passed away. The novelist purchased the house and grounds, in 1856, of the late Mrs E. Lynn Linton, who then resided there with her father, the Rev. Lynn Linton. It was not until four years later, however, that he made it his permanent home; during that interval Tavistock House (the lease not having expired) continued to be his headquarters, with occasional visits to Gadshill Place, which had been furnished as a temporary summer residence. On giving up possession of Tavistock House (now quite demolished), he set about beautifying his Kentish property, making it thoroughly comfortable and homelike. Here he completed *A Tale of Two*

Cities, and wrote *Great Expectations*, *Our Mutual Friend*, and *The Mystery of Edwin Drood*. It was in the Swiss chalet (given to him by Fechter the actor), which stood in the grounds near the house, that he penned the last lines of his unfinished story. The literary and artistic associations of Gadshill Place impart to it much of the charm which continues to characterize the hallowed spot, for here Dickens received as guests a host of cherished friends whose names are as "familiar in our mouths as household words".

ALSO AVAILABLE FROM NONSUCH PUBLISHING

For forthcoming titles and sales information see

www.nonsuch-publishing.com